RITUAL TEXTS FOR
THE AFTERLIFE

Fascinating texts written on small gold tablets and deposited in graves provide a unique source of information about what the Greeks and Romans believed regarding the afterlife, and how they could influence it. These texts, which stretch from the fifth century BCE to the second century CE, have provoked debate for almost a century and a half. The tablets belonged to those who had been initiated into the mysteries of Dionysus; the words the tablets carried drew upon poems ascribed to the extraordinary singer and sage Orpheus.

In this new edition of *Ritual Texts for the Afterlife*, Graf and Johnston present additional finds and engage with recent interpretations. After providing the Greek text and a translation of all the known tablets, the authors analyze their role in the mysteries of Dionysus, and present an outline of the myths concerning the origins of humanity and of the sacred texts that the Greeks ascribed to Orpheus. In addition to their earlier appendix of related ancient texts in translation, the authors offer appendices on similar gold tablets from Roman Palestine, the tablets from Pherae and their mythic context, and a fresh look at the contested category of "Orphism." Providing the first book-length coverage of these enigmatic texts in English, *Ritual Texts for the Afterlife* will remain essential to the study of ancient Greek religion.

Fritz Graf is Distinguished University Professor at The Ohio State University, where he teaches in the Department of Classics and directs the Epigraphy Section of the Center for Epigraphical and Palaeographical Studies.

Sarah Iles Johnston is Arts and Humanities Distinguished Professor of Religion and Professor of Classics at The Ohio State University.

RITUAL TEXTS FOR THE AFTERLIFE

Orpheus and the Bacchic
Gold Tablets

Second edition

*Fritz Graf and
Sarah Iles Johnston*

Routledge
Taylor & Francis Group

LONDON AND NEW YORK

Walter Burkert, Fritz Graf, and Sarah Iles Johnston (courtesy Martin L. West).

For Walter Burkert,
teacher and friend

First published 2007.
This second edition published 2013 by Routledge
2 Park Square, Milton Park, Abingdon, Oxon OX14 4RN

Simultaneously published in the USA and Canada
by Routledge
711 Third Avenue, New York, NY 10017

Routledge is an imprint of the Taylor & Francis Group, an informa business

© 2013, 2007 Fritz Graf and Sarah Iles Johnston

The right of Fritz Graf and Sarah Iles Johnston to be identified as author of this work has been asserted by him/her in accordance with sections 77 and 78 of the Copyright, Designs and Patents Act 1988.

British Library Cataloguing in Publication Data
A catalogue record for this book is available from the British Library

Library of Congress Cataloging in Publication Data
Ritual texts for the afterlife : Orpheus and the Bacchic Gold
Tablets / Fritz Graf and Sarah Iles Johnston.
p.   cm.
Includes bibliographical references and index.
1. Greece – Religion. 2. Future life. 3. Orpheus (Greek mythology) 4. Dionysus (Greek deity)
I. Graf, Fritz. II. Johnston, Sarah Iles, 1957–
BL790.R58 2007
292.8'5 – dc22   2006033828

ISBN: 978-0-415-50802-5 (hbk)
ISBN: 978-0-415-50803-2 (pbk)
ISBN: 978-0-203-56424-0 (ebk)

Typeset in Minion Pro by The Running Head Limited, Cambridge

CONTENTS

ILLUSTRATIONS

Figures

Map

PREFACE TO THE FIRST EDITION

In the past, scholarship on the so-called Orphic Gold Tablets has had a checkered career. For a short while, at the beginning of the last century, the tablets were at the center of attention, to the extent that one scholar, Alexander Olivieri, even produced an edition for academic seminars. They soon relinquished that position, however, and for many years since have barely been visible to most scholars of ancient religion: they were epigraphical curiosities, read only by a few specialists. Günther Zuntz's 1971 edition of these texts, in the context of his research into the religion and philosophy of Southern Italy, did not help much. Neither Martin Nilsson nor Walter Burkert devoted much space to them in their authoritative accounts of Greek religion, and only Margherita Guarducci valued them highly enough to include them in her manual of Greek epigraphy.

A steadily growing number of additions to Zuntz's small corpus, from excavations all over the Greek world, has considerably enhanced our understanding of these texts, however, even if their religious affiliation has become hazy again in recent years. This body of texts calls for a new, collective publication and interpretation that make them accessible both to students of ancient religions and to others who are interested in Greek beliefs in the afterlife. (Although Pugliese Carratelli has recently produced several editions and translations into Italian and French, and Bernabé and Jiménez San Cristóbal have presented the tablets in Spanish, nothing has been recently produced for the English-language reader.) The present book attempts to fill this gap. The edition we offer aims to present the texts in a form that is not too far from their actual appearance; the translation and the five interpretative chapters will introduce the reader to the beliefs and rituals that we can see, or more often guess, lay behind these fragile texts.

This book is a joint undertaking, and it has kept its two authors busy for several years. We thank each other for elucidation and patience, and we thank many friends – more than can be mentioned here – for their help and advice. Paramount are four scholars who shared their materials with us well before their publication – Alberto Bernabé, who gave us the indexes of his splendid Teubner edition of the *Orphica* long before they were published; Robert Parker and Maria Stamatopoulou, who made their exciting new text accessible to us; and Yannis Tzifopoulos for sharing with us his Cretan texts. Jan Bremmer read the entire manuscript and contributed many suggestions. Our students Anna Peterson and Agapi Stefanidou helped with the proofreading; Wendy Watkins, Curator of Epigraphy at the Center for Epigraphical and Palaeographical Studies at The Ohio State University, created the map of find-spots.

We dedicate this book to the scholar whose work has been our source of continuing inspiration on this and other topics for many years, Walter Burkert.

Abbreviations

Our abbreviations and mode of spelling ancient names usually follow the *Oxford Classical Dictionary*, 3rd edn.; note the following:

ABV	J. D. Beazley, *Attic Black-Figure Vase Painters*, 2nd edn. (Oxford: Clarendon Press, 1971 [1956])
DK	Hermann Diels, *Die Fragmente der Vorsokratiker*, 6th edn. by Walther Kranz (Berlin: Weidmann, 1951 [and reprints])
Inscr. Cret.	*Inscriptiones Creticae, opera et consilio Friderici Halbherr collectae*, ed. Marguerita Guarducci. 4 vols. (Rome: Libreria dello Stato, 1935–50)
LIMC	*Lexicon Iconographicum Mythologiae Classicae*. 8 vols. (Zurich and Munich: Artemis, 1981–2004)
OF	Alberto Bernabé, ed. *Poetae Epici Graeci*. II *Orphicorum et Orphicis similium testimonia et fragmenta*. Fasc. 1/2 (Munich and Leipzig: Sauer, 2004, 2005)
OF . . . Kern	Otto Kern, ed. *Orphicorum Fragmenta* (Berlin: Weidmann, 1922 [repr. 1963])
SGOst	Reinhold Merkelbach and Josef Stauber, eds. *Steinepigramme aus dem griechischen Osten*, 5 vols. (Stuttgart and Leipzig: Teubner and Munich: Saur 1998–2004)

PREFACE TO THE
SECOND EDITION

After five years, a new edition of this book gives us the opportunity to bring our edition and discussions into line with recent scholarship. This period has seen the publication of Yannis Tzifopoulos' important book on the Cretan texts (2010), which offers a comprehensive edition and interpretation of the *epistomia*, or "mouth cover" tablets; the translation into English (and updating) of Alberto Bernabé and Ana Isabel Jiménez San Cristobal's *Instrucciones para el más allá* (2008); and Radcliffe G. Edmonds III's edited volume of essays on the tablets (with its own edition of the texts [2011]), as well as many shorter treatments of individual tablets or topics related to the tablets.

Our discussions now reflect these new developments, and especially take into fuller consideration the consequences of the newest tablet from Pherae (our no. 28), which had become available to us only at the very moment that we were finishing the first edition. We have also reflected upon yet another document that appeared very recently, the Dionysiac papyrus from the Green Family Collection, which Dirk Obbink made available in a preliminary edition in 2012. Some of these recent developments necessitated changes in our six original chapters. Others are reflected in our new Appendix 2, on the Pherae tablets, and in our new Appendix 3, we present and discuss some intriguing parallel documents from Roman Palestine. Finally, in a discussion that is now called Appendix 1 (the former Appendix 1 taking a new place as Appendix 4) we stand back and reconsider, in the face of new evidence and recent discussions, the question of how "Orphism" might best be defined, drawing in particular on late antique evidence.

Given that Bernabé's *Orphicorum Fragmenta* offers a very thorough critical edition of all the tablets, including (in the supplements to vol. 3 of 2007) the new ones, we saw no need to change our policy of offering a readable but not fully critical text.

Although this new edition, like the original book, is the result of intensive discussion between the two authors, we have continued our practice of indicating which of us took the main responsibility for shaping and writing each chapter or appendix. We thank Katrina Väänänen, graduate student in the Department of Classics at OSU, for her great help with the indexes.

Columbus, Ohio, September 1, 2012

1

THE TABLETS

An edition and translation

Fritz Graf (edition) and Sarah Iles Johnston (translation)

Preface

The edition has a double aim: to present a readable text, and to give an impression of the physical appearance of each individual document. Thus, we do not give a critical text, either in a philological or an epigraphical sense – we use the often threatening panoply of such an edition as sparingly as possible, and we indicate readings and scholarly conjectures only where absolutely necessary.[1] Readers interested in these matters should consult one of the more recent critical editions, preferably Bernabé's Teubner text. None of these editions preserve the Greek in the form it appears on the tablets, instead translating it into uniform Attic spelling and sometimes reconstructing words that the writer did not intend to write. One needs to retain the exact spelling of words as they appear on the tablets in order to understand the degree of literacy possessed by these local writers, and to judge the editorial decisions of modern editors.

To give two examples, one trivial, one less so. First, the most complete and least corrupt tablet from the Timpone Piccolo in Thurii (Zuntz A 1, our no. 5) twice writes double-s before a hard consonant inside of a word (ἀσστεροβλῆτα 4, δεσσποίνας 7; against μακάριστε in 9): the gemination of -σ- in this position is common in Greek, and no editor should normalize it.[2] Second, line 14 of the Hipponion tablet ends with the word ΒΑΣΙΛΕΙ, i.e., βασιλεῖ, "to the king," after which there is ample space: the writer thus wanted his line to end like this. Although this text is metrically correct, many editors have changed the final word to the metrically equally correct βασιλείαι, "to the queen," for reasons of mythology: in "Orphic" myth, Persephone, the Queen of the Underworld, is much more prominent than her husband. But mythology is a somewhat uncertain guide: at least in South Italian vase images, such as the one in Toledo (Figure 4, p. 64), Hades is as much present as is his queen.

1

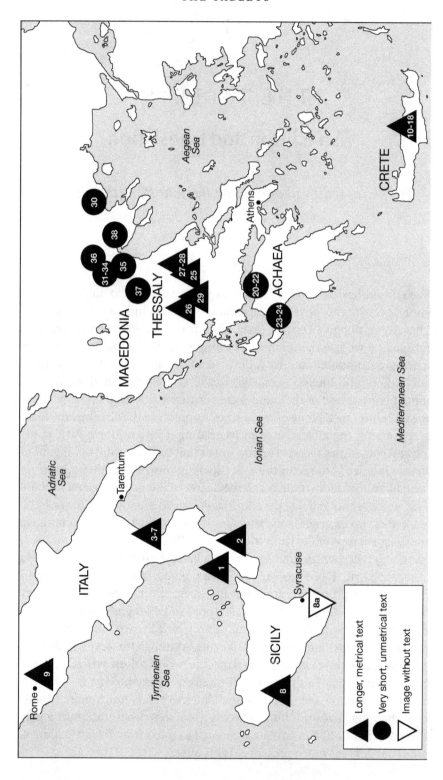

Unlike in any other edition, the arrangement of the texts here follows geographical criteria. To group them in A and B texts, following Zuntz's arrangement, is impossible because some of the more recent texts clearly override such a neat dichotomy; to group them according to a reconstructed narrative, as Bernabé and Jiménez San Cristóbal do, begs the question of how they belong together. A geographically determined arrangement not only avoids these problems, but also makes manifest the local groupings and idiosyncracies of these texts: after all, they sometimes belonged to local groups and always attest to the activities of a local *orpheotelestēs*.[3]

We use quotation marks to indicate portions of the texts that either are phrases to be repeated by the addressee, i.e., by the soul of the deceased, or are spoken by someone other than the main voice of the tablet in question.

The bibliographical data we have provided list the most important first editions and refer, in an abbreviated form, to the most recent critical editions:

G. Zuntz, *Persephone. Three Essays on Religion and Thought in Magna Graecia* (Oxford: Clarendon Press, 1971).

C. Riedweg, "Anhang: Übersicht und Texte der bisher publizierten Goldblättchen," in: Riedweg 1998, 389–98 [uses the expanded classification of Zuntz].

G. Pugliese Carratelli, *Le lamine d'oro orfiche. Istruzioni per il viaggio oltremondano degli iniziati Greci* (Milan: Adelphi. 2001) (with an important correction in *La Parola del Passato* 53, 2002, 228–30).[4]

Alberto Bernabé, *Poetae Epici Graeci*. II *Orphicorum et Orphicis similium testimonia et fragmenta*, fasc. 2 (Munich: Saur, 2004); the numbers with the prefix L refer to the edition in Bernabé and Jiménez San Cristóbal 2008, 245–71.

Robert Parker and Maria Stamatopoulou, "A new funerary gold leaf from Pherai," *Arkhaiologike Ephemeris* 143 (2004 [2007]), 1–32.

Marisa Tortorelli-Ghidini, *Figli della terra e del cielo stellato. Testi Orfici con traduzione e commento* (Naples: D'Auria Editore, 2006) [only the long texts; abbreviated MTG].

Yannis Tzifopoulos, *"Paradise" Earned. The Bacchic-Orphic Gold Lamellae of Crete*. Hellenic Studies 23 (Washington, DC: Center for Hellenic Studies, 2010), 255–80 [uses an expanded classification of Zuntz/Riedweg].

Radcliffe G. Edmonds III, ed., *The "Orphic" Gold Tablets and Greek Religion. Further Along the Path* (Cambridge: Cambridge University Press, 2011), 16–48 [uses the same expanded classification of Zuntz/Riedweg as Tzifopoulos].

Magna Graecia

Calabria

1 *Hipponion*

From the cist-grave of a woman, around 400 BCE; now in the Museo Archeologico Statale di Vibo. The rectangular gold tablet, folded several times, was found lying on the upper chest of the skeleton and was perhaps attached to its neck by a tiny string.

Ed. princ.: Pugliese Carratelli and Foti 1974; new readings Russo 1996. *Coll.*: Riedweg/Tzifopoulos/Edmonds B 10 [not in Zuntz]; Pugliese Carratelli 2001, I A 1; Bernabé, *OF* 474 (= L 1); MTG 1.

Μναμοσύνας τόδε ἔργον, ἐπεὶ ἂν μέλλε̄ισι θανε̄σθαι
εἰς Ἀΐδαο δόμο̄ς εὐέρεας. ἔστ' ἐπὶ δ<ε>ξιὰ κρε̄να,
πὰρ δ'αὐτὰν ἑστακῦα λευκὰ κυπάρισος·
ἔνθα κατερχόμεναι ψυκαὶ νεκύο̄ν ψύχονται.   4
ταύτας τᾶς κράνας με̄δὲ σχεδὸν ἐνγύθεν ἔλθε̄ις.
πρόσθεν δὲ hευρε̄σεις τᾶς Μναμοσύνας ἀπὸ λίμνας
ψυχρὸν ὕδο̄ρ προρέον· φύλακες δὲ ἐπύπερθεν ἔασι.
τοὶ δέ σε εἰρε̄σονται ἐν φρασὶ πευκαλίμαισι   8
ὅ τι δὲ̄ ἐξερέεις Ἄϊδος σκότος ὀρφε̄εντος.
εἶπον· hυὸς Γᾶς ἔμι καὶ Ὀρανο̄ ἀστερόεντος.
δίψαι δ' ἔμ' αὖος καὶ ἀπόλλυμαι· ἀλὰ δότ' ὄ[κα
ψυχρὸν ὕδο̄ρ πιέναι τε̄ς Μνε̄μοσύνε̄ς ἀπὸ λίμν[α]ς.   12
καὶ δή τοι ἐρέο̄σιν hυποχθονίδι βασιλε̄ϊ·
καὶ δέ̄ τοι δό̄σο̄σι πιὲν τῆς Μναμοσύνας ἀπὸ λίμνα[ς].
καὶ δὲ̄ καὶ σὺ πιὼ̄ν ὁδὸν ἔρχεα<ι>, hάν τε καὶ ἄλλοι
μύσται καὶ βάχχοι hιερὰν στείχο̄σι κλεινοί.   16

1 ἔργον Burkert; EPION tablet.
9 ὀρφ<ν>ήεντος Ebert, in Luppe, *ZPE* 30 (1978), 25; ΟΡΟΕΕΝΤΟΣ tablet.
10 ΙΟΣΙ ΑΡΙ ΜΙ tablet, Sacco, *ZPE* 137 (2001), 27; <hυ>ιὸς Βαρέας καὶ Pugliese Carratelli, *ed. princ.*; ΥΟΣΓΑΣΕΜΙ, i.e., hυὸς Γᾶς ἔμι Russo 1996 (Γᾱς or Γαίας earlier editors).
13 ΕΡΕΟΣΙ Lazzarini, *Annali Pisa* 17 (1982), 331; ΕΛΕΟΣΙ Pugliese Carratelli, *ed. princ.*; ΗΥΠΟΧΘΟΝΙΟΙΒΑΣΙΛΕΙ tablet; some editors prefer βασιλεί<αι>.

1

1 This is the work of Memory, when you are about to die

2 down to the well-built house of Hades. There is a spring at the right side,

3 and standing by it a white cypress.

4 Descending to it, the souls of the dead refresh themselves.

5 Do not even go near this spring!

6 Ahead you will find from the Lake of Memory,

7 cold water pouring forth; there are guards before it.

8 They will ask you, with astute wisdom,

9 what you are seeking in the darkness of murky Hades.

10 Say, "I am a son of Earth and starry Sky,

11 I (masculine) am parched with thirst and am dying; but quickly grant me

12 cold water from the Lake of Memory to drink."

13 And they will announce you to the Chthonian King,

14 and they will grant you to drink from the Lake of Memory.

15 And you, too, having drunk, will go along the sacred road on which other

16 glorious initiates and *bacchoi* travel.

2 Petelia

Said to come from a grave in Petelia (modern Strongoli), 4th cent. BCE. The tablet was rolled up in a golden amulet case from the Imperial epoch. Bought *c.* 1830 from a local by Baron Millingen; now in the British Museum (inv. 3155). Rectangular tablet, damaged at the bottom because it was, in a secondary use, cut to fit into the amulet case. A final line runs along the right margin.

Eds.: G. Franz, "Epigrafe greca sopra lamina d'oro spettante al Sig. Millingen," *Bolletino di Corrispondenza Archeologica* (1836), 149f.; Cecil Smith and Domenico Comparetti, "The Petelia Gold Tablet," *Journal of Hellenic Studies* 3 (1882), 111–18; cp. Marshall 1911, 380 no. 3155.
Coll.: Zuntz (Riedweg/Tzifopoulos/Edmonds) B 1; Pugliese Carratelli 2001, I A 2; Bernabé, *OF* 476 (= L 3).

Εὑρήσσεις δ' Ἀΐδαο δόμων ἐπ' ἀριστερὰ κρήνην,
πὰρ δ'αυτῆι λευκὴν ἑστηκυῖαν κυπάρισσον.
ταύτης τῆς κρήνης μηδὲ σχεδὸν ἐμπελάσειας.
εὑρήσεις δ' ἑτέραν, τῆς Μνημοσύνης ἀπὸ λίμνης   4
ψυχρὸν ὕδωρ προρέον· φύλακες δ' ἐπίπροσθεν ἔασιν.
εἰπεῖν· Γῆς παῖς εἰμι καὶ Οὐρανοῦ ἀστερόεντος,
αὐτὰρ ἐμοὶ γένος οὐράνιον· τόδε δ' ἴστε καὶ αὐτοί.
δίψαι δ' εἰμὶ αὔη καὶ ἀπόλλυμαι. ἀλλὰ δότ' αἶψα   8
ψυχρὸν ὕδωρ προρέον τῆς Μνημοσύνης ἀπὸ λίμνης.
καὺτ[οί] σ[οι] δώσουσι πιεῖν θείης ἀπ[ὸ κρή]νης,
καὶ τότ' ἔπειτ' ἄ[λλοισι μεθ'] ἡρώεσσιν ἀνάξει[ς].
[Μνημοσύ]νης τόδ<ε> ἔ[ργον – – –   12
θανεῖσθ[αι – –] τόδε γραψ[– –
in marg. – –]τογλωσειπα σκότος ἀμφικαλύψας.

10 λίμ]μνης would be equally possible.
11 [τέλη σὺθ'] Edmonds, deriving ἀνάξεις from ἀνάγω "to celebrate"; see Edmonds in Herrero de Jáuregui et al. 2011: 185–8.

2

1   You will find to the left of the house of Hades a spring

2   and standing by it a white cypress.

3   Do not even approach this spring!

4   You will find another, from the Lake of Memory,

5   cold water pouring forth; there are guards before it.

6   Say, "I am a child of Earth and starry Sky,

7   but my race is heavenly. You yourselves know this.

8   I (feminine) am parched with thirst and am dying; but quickly grant me

9   cold water flowing from the Lake of Memory."

10 And they themselves will grant you to drink from the sacred spring.

11 And thereafter you will rule among the other heroes.

12 This is the work of Memory. When you are about to die

13 to die   write this

14   enwrapped . . . darkness.

Lucania

3 *Thurii 1*

From a tumulus (Timpone Grande) in Thurii, now in the Museo Nazionale in Naples, inv. no. 11463; 4th cent. BCE. The thin gold tablet was folded several times and put inside a larger and thicker tablet, folded like an envelope (below no. 4), next to the cranium of the deceased, who had been cremated in his wooden coffin.

Ed. princ.: *Not. Scav.* 1879, 156–9 (facsimile by Barnabei, ed. and commentary by D. Comparetti); *IG* XIV 642.
Coll.: Zuntz (Riedweg/Tzifopoulos/Edmonds) A 4; Pugliese Carratelli 2001, II B 2; Bernabé, *OF* 487 (= L 8); MTG 4.

Ἀλλ' ὁπόταμ ψυχὴ προλίπηι φάος ἀελίοιο,|
δεξιὸν Ε.ΘΙΑΣ δ' ἐξιέναι πεφυλαγμένον | εὖ μάλα πάντα·
χαῖρε παθὼν τὸ πάθη|μα τὸ δ' οὔπω πρόσθε ἐπεπόνθεις.
   θεὸς ἐγ|ένου ἐξ ἀνθρώπου· ἔριφος ἐς γάλα | ἔπετες.   4
   χαῖρ<ε>, χαῖρε· δεξιὰν ὁδοιπόρ[ει] |
λειμῶνας τε ἱεροὺς καὶ ἄλσεα | Φερσεφονείας.

2   εὐθείας Pugliese Carratelli (a very uncertain reading).

3

1   But as soon as the soul has left the light of the sun,

2   Go to the right [. . . .] being very careful of all things.

3   "Greetings, you who have suffered the painful thing; you
     have never endured this before.

4   You have become a god instead of a mortal. A kid you fell into
     milk.

5   Rejoice, rejoice." Journey on the right-hand road

6   to holy meadows and groves of Persephone.

4 Thurii 2

From the same findspot as no. 3. Napoli, Museo Nazionale inv. no. 111464.
4th cent. BCE. A larger and thicker tablet, folded around no. 3 like an
envelope.

Ed. princ.: Hermann Diels, "Ein orphischer Demeterhymnus," in *Festschrift Theodor Gomperz* (Vienna, 1902), 1–15.
Coll.: Zuntz (Riedweg/Tzifopoulos/Edmonds) C; Pugliese Carratelli 2001,
III 1; Bernabé, *OF* 492 (= L 12); MTG 3.

Πρωτογόνῳ<ι> ΤΗΜΑΙΤΙΕΤΗ Γᾶ<ι> ματρί ΕΠΑ Κυβε-
   λεία<ι> Κόρρα<ι> ΟΣΕΝΤΑΙΗ Δήμητρος ΗΤ

ΤΑΤΑΙΤΤΑΠΤΑ Ζεῦ ΙΑΤΗΤΥ ἀέρ ΣΑΠΤΑ ῞Ηλιε πῦρ
   δὴ πάντα ΣΤΗΙΝΤΑΣΤΗΝΙΣΑΤΟΠΕ νικᾶι Μ

ΣΗΔΕ Τύχα ΙΤΕ Φάνης πάμνηστοι Μοῖραι ΣΣΤΗΤΟΙΓΝ
   ΝΥΑΠΙΑΝΤΗ σὺ κλυτὲ δαῖμον ΔΕΥΧΙ

Σ πάτερ ΑΤΙΚ παντοδαμάστα ΠΑΝΤΗΡΝΥΝΤΑΙΣΕΛΑΒ
   ΔΟΝΤΑΔΕΠ ἀνταμοιβή ΣΤΛΗΤΕΑΣΤΛ   4

ΤΗΜΗ ἀέρ Ι πῦρ ΜΕΜ Μᾶτερ ΛΥΕΣΤΙΣΟΙΛ·ΕΝΤΑΤΟ
   Νῆστι Ν Νὺξ ΙΝΗΜΕΦ ἡμέρα ΜΕΡΑΝΕΓΛΧΥΕΣ

ἐπτῆμαρ ΤΙ νήστιας ΤΑΝ Ζεῦ ἐνορύττιε (?) καὶ πανόπτα
   αἰέν ΑΙΜΙΥΟ μᾶτερ ἐμᾶς ἐπ-

άκουσον ΕΟ εὐχᾶς ΤΑΚΤΑΠΥΑΡΣΥΟΛΚΑΠΕΔΙΩΧΑ
   ΜΑΤΕΜΑΝ καλΗὰ Δ ἱερά ΔΑΜΝΕΥΔΑΜΝΟΙ

ΩΤΑΚΤΗΡ ἱερά ΜΑΡ Δημήτερ πῦρ Ζεῦ Κόρη Χθονία
   ΤΡΑΒΔΑΗΤΡΟΣΗΝΙΣΤΗΟΙΣΤΝ   8

ἥρως ΝΗΓΑΥΝΗ φάος ἐς φρένα ΜΑΤΑΙΜΗΝΝΤΗΣΝ
   ΥΣΧΑ μήστωρ εἷλε κούρην

αἶα ΦΗΡΤΟΝΟΣΣΜΜΟ·ΕΣΤΟΝ ἀέρ ΤΑΙΠΛΝΙΛΛΥ ἐς
   φρένα ΜΑΡ*ΤῼΣ

Our text and translation follow Bernabé, *OF* 492 and L 12, see Bernabé and Jiménez
San Cristóbal 2008: 137–50 and Betegh 2004: 333–7 who follows and connects it
with the cosmological theory of the Derveni Papyrus. This understanding takes
up a suggestion of Comparetti 1910: 12 and reads the text as a conscious mixture
of meaningful words and meaningless letter groups; the nonsensical sequences
contain as few as one or two letters, or as many as two dozen. The most important
details (for the rest see Bernabé's edition):

4

1 To Protogonos [untranslatable letters] Earth Mother [ditto] Cybele [ditto] Girl [ditto] of Demeter [ditto]

2 [ditto] Zeus [ditto] Air [ditto] Sun, Fire that overcomes [ditto] all.

3 [ditto] Fortune [ditto] Phanes, All-remembering Moirai [ditto] you famous *daimon* [ditto]

4 Father [ditto] Master of All [ditto] correspondence [ditto]

5 [ditto] Air, Fire [ditto] Mother [ditto] Fasting, Night [ditto] Day [ditto]

6 Seventh day [ditto] of a fast, Zeus Who-Digs-In (?) and Watcher-Over-All, always [ditto] Mother, hear

7 my [ditto] prayers [ditto] beautiful [ditto] sacred things [ditto]

8 [ditto] sacred things [ditto] Demeter, Fire, Zeus, Chthonic Kore [ditto]

9 Hero [ditto] Light to the mind [ditto] the mindful one seizes Kore

10 land [ditto]Air [ditto] to the mind.

1 ΠΡΩΤΟΓΟΝΟΤΗ etc. tablet, Bernabé also suggests (with earlier editors) Πρωτόγονο<ς> (?): ΓΑΜΜΑΤΡΙ etc.

3 πάμνηστοι: ΠΑΜΜΗΣΤΟΙ tablet; κλυτὲ δαῖμον Diels: ΚΛΗΤΕΔΑΡΜΟΝ tablet.

7 ἐπ|άκουσον Olivieri 1915: ΕΠ|..ΩΥΣΟΝ or ΕΠ|ννΩΣΟΝ tablet.

According to Bernabé, the understandable text adds up to:

Πρωτογόνωι, Γᾶι ματρί, Κυβελείαι Κόρραι Δήμητρος. |Ζεῦ, ἀέρ, Ἥλιε. πῦρ δὴ πάντα νικᾶι. | Τύχα, Φάνης, πάμνηστοι Μοῖραι. σὺ, κλυτὲ δαῖμον, | πάτερ παντοδαμάστα | ἀνταμοιβή |ἀέρ, πῦρ, Μᾶτερ, Νῆστι, νύξ, ἡμέρα | ἑπτῆμαρ νήστιας, Ζεῦ ἐνορύττιε (?) καὶ πανόπτα. αἰέν, μᾶτερ, ἐμᾶς ἐπάκουσον εὐχᾶς, καλὰ ἱερά,| ἱερά Δημῆτερ, πῦρ, Ζεῦ, Κόρη Χθονία, | ἥρως, φάος ἐς φρένα. μήστωρ εἶλε κούρην. | αἶα, ἀέρ, ἐς φρένα.

5 *Thurii 3*

From a smaller tumulus (Timpone Piccolo) in Thurii, 4th cent. BCE; Napoli, Museo Nazionale inv. no. 111625. Rectangular gold tablet, folded, found in the topmost of the three cist-graves contained in the tumulus, next to the right hand of the deceased.

Ed. princ.: *Not. Scav.* 1880, 155 (Barnabei's facsimile). 156–62 (Comparetti's commentary).
Coll.: Zuntz (Riedweg/Tzifopoulos/Edmonds) A 1; Pugliese Carratelli 2001, II B 1; Bernabé, *OF* 488 (= L 9); MTG 5

Ἔρχομαι ἐκ κοθαρῶ\<ν> κοθαρά, χθονί\<ων> βα|σίλεια,

Εὐκλῆς Εὐβōλεύς τε καὶ ἀ|θάνατοι θεοὶ ἄλλοι.

καὶ γὰρ ἐγὼν | ὑμῶν γένος ὄλβιον εὔχομαι | εἶμεν.

ἀλά με Μο\<ῖ>ρα ἐδάμασε | καὶ ἀθάνατοι θεοὶ ἄλλοι   4a

              καὶ ασ|στεροβλῆτα κεραυνόν.   4b

κύκλō | δ' ἐξέπταν βαρυπενθέος ἀργα|λέοιο,

ἱμερτō δ' ἐπέβαν στεφά|νō ποσὶ καρπαλίμοισι·

Δεσποί|νας δὲ ὑπὸ κόλπον ἔδυν χθονί|ας βασιλείας.

ἱμερτō δ' ἐπέβαν | στεφάνō ποσὶ καρπαλίμοι|σι.   8

ὄλβιε καὶ μακαριστέ, θεὸς δ' ἔσ|ηι ἀντὶ βροτοῖο.

ἔριφος ἐς γάλ' ἔπετο|ν.

4a καὶ ἀθάνατοι θεοὶ ἄλλοι and 4b καὶ ασ|στεροβλῆτα κεραυνῶι are metrically equivalent; each adds up to a good hexameter after ἐδάμασε. Semantically as well, they are variations; there is no need to decide between either of them as more authentic, even if we could.
8 ΣΤΕΜΑΝΟ tablet; some editors delete the verse as a doublet of 6.

5

1 I come pure from the pure, Queen of the Chthonian Ones,

2 Eucles, Euboleus and the other immortal gods.

3 For I also claim to be of your happy race.

4 But Moira overcame me and the other immortal gods   4a

                  and the star-flinger with lightning.   4b

5 I have flown out of the heavy, difficult circle,

6 I have approached the longed-for crown with swift feet,

7 I have sunk beneath the breast of the Lady, the Chthonian Queen,

8 I have approached the longed-for crown with swift feet.

9 "Happy and blessed, you will be a god instead of a mortal."

10 A kid I fell into milk.

6 Thurii 4

rom the same tumulus, 4th cent. BCE; Napoli, Museo Nazionale inv. 111624. Rectangular gold tablet, folded, found next to the right hand of the deceased in the second cist-grave, deeper down; inscribed on both sides.

Ed. princ.: Not. Scav. 1870, 156 (Barnabei's facsimile), 156–62 (Comparetti's commentary).
Coll.: Zuntz (Riedweg/Tzifopoulos/Edmonds) A 3; Pugliese Carratelli 2001, II A 2; Bernabé, OF 490 (= L 10b); MTG 7.

^{to} Ἔρχομαι ἐκ <κ>αθαρῶ<ν> καθα<ρά, χθ>|ο<νίων> βασίλ<ει>α,

κλε {υα} κα<ὶ> Εὐ|βōλεῦ καὶ θεοὶ ὅσοι δ<αί>μο|νες ἄλλοι.

καὶ γὰρ ἐ<γ>ὼ ὑ|<μῶν> γένος εὔχομα<ι> ἐ<ῖ>να<ι> | ὄλβιο<ν>.

ινὰν {ν}ἀ<ν>ταπ|έτε<ισ'> ἔργω<ν ἕνεκ'> ὅτι δικ||^{verso}α<ί>ων.

<ε> με Μοῖρα <ἐδάμασ'> ἔ̆<τε ἀσ>τεροπῆτα {κη} κερα<υ>|νῶ<ι>.

ν δὲ <ἱ>κ<έτις> ἥκω, | ἥκω παρὰ Φ<ερ>σεφ<όνειαν>.

{λ} με <π>ρόφ<ρων> πέ[μ]ψει {μ}| ἕδρας ἐς εὐ<α>γ<έων>.

7 Thurii 5

rom the same tumulus, 4th cent. BCE; Napoli, Museo Nazionale inv. 111623. Rectangular gold foil, folded, found in a third cist-grave, "next to the skeleton" (according to the excavation report).

Ed. princ.: Not. Scav. 1870, 156 (Barnabei's facsimile), 156–62 (Comparetti's commentary).
Coll.: Zuntz (Riedweg/Tzifopoulos/Edmonds) A 2; Pugliese 2001, II A 1; Bernabé, OF 489 = (L 10a); MTG 6.

ρχομα<ι> ἐκ <κ>α<θα>ρῶν {σχονων}| καθαρά, χθονί<ων>

βασίλ{η}ει<α>|,

Εὐκλε καὶ Εὐβουλεῦ καὶ θεοὶ <καὶ> δαίμον|ε<ς> ἄλλοι.

καὶ γὰ<ρ> ἐγὼν ὑμῶ<ν> γένο<ς> εὔχομα|ι ὄλβιον εἶναι.

<ι>νὰν δ' ἀνταπέ{ι}τε<ισ'>| ἔργων ἕνεκα οὔτι δικα<ί>ων.   4

τε με Μο<ί>ρα ἐδαμά<σ>σατο εἴτε ἀστεροπῆτα κ<ε>ραύνων.

ν δ' ἱκέτ<ις> ἥκω πα<ρα>ὶ ἁγνη<ν> Φε<ρ>σέ|φονειαν,

ς με{ι} πρόφρων πέμψη<ι>| ἕδρας ἐς εὐαγέ{ι}ων.

6

1   I come pure from the pure, Queen of the Chthonian Ones,

2   Eucles and Euboleus and other gods – as many *daimones* (as do exist).

3   For I also claim to be of your happy race.

4   I have paid the penalty for unrighteous deeds.

5   Either Moira overcame me or the star-flinger with lightning.

6   Now I come, come as a suppliant (feminine) to Persephone,

7   so that she may kindly send me to the seats of the pure.

7

1   I come pure from the pure, Queen of the Chthonian Ones,

2   Eucles and Eubouleus and the gods and other *daimones*.

3   For I also claim to be of your happy race.

4   I have paid the penalty for unrighteous deeds.

5   Either Moira overcame me or the star-flinger of lightnings.

6   Now I come as a suppliant (feminine) to holy Persephone,

7   so that she may kindly send me to the seats of the pure.

Sicily

8 Entella

Fragment of a rectangular gold foil said to come from Entella, now in a private collection in Geneva, Switzerland. Found in a field (the region of the archaic and classical cemetery?) inside a terracotta lamp, perhaps 3rd cent. BCE. The only tablet with a text written in two columns.

Ed. princ.: Jiři Frel, "Una nuova laminella 'orfica'," *Eirene* 30 (1994), 183f. (*SEG* 44.750) – no photograph available.
Coll.: Riedweg/Tzifopoulos/Edmonds B11 [not yet in Zuntz]; Pugliese Carratelli 2001, I A 4; Bernabé, *OF* 475 (= L 2); MTG 13.

col. I[ἐπεὶ ἂν μέλ]ληισι θανεῖσθαι
[μ]εμνημέ<ν>ος ἥρως
[   ]σκότος ἀμφικαλύψας
[ἐπὶ] δεξιὰ λίμνην,   4
[πὰρ' αὐτῆι λευκὴν ἑστη]κῦαν κυπάρισσον·
[ἔνθα κατερχόμεναι ψυ]χαὶ νεκύων ψύχονται.
[ταύτης τῆς κρήνης μη]δὲ σχεδὸν ἐ<μ>πελάσ<ασ>θαι.
[πρόσθεν δ' εὑρήσεις τῆς] Μνημοσύνης ἀπὸ λίμνης   8
[ψυχρὸν ὕδωρ προρέον·] φυλακοὶ δ' ἐπύπε<ρ>θε<ν ἔ>ασιν.
[τοὶ δέ σε εἰρήσονται ἐνὶ] φρασὶ πευκαλίμησιν,
[ὅττι δὴ ἐξερέεις Ἄιδος σκότο]ς ὀρφονήεντος.
[εἶπον· Γῆς παῖς εἰμι καὶ] Οὐρανοῦ ἀστερόεντος.   12
[δίψαι δ' εἰμ' αὖος καὶ ἀπόλλ]υμαι· ἀλλὰ δότε μμοι
[ψυχρὸν ὕδωρ πιέναι τῆς] Μνημοσύνης ἀπὸ λίμνης.
col. II αὐτὰρ ἐ[μοὶ γένος οὐράνιον· τόδε δ' ἴστε καὶ αὐτοί.]
καί τοι δὴ [ἐρέουσι ὑποχθωνίωι βασιλῆϊ·   16
καὶ τότε τ[οι δώσουσι πιεῖν τῆς Μνημοσύνης ἀπὸ λίμνης
καὶ τότε δ[ὴ -
σύμβολα φ[- - - - - - - - - - - - - - - - - - - -
καὶ φε[-   20
σεν[

8

1   when you are about to die

2   remembering hero

3   darkness enwrapping

4   upon the right a lake

5   and standing by it a white cypress.

6   Descending to it, the souls of the dead refresh themselves.

7   Do not even approach this spring!

8   Ahead you will find from the Lake of Memory,

9   cold water pouring forth; there are guards before it.

10   They will ask you, with astute wisdom,

11   what you are seeking in the darkness of murky Hades.

12   Say, "I am a child of Earth and starry Sky,

13   I am parched with thirst and am dying; but grant me

14   cold water from the Lake of Memory to drink.

15   But my race is heavenly. You yourselves know this."

16   And they will announce you to the Chthonian Queen.

17   and then they will grant you to drink from the Lake of Memory.

18   and then

19   symbols

20   and

21   (fragment of a word)

Most restitutions are given in order to show how we imagine the sense of the text, without necessarily reconstructing the exact wording (an obvious source for the reconstruction is no. 1). There is still no reliable transcription, photograph, or facsimile available.

11 ὀρφονήεντος spoken variation of ὀρφνήεντος?

8a Syracuse 1/2

Two uninscribed pieces of gold leaf from two graves (Fusco necropolis), between late 5th and early 3rd cent BCE. One is a rectangular piece (20 mm : 12 mm) with an engraved image of a woman with a Janus-head (Demeter/Kore?), found in the mouth of the deceased, the second is longish oval (34mm : 10 mm), found on the chest.

P. Orsi, in *Not. Scav ser.* 5, vol. 4 (1906), 741 no. 561 and 747 no. 567, with a drawing 743 fig. 2.

Italy

9 Rome

From Rome, perhaps from the necropolis at Via Ostiense; now in the British Museum. A rectangular gold tablet, mid-2nd or 3rd cent. CE.

Ed. princ.: Comparetti 1903; cp. Murray in Harrison 1922 (1903): 672 no. VIII; Marshall 1911: 380 no. 3154.
Coll.: Zuntz (Riedweg/Tzifopoulos/Edmonds) A 5; Pugliese Carratelli 2001, I C I; Bernabé, *OF* 491 (= L 11); Kotansky 1994: 107 no. 27 (with ample commentary); MTG 23.

Ἔρχεται ἐκ καθαρῶν καθαρά, | χθονίων βασίλεια
Εὔκλεες Εὐβου|λεῦ τε, Διὸς τέκος, ἀλλὰ δέχε<σ>θε
Μνημο|σύνης τόδε δῶρον ἀοίδιμον ἀνθρώ|ποισιν.
Καικιλία Σεκουνδεῖνα, νόμωι | ἴθι δῖα γεγῶσα.

2 ἀλλὰ δέχε<σ>θε West, *ZPE* 18 (1975), 231: ΑΓΛΑΑΕΧΩΔΕ tablet, ἀγλαά· ἔχω δὲ editors.

9

1   She comes pure from the pure, Queen of the Chthonian Ones.

2   Eucles and Eubouleus, child of Zeus. "But accept

3   this gift of Memory, sung of among mortals."

4   "Caecilia Secundina, come, by law grown to be divine."

Greece, Islands

Crete

10 Eleutherna 1

From Eleutherna in central Crete, now in the National Museum, Athens; 2nd/1st cent. BCE, presumably from a cemetery. Small rectangular gold tablet, folded several times.

Ed. princ.: Joubin 1893; cp. Comparetti 1910, 38; *Inscr. Cret.* II, XII no. 31a.
Coll.: Zuntz (Riedweg/Tzifopoulos/Edmonds) B 3; Pugliese Carratelli 2001, I B 1; Bernabé, *OF* 478 (= L 5a); MTG 14a.

Δίψαι αὖος ἐγὼ καὶ ἀπόλλυμαι· ἀλλὰ πιέ<ν> μοι |

κράνας αἰειρόω ἐπὶ δεξιά, τῆ{ς} κυφάριΖος.|

τίς δ' ἐΖί; πῶ δ' ἐΖί; Γᾶς υἱός ἠμι καὶ Ὠρανῶ| ἀστερόεντος.

In the local alphabet, Z stands for the sharp double -σσ

11 Eleutherna 2

Presumably from the same cemetery; now in the National Museum, Athens; 2nd/1st cent. BCE. Small rectangular gold tablet, folded.

Ed. princ.: Myres 1893: 629 no. 1; cp. Comparetti 1910, 38; *Inscr. Cret.* II, XII no. 31b.
Coll.: Zuntz (Riedweg/Tzifopoulos/Edmonds) B 4; Pugliese Carratelli 2001, I B 2; Bernabé, *OF* 479 (= L 5b); MTG 14b.

Δίψαι αὖος ἐγὼ καὶ ἀπόλλυ{μα}μαι· ἀλλὰ πιέ<ν> μοι |

κράνας αἰειρόω ἐπὶ δεξιά, τῆ κυφάριΖος.|

τίς δ' ἐΖί; πῶ δ' ἐΖί; Γᾶς υἱός ἠμι καὶ Ὠρανῶ | ἀστερόεντος.

10

1   I (masculine) am parched with thirst and am dying; but grant me to drink

2   from the ever-flowing spring on the right, where the cypress is.

3   "Who are you? Where are you from?" I am a son of Earth and starry Sky.

11

1   I (masculine) am parched with thirst and am dying; but grant me to drink

2   from the ever-flowing spring on the right, where the cypress is.

3   "Who are you? Where are you from?" I am a son of Earth and starry Sky.

12 Eleutherna 3

Presumably from the same cemetery; now in the National Museum, Athens; 2nd/1st cent. BCE. Small rectangular gold tablet, folded.

Ed. princ.: Myres 1893: 629 no. 2; cp. Comparetti 1910: 38; *Inscr. Cret.* II, XII no. 31c.
Coll.: Zuntz (Riedweg/Tzifopoulos/Edmonds) B 5; Pugliese Carratelli 2001, I B 3; Bernabé, *OF* 480 (= L 5c); MTG 14c.

Δίψαι αὖος {λα.ος} ἐγὼ καὶ ἀπόλλυμαι· ἀλλὰ πιέμ μοι |

κράνας αἰενάω ἐπὶ δε[ξ]ιά, τῇ κυφάρισℨος. |

τίς δ' ἐℨί; πῶ δ' ἐℨί; Γᾶς υἱός ἠμ<ι> καὶ Ὠρανῶ | ἀστερόεντ[ο]ς.

13 Eleutherna 4

Found near Eleutherna, now in the National Museum, Athens (Hélène Stathatos Collection). 2nd/1st cent. BCE. Small rectangular gold tablet, folded

Ed. princ.: N. Verdelis, "Ὀρφικὰ ἐλάσματα ἐκ Κρήτης," *Arch. Eph.* 2 (1953–4), 56–60.
Coll.: Zuntz (Riedweg/Tzifopoulos/Edmonds) B 7; Pugliese Carratelli 2001, I B 5; Bernabé, *OF* 482 (= L 5e); MTG 14c; Tzifopoulos (2010), 5; (1953–4), 56–60.

Δίψαι αὖος ἐγὼ καὶ ἀπόλλυμαι· ἀλλὰ πιὲν ἐμοὶ |

κράνας <α>ἰ<ε>ιρ<ό>ω ἐπ<ὶ> δεξιά, τῇ κυφάριℨος. |

τίς δ' {εδ} ἐℨί; πῶ δ' ἐℨί; Γᾶς υἱός ἠμι καὶ <Ω>ρανῶ | ἀστερόεντος.

12

1   I (masculine) am parched with thirst and am dying; but grant me to drink

2   from the ever-flowing spring on the right, where the cypress is.

3   "Who are you? Where are you from?" I am a son of Earth and starry Sky.

13

1   I (masculine) am parched with thirst and am dying; but grant me to drink

2   from the ever-flowing spring on the right, where the cypress is.

3   "Who are you? Where are you from?" I am a son of Earth and starry Sky.

14 Eleutherna 5

From the same place, now in the National Museum, Athens (Hélène Stathatos Collection). 2nd/1st cent. BCE. Small rectangular gold tablet, folded.

Ed. princ.: N. Verdelis, "Ὀρφικὰ ἐλάσματα ἐκ Κρήτης," *Arch. Eph.* 2 (1953–4), 56–60.
Coll.: Zuntz (Riedweg/Tzifopoulos/Edmonds) B 8; Pugliese Carratelli 2001, I B 6; Bernabé, *OF* 483 (= L 5f); MTG 14f.

Δίψα<ι> δ' αὖος ἐγὼ καὶ ἀπόλ<λ>υμαι· ἀλ|λὰ π<ι>έμ μο<ι>

κράνας αἰενάω ἐπὶ δ|<ε>ξιά, τῆ κυφάριΖος.

τίς δ' ἐΖί; πῶ | δ' <ἐ>Ζί; Γᾶς υἱός <ἠ>μι καὶ Ὠρανῶ ἀστερό|εντος.

15 Eleutherna 6

From the same cemetery as Eleutherna 1, 2, and 3; National Museum, Athens; 2nd/1st cent. BCE. Rectangular gold tablet, left part missing (broken over the fold?).

Ed. princ.: Myres 1893: 629 no. 3; cp. Comparetti 1910: 40; *Inscr. Cret.* II, XII no. 31 bis.
Coll.: Pugliese Carratelli 2001, II C 1; Bernabé, *OF* 495 (= L 15); MTG 20: Tzifopoulos E1; Edmonds E2.

[Πλού]τωνι καὶ Φ-
[ερσ]οπόνει χαίρεν.

14

1 I (masculine) am parched with thirst and am dying; but grant me to drink

2 from the ever-flowing spring on the right, where the cypress is.

3 "Who are you? Where are you from?" I am a son of Earth and starry Sky.

15

1 To Pluton and

2 Persephone, greetings

16 Mylopotamos

From the region of Mylopotamos (between Eleutherna and Axos); exact location unknown. Now in the Archeological Museum, Iraklion. 2nd cent. BCE. Half-moon shaped gold tablet (top straight), not folded: an *epistomion* (mouth cover), as no. 17.

Ed. princ.: *Inscr. Cret.* II, XXX no. 4.
Coll.: Zuntz (Riedweg/Tzifopoulos/Edmonds) B 6; Pugliese Carratelli 2001, I B 4; Bernabé, *OF* 481 (= L 5d); MTG 17.

Δίψα<ι> δ' ἠμ' αὖος καὶ ἀπόλυμαι· ἀλὰ | πιέν μοι

κράνας αἰε<ρ>όω ἐπὶ | δεξιά, τê κυπαρί⟨ος.

τίς δ' ἐ⟨ί; π|ῶ δ' ἐ⟨ί; Γᾶς ἠμὶ <θ>υ<γ>άτηρ καὶ | Ὠρανῶ ἀστερόεντο

17 Rethymnon 1

From a grave of early Imperial times (between 25 BCE and 40 CE) in Sfakaki; Museum Rethymno. An ellipsoid piece of gold foil, unfolded; found at the base of the skull and quite probably originally covering the mouth.

Ed. princ.: Gavrilaki and Tzifopoulos 1998 (*SEG* 48.1227).
Coll.: Bernabé, *OF* 494 (= L 14); MTG 22; Tzifopoulos E 4; Edmonds E 5.

Πλούτωνι

Φερσεφόνη[ι]

It is unclear whether after Πλούτωνι one should add [καὶ].

16

1 I (masculine) am parched with thirst and am dying; but grant me to drink

2 from the ever-flowing spring on the right, where the cypress is.

3 "Who are you? Where are you from?" I am a daughter of Earth and starry Sky.

17

1 To Pluton

2 to Persephone

18 Rethymnon 2

From a disturbed grave in Sfakaki; 2nd/1st cent. BCE; Museum Rethymno. An oblong piece of gold foil, unfolded.

Ed. princ. = *Coll.*: Bernabé, *OF* 484a (= L 6a); MTG 21; Tzifopoulos/ Edmonds B12.

δίψαι τοι <α>ῦος παραπ<ό>λλυται. ἀλλὰ π{α}ιέν μοι
κράνας αἰ<ει>|ρ<ό>ου ἐπ' ἀ{α}ρι<σ>τερὰ τᾶς κυφα{σ}|ρίΖω.
τίς δ'εῖ ἤ πῶ δ'εῖ; Γᾶ|ς ἠμ{ο}ὶ μάτηρ ΠΩΤΙΑΕΤ| <κ>αὶ <Ο>ὐρανῶ
    <ἀ>στε<ρόεν>τ<ο>ς.
δίψαι το|ιΛΤΟΠΥΤΟΟΠΑСΡΑΝΗΟ

A number of gold tablets or reused flattened gold coins from Cretan graves bear personal names or are uninscribed; Tzifopoulos (2010) understands them as *epistomia*, to be put over the mouth of the deceased.

19 Lesbos

From a Hellenistic cist-grave, "an inscribed sheet with an Orphic text" has been reported, *Arch. Rep.* 1988–9, 93; unpublished.

18

1   He is parched with thirst and almost dying, but grant me to drink

2   from the ever-flowing spring on the left of the cypress.

3   "Who are you? And where are you from?" I am of Earth, mother
      [untranslatable letters] and of starry Sky.

4   Thirst [untranslatable]

Mainland Greece

Achaia

20 Aigion 1

From a Hellenistic cist-grave of a woman (ear-rings); small piece of gold foil, a "laurel leaf" (in reality in the shape of a lens or almond); the inscription with a lunar sigma.

Ed. princ.: *Arch. Delt.* 32B (1977), 94, with pl. 63b.
Coll.: Bernabé, *OF* 496e (= L 16e); Tzifopoulos/Edmonds F2.

Μύστης

21 Aigion 2

From a Hellenistic cist-grave; small piece of gold foil, leaf-shaped.

Ed. princ.: *Arch. Delt.* 42B (1987), 153.
Coll.: Bernabé *OF* 496c (= L 16c); Tzifopoulos/Edmonds F4.

Δεξίλαος μύστας

22 Aigion 3

From a Hellenistic cist-grave; small piece of gold foil, "almond-shaped."

Ed. princ.: *Arch. Delt.* 42B (1987), 153.
Coll.: Bernabé, *OF* 496d (= L 16d); Tzifopoulos/Edmonds F5.

Φίλων μύστας

20

Initiate

21

Dexilaos (is an) initiate

22

Philon (is an) initiate

Elis

23 Elis 1

From a pithos-shaped grave of a woman (rich jewelry, including a diadem); a small rectangular piece of gold foil, with rounded short sides; early 3rd cent. BCE

Ed. princ.: G. P. Papathanatsopoulos, *Deltion* 24B (1969), 153 and pl. 153β.
Coll.: Bernabé, *OF* 496i (= L 16i); Tzifopoulos/Edmonds F1.

Εὐξένη

24 Elis 2

From a 3rd-cent. BCE grave of a young woman; a piece of gold foil like a "myrtle leaf(?)" (Themelis), found under the cranium, i.e., probably placed in the mouth of the deceased.

Ed. princ.: Petros Themelis, in *Γ Ἐπιστημονική Συνάντηση για την Ἑλληνιστική κεραμική* (Thessalonica, 1994), 154 no. 15 and pl. 82b.
Coll.: Bernabé, *OF* 496j (= L 16j); Tzifopoulos/Edmonds F7.

Φιλημήνα

24a Elis 3

From a cist-grave of a woman (mirror) in Daphiotissa near Elis (chance find); "a small olive leaf" (Lazaridis), end 4th/early 3rd cent. BCE.

Ed. princ.: A. Lazaridis, *ADelt* 36B (1981) 151. 37B (1982) 135 (*SEG* 38.363).
Coll.: Edmonds F13 (not in Tzifopoulos).

Πάλαθα

On the name see *SEG* 41.809.

23

Euxene

24

Philemena

24a

Palatha

Thessaly

25 Pharsalos

From a grave of 350–300 BCE; now in the Volos Museum. The tablet was inside a richly decorated Attic bronze hydria (representing Boreas abducting Oreithyia) that contained the ashes of the deceased.

Ed. princ.: N. Verdelis, *Arch. Eph.* (1950–1), 80–105; cp. J.-C. Decourt, *Inscriptions de Thessalie I. Les cités de la vallée de l'Enipeus* (Paris, 1995), 128 no. 115.
Coll.: Zuntz (Riedweg/Tzifopoulos/Edmonds) B 2; Pugliese Carratelli 2001, I A 3; Bernabé, *OF* 477 (= L 4); MTG 8.

Εὑρήσεις Ἀΐδαο δόμοις ἐνδέξια κρήνην,
πὰρ δ' αὐτῆι | λευκὴν ἑστηκυῖαν κυπάρισσον.
ταύτης τῆς κρήνης | μηδὲ σχεδόθεν πελάσηισθα.
πρόσσω δ' εὑρήσεις τὸ Μνη|μοσύνης ἀπὸ λίμνης   4
ψυχρὸν ὕδωρ προ(ρέον), φύλακες | δ' ἐπύπερθεν ἔασιν.
οἵδε σ' εἰρήσονται ὅ τι χρέος | εἰσαφικάνεις.
τοῖς δὲ σὺ εὖ μάλα πᾶσαν ἀληθείην | καταλέξαι.
εἰπεῖν· Γῆς παῖς εἰμι καὶ Οὐρανοῦ ἀστ(ερόεντος),| 8
Ἀστέριος ὄνομα, δίψηι δ' εἰμ' αὖος· ἀλλὰ δότε μοι|
πίεν' ἀπὸ τῆς κρήνης.

25

1   You will find in the house of Hades, on the right side, a spring,

2   and standing by it a white cypress.

3   Do not even approach this spring!

4   Ahead you will find from the Lake of Memory,

5   cold water pouring forth; there are guards before it.

6   They will ask you by what necessity you have come.

7   You, tell them the whole entire truth.

8   Say, "I am a child of Earth and starry Sky.

9   My name is 'Starry.' I (masculine) am parched with thirst. But grant me

10 to drink from the spring."

26 a, b Pelinna

From a woman's grave in a sarcophagus in Pelinna (modern Palaio-gardiki); late 4th cent. BCE. Two ivy-shaped tablets, lying on the chest of the deceased.

Ed. princ.: K. Tsantsanoglou and G. M. Parassoglou, "Two Gold Lamellae From Thessaly," *Ελληνικά* 38 (1987), 3–16.
Coll.: Pugliese Carratelli 2001, II B 3 and 4; Bernabé, *OF* 485 and 486 (= L 7a, b); MTG 10, 11; Tzifopoulos/Edmonds D1, D2.

Text a

Νῦν ἔθανες | καὶ νῦν ἐγ|ένου, τρισόλβ|ιε, ἄματι τωῖδε.
εἰπεῖν Φερσεφόν|αι σ' ὅτι Β<ακ>χιος αὐτὸς | ἔλυσε.
τα{ι}ῦρος | εἰς γάλα ἔθορες,
αἶ|ψα εἰς γ<ά>λα ἔθορες,| 4
κριὸς εἰς γάλα ἔπεσ<ες>.
οἶνον ἔχεις εὐ|δ<α>ίμονα τιμή<ν>
κἀπιμένει σ' ὑπὸ | γῆν τέλεα ἄσσαπερ ὄλ|βιοι ἄλ|λοι.

5   χρίος tablet
7   τελέσας ἄπερ Bernabé: ΤΕ|ΛΕΑΑCΑ|ΠΕΡ tablet: τέ|λεα ἄσσα|περ editors.

Text b

Νῦν ἔθανε<ς> | καὶ νῦν ἐ|γένου, τρισόλ|βιε, ἄματι <τωῖ>|δε.
<ε>ἰπεῖν Φερ|σεφό<ναι σ'> ὅτι Βά<κ>χιο|ς αὐτὸς ἔλυσε.|
ταῦρος εἰς γάλα ἔθορες,
κριὸς εἰς γάλα ἔπεσε<ς>.
οἶνον ἔ|χεις εὐδ<αί>μον<α>| τιμ|ήν.

26 a, b

1   Now you have died and now you have come into being, O thrice happy one, on this same day.

2   Tell Persephone that the Bacchic One himself released you.

3   Bull, you jumped into milk.

4   Quickly, you jumped into milk. [*This line is missing from b*]

5   Ram, you fell into milk.

6   You have wine as your fortunate honor.

7   And below the earth there are ready for you the same offices [*or* rites] as for the other blessed ones. [*This line is missing from b*]

27 Pherae 1

From the south cemetery of Pherae, now in the Museum of Volos; 350–300 BCE. Rectangular gold band, originally rolled in the form of a cylinder.

Ed. princ.: Pavlos Chrysostomou, *Hypereia* 2 (1994), 127–38 (*SEG* 45.646); idem, *Η Θεσσαλική θεά Εν(ν)οδία η Φεραία θεά* (Athens, 1998), 210–20.
Coll.: Bernabé, *OF* 493 (= L 13); MTG 12; Tzifopoulos/Edmonds D3.

Σύμβολα· Ἀν<δ>ρικε-
παιδόθυρσον, ἀνδρικεπαι-
δόθυρσον· Βριμώ, Βριμώ. εἴσιθ<ι>
ἱερὸν λειμῶνα· ἄποινος   4
γὰρ ὁ μύστης.
ΓΑΠΕΔΟΝ

The last word is written upside down.

28 Pherae 2

Found 1904 in clandestine excavations in a tomb ("of historical times") near the Neolithic settlement at the Magoula Mati (A. Arvanitopoulos, *Praktika* 1907, 160), in a marble repository (*osteotheke*); now in the National Museum, Athens. Later 4th/earlier 3rd cent. BCE.

Ed. princ.: Robert Parker and Maria Stamatopoulou, *Arch. Eph.* 2004 (publ. 2007), 1–32. We thank the authors for making the proofs of their article available to us.
Coll.: Bernabé, *OF* 493A (= L 13a); Tzifopoulos/Edmonds D5.

πέμπε με πρὸς μυστῶ<ν> θιάσους· ἔχω ὄργια [-x]
Δήμητρος Χθονίας τε <τέ>λη καὶ Μητρὸς Ὀρεί[ας].

1 ΜΥΣΤΩΧ tablet; Βάκχου suggested but rejected by Parker and Stamatopoulou who prefer [ἰδοῦσα] (K. Bouraselis).
2 <τέ> Parker and Stamatopoulou; Burkert (orally)

On the problems of restoration see below pp. 205–7.

27

1   Passwords: Man-and-
2   child-thyrsus. Man-and-child-
3   thyrsus. Brimo, Brimo. Enter
4   the holy meadow, for the initiate
5   is redeemed.
6   GAPEDON (apparently a nonsense word, written upside down)

28

Send me to the *thiasoi* of the initiates; I possess the tokens [ ]
the rites [or offices] of Demeter Chthonia and of the Mountain
Mother.

29 Unknown place in Thessaly

From a grave of an unknown location in Thessaly, mid-4th cent. BCE; now in the J. Paul Getty Museum, Malibu, California. Rectangular gold tablet, found in a bronze hydria used as a crematory urn (see Figure 1, p. 51).

Ed. princ.: J. Breslin, *Greek Prayer* (Pasadena, CA 1977); repr. *Colloquy* 28 (1977), 10.
Coll.: Riedweg/Tzifopoulos/Edmonds B 9 (not yet in Zuntz); Pugliese Carratelli 2001, I B 7; Bernabé, *OF* 484 (= L 6); MTG 9.

Δίψαι αὖος ἐγὼ κἀπόλλυμαι·| ἀλλὰ πίεμ <μ>ου
κράνας αἰειρόω.| ἐπὶ δεξιὰ λευκὴ κυπάρισσος.|
τίς δ'εσί; πῶ δ'ἐσί; Γᾶς υἱός εἰμι |καὶ Οὐρανοῦ ἀστερόεντος·|
αὐτὰρ ἐμοὶ γένος οὐράνιον.

Macedonia

30 Amphipolis

From a grave in the Eastern Cemetery; found in a sarcophagus (T 45), folded on the chest of the deceased woman. Late 4th to early 3rd cent. BCE.

Ed. princ.: P. Malama, *Το Αρχαιολογικό έργο στη Μακεδονία και Θράκη* 15 (2001) [2003], 118 (A. Chaniotis, "Epigraphical Bulletin for Greek Religion 2001," *Kernos* (2004), 225 no. 118; *SEG* 51.788).
Coll.: Bernabé, *OF* 496n (= L 16n); Tzifopoulos/Edmonds D 4.

Εὐαγὴς ἱερὰ Διονύ-
σου Βαχχίου εἰμί,
Ἀρχεβού[λ]η
Ἀντιδώρου.

3 suppl. Chaniotis.

29

1 I (masculine) am parched with thirst and am dying; but grant me to drink

2 from the ever-flowing spring. On the right is a white cypress.

3 "Who are you? Where are you from?" I am a son of Earth and starry Sky.

4 But my race is heavenly.

30

1 Pure and sacred to Dionysus

2 Bacchius am I;

3 Archeboule

4 (daughter of) Antidoros.

31 Pella/Dion 1

From a well-built cist-grave in the immediate vicinity of a temple-like building; end of the 4th cent. BCE. Shaped like a leaf: laurel or, more likely, myrtle.

Ed. princ.: Maria Lilimbake-Akamate, *Το Αρχαιολογικό έργο στη Μακεδονία και Θράκη* 3 (1989 [1992]), 95 with fig. 8; eadem, *Arch. Delt.* 44–6 (1989–91), Meletemata 80 with fig. 27a (*SEG* 45.782).
Coll.: Bernabé, *OF* 496b (= L 16b); Tzifopoulos E 3; Edmonds E 4.

Φερσεφόνηι
Ποσείδιππος μύστης
εὐσεβής.

32 Pella/Dion 2

From a girl's grave (T3, with female jewelry) close by, similar to and contemporary with no. 31; an almost identical leaf, the inscription scratched lengthwise in the bottom half.

Ed. princ.: Maria Lilimbake-Akamate, *Το Αρχαιολογικό έργο στη Μακεδονία και Θράκη* 3 (1989 [1992]), 101 with fig. 8; eadem, *Arch. Delt.* 44–6 (1989–91), Meletemata 80 with fig. 29a (*SEG* 45.782).
Coll.: Bernabé, *OF* 496a (= L 16a); Tzifopoulos/Edmonds F 6.

Φιλόξενα

33 Pella/Dion 3

From a Hellenistic grave; gold disk.

SEG 49.703; Tzifopoulos/Edmonds F 12.

Ἐπιγένης

31

1   To Persephone,

2   Poseidippos,

3   pious initiate.

32

Philoxena

33

Epigenes

34 Pella/Dion 4

From the cist-grave of a girl of late 4th cent. BCE; a small gold leaf.

Ed. princ.: M. Lilibaki-Akamanti, "Από την τοποφραφίαν και τα νεκρο-
ταφεία της Πέλλας," *Το Αρχαιολογικό έργο στη Μακεδονία και Θράκη* 6
(1992), 127–35 (*SEG* 45.783).
Coll.: Bernabé, *OF* 496f (= L 16f); Tzifopoulos/Edmonds F 11.

Ἡγησίσκα

35 Methone

From a 4th-cent. BCE cist-grave; placed inside the skull (i.e., in the mouth)
of the deceased; presumably rectangular piece of gold foil; the grave couch
with Dionysiac ornaments.

Ed. princ.: M. Besios, *Arch. Delt.* 41B (1986), 142f. (*SEG* 40 (1990),
no. 541).
Coll.: Bernabé, *OF* 496h (= L 16h); Tzifopoulos/Edmonds F 3.

Φυλομάγα

36 Europos

From tumulus β in modern Toumba Paionias, north of Europos (= ancient
Gortynia, Hatzopoulos, *BE* 1996, no. 261?); a rectangular piece of gold
foil; late 4th/early 3rd cent. BCE.

Ed. princ.: Th. Savvopoulou, *Το Αρχαιολογικό έργο στη Μακεδονία και
Θράκη* 6 (1992), 427–8 with fig. 4 on p. 430 (*SEG* 45.762).
Coll.: Bernabé, *OF* 496g (= L 16g); Tzifopoulos/Edmonds F 10.

Βόττακος

34

Hegesiska

35

Phylomaga

36

Bottakos

36a Pella/Dion

Undisclosed number of gold-tablets from fifteen cist-graves, 4th cent. BCE, each placed in the mouth of a deceased. Each contained a personal name.

A. Pariente, *BCH* 14 (1990) 787.

37 Vergina (Aigai)

From a Hellenistic grave.

Ed. princ.: Ph. Petsas, *Deltion* 17A (1961/62), 259.
Coll.: Bernabé, *OF* 496k (= L 16k); Tzifopoulos E 2; Edmonds E 3.

Φιλίστη Φερσεφόνηι χαίρειν.

38 Hagios Athanasios (near Thessalonica)

A carelessly inscribed gold tablet from a looted grave; Hellenistic.

Ed. princ.: Ph. Petas, *Deltion* 22B (1967), 2, 399–400, fig. 21 (see also *Makedonika* 9, 1969, 466); better text M. Hatzopoulos, in Aphrodite Avagiannou, ed., *Λατρείες στην περιφερείαν του αρχαίου Ελληνικου κόσμου* (Athens, 2002), 28 (*SEG* 52.607).
Coll.: Bernabé, *OF* 496l; (= L 16k); Tzifopoulos E 5; Edmonds E 6.

Φιλωτέρα
τῶι Δεσπό-
τει χέρε(ιν)

37

Philiste greets Persephone

38

Philotera

greets

the Lord

CONCORDANCE

Graf/Johnston	Bernabé, OF	Zuntz	Riedweg	Pugliese	Bernabé/Jiménez	Tzifo-poulos	Edmonds
1 Hipponion	474	—	B10	I A1	L1	B10	B10
2 Petelia	476	B 1	B1	I A2	L3	B1	B1
3 Thurii 1	487	A4	A4	II B2	L8	A4	A4
4 Thurii 2	492	C	C	III 1	L12	C	C
5 Thurii 3	488	A1	A1	II B1	L9	A1	A1
6 Thurii 4	490	A3	A3	II A2	L10b	A3	A3
7 Thurii 5	489	A2	A2	II A1	L10a	A2	A2
8 Entella	475	—	B11	—	L2	B11	B11
8a Syracuse	—	—	—	—	—	—	—
9 Rome	491	A5	A5	I A3	L11	A5	A5
10 Eleutherna 1	478	B3	B3	I C1	L5a	B3	B3
11 Eleutherna 2	479	B4	B4	I B1	L5b	B4	B4
12 Eleutherna 3	480	B5	B5	I B2	L5c	B5	B5
13 Eleutherna 4	482	B7	B7	I B3	L5e	B7	B7
14 Eleutherna 5	483	B3	B3	I B5	L5f	B8	B8
15 Eleutherna 6	495	—	—	I B1	L15	E1	E2
16 Milopotamo	481	B6	B6	II C1	L5d	B6	B6
17 Rethymno 1	494	B7	B7	I B4	L14	E4	E5
18 Rethymno 2	484a	—	—	—	L6a	B12	B12
[19 Lesbos]	—	—	—	—	—	—	—
20 Aigion 1	496e	—	—	—	L16e	F2	F2
21 Aigion 2	469c	—	—	—	L16c	F4	F4
22 Aigion 3	469d	—	—	—	L16d	F5	F5
23 Elis 1	469i	—	—	—	L16i	F1	E1
24 Elis 2	469j	—	—	—	L16j	F7	F7
24a Elis 3	—	—	—	—	—	—	—
25 Pharsalos	477	B2	B2	I A3	L4	B2	B2
26 Pelinna a	485	—	—	—	L7a	D2A	D1
Pelinna b	486	—	—	—	L7b	D2B	D2

Graf/ Johnston	Bernabé, OF	Zuntz	Riedweg	Pugliese	Bernabé/ Jiménez	Tzifó- poulos	Edmonds
27 Pherai 1	493	—	—	—	L13	D3	D3
28 Pherai 2	493a	—	—	—	L13a	D5	D5
29 (Thessaly)	484	—	B9	—	L6	B9	B9
30 Amphipolis	496n	—	—	—	L16b	D4	D4
31 Pella 1	496b	—	—	—	L16a	E3	E4
32 Pella 2	496a	—	—	—	—	F6	F6
33 Pella 3	—	—	—	—	—	F12	F12
34 Pella 4	496f	—	—	—	L16f	F11	F11
35 Methone	496h	—	—	—	L16h	F3	F3
36 Europos	496g	—	—	—	L16g	F10	F10
37 Vergina	496k	—	—	—	L16k	E2	E3
38 Heraclea	496l/495a	—	—	—	L15A	E5	E6

In the first edition, our no. *39 ("uncertain") – the fragment of a gold foil in the museum of Manisa (Hasan Malay, *Greek and Latin Inscriptions in the Manisa Museum*, Vienna: 1994, 139 no. 488 = Bernabé 494) – has been provided with a better text by David Jordan and Elena Pachoumi, *Epigraphica Anatolica* 44 (2011), 163–4. The new text makes it clear that it is a phylactery of a known type – see David Jordan in Bernabé *OF* after no. 494.

A HISTORY OF SCHOLARSHIP
ON THE TABLETS

Fritz Graf

Before philology

Orpheus, the son of Apollo (or a Thracian king) and a Muse, was first and foremost a poet, the earliest poet the Greeks claimed to have. Byzantine manuscripts transmit several hexametrical works under his name: the *Argonautica* on the voyage of Jason and his crew (which included Orpheus, the narrator of the story); the *Lithica*, which discussed the magical properties of stones and gems; the *Hymns*, a collection of short hymns to a large variety of Greek divinities. Many more works are known to us by their titles, and fragments are preserved in other Greek works; foremost among them is a *Theogony* in twenty-four rhapsodies that is repeatedly cited by Neoplatonic commentators on Plato. With some notable and early exceptions, the Greeks did not doubt Orpheus' authorship of these works, and early modern Europe initially concurred; the great Joseph Justus Scaliger (1520–1609) even made a translation of the *Hymns* into somewhat archaizing Latin (1561). Slowly, however, textual scholars recognized the late date and therefore the spurious character of these texts; this is why Gottfried Hermann (1772–1848), Germany's leading classical scholar of the time, entitled his collection of these texts and fragments, the first collection ever made and published in 1805, not the "Works of Orpheus" but simply "Things Having to Do With Orpheus," *Orphica*.[1]

To the Greeks, Orpheus also was an inventor and teacher of rituals (*teletai*), from Aristophanes onwards (*Frogs* 1032). More specifically, these rituals were described as mystery rites (*mystēria*), especially those of Dionysus. Diodorus of Sicily is the first to write about Orphic mystery rites, *Orphikai teletai*, a phrase that to him is just another name for the mystery rites of Dionysus (*Bibl.* 3.65.6); perhaps he followed the terminology of an earlier historian. Four centuries earlier, Herodotus combined "Orphic and Bacchic" burial customs that in reality were "Egyptian and

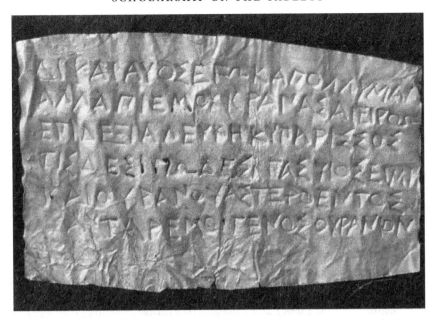

Figure 1 Gold Tablet from Thessaly (no. 29). The J. Paul Getty Museum, Villa Collection, Malibu, California, gift of Lenore Barozzi.

Pythagorean" (2.8). The Neoplatonists, in their enthusiasm for mysteries, developed the image of Orpheus as the founder of mystery cults, and early modern Europe accepted and elaborated upon it, sometimes wildly; this is not the place to go into details.[2] The late eighteenth and early nineteenth centuries saw many authors who turned Orpheus into a major religious leader of early Greece, most prominently perhaps the greatly admired Heidelberg professor Friedrich Creuzer (1771–1858), who was, in spite of his sometimes outrageous ideas, no mean scholar: in his widely read *Symbolik und Mythologie der Alten Völker* (four volumes in its third edition, 1810–12), Orpheus and his mysteries play a major role in the civilizing of early Greece by religious reformers who (he thought) had come from India. This wild theory quickly provoked the Hellenists, who could accept neither such a dominant Eastern influence nor such a key role for the mystery rituals in early Greece.[3] In 1829, in the most thorough attack on Creuzer's "pan-Orphism," Christian August Lobeck, a strict philologist who almost by nature distrusted the vagueness of mysteries, tried to set the record straight: the second book of his *Aglaophamus sive de theologiae mysticae Graecorum causis libri tres*, which dealt with the *Orphica*, still remains a sound if polemical account of what antiquity really knew about Orpheus and his religious inventions.[4]

The first Gold Tablets

Such early scholarship on Orpheus and his mysteries does not mention the Gold Tablets or gold leaves, *lamellae aureae*: these direct witnesses to the mysteries of Dionysus Bacchius and to the hopes of the initiates were still hidden in the graves of their bearers. The first gold leaf to be known, the somewhat damaged text from Petelia, came to light not long after *Aglaophamus* was published (it would have been tidy if it had been found in the same year that *Aglaophamus* appeared, but this cannot be demonstrated). It did not, however, make an impact, since its nature remained enigmatic or was misunderstood for most of the nineteenth century, a not uncommon fate for isolated archeological objects. In 1834, it was for sale somewhere in the kingdom of Naples, and it was purchased by James Millingen (1774–1845), an engraver and antiquarian who was for some time in the service of that famous and colorful British ambassador at the court of Naples, Sir William Hamilton; Sir William himself was an ardent collector, besides being the lover and husband of Emma, *née* Hart (1761–1815) who in turn was the lover of Horatio Nelson. Millingen's service to Sir William accounts for his excellent connections in Southern Italy, and his impressive status in the world of antiquarians of the period.[5] Millingen's acquistion provoked the comment of another collector, who described it to the then secretary of the German Archeological Institute in Rome, Eduard Gerhard, in a letter that makes it very clear that no one, including Millingen, really understood what it was they had found or bought.[6] Speculations ranged from a text in an unknown language to an amulet or an oracle: it was as an oracle that the tablet was reprinted in some of the major epigraphical collections of the nineteenth century.[7] In one sense, the Petelia tablet really was an amulet: the thin foil was found, tightly rolled, in an amulet case that was hanging on a golden chain: this amuletic necklace dates to perhaps the second century CE. But this was its second, later use by someone who thought the text so powerful that it would protect her against the evil powers of the Underworld; in order to fit into the case, its bottom part had been cut away when already rolled up.[8]

Things changed radically only toward the end of the nineteenth century, when the Petelia tablet (which was lost from sight after the dispersal of the Millingen collection, although it had arrived, with a large part of this collection, at the British Museum[9]) was freed from its status as an isolated object without parallels or, perhaps more importantly, without an archeological context (a concept that, in any case, did not yet exist in the earlier nineteenth century). In 1879, an enterprising local engineer, Francesco Cavallari, began to excavate the impressive burial mounds in the region of Thurii in Southern Italy. The careful excavation of the largest mound, the

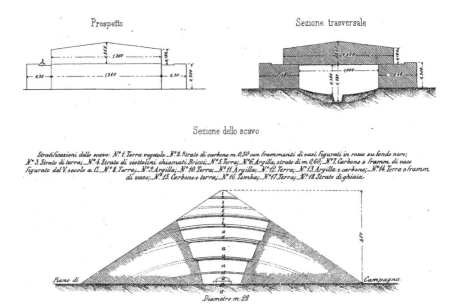

Figure 2 Cavallari's drawings of the Timpone Grande, after *Notizie degli Scavi d'Antichità* (1879), plate VI.

Timpone Grande (Figure 2), yielded two texts, a larger leaf enveloping a second, smaller one (our nos. 3 and 4). In the following year, the excavation of a smaller mound, the Timpone Piccolo, brought three more texts to light that were almost identical among themselves (our nos. 5–7). The prestigious *Notizie degli Scavi di Antichità* that were edited by the famous and old Roman Accademia dei Lincei published excavation reports at the end of both seasons.[10] These reports also contained the texts and interpretations of the Gold Tablets by Domenico Comparetti (1835–1927), one of Italy's most active scholars at the time. These editions and commentaries make Comparetti the very founder and ancestor of all scholarly work on the Gold Tablets.

Comparetti was a scholar whose career still astonishes us.[11] Having acquired a degree in mathematics and science from the University of Rome, he started out in life as assistant in his uncle's Roman pharmacy. This must have given him enough leisure that he could teach himself ancient and modern Greek (the latter simply by chatting with Greek students in Rome). In 1859, at the age of twenty-four, he became Professor of Ancient Greek in Pisa. Later he moved to the University of Florence, then perhaps the most prestigious of all Italian universities, all the while retaining a position as professor emeritus at Pisa. Comparetti was, as a recent admirer has formulated it, "hardly a one-project scholar":[12] his interests went well beyond Greek culture and religion and embraced, among other things, folklore studies. Many of his books were quickly translated into English and some of them are still read or at least cited with respect bordering on awe. Among them are a study of the Finnish epic poem *Kalevala* that showed a vivid interest in orality well before it became *de rigueur* in classical studies (*Kalevala o la poesia tradizionale dei Finni. Studio storico-critico sulle origini delle grandi epopee nazionali*, 1891; English 1898);[13] a book on Sindbad the Sailor that impressed the learned world (*Ricerche intorno al libro di Sindibad*, 1869; English 1881); and a collection of medieval Italian poetry from manuscripts, organized together with a colleague. His most lasting achievement, however, was the two volumes on *Vergil in the Middle Ages*: they still are the authoritative account of how Rome's most famous poet was seen in the Middle Ages and beyond.[14]

In 1875, Comparetti was elected to the venerable Roman Accademia dei Lincei that had just become the national academy of unified Italy; the election confirmed his stature as one of the leading scholars of antiquity in Italy. This and, more specifically, his well-known competence with regard to early Greek and Roman inscriptions, must have been the reason that the excavator of the Thurian grave mounds immediately consulted him on these texts. In 1879, having only the two tablets from the Timpone Grande, the larger of which baffled him (as it still baffles most scholars today), Comparetti saw the connection to mystery cults (although he thought of Eleusis) and was reminded of Pindar's description of the soul's way to the Isles of the Blessed in *Olympian* 2, as we still are. A year later, with the three tablets from the Timpone Piccolo, he could be more elaborate, and more precise; most importantly perhaps, he recalled the other South Italian Gold Tablet, the one from Petelia, and showed that it was not an oracle at all but belonged to the same group of mystery texts; when the British Museum, reacting to his report, informed him of its whereabouts, he published an excellent edition of it.[15] He now defined the mystery cult into which the deceased were initiated as "Orphic and Bacchic," rejecting the association with Pythagoreanism that would have been natural in Southern Italy and that was still important to Zuntz in 1971, in favor of an association with the mysteries of Dionysus; he called this Orphic Dionysus "Zagreus," using a divine name that the learned Greek poets Euripides and Callimachus had connected with Dionysus. He associated the eschatology of the tablets with the Orphic anthropogony and assumed that the hexameters in the Gold Tablets would have been derived from three *Descent Poems* attributed to Orpheus. Furthermore, he connected all these texts and rituals with the *orpheotelestai*, the "begging priests and seers" whom we know from Plato, and with the Bacchic movement that spread from

Southern Italy to Etruria and to Rome, where it caused, in 186 BCE, what has become known as the "Bacchanalia scandal." Plato describes these itinerant religious practitioners as specialists in harmful magic and initiation rites that would heal the consequences of unjust deeds; he ascribes to them the use of "a hubbub of books by Musaeus and Orpheus according to which they perform sacrifices" in order to remove the fear of postmortem punishment.[16] It was an itinerant priest such as this (*sacrificulus et vates*, Livy 39.8.4) who spread the Bacchic mysteries from Campania to Etruria and Rome. Here they became a major threat to order and morals, at least according to the Roman authorities who were quick to punish the major participants and *de facto* forbid these mysteries.

It is difficult not to be impressed by Comparetti's achievement. With only six tablets at his disposal, one of which he did not understand and three of which were basically identical, he nevertheless shaped interpretation of the Gold Tablets in a decisive way; it still is the frame for our way of thinking about them, more than a century and many tablets later. There have been those who contradicted him, most famously Günther Zuntz and most recently Radcliffe Edmonds, but these voices always have been dissenters from a large *communis opinio* shaped by Comparetti. It is tempting to speculate on what the course of scholarship would have been if it had not been the Thurii tablets but the shorter Cretan ones or that of Caecilia Secundina that had been found first. Without the reference to reincarnation, Comparetti might not have seen a connection with Pythagoras and Orpheus; without the claim that the deceased "paid the penalty for unrighteous deeds," he would not have adduced Pindar's frg. 133 and Orphic anthropogony; and without the name of Eucles, whom he understood as perhaps "*Dionysus* infernale o *Zagreus* degli Orfici,"[17] he would not have spotted the Bacchic character of the rites. Perhaps then, one would have had to wait much longer for the correct understanding of these texts as Instructions for the Beyond, *Totenpässe*, belonging to Bacchic initiates and embedded within a mythological framework expressed in hexametrical poems ascribed to Orpheus.

Due to the wide distribution of the *Notizie degli Scavi*, the South Italian texts soon became known outside of Italy. In his *Habilitationsschrift* of 1891 on the Orphic *Hymns*, written under the guidance of the great Hermann Usener, the young German scholar Albrecht Dieterich (1866–1908) devoted an entire chapter to the tablets and tried to show that they all derived from the same "Orphico-Pythagorean" poem: despite Comparetti, the Pythagoreans could not be left out of his reading. He repeated his thesis in his widely read book *Nekyia* (1893, 2nd edn. 1913). On the surface, this book dealt with a range of questions relating to a recently published fragment of the *Apocalypse of Peter* from Egypt.[18] In its substance, however,

Nekyia was a pivotal study of Greek eschatological beliefs from Homer to late antiquity, including "Greek folk beliefs about the realm of the dead" ("*griechischer Volksglaube vom Totenreich*"); its third chapter explicitly deals with "Orphico-Pythagorean Books on the Underworld" ("*orphisch-pythagoreische Hadesbücher*").[19] The other, even more fundamental study on these beliefs appeared a year later: Erwin Rohde (1845–98) included the tablets in his epoch-making *Psyche. Seelencult und Unsterblichkeits-glaube der Griechen* (1894, 2nd edn. 1898) and, like Comparetti,*f* ascribed them to a religious sect that performed Dionysiac mystery rites.[20] From the pages of these two highly influential German scholars, the Orphic or "Orphico-Pythagorean" Gold Tablets were firmly established in the modern scholarship on Greek eschatology.

A few more Greek texts were found not much later. The first four of the short Cretan texts were published, somewhat hastily, in 1893 by two archeologists and in 1910, more authoritatively, by Domenico Comparetti (our nos. 10–12, 16);[21] in 1903, Comparetti published the considerably later text of Caecilia Secundina from Rome (our no. 9). This expanded the geographical and temporal range from fourth-century Southern Italy to Crete, and to Rome in the Imperial epoch. These new texts did not change much, however: Comparetti's assessment seemed confirmed, and to assume Pythagoreanism as a vehicle became even more difficult.

The importance that the Gold Tablets acquired for the study of Greek religion and thought manifested itself in the four editions that followed each other within a short period of time at the beginning of the twentieth century. The first monograph edition to be printed was due to Comparetti; it appeared in 1910, provided with ample commentaries and lavish illustrations. In 1915, another Italian, Alexander Olivieri, edited the texts in a series that was destined for use in the academic classroom: by now, they were important enough to be the subject of university teaching. Well before that, Gilbert Murray, Regius Professor of Greek at the University of Oxford, had contributed a "Critical Appendix on the Orphic Tablets" (fifteen pages of drawings, a Greek text, an English translation and explanatory notes) to the highly influential book of his Cambridge friend Jane Ellen Harrison, *Prolegomena to the Study of Greek Religion* (1903); the appendix bolstered the arguments of Harrison's long account of Orphism with its main thesis that "Orpheus took an ancient superstition, deep-rooted in the savage ritual of Dionysus, and lent to it a new spiritual significance."[22] For Harrison, that is, the texts all belonged to a reformed version of the ecstatic cult of Dionysus; Orpheus, the poet from Thrace, had become a religious reformer who turned the primitivism of Greek religion into something new, spiritual, and modern. Orpheus and the Orphic movement thus attested to the philosophical force of Greek religion before the rise of true philosophy, and the Gold Tablets with their hint of reincarnation and theology were crucial. This also explains why Hermann Diels included them in his highly successful and still fundamental *Fragmente der Vorsokratiker* (first edition 1906) among the fragments of Orpheus, the first and foremost of the pre-philosophical thinkers;[23] the radical reshuffling of the collection done by Walter Kranz for its fifth edition (1934) did not affect Orpheus' inclusion.[24] This conferred the blessings of German scholarship on the interpretations of Comparetti. When Otto Kern published his Orphic fragments (*Orphicorum fragmenta*, 1922, a Latin title that left blissfully open whether the book dealt with the fragments of Things Orphic or fragments written by Orphics), the Gold Tablets had to be included as important documents for the pre-Hellenistic history of Orphism.

Kern's collection had made a very different choice from Hermann's, which had been published more than a century earlier. Kern decided not to print the extant texts of Orpheus – the *Hymns*, *Lithica*, and *Argonautica* – and focused entirely on the fragments of poems ascribed to Orpheus. Unlike Hermann, whose Orpheus was basically a poet, Kern's Orpheus was a religious founder, the prophet of what was seen as an important religious movement in Greek religion, called "Orphism." In research on ancient religion, Orphism had established itself as a major topic, and a rather impatient comment made by Wilamowitz in his old age, to the effect that his contemporaries were talking much too much about Orphics ("die Modernen reden so entsetzlich viel von Orphikern"), simply confirmed this state of affairs. Wilamowitz had become quite skeptical about the very existence of something called Orphism; he rejected the term *die Orphik* as a hideous neologism and refused to connect it in any way with the mysteries of Dionysus. If anything, the Gold Tablets were un-Greek, Egyptian in their inspiration.[25] If this position was at least in part due to his life-long aversion to Nietzsche (whose friend Rohde was) and to the school of Bonn (where Albrecht Dieterich earned his doctorate), it also made him contradict his friend and colleague Hermann Diels, and take back things he himself had said in his youth. This shows how the evidence could be read in a much less maximalist way than many had read it, and it remains part of the methodological problem facing any study of Orphism: how far is it legitimate to explain isolated pieces of information from the late archaic and classical age by means of the full picture provided only by Neoplatonic sources? Or, to put it differently: should we choose the most economical hypothesis that combines all the facts we have at our disposition, or should we choose other explanations, or even prefer to leave isolated details unexplained because there is no continuity between Greece of the fifth century BCE and that of the third century CE?[26]

Orphism and Christianity

The contemporaries against whom Wilamowitz grumbled were many, and among the first was a student of his (the belief in Orphism was not the prerogative of Rohde or the Bonn crowd). In 1895, shortly after the first appearance of *Psyche*, Ernst Maass (1856–1929), a somewhat renegade student of Wilamowitz, published *Orpheus. Untersuchungen zur griechischen, römischen, altchristlichen Jenseitsdichtung und Religion*, a book that was as well received at its time as it is thoroughly forgotten today. It unites studies on Eleusis and "the Orphic religion," Orpheus "a Greek god," the Orphic *Hymns*, the "*Katabasis* of Vibia," and the Orphic background of some Christian apocalypses.[27] Its common denominator is the central place of poetry ascribed to Orpheus or rather of the religious movement called Orphism ("die orphische Religion") in Greek thought about the afterlife. For Maass, as for Rohde and for Albrecht Dieterich, Greek religion was far from being a religion focused on sacrificial ritual on the one side, and on a rather amoral divine mythology on the other side. This was the polemical stance that the early Christian apologetics had taken when fighting against pagan religion; in reality, scholars now insisted, Greek religion contained a strain of religious practice and thought that was very much concerned with the fate of the individual soul and with life after death. Jane Ellen Harrison's Orpheus, who infused spiritual values into primitive Dionysiac ritual, follows this same paradigm, enriched only by the exciting primitivism of the Cambridge School.

But there was much more behind this intensive talk about Orphism than just a philological fashion: Orphism had joined a major debate, almost a "culture war" (to use a contemporary term) that characterized late nineteenth- and early twentieth-century Europe. The debate was about the role of institutional religion in a modern, secular state, not least about the role of the Catholic Church, the most powerful religious institution in the Western world but one that, in the course of the nineteenth century, felt severely threatened and reacted with aggressive positions such as the dogma of the Pope's infallibility. The debate coincided with the foundation of two major European nation-states, Germany and Italy, both of which had to struggle for independendence from the Vatican; in Germany, this resulted in what contemporaries called *Kulturkampf*, "culture war"; one side-effect of the debate was the foundation of chairs in the History of Religion in The Netherlands, France, and Germany. One way to break the power of the Church was to historicize Christianity: far from being the divinely revealed religion, much (or, according to some people, all) of its ritual and theological content had pre-Christian roots and derived from Greek and Roman paganism. This move extended a much older Protestant criticism of Catholicism to Christianity as such.[28] Since nineteenth-century Christianity very much defined itself through its care for the soul and its fate after death, it was important to find this same content already among the pagans. It was found in the mystery religions that became pagan religions of individual salvation, sometimes with structures that were reminiscent of Christian institutions. This was in part the result of an attitude toward Greek and Roman paganism that now became circular. For a long time already, scholars had unconsciously projected their Christian notions of religion and its institutions on pagan religion, especially on what they called the mystery religions. This was especially true for itinerant cults such as the mystery cult of Isis or of Dionysus, where Livy and Apuleius could be used as reliable witnesses for "missionary" expansions.[29] Now, in the heated atmosphere of *Kulturkampf*, they used these parallels as an argument for historical ties between the two phenomena.[30] Emblematic for this move is the life and work of the French Roman Catholic priest and theologian Alfred Loisy (1857–1940). Loisy was a major force in the historical approach to the origins of Christianity already when he was teaching at the Institut Catholique in Paris; the Church, feeling threatened by Loisy's work, soon removed Loisy from this teaching position. After first the École Pratique des Hautes Études and later the Collège de France gave him positions to continue his research and his teaching, Pope Pius X excommunicated him in 1908. He summed up much of his research in *Les mystères païens et le mystère chrétien*, a book that was finished in summer 1914 but released, due to the war, only in 1919 and re-edited in 1924.[31] One result of Loisy's work was his insight that the mystery cults, not the least the Orphic mysteries of Dionysus, expressed the very same spiritual world of individual salvation that also expressed itself in the rise of Catholic Christianity; Loisy was very careful not to derive Christianity directly from the pagan mystery religions but to embed them in the same general need for personal salvation of the times.

The Gold Tablets, under these circumstances, were a real god-send: they confirmed the eschatological and spiritual hopes of the initiates of Dionysus Bacchius as far back as the fourth century BCE, and thus, they played a role in the monographs on Orphism that summed up and continued the work of Rohde, Maass, and Harrison between the two world wars – André Boulanger's *Orphée. Rapports de l'orphisme et du christianisme* (1924), Vittorio Macchioro's *Zagreus. Studi intorno al Orfismo* (1930), William K. C. Guthrie's *Orpheus and Greek Religion* (1935), and Father Marie-Joseph Lagrange's *L'Orphisme* (1937), part of a much larger introduction to the New Testament that mainly answered and corrected Loisy. They all share, to a larger or smaller degree, a maximalist approach to Orphism: there was an Orphic movement that was part of or even identical with the mysteries of Dionysus; there were religious communities that shared the eschatological beliefs expressed in the Gold Tablets; and there were religious leaders and initiators, the itinerant *orpheotelestai* who were the missionaries of the cult.

The ideological basis of this concept of an Orphic movement or even an Orphic church is much clearer with Macchioro and Father Lagrange than it is with the Hellenists Boulanger and Guthrie, who were less interested in the roots of Christianity. Macchioro's *Zagreus* is the sum of his long study of the role the Orphic movement played in Greek civilization; in its preface he lists all his earlier publications, which the present book was intended to supersede.[32] He constructed the Orphic mysteries as a Dionysiac movement of great power and long duration. The eschatology of these mysteries was a major spiritualizing force of Greek religious ritualism; it was expressed in the Gold Tablets and formulated in the Orphic mythology whose fragments were preserved by the Neoplatonic commentators of Plato. Orphic religious thought influenced the most prominent Greek thinkers, from Heraclitus and Plato to the apostle Paul and the Gnostic reformer Marcion, whose importance for early Christianity had been recovered, not so long before, by the leading German church historian Adolf von Harnack.[33] It is obvious how Macchioro reduces Christianity to yet another extension of pagan spiritualism, and this was not lost on contemporary readers. During the winter of 1929/1930, he was invited to give a series of lectures on this very topic at New York's Columbia University, which were immediately published as *From Orpheus to Paul. A History of Orphism*. The book made Macchioro's position available to the Anglophone world (where the book is still in print). The Columbia faculty, whom Macchioro thanks in his preface and who must have been instrumental in his invitation, were less interested in Greek religion than in this historical reductionism of dogmatic and totalitarian Christianity. They all were members of Columbia's philosophy department with a deep interest in Pragmatism. Wendell T. Bush was a close friend and ally of John Dewey, one of the founders of American Pragmatism. Herbert W. Schneider, who had been Dewey's research assistant, had just become professor of religion and philosophy in 1929. Schneider had worked in Italy, studying the totalitarian Fascist movement;[34] Macchioro in turn is remembered for his distance from Fascism, which cost him his post as director of the Naples Archeological Museum in 1929.[35] Schneider's fellow student Irwin Erdman is still being vilified as an atheist on a Fundamentalist website,[36] a fate he shares with John Dewey whose philosophy of education still angers evangelical Christians.[37]

Marie-Joseph Lagrange, the Dominican monk and scholar who founded the École Pratique d'Études Bibliques in Jerusalem, comes from the opposite side. His book was part of an introduction to the New Testament in which he addressed the question of how greatly Christianity was influenced by pagan religion. In his preface, he squarely faces the challenge that history poses to a revealed religion. History is inescapable, because "Christian religion has been revealed by God through history," and only a critical historian can refute the many wrong historical theories of the past. Even if "one has perhaps exaggerated the importance of mystery cults in ancient religion," these cults existed, and they were *des religions de salut*.[38] He accepts the reality of an Orphic movement, almost an Orphic church, and he sees the Gold Tablets as belonging to "the center of Orphism,"[39] only to stress its difference from other religious traditions in the pagan world: Christianity then could feel free to adopt those forms of pagan religion that were close to its own revealed message and tradition.

The reaction to these maximalist positions was not slow in coming.[40] In 1941, Ivan Linforth, a historian of Greek philosophy and religion at Berkeley, published *The Arts of Orpheus*, an immensely skeptical book that methodically goes through all the evidence for Orpheus and Orphism before the end of the fourth century and attempts to destroy the claims of the maximalists. Beyond the hexametrical texts attributed to Orpheus, not much was left. When he gave his Sather Lectures at Berkeley ten years later, Eric Robertson Dodds could but acknowledge the impact Linforth's book had had on him: "The edifice reared by an ingenious scholarship upon these foundations remains for me a house of dreams."[41] This set the tone for many years to come. And along with Orphism, the Gold Tablets almost disappeared from scholarly discourse. Symptomatic is the treatment Martin P. Nilsson gave them in his magisterial history of Greek religion, the manual that dominated scholarship for many decades. In his first volume, which treated the time before Alexander, he banished them into a footnote; in his second volume, on the religion of the Hellenistic and Imperial epochs, he relegated them to the section on Hellenistic eschatology, squeezing them in between a chapter on "Superstition" and one on "Mysticism and Syncretism."[42]

Zuntz and after

Skepticism was still prevalent twenty years later when Günther Zuntz published his edition and commentary of the Gold Tablets in 1971.[43] Zuntz had few new texts to offer. Since the time of Comparetti and Kern, the number of tablets had not much increased: excavations in Pharsalos in Thessaly had yielded another long text (our no. 25), and finds in Crete added three new texts to the three already known (our nos. 13–15). Following Olivieri's 1915 edition, Zuntz proposed a simple classification for all the texts: he divided them into two classes, A and B. The A texts all came from the two mounds of Thurii; in them, the soul addresses the Underworld divinities and expects release from a cycle of reincarnation. All other texts belong to the B group: they were guides to the Underworld, partly addressed to the deceased, partly telling the deceased what he had to say when challenged by the powers of the beyond. The six short Cretan texts were seen as the oldest and as the source for the expansions of the longer texts from Petelia and Pharsalos. The presence of reincarnation in one of the tablets from Thurii (our no. 5) made Zuntz attribute group A to Pythagoreanism, as a "Pythagorean *missa pro defunctis*"; the B texts, although lacking such a telling detail, nevertheless in his opinion belonged to the same philosophical and religious movement. Against Comparetti, Zuntz thus asserted that the tablets did not contain verses of Orpheus, but of Pythagoras, "a far greater poet than one would expect" when reading the late Pythagorean *Golden Verses*.[44]

But almost as soon as Zuntz, in the wake of Wilamowitz and Linforth, had hoped to have finally exorcized the ghosts of Comparetti and Macchioro, they were back: new finds again caused radical changes away from the minimalist position. At the very time that Zuntz was working on his commentary, Italian archeologists found yet another tablet, the earliest of all, in Vibo Valentia, the ancient Hipponion (our no. 1). In the fall of 1973, Giovanni Pugliese Carratelli, whom the excavators had charged with its publication, presented it to the annual Magna Grecia conference in Taranto. The conference topic was "Orfismo in Magna Grecia," and Günther Zuntz was among the participants. The Hipponion tablet immediately changed the debate: it not only had the most elaborate description of the Underworld path of the initiate, it also situated him among "the other initiates and *bacchoi*." The text not only belonged to a mystery group, the god of this group must have been Dionysus. Comparetti's original attribution of the tablets to Dionysiac mysteries was finally confirmed by a text. The A tablets, found only in the two impressive mounds in Thurii, could still be separated out and understood as being Pythagorean, if one wished to do so – if anything, the Hipponion tablets seemed to have cofirmed Zuntz's categories and to have widened the gap between A and B tablets. This again changed radically after the publication of the two identical ivy leaves from Pelinna in 1987 (our nos. 26a and b). Among otherwise unparalled wording, these texts also contained the "kid in the milk" formula that was typical for the A group; at the same time, they claimed that Dionysus Bacchius had released the soul. Thus, they belonged to Dionysiac mysteries, as did the Hipponion tablet; their shape, ivy leaves, and the statuette of a maenad found in the same grave confirmed the Dionysiac associations. They thus combined a characteristic of the A group with the Diony-

Figure 3 Apulian amphora by the Ganymede Painter, *c.* 340 BCE. Antikenmuseum Basel und Sammlung Ludwig, inv. no. S40.

siac associations of the B group, showing that Zuntz's classification was not watertight. More recent texts have since confirmed this: all of these texts must have belonged to Dionysiac mysteries. More important still, the reference to Dionysus' releasing the soul in the Pelinna tablets made full sense only in the framework of Orphic anthropogony.[45] The Pelinna texts, dated to about 320 BCE, belong among the early attestations for this anthropogony. Two more recent texts, however, suggest that local mystery groups using the tablets were not exclusively focused on Dionysus alone. A text from Thessalian Pherae, published in 1994, combined Dionysiac elements with Brimo, a rather enigmatic goddess (our no. 27);[46] another

Figure 4 Apulian volute crater by the Darius Painter, *c.* 380 BCE, Toledo Museum of Art, Toledo, OH. Gift of Edward Drummond Libbey, Florence Scott Libbey, and the Egypt Exploration Society, by exchange.

one from the same place, found in 1907 and published in 2007, invoked Demeter Chthonia and the Mountain Mother (see Appendix 2).[47] Similar local variations are present in the Orphic *Hymns* and in the ritual text from Egyptian Gurôb.[48]

A small group of related texts helped to suggest what the "Orphic" rites of Dionysus could be. In 1978, the Russian archeologist Anna Rusyayeva published a set of bone plaques from fifth-century BCE Olbia, found in 1951 during the Russian excavations of the city.[49] The small plaques contain enigmatic texts, all connected through the name of Διόν(υσος); one combines in its first lines a chain of nouns – "life," "death," "life," "truth" – with the god's name and, in the left-hand bottom corner, what must be Ὀρφικοί or, perhaps, Ὀρφικόν; another one has "truth," "soul" and the god's name. The first sequence seems to sketch a movement from life to death to a new life, firmly asserting this as the truth, and connecting this truth with Dionysus and the Orphics; the other text at least seems to concern the soul. Whatever the detailed and highly debated meaning and function of these small texts, they attest to Orphics or Orphic lore in a context that combined Dionysus, eschatology, and the emphatic claim of a truth that was different.[50]

The third archeological find that changed the debate about Orphism was the so-called Derveni Papyrus. Greek excavations near Derveni east of Thessalonica brought to light the carbonized fragments of a papyrus book that cited, among other things, a theogonical poem of Orpheus. The find was announced in 1968, with some samples of the intriguing text. The official and full publication of the text appeared recently, after the scholarly world had relied for many years on texts that were obtained through a combination of rather clandestine means and ingenuity, in the face of the museum's long and annoying reticence.[51] The book was burned and buried around 330 BCE; its main text, however, which comprises philosophical comments on a poem by Orpheus, easily goes back to the late fifth century; this in turn dates Orpheus' poem even earlier. The poem attests to Zeus' incest with his mother, Rhea-Demeter, and the birth of their daughter, Persephone. This is the framework of the story of Persephone giving birth to Dionysus: the Derveni text thus seems to accept the Orphic story of Dionysus, who was the son of Zeus and Persephone and, through his murder by the Titans, the ancestor of humankind.

Recent finds of South Italian art, finally, have given an even better insight into the importance of Orpheus and Dionysus in eschatological beliefs.[52] An Apulian grave vase by the Ganymede Painter (Figure 3, p. 63), published in 1976, depicts a singing Orpheus in front of the deceased, who sits, holding a papyrus scroll in his hand: this attests to the combination of Orpheus, written texts, and the fate of the deceased in Southern Italian eschatological belief.[53] Another Apulian vase by the Darius Painter (Figure 4, opposite), published in 1993, confronts Hades and Dionysus in a handshake that seems to give Dionysus a special role in the Underworld; this again points to the world of Bacchic mystery cults.[54] The statue group of a singing Orpheus among Sirens from a late fourth-century BCE grave in Tarentum, published in the same year, might point to an eschatological reading of the myth of how Orpheus' song overcame the dangers of the Sirens.[55]

Like our ancestors in the early twentieth century, most contemporary scholars seem again to lean toward a maximalist definition of Orphism, against the minimalist approach of Wilamowitz, Linforth, and Zuntz:[56] by now, the textual foundation for such a position has become much better. But unlike the scholars of a century ago, even among contemporary maximalists no one would call the Orphic movement a religion or claim that early Christianity depended on Orphism. To derive Christianity directly from the pagan mystery cults still smacks of an ideological stance,[57] and when religions are understood as systems, the Bacchic mysteries are, if anything, only a sub-system (see further Appendix 1).

3

THE MYTH OF DIONYSUS

Sarah Iles Johnston

What we commonly call the Orphic myth of Dionysus does not survive in anything approaching a complete form earlier than Olympiodorus, a Neoplatonic philosopher of the sixth century CE. Olympiodorus narrated it briefly in the course of writing a commentary on a passage from Plato's *Phaedo*, where Socrates and his friends are debating whether it is right to commit suicide.[1] Socrates argues against suicide by claiming that humans are under the guardianship of the gods, and alludes to a myth "told secretly" that explains how this is so. In attempting to clarify Socrates' allusion Olympiodorus gives us the Orphic story. He says:

> According to Orpheus there were four cosmic reigns. First was the reign of Uranus, then Cronus received the kingship, having cut off his father's genitals. Zeus ruled after Cronus, having cast his father into Tartarus. Next, Dionysus succeeded Zeus. They say that through Hera's treachery, the Titans who were around Dionysus tore him to pieces and ate his flesh. And Zeus, being angry at this, struck the Titans with thunderbolts, and from the soot of the vapors that arose from [the incinerated Titans] came the matter from which humanity came into existence. Therefore, we must not commit suicide – not because, as [Socrates] seems to say, we are in our body as if in a prison, since that is obvious and [Socrates] would not call such an idea secret, but rather because our bodies are Dionysiac. We are, indeed, part of Dionysus if we are composed from the soot of the Titans who ate Dionysus' flesh.

Many other authors – some as early as Pindar and Plato himself[2] – fill in details or offer variations on what Olympiodorus said; some of this additional material will be discussed as it becomes relevant below. Before we begin our discussion, however, it would be good to see the story in its entirety. Parts of the story taken from sources other than Olympiodorus are italicized; in other parts, Olympiodorus' words have been changed slightly to reflect a fuller range of the versions available, most of which will be discussed in more detail below:

> *Dionysus was the child of Zeus and Zeus' daughter Persephone.* Dionysus succeeded Zeus; *Zeus himself placed the child on his throne and declared him the new king of the cosmos.*[3] The Titans, jealous of Dionysus' new power and perhaps encouraged by Hera, *used various toys, and a mirror, to lure Dionysus away from his guardians, the Curetes,* and dismembered him.[4] *They cooked his flesh* and ate it.[5] Zeus, being angry at this, killed the Titans, and from their remains, humanity arose.[6] *Because humanity arose from material that was predominantly Titanic in nature, each human is born with the stain of the Titans' crime,* but a remnant of Dionysus leavens the mixture.[7] *Each human must expiate the Titans' crime by performing rituals in honor of Dionysus and Persephone, who still suffers from the "ancient grief" of losing her child; by doing so, humans can win better afterlives.*[8] *Meanwhile Dionysus was in some manner revived or reborn.*[9]

The story has struck modern readers as both weird and familiar. Its reputation for weirdness arises from the fact that the typical reader approaches it from better known myths that make Semele alone, not Persephone, the mother of Dionysus, and make Zeus defeat the Titans at the beginning of his reign and then cast them, still intact, into Tartarus. In myths that we encounter through popular literary texts – Hesiod, Homer, the tragedians, Apollodorus, Ovid – we hear nothing about Titans dismembering Dionysus, much less consuming him; nothing about Titans being killed and giving rise to humanity; and nothing about a second conception and birth of Dionysus. Most modern readers, therefore, find the Orphic myth as strange as they would find a story of Joseph tucking Mary into a cave when she was in labor with Christ, leaving her in the care of his older sons, and then setting out to fetch a midwife – meanwhile missing the birth altogether.

And yet, just as this alternative tale of Christ's birth was accepted by some early Christians,[10] so also was the Orphic story of Dionysus' birth, death, and rebirth accepted by some people in antiquity. There is nothing apocryphal about it, particularly when we remember that in contrast to Christianity, Judaism, and Islam, the religions of ancient Greece had no canonical, sacred texts. Myths, and especially myths associated with cults, were fluid; now one version of a story and now another was invoked to suit particular circumstances. Nor was our myth really "secret," given that we find it referred or alluded to in sources such as Pindar, Plato, and Callimachus. The cult that used it as an *aition* may have had secret interpretations of it, or secret rituals that reflected it, just as Eleusis had secret interpretations and rituals centering on the familiar story of Demeter's search for her daughter, but the myth's existence and its basic plot-line were well known.

Why have many modern people also perceived the Orphic story as familiar, even in the midst of claiming that it is strange? The answer lies in its broad thematic similarity to foundational Christian stories: a god dies and is revived; the human race carries within itself a stain that each individual member must expunge through rituals paid to that god or else risk eternal misery in the afterlife. Some scholars recently have shown how deeply such perceived similarities have affected study of the myth and related cults, including those that used the Gold Tablets; I need not repeat their analyses here.[11] What I would point out instead is that ironically, the apparent similarity between the Orphic myth and the Christian story is likely to have made the myth's perceived weirdness all the more highly prized, for the weirdness was sometimes credited, explicitly or implicitly, to the fact that the myth and the cult were precursors of another religion that allegedly was more spiritual and more personally fulfilling than "mainstream" Greek religion. The very title of Vittorio Macchioro's book, *From Orpheus to Paul*, rests on this idea. Once one had accepted that premise, it seemed natural that the Dionysiac myth and cult didn't align well with better known Greek myths and cults.

We need to take a fresh look at the myth, approaching it as neither excessively strange nor excessively familiar. Doing so requires us to start by considering how both it and its associated mysteries came into existence.

The origin of the myth and cult: when

A fragment from one of Pindar's threnodies, quoted by Plato at *Meno* 81b8–c4, tells us that:

> But for those from whom Persephone accepts retribution
> for her ancient grief, in the ninth year she returns their souls
> to the upper sunlight; from them arise
> proud kings and men who are swift in strength
> and greatest in wisdom, and for the rest of time
> they are called sacred heroes by mortals.
> (frg. 133; W. H. Race's Loeb translation, slightly adapted)

Most scholars are agreed that "Persephone's ancient grief" refers to the loss of her child, Dionysus, which gave rise, in the long run, to the birth of humanity – and therefore to humanity's debt to Persephone.[12] Pindar's threnody thus places our myth in the mid-fifth century; the Gold Tablet from Hipponion (our no. 1) comes a few decades later. If the myth and the cult were around for a while before these materials began to show up in our textual record, then we must go back to the early fifth or late sixth century for their debut – which might align with a reference by Heraclitus to some kind of eschatological mysteries honoring Dionysus.[13] Much of the material that circulated in the same orbit as our myth and cult (most importantly, cosmogonies and theogonies similar to those used in our myth) has also been dated to the late sixth century[14] – this seems to have been the time when such ideas were newly in the air. More broadly, our myth and cult, as well as the Orphic theogonies, fit into a spectrum of other religious and philosophical ideas that developed during the late sixth and early fifth centuries, particularly Pythagoreanism; the nature of the individual soul and its ultimate fate were questions of heightened interest during this period.[15]

But is it possibly just a matter of chance survival that our evidence begins to appear when it does? Could the story and the cult have been around earlier, without leaving a trace? Several things argue against this. First, not only is any trace of our myth *per se* missing from Homer, Hesiod, and fragments of other epic poets, but so also is mention of any relationship at all between Dionysus and Persephone or between Dionysus and the Titans. One might argue that these were deliberate omissions – that the poets wanted to present a unified picture of a world in which the Titans were punished in one particular way for one particular crime, and in which Dionysus was the son of Semele – and that therefore, the poets would have repressed inconvenient mythic variants. But we know that variants crept into other theogonic and cosmogonic episodes during the period in which these poems reached their final forms. At times, for example, Aphrodite is called the child of Dione and at other times she is said to have been born from Uranus' severed genitals. At times, Hephaestus is called the son of Hera alone, whom she conceived parthenogenically while she was angry at Zeus, and at other times Hephaestus is called the son of both Zeus and Hera. If the stories of Dionysus' birth from Persephone, his rending at the Titans' hands or humanity's birth from the aftermath of these acts were available when the Homeric, Hesiodic, and other epic poems were being composed, then it is surprising that we find absolutely no trace of them. It is also significant that when authors refer to the cult during the fifth and early fourth centuries (i.e., within a hundred years after the cult's apparent debut), they treat it in ways suggesting that, in contrast to the Eleusinian Mysteries, this cult was far from being well entrenched and respected:

Euripides' Theseus scorns the rites that Orpheus teaches as a screen for immoral behavior; Plato connects wandering con-men priests with the writings of Orpheus; Theophrastus' ridiculously superstitious man visits the *orpheotelestēs* once a month. According to Herodotus, the Scythian king Scyles' decision to be initiated so disturbed his people that they handed the throne to his brother – and Scyles ended up losing his head.[16]

One final note: Pausanias tells us that Onomacritus composed *orgia* (rituals) for Dionysus that included a story about the Titans (Paus. 8.37.5 = OF 39); Onomacritus brings us to the late sixth century. Although we cannot be sure that Pausanias has his facts right, this is certainly the sort of thing we would expect from Onomacritus, who was an expert in sacred poetry, particularly that of Orpheus and Musaeus, and its applications. The backward glance of late antiquity places the development of the cult at the same time that other evidence does.

The origin of the myth and cult: how and why

Why did the myth and cult develop into the particular forms that they did? The general fact that certain raw materials were around, such as an increased interest in the fate of the individual soul and the beliefs that Orpheus had composed poems revealing cosmogonic truths, doesn't explain the development of particular ideas. This section will address these issues.

Greek myths, as we have them, are deliberate creations; the Oedipus whom most of us know best is a creation of Sophocles, and Euripides created our most familiar Medea. Although each such author was influenced by earlier literary and artistic creations, they borrowed only what they wished and then innovated upon it. Visual artists did the same, each one drawing upon earlier artistic and literary versions of myths but adding touches that made the presentation uniquely his own.

This point is well known, but we tend to restrict its application to literary texts and their visual equivalents, rather than to cultic *aitia*. We are willing to imagine Sophocles or the painter Polygnotus as a *bricoleur* who combined older ideas with his own insights (indeed, we praise them for the brilliance of their *bricolages*),[17] but even as we concede that cultic *aitia* are known to us primarily through such deliberately composed literary and artistic sources, we nonetheless assume that there must have been "original" *aitia* lying behind them, reflecting feelings and beliefs that were so deeply ingrained in the culture as to spring forth unsummoned, fully formed, from its collective unconscious. We don't entertain the possibility that a discrete person or persons consciously *created* myths to accompany cults or rituals in anything like the way that Sophocles created his story of

Oedipus. Typically, we instead try to "explain" origins by adducing parallels – implying, again, that the myth in question grew up on its own out of a great Mediterranean soup of shared concerns and concepts.

I will not suggest that the approach I have just described is completely incorrect, not only because it does indeed have value (I will be adducing parallels from other Mediterranean myths myself to help clarify what the Orphic myth was about) but also because it is fruitless to argue exclusively for either side of this issue in the case of most myths. Very seldom can we gather the evidence we would need if we were to say anything definite about the origin or early history of an *aition*.[18] But I have sketched the question and its implications to stress the fact that we typically approach cultic *aitia* with a different, and not very well examined, set of questions and assumptions about their origins from when we approach literary myths – most significantly, we forget to consider the deliberate choices that might have been made as the *aition* developed or to ask how and why separate parts of an *aition* were joined together into a whole.

These issues become more pressing when we consider a particular type of cultic *aitia*: those that were transmitted through hexameters attributed to an inspired poet, such as Orpheus. Although they are pseudonymous, these *aitia* are not authorless, and whoever composed the hexameters had to make especially deliberate choices about what forms the *aitia* would take because they were trying to align themselves not only with mythic models but with literary models – the Homeric poems and Hesiod, for example – as well. Recognizing this compels us all the more so to look beyond that filmy realm of "collective unconscious" to which *aitia* usually are condemned, asking why and how an *aition* was given the form it was given.

Before we move on to specifics, let us consider, as best we can, the broader question of what the author of our *aition* may have understood himself to be doing.[19] Four possible models present themselves. According to the first, the myth itself might have been around for a considerable time before it was put into hexameters. The "author" was an author only in the sense of choosing the poetic words through which to transmit it. He attributed the poem to Orpheus in the belief that the sacred stories he was transmitting had been revealed to Orpheus; the common practice of attributing poems to legendary poets would have made this a natural thing to do. The problem with this thesis, however, is that there is no trace of our myth before the mid-fifth century; if it had been circulating for any significant length of time before the Orphic hexameters that narrate it came into existence, we might expect to hear about it, as I noted earlier.

All three of the other models take us into the realm of men such as the itinerant *orpheotelestai* who recited the poems attributed to Orpheus and presided over the cults that the poems validated. All three models assume that one or more of these "entrepreneurs of the sacred" developed a new mystery cult (perhaps in imitation of Eleusis' success) and a new myth to accompany it. The three models diverge, however, when it comes to imagining the intentions of this entrepreneur. Was he consciously misrepresenting the origin of the myth and cult to his audience by attaching them to Orpheus' name? Should we see him as akin to Onomacritus, who was accused by Lasus of Hermione of interpolating his own verses into a compilation of Musaeus' oracles?[20] Or did our imaginary entrepreneur truly believe himself to be some new recorder of Orpheus' previously unrecorded words? Musaeus, according to legend, had acted as Orpheus' amanuensis; it is possible that someone else might have thought that Orpheus was speaking to or through him, as well, in order to deliver divinely inspired information. Or, finally, did our entrepreneur believe that he himself was divinely inspired with the hexameters he recorded and, as was the custom of the time, attribute them to a legendary poet of greater renown, a poet whose name was already associated with cosmogonic and eschatological poetry?

Any of these three models would suit a poetically expressed *aition* that began to develop in the late sixth century. Nor are the models mutually exclusive so far as the way the public would have perceived the figure(s) who created the *aition* and its cult is concerned. Not only do we have evidence, beginning already in the sixth century, that Orphic lore, Dionysiac cult, and the men who purveyed them were scorned by some as fraudulent (Heraclitus, Euripides, Plato, Theophrastus, etc.) even as they were embraced by others, but history presents plenty of other examples of religious innovators who were praised by some and mocked by others. To take an example from later antiquity: Alexander of Abonuteichos was derided by Lucian as a villainous cheat who invented a new cult and myth to fill his pockets and satisfy his lusts, but he was revered by thousands as a holy man – his cult endured for at least two centuries after his death.[21] A parallel from our own time is Joseph Smith. Many of his contemporaries called him a cozener. His own Gold Tablets, which narrated Mormonism's sacred history, mysteriously vanished as soon as Smith had deciphered them, or so he said, with the aid of magical stones, and other sacred writings that he translated from the linen bandages wrapped around a mummy were subsequently shown by Egyptologists to be the most banal of bookkeeping accounts – and yet none of this has slowed Mormonism's success.[22]

We will never know to which of these three models the creator(s) of our cult and myth belongs – it is impossible for the most exacting scholars of even contemporary religions to determine whether or not their spokesmen sincerely believe in their spiritual wares. One final thing that we can learn from the models, however, is that for the best chance at success, new myths and cults need to tie in to established ones: Joseph Smith's tablets traced Mormonism to the lost tribe of Israel, which (his tablets said) had made its way to America and there experienced a new epiphany of Christ. Alexander of Abonuteichos claimed that his sacred snake was Asclepius reborn and modeled his mystery cult on Eleusis. In other words, the successful creator of a new cult or *aition* must be a *bricoleur* in much the same way that Sophocles was: he must weave together older ideas with his new ones. This, as we will see in the sections that follow, was exactly what the creator of our Dionysiac myth did.

The myth: Dionysus' birth – and rebirth

Let us start from two observations. First, the Eleusinian Mysteries were already thriving at the time that our myth and cult were developing; they undoubtedly served as an inspiration and perhaps even as a specific model for our *bricoleur*.

Second, if one were inspired by Eleusis to create a new mystery cult and sought a god who could be drafted into a role comparable to those played by Demeter and Persephone – that is, a god with ties to the world of the dead who could offer eschatological advantages – Dionysus would be the most obvious choice. His connection to death is already alluded to by Heraclitus, who says "Hades is the same as Dionysus" (*DK* 22 B 15). Two of the Olbia tablets, dated to the fifth century, connect Dionysus to a concern with death and the fate of the soul, if our readings are correct (see Appendix 4, 1A and C). The Anthesteria – one of Dionysus' oldest festivals and one that was celebrated all over the parts of Greece influenced by Ionia – included rituals designed to insure that the dead were happy in the afterlife.[23] Another element that would have encouraged Dionysus' election as the god of new mysteries was his marginalization from the Olympic pantheon, especially as it was known in epic poetry, and his marginalization from civic cult in most locales. Eschatology is never a central concern of a divinity who, like Zeus, Apollo, or Athena, represents the daily life of the *polis*; rather, it typically falls to divinities such as Demeter, Persephone, and Dionysus who are important primarily to particular portions of the population or important only at particular times of the year or times of life. An epic fragment attributed to Eumelus (frg. 27 West = frg. 11 Bernabé) reflects this idea by claiming that Dionysus learned how to perform initiations (*teletai*) in Phrygia (an exotic, marginal place), from Rhea (a name used in literary texts for a goddess called the Mother, who was herself exotic and marginal; see further discussion of this fragment in Chapter 5 and Appendix 2).

Another early indication of Dionysus' connection with the welfare of the dead is found in the story of his retrieval of Semele from Hades. It is likely that this story was known at least by the late sixth century: several late sixth- and early fifth-century black-figure vases show Dionysus leading forth a woman, who sometimes stands in a chariot. Her lack of a veil makes it unlikely that she is Dionysus' bride, which leaves Semele as the most obvious choice and Dionysus' retrieval of her from Hades as the most obvious situation. Hermes' presence on some of these vases may point in this direction, too, as he is well known in literature and art as a *psychopompos*.[24] We know that the story was treated in a tragedy by Sophocles' son Iophon, in the late fifth century (*TGF* 22 F 3); we next hear about it in Diodorus Siculus, who describes it with a verb (*mythologein*) that typically is used in connection with stories credited to Homer or stories that are otherwise of considerable age.[25] Myth, as usual, sketches a far brighter reward than ritual ever promises; no initiate into Dionysiac mysteries would have expected Dionysus literally to lead him out of Hades as he had led Semele, any more than an initiate at Eleusis would have expected to return from Hades as Persephone had. Nonetheless, the myth further suggests that Dionysus was understood to have special privileges in the Underworld, which in turn suggests that his role as an advocate of the dead was well established by the time of our first evidence for Dionysiac mysteries.

Semele brings us to Dionysus' other mother, Persephone, and an important question: if, in our earliest sources, Semele is always Dionysus' mother, why did Persephone take on this role in the new myth and cult that developed in the later sixth century? Undoubtedly, it was first and foremost her existing connection to the dead, as their queen and as one of the two goddesses worshipped at Eleusis, that made Persephone an attractive partner for Dionysus. Forging a close connection between the two would have been the best way to mark the new cult and myth both as eschatologically important and more specifically as correlative to those at Eleusis.

But the means of forging the connection were limited. Persephone was well known as Hades' wife from both epic poems and Eleusinian legend; linking her to Dionysus through marriage would have been too daring, particularly if the new cult wanted to claim some relationship to Eleusinian myth, as various fragments of Orphic poems suggest. This left two possibilities: a brother–sister link or a mother–child link. The former had been used in Sumerian myth: Dumuzi's sister pleaded for his release from the Underworld and in one version agreed to spend part of her time there in place of him. In Greece, the same story was told about the brothers Castor and Polydeuces. Persephone and Dionysus, both of whom were children of Zeus, would have been eligible for similar treatment.

Two factors made the mother–child option more appealing, however. First, in Greek culture, sisters were the weaker partners in sibling relationships. Brothers defended their sisters' honor until the sisters married; sisters seldom had either the opportunity or the resources to come to their brothers' aid. Once a sister had married, her relationship to her brother diminished.[26] Thus, a mother–child relationship would prove stronger than a sister–brother relationship. Second, a mother–child relationship between Persephone and Dionysus would echo the Eleusinian Mysteries, which according to myth had been founded to help assuage the grief of another mother (Demeter) over the loss of her child (Persephone). The Dionysiac myth in effect carried the Eleusinian saga into the next generation by making Persephone the mourning mother instead of the stolen child.

If Dionysus became Persephone's son in order to bind him more closely to the Underworld, why didn't he become Hades' son as well? Three things spoke against it: first, this would have introduced yet another change between the new myth and the older, familiar myth, in which Dionysus was Zeus' son. Already, Persephone's replacement of Semele was a significant alteration. Second, as the son of Hades and Persephone, Dionysus' link to the world of the dead would have been too strong. It would have jarred with other aspects of his mythic and cultic persona and diminished his appropriateness as a *mediator* between the two worlds, the very role that the new cult demanded from him. He needed a foot in each camp, and Zeus' paternity ensured him of this. Finally, it also gave him, as our myth tells us, a claim to Zeus' throne, an important point that will be discussed below.

Once Persephone was in place as Dionysus' mother, our *bricoleur* had either to dispense with Semele altogether or work her into some other part of the story. This brings us to the topic of Dionysus' multiple births. In our earliest sources, the story that involved Semele already talked about the god being born twice – once from her and once from the thigh of his father, Zeus. Once the episode with the Titans was added to the story, this changed. After this, the god's first birth typically was said to be from Persephone, but then, after his dismemberment, his second and sometimes third births were arranged in any of various ways. According to one tradition, Rhea brought together the pieces of the dismembered god and then revived him. Philodemus relates this story in the service of explaining why Dionysus is said to have been born thrice: once from "his mother," he says, a second time from Zeus' thigh and a third time, after his dismemberment by the Titans, when Rhea collected the pieces and revived him.[27] Philodemus claims that the Hellenistic poet Euphorion "agrees with these things" and that "the Orphics are absolutely fixated on them." In the first century CE, Cornutus reports that "according to myth" Rhea revived Dionysus after he had been torn apart by the Titans.[28] Similarly, Diodorus Siculus says that Demeter (who was occasionally equated with Rhea from the fifth century onwards, including in Orphic contexts; see n. 32 below) arranged the pieces of Dionysus "from which he was born anew" and that "the teachings set forth in the Orphic poems, which are introduced into their rites," agree with them, but "it is not lawful to reveal them in detail to the uninitiated."[29]

The following points seem clear, then: at least as early as Euphorion, there was a story that Rhea revived Dionysus after his dismemberment that could be regarded as "Orphic." What can we say about its origins?

Certainly, such a tale would have found itself at home amid panhellenic poetry and myth. Bacchylides told of Rhea reviving Pelops after his father had killed him and cut him up into a kettle (frg. 42). Both this tale and that of Dionysus, in turn, nod to Rhea's instrumental role in protecting and aiding the infant Zeus in popular theogonic myths (as well as in Orphic myth)[30] and more generally to her identity as a goddess concerned with the birth and nurture of children (she is one of the goddesses singled out as aiding Leto when she bears Apollo and Artemis, for example: Hom. *Hymn Ap.* 93). Similarly, the story of Demeter attempting to immortalize an infant for whom she was caring, known from the Homeric *Hymn to Demeter* and other sources, as well as her cultic roles as a *kourotrophos*, form a background for the idea that Demeter revived the young Dionysus, even apart from Demeter's frequent identification with Rhea.

Further impetus for involving Rhea or Demeter in the story of Dionysus' dismemberment would have come from the tale of Isis' search for her dismembered husband, Osiris. Particularly in the context of mystery cults, Dionysus had been equated with Osiris by at least the late sixth or early fifth century[31] and Demeter had been equated with Isis by at least the time of Herodotus.[32] This is not to imply that the entire story of Dionysus' own dismemberment was simply borrowed from Egyptian myth, however, as both ancient and modern authors have sometimes concluded[33] – on the contrary, dismemberment was probably one of the features that drew Dionysus and Osiris together in the first place, for it was an important theme in Dionysiac myths from a very early period. Even before allusions to Dionysus' dismemberment begin to show up, we see his enemies – Pentheus, Orpheus, the Minyads' child, Actaeon – undergo it.[34] The god's fate, then, may be taken to mirror that of the mythic characters who offended him, in somewhat the same way that Artemis' eternal virginity mirrors that of the maidens who follow her in myth. Even if Dionysus' dismemberment *per se* was not borrowed from Egyptian myth, however, details might have moved back and forth between the two stories. Specifically, the part that Isis played in Osiris' myth might have given Greek mythmakers – poets, itinerant initiators, or both – further reason to make Demeter or Rhea responsible for the aftermath of Dionysus' dismemberment.[35]

In contrast to this first tradition, which aligns well with several other traditions available during the archaic and classical periods, the second tradition that attempts to account for Dionysus' revival is not at all an easy fit with earlier myth or cult. According to Damascius, it was Apollo, rather than Rhea or Demeter, who resurrected the god.[36] Damascius specifically credits Orpheus with this story.

Nowhere else in Greek myth does Apollo act to revive the dead or bring anyone to birth; the story looks more like a variation of the first tale we have examined than anything else. Its development in Neoplatonic circles would have been encouraged by three other elements. The first is the tendency, from the late classical period onwards but especially in late antique mysticism, to identify Apollo with Helios (explicitly mentioned in Damascius' discussion of the story and compare, e.g., *OF* 102 and 322); the second element is the tendency, in late antique mysticism, to make Helios (and therefore by association, Apollo) an important source of both generative powers and the soul's salvation. Given that the Neoplatonists sometimes identified Dionysus with the individual soul, making Apollo/Helios the savior of Dionysus would have worked well within their soteriological systems.

The third element is a story that we can trace back much further – at least as far as Callimachus and Euphorion. Some version of it was probably included in the Eudemian Theogony (from the early Hellenistic period), and perhaps even in an earlier Orphic poem: Apollo either gathered up the dismembered pieces of Dionysus or received them (from the Titans, Zeus, or Athena, according to various sources), took them to Delphi and then buried them near the sacred tripod.[37] Although this story undoubtedly contributed to Apollo's Neoplatonic role as Dionysus' resurrector, we find it narrated independently of that story as well. It comprises, indeed, what I will call our third tradition.

This third tradition – this story of Apollo collecting the pieces of Dionysus and burying them – was probably built, in turn, upon the fact that Dionysus was reputed to have a tomb at Delphi, which Philochorus (late fourth or early third century BCE) says that he saw himself. Another fourth-century author, Dinarchus, claims that Dionysus actually died in the Delphic temple.[38] Philochorus says that the inscription on the tomb in Delphi read "Dionysus, son of *Semele*." If this is right, then either those who told the Orphic story of Dionysus' burial at Apollo's hands arrogated the tomb for their own purposes, in spite of the inscription, or the inscription was added later, perhaps by someone who wanted to reassert Dionysus' Theban identity against the stories that had written Semele out of the picture. It is also possible that the tomb had been connected earlier with some other, heroic figure associated with Apollo's cult before it became known as Dionysus' tomb. If so, its reassignment to Dionysus would have been encouraged not only by the Orphic story but also by another practice at Delphi: the biennial "awakening" of Liknites, who was understood to be Dionysus in the form of a child, by priestesses called the Thyiades.

Notably, Euphorion said both that Apollo collected the pieces and that Rhea arranged them and revived the god; Euphorion implies that the process had two different stages and involved two different gods. As we'll see shortly below, the story of Apollo taking the pieces to Delphi could also be combined with yet another version of how Dionysus was resurrected, as could our second tradition, according to which Apollo resurrected the god. The tradition whereby Apollo collected the pieces and carried them to Delphi, in other words, could be continued in any of various ways in order to explain Dionysus' revival; in this sense, it is not so much a tradition about the god's rebirth *per se* as it is an additional stage to which other traditions could be joined as sequels.

The fourth tradition concerning Dionysus' revival finally brings us back to Semele. Quite a few late sources say that Athena snatched Dionysus' heart from the Titans while it was still beating.[39] Some authors tell us no more than this, but Proclus, in his *Hymn to Athena*, goes on to say that Zeus used the rescued heart to create Dionysus anew in Semele and Nonnus says that the second Dionysus, Semele's son, was linked to the first Dionysus through the heart that the two shared. Allusions to this story show up in the Orphic *Hymns* as well. Hyginus provides more specific details, saying that Zeus minced up the heart, created a stew, and fed it to Semele so that she might conceive Dionysus.[40] Clement combines this tradition with the one we have just examined: Apollo buried all of the pieces of Dionysus at Delphi except his heart.[41]

Obviously this tradition, far more than any of the others, addresses what would have been a considerable problem for a *bricoleur*, namely, what to do with the old and well-established idea that Semele was Dionysus' mother. It also would have been appealing because at least in the version conveyed by Hyginus it is thematically similar to a tale found elsewhere in Orphic cosmogonies, in which Zeus swallowed Phanes (who in late sources was also called Erikepaios and Bromios, which potentially identifies him with Dionysus) and then recreated the whole cosmos from within himself. Zeus' act is but one example of a motif found in creation stories from several Mediterranean cultures, in which birth or rebirth follows ingestion: Kumarbi swallows Anu's phallus in Hurrian myth and subsequently bears gods who are Anu's offspring; Cronus swallows and subsequently disgorges (thus giving a second birth to) his offspring; Zeus swallows his consort Metis and subsequently gives birth to their child, Athena.[42] The idea of Semele eating in order to give birth, then, fits beautifully into the mentality underlying Mediterranean cosmogonic and theogonic myth.

This tradition probably also reflects real Dionysiac ritual as practiced in at least some places. A sacred law from second-century CE Smyrna that has a Bacchic context prohibits placing the heart of the sacrificial animal on the altar, which aligns with the idea that this part of the god's body was rescued by Athena.[43] Firmicus Maternus, in a euhemerizing mode, says that Zeus placed the dead child's heart in a gypsum figure and instituted a cult in its honor. During the annual celebration of this cult, the box (*kistē*) in which Athena had placed the heart was carried in procession. Firmicus sets the cult on Crete but it is possible that the practices, or something like them, were more widely spread (Firm. Mat. *Err. prof. rel.* 6.4 [89 Turcan] = *OF* 325). Which came first, the myth or the ritual? It is impossible to be sure, but the existence of both suggests that the myth was more than just the fantasy of late antique authors.

But is the tradition of Dionysus' rebirth from Semele "Orphic"? Earlier scholars rejected this possibility because most of the sources that convey it fail to attribute it to Orpheus. The exceptions, the Orphic *Hymns*, have been viewed suspiciously because they are late (second century CE) and apparently the products of a private cult, as opposed to the theogonic poems from which other Orphic myths are assumed to derive (or so the argument goes). Jean Rudhardt demonstrated how misplaced this attitude is; the *Hymns* have just as much claim to be transmitting earlier Orphic lore about Dionysus as other sources – some of which are much later than the *Hymns* and not all of which include Orpheus' name, either. Moreover, as Rudhardt notes, Proclus, who knew his Orphic theogonies extremely well, also transmits the story of Semele and the heart. Further support for the inclusion of Semele in Orphic myth can be found in Aristides and Proclus' designation of the story of Dionysus being born from Zeus' thigh as Orphic. Although Semele is not explicitly mentioned in these passages, it is hard to imagine what episode other than Semele's premature death could have led to the embryo's placement in Zeus' thigh. And if the Orphics told one part of that story, they surely told the other.[44]

To sum up: we have four main traditions concerning what happened to Dionysus once he had been dismembered by the Titans, all of which were considered Orphic by at least some of the sources that conveyed them:

1   he was revived by Rhea or Demeter
2   he was revived by Apollo
3   his body parts were collected and then hidden or buried by Apollo at Delphi; rebirth subsequently was accomplished by the means described in any of the three other traditions
4   his heart was used to create a new Dionysus in Semele.

Tradition 2, as I have noted, is not likely to have been circulating very early, given its Neoplatonic hallmarks, but it is possible – even probable, given the decentralized nature of a cult relying on independent, itinerant practitioners who crafted their material to suit local clientele as well as their own beliefs – that the three other traditions all were circulating at a fairly early stage. It is impossible to go much further with complete confidence, but I would also suggest that although Tradition 3 surely developed earlier than Tradition 2, it probably developed later than Traditions 1 and 4. Traditions 1 and 4 are "sequels" to Tradition 3 insofar as within the chronology of the story they finish an act that begins in Tradition 3, but outside of the narrative frame they could have existed independently without Tradition 3 or any other "prequel." Tradition 3, on the other hand, could not exist independently in any *milieu* that required Dionysus' revivification. It is easy to imagine that Tradition 3 was added to either Tradition 1, Tradition 4 or both during the Hellenistic period in order to incorporate what was by then a famous sight at a panhellenic sanctuary: Dionysus' tomb.

The myth: Dionysus' death

In jumping from Dionysus' birth to his rebirth, we have gotten ahead of ourselves; his death intervened between the two.

Near the center of the story of Dionysus' death lies the theme of sacrifice.[45] The Titans lure Dionysus away with toys to ensure that, like an animal at a sacrifice, he will go willingly to the slaughter. They disjoint their victim, cook him, and consume him, as one would a sacrificial animal. To make this more pointed, in some late versions of the story, Zeus discovers the Titans *in flagrante* after he is drawn to the scene by the odor of what he thinks is roasting lamb; he hopes for his usual portion of the sacrifice, but discovers the dismembered corpse of his son lying on the fire instead.[46] Some sources attempt to explain an unusual aspect of real Dionysiac animal sacrifice (the preservation of the victim's heart) with reference to what happened to Dionysus at the Titans' hands, indicating that they understood the two acts to be parallel.

But Dionysus is not an animal, of course. He is a god, slaughtered and consumed by other gods. The situation is analogous to that of human sacrifice, in which one human is slaughtered and consumed by others. This feature makes the Titans' sacrifice abnormal, perverse – corrupted. Further details underscore its distance from normal sacrifice. In many versions of the tale, the Titans perform *sparagmos* on Dionysus – that is, he is torn apart while still alive rather than disjointed after being killed, as sacrificial animals normally are.[47] *Sparagmos* collapses killing and butchering, processes that are marked as separate in normal sacrifice, into a single action. Its crude means of dividing up its victims prevents the careful apportioning of sacrificial meat into shares for the mortals and shares for the gods – much less into a special share for a particular god or priest. (Although Orphic fragment 311 tells us that the Titans tore Dionysus into seven pieces, there is no indication that these pieces approximated the carefully apportioned shares of a normal sacrifice.) The means by which the Titans cook Dionysus' flesh also sets their act against normal sacrifice: they first boil and then roast the meat instead of roasting some parts and then boiling others, as was typical.[48]

The theme of corrupted sacrifice – especially in the form of human sacrifice and cannibalism – runs throughout Greek myth. Children, as here, are frequently the victims. Tantalus sacrifices, cooks in a kettle and serves up his son Pelops, Lycaon does the same to a young boy (in some versions, his own son or grandson), and Atreus sacrifices his nieces and nephews and then serves them up to their father, his brother Thyestes. Herodotus offers another, allegedly historical, instance in the story of Astyages, who sacrificed and served up the children of Harpagus. The Greeks and Romans later accused early Christians of doing the same.[49]

Scholars have suggested that the stories of Tantalus and Lycaon also exhibit an initiatory theme; that is, that the child's death and consumption symbolizes the dangerous transition from youth to adulthood, and that the subsequent revivification of Pelops (and in some versions, Lycaon's son or grandson) represents its successful completion.[50] They have supported this through various arguments, including the fact that a festival with which the myth of Lycaon's victim is connected (the Lykaia) facilitated the maturation of young men. Some scholars, using these and other myths as correlates, have gone on to suggest that the sacrifice of Dionysus is also about passage into adulthood.[51] In other words, a myth evoking the passage of adolescents into adulthood was adapted for use as an *aition* for mystery initiation; Dionysus, the paradigmatic young-man-in-transition, became paradigmatic for initiates entering into a state of enhanced eschatological expectations.

We must be cautious about this for several reasons. First of all, by the late sixth century, the time at which I have suggested our myth was invented, rituals of adolescent initiation had long since disappeared from all but perhaps two Greek locales, Crete and Sparta; formal initiation rites were no longer an active concern of Greek men. To argue that the *bricoleur* purposefully introduced an initiatory theme into the story he was creating requires us to presume that he could conceptualize and recreate, in approximately the same manner as we do, an adolescent initiatory pattern that at the time existed only in traces in various other myths, and also that he could discern a phenomenological similarity between that initiatory pattern and the sort of initiation associated with mystery rites. This seems unlikely.

There is another, very different methodological problem as well. Greek myths are seldom "about" just one thing; no single theme can provide the key to a myth's meaning. Themes combine and recombine with one another in kaleidoscopic variations; it is the whole picture presented by a mythic narration, not the individual theme, that is meaningful. This is especially true in cases like ours, where a myth has been constructed by someone who could draw on a large repertoire of themes and choose to convey particular meanings by deliberately combining them in new forms. A second caveat follows: because of this kaleidoscopic quality of myths – and again, especially when the kaleidoscope is being turned by a skilled and purposeful hand – it is dangerous to transfer comprehensive interpretations from one myth to another on the basis of a single shared theme, however prominent that theme may be. The myth of Dionysus is similar to those of Pelops, Lycaon's son, and various other children insofar as all of them include the theme of child sacrifice – but this need not mean that all of them have the same central concern.

In fact, closer comparison of these myths will reveal differences that enhance our understanding of Dionysus' myth. Scholars who see adolescent initiation behind Dionysus' myth further support their argument by noting that the Curetes – paradigmatic young men, after whom an initiate might be expected to pattern himself – guard Dionysus in the early part of the story.[52] But ironically, this is actually one element that distinguishes Dionysus' story from the other, purportedly initiatory stories with which it has often been compared: there are no guardians in the tales of Pelops, Lycaon's son, Thyestes' children, or Harpagus' children. This is not to say that guardians who serve as models for young men can never appear in initiatory myths, or that the Curetes never have initiatory overtones. Rather, it is to caution that the *bricoleur* may have included them for some other reason.

And in fact, there is another, very good reason. The Curetes' protection of Dionysus, combined with the setting of the whole episode on Crete and Dionysus' consumption by Titans, immediately would have reminded ancient listeners of the story of Zeus, who similarly was born and spent his boyhood on Crete and similarly was guarded by Curetes lest he be consumed by one particular Titan, his father Cronus. These were central episodes in the known Greek theogonic myth; by invoking them, our *bricoleur* surely meant Dionysus' experiences to be compared to those of Zeus.[53] To understand what this part of Dionysus' story was intended to be "about," therefore, we have to understand what Zeus' story was meant to be "about." Was it initiatory?

Originally, perhaps, yes. As Jane Harrison argued long ago, the Curetes probably were meant, in Zeus' case, as models after whom the young man whom they guarded could pattern himself. Moreover, Zeus' victorious combat against the dragon-like Typhoeus, whom he confronts later in the story of his rise to power, is typical of myths in which youths grow up and test themselves against the world. But by the sixth century and particularly within the context of panhellenic poetry, such initiatory elements in Zeus' story had been subordinated to a different, although potentially related, theme: succession to rule. It is Zeus' father against whom he must be protected and it is his father whom he must eventually conquer. It is his father's authority as king of the cosmos that Zeus acquires when he topples Cronus, just as Cronus had won that authority by toppling his father Uranus. In myth, the theme of succession sometimes intersects with the initiatory theme insofar as it focuses on the maturation of a young man and his acquisition of adult status and rights, but succession myths set themselves apart from initiatory myths by focusing attention on the displacement of an older generation and the changes that this displacement will bring – within a kingdom or, as so often in the ancient Mediterranean, within an entire cosmos. Zeus' succession brings a change from a cosmos ruled by violence to a cosmos ruled by law and order, for example. In contrast, we hear nothing about any resultant changes in the government of Arcadia after Lycaon's act, nor do we hear about such changes in the myth of Tantalus and Pelops or any of the other initiatory myths we have surveyed – indeed, far from inheriting his father's throne, Pelops travels far away to Elis, where he wins both the local throne and the daughter of the king, Oenomaus. The difference might be summed up as follows: initiation myths are about the experiences of the initiate and the changes he undergoes, whereas succession myths focus on how the passage of a particular youth into adulthood (or of a particular adult into a higher office) affects his society as a whole.

We hear nothing about changes to Dionysus himself in the Orphic story, other than that he is killed and reborn. He does not marry, for example, fight monsters, or pursue a quest, as adolescent initiates typically do. The biggest changes in the story are to the cosmos itself: first Zeus makes

Dionysus its ruler, by which he intends to usher in a fourth and greater era of cosmic history, and then Zeus regretfully resumes his rule; the new era is truncated before it can really start. In addition, the cosmos is burdened with a new race of inhabitants, which will change forever more the way that it functions. The succession theme is further emphasized by the motif of ingestion, which not only is the sequel to many stories of human sacrifice, as we will see shortly below, but which also evokes a variety of Mediterranean succession myths in which older gods consume younger gods in order to prevent their rise. The motive for the Titans' actions is also important in this respect: all of our sources agree that they killed Dionysus because they envied his rise to cosmic power.

Once we understand that the *bricoleur* was creating a new succession myth (or rather, that he was extending a panhellenically famous succession myth into a new generation), it becomes clear that Dionysus is meant to be understood as a Zeus *manqué*. Like his father, he is destined to usher in the next, even greater phase of cosmic history, but unlike his father, he falls prey to the Titans. The *bricoleur* thus manages to have his cake and eat it, too: Zeus is retained as the monarchic ruler of the universe (changing this fact would have been far too bold a move for any *bricoleur*; he had to work around it) and yet Dionysus is presented as having been worthy of ruling it, perhaps even worthier than Zeus; the unfulfilled promise of his truncated kingship glimmers behind the different role he takes on, once he is reborn, as a mediator between the world of the living and that of the dead.

At this point we might ask specifically what the *bricoleur* has gained by combining the two themes that I have suggested underlie his version of Dionysus' death: succession and corrupted (i.e., human) sacrifice. Granted that it was important to present Dionysus as Zeus' failed heir; granted that an attack by Titans solidified the identification between Zeus and Dionysus; and granted that ingestion was a common theogonic motif, nonetheless we must ask why it was desirable to make the Titans consume Dionysus in a *sacrificial* setting that had no parallel in theogonic myth. What was the advantage of introducing this theme?

Two things. First, some victims of human sacrifice, including the two whose stories most closely parallel Dionysus' tale (Pelops and Lycaon's son or grandson) die but are subsequently resurrected, as Dionysus will be. Similarly, some other children miraculously re-emerge from their elders' culinary experiments, as well: Demeter and Isis place their nurslings in the hearth fire, Thetis does the same to Achilles, and some such action was performed by Medea as well.[54] Although the action is intended to improve the child in those cases, rather than harm him, the general structure of the story is the same as that of Pelops, Lycaon's son, and Dionysus, and suggests that to be cooked is not necessarily the end of one's story. In choosing to truncate Dionysus' kingship through death in a sacrifice, then, the *bricoleur* could lay the groundwork for the next chapter in Dionysus' history.

Second, corrupted sacrifice brings on disaster not only for the individual who performs it (Tantalus, Lycaon, Thyestes, and Astyages lose their kingdoms), but also, potentially, on a cosmic scale, for all humans. It is after Lycaon's sacrifice that the gods flood the earth in order to wipe out humanity, and after Thyestes' meal that they cause the sun to reverse its course.[55] By corrupting sacrifice, an act that underpins the relationship amongst humans and the relationship between humans and gods, these men put all mortals at risk. The same message underlies Prometheus' institution of the first sacrifice. Given that he is inventing the practice *ex nihilo*, Prometheus cannot be said to corrupt it, exactly, but by deceiving Zeus as he divides up the sacrificial meat for the first time, Prometheus establishes upon faulty ground both the institution of sacrifice and the relationship between gods and mortals that sacrifice instantiates. In doing so, Prometheus brings punishment both upon himself and upon all of humanity, forever more.[56] By choosing to present Dionysus' death as a corrupted sacrifice, the *bricoleur* suggests that it similarly will have dire effects for the cosmos, humanity, or both. It is to this topic that we now turn.

The myth: humanity's birth

Greek myth seldom exalts humanity. Far from suggesting that humans are the culmination of all creation, as does Genesis chapter 1 for example, Greek myth typically implies that they are the cause of problems – for the gods, for the cosmos, for each other. The very fact that humanity's origin lies within the Titans' corrupted sacrifice of Dionysus, then, can be taken as yet another example of corrupted sacrifice leading to cosmic disaster. Or, to look at it the other way around, by locating the beginning of the human race within a corrupted sacrifice, the *bricoleur* offers a new and very powerful explanation of why the human condition is so hopelessly flawed. In this sense, the Orphic anthropogony is a particularly pointed variation of another well known mythic theme, "primal error," according to which an early human or a god representing humanity makes a mistake or commits a crime that adversely affects humans thereafter – Eve ate the apple, Prometheus stole fire, Epimetheus accepted the dangerous gift of Pandora, and Pandora herself opened the jar. But by locating the fault immediately *before* the birth of humanity – by making it "pre-primal," in fact – the *bricoleur* makes humanity's nature defective from its very inception. This is ideologically important to the mystery cult that the myth underpins, for the bleaker the prospects facing humanity as a whole, the more brightly, in contrast, will shine the promise that Dionysus offers to individual humans. This is also important to the mystery cult insofar as, in contrast to the mysteries of Eleusis, which situated an error in Eleusis itself and linked it to an early Eleusinian queen (Metanira's interruption of Demeter's immortalization of Demophon, which finally drove Demeter into angry seclusion), the Orphic story situated primal error completely outside of any human geography. For a cult that was dispersed by itinerant priests throughout the Greek world, this was a big advantage.

The *bricoleur* further accentuates the innate defectiveness of humanity in several ways. First are the materials from which humanity is constructed. In one variation of the Orphic tradition that comes down to us, humans spring from the earth wherever drops of the Titans' blood fall upon it. In another, humanity emerges out of the sooty remains of the incinerated Titans. A third version combines features of the two others: humanity emerges from a mixture of the Titans' blood and bodily remains, which is enlivened, Frankenstein-like, by the lightning bolts that killed them.[57] The immediate parallel, to a Greek mind, would come from Hesiod's *Theogony*: when blood from Uranus' castrated genitals fell upon the earth, it generated the Giants, the Erinyes and the Ash tree nymphs (*Theog.* 183–7). Tradition told of the Giants rebelling against the gods and made them paradigmatic examples of hubristic behavior.[58] The Erinyes, although not rebellious or evil, were dire – an unpleasant reminder that humans could behave unjustly and thus merit punishment. The Ash tree nymphs, as Glenn Most and M. L. West have noted, were the mothers of humanity in some Greek traditions to which Hesiod seems to have alluded at *Works and Days* 187. These nymphs might thus be considered defective as well – or at least the parents of a defective race.[59] The point is clear: when touched by the blood of a dreadful god, the earth sends forth dreadful creatures.[60]

A variation that brings us even closer to our Orphic tale appears in Ovid's *Metamorphoses*, although it has migrated to a different cosmogonical stage: when the Giants hubristically try to scale the heavens by piling Mount Pelion upon Mount Ossa, they are dashed down by Zeus' thunderbolts, and the earth, drenched in their blood, sends up a race of humans who like their progenitors are "contemptuous of the gods" (*Met.* 1.151–62).[61] Near Eastern parallels lie near as well: according to the *Enuma elish* the gods Marduk and Ea built the physical world out of the remains of their enemy Tiamat and then created humans from the blood of Tiamat's vizier, Kingu. The *Atrahasis* similarly says that Ea and the mother goddess Mami mixed clay with the blood of the slain god Geshtu-e to create humanity, and several other, more fragmentary Babylonian sources offer further variations on the tale.[62] We do not possess any Greek reports of Babylonian myths before Berossus, a third-century BCE Babylonian scholar who wrote in Greek, but given the enormous influence of Near Eastern creation myths on Greek cosmogonies and theogonies, it is probable that the idea of humanity being created from the remains of a divine enemy was available in Greece much earlier. The Greeks have left us with scarcely a trace of any panhellenically celebrated anthropogony on the scale of their theogonies and cosmogonies – the origin of humanity does not seem to have interested their poets much – which might explain why we glimpse a motif that was central to Near Eastern thought only later, in our Orphic tale, whose *bricoleur* had good reason to adopt it.

This brings us to another significant insight. If we are right in dating the origin of our Orphic story to the late sixth or early fifth century, then it represents the earliest Greek attempt we know of to create an anthropogony that would be panhellenically relevant. There were numerous myths that narrated the origin of specific races or groups of people – Erichthonius, one of the earliest Athenians, sprang from Attic soil, for example – but these myths were not interested in claiming anything of wider applicability.[63] Stories such as the one that Plato offers at *Protagoras* 321c–e, where gods mold the very first humans, may have been drawn from various popular tales (they express a motif found world-wide), but these were never conveyed through poetry and gained little authority.

The poets to whom one might have looked for a panhellenically acceptable anthropogony, such as Hesiod, had left a gap – or rather, an opportunity. For example, although Hesiod's myth of the Five Ages said that the people of the four first ages were created by the gods or by Zeus, it made no explicit statement about the origin of the people of the fifth age – our own age.[64] This silence has been interpreted in various ways by ancient and modern commentators: among the moderns, Most has persuasively argued that Hesiod left the issue of our specific origins vague because this allowed him to simultaneously suggest a number of different things about the qualities and potential of our race; precision would have restricted him.[65] Whatever Hesiod may have intended, however, his silence could be exploited by the Orphic *bricoleur* insofar as the story that he wished to market panhellenically would not have openly contradicted anything that Hesiod had actually said. In fact, the *bricoleur's* story could be understood to supplement Hesiod's narrative in two ways: it explained exactly where our race came from and it gave a specific reason for its wretched condition. What was in some ways a bold innovation – a panhellenic anthropogony – fit perfectly into the existing poetic tradition.

The second way in which the *bricoleur* accentuated humanity's defectiveness was to portray the birth of humanity as utterly spontaneous and without purpose. According to the Babylonian anthropogony, the gods deliberately fashioned humans because they desired servants who would take over their burdens and bring them sacrifices.[66] Although this is not the most promising beginning, at least it gives the human race a function and purpose. Most Greek creation stories similarly imply a purpose or at least an intention behind anthropogony. In some, the gods craft the first humans and endow them with specific talents.[67] In others, heroic figures engender humans by deliberately throwing special objects onto the ground.[68] In yet others, the first humans are children of gods, the products of sexual unions, and in this sense can at least be said to have been born out of the same procreative drive as are other humans and most of the gods themselves.

In striking contrast to all of these is the Orphic anthropogony, which is not, in fact, a *creation* story at all in the strict sense of that term. In this story, no deliberate design, action, or volition brings humanity to light – rather, humanity is generated spontaneously, without plan, intention, or desire. Other myths of spontaneous generation underscore how bleak an origin this is. A Greek of the early fifth century would have thought first of the passage from Hesiod's *Theogony* mentioned above, which describes spontaneous generation of giants, Erinyes, and Ash tree nymphs when Uranus' castrated genitals drip blood onto the earth.[69] The story we read in Ovid, if its roots go back far enough, would have provided another parallel. In portraying the birth of humanity as an accident, an incidental occurrence, the *bricoleur* again underscores humanity's innate defectiveness.

There was a fourth version of the Orphic anthropogony that, in contrast to the three others I have just surveyed, does introduce divine volition into the story. As I will show, this version is probably a late and idiosyncratic invention, but it is worth our attention because it has had a pervasive effect: it is the version offered in some mythology textbooks, for example, and in one recent, influential study of Orphic poetry.[70]

In the course of his commentary on Plato's *Republic* 8, 546e–547e, Proclus tells us that according to Orpheus, Zeus "put together" (*systēsasthai*) humanity out of the dismembered limbs of the Titans.[71] This is part of a longer account that Proclus is examining, according to which Orpheus had described three races of humanity: a golden one, which flourished under the reign of Phanes; a silver one, over which Cronus ruled; and a third race, for which Zeus was responsible. We perhaps glimpse the same tradition concerning three ages or races of humanity behind the remarks of Olympiodorus that opened this chapter: only three cosmic rulers reigned for any significant period of time (in Olympiodorus' account these were

Uranus, Cronus, and Zeus rather than Phanes, Cronus, and Zeus) and it was under the reign of the third ruler, Zeus, that the current race of humans came into existence.[72] The Orphic tradition of three human ages probably drew on or reacted to the Hesiodic tale of five human ages (which Plato discussed in the passage of *Republic* 8 that Proclus was commenting on, and which Proclus himself went on to discuss after finishing with the Orphic idea that interests us). Because the Orphic tradition wished to link each race with the reign of a specific cosmic ruler, however, and since there were only three such rulers in the Orphic system, five races were telescoped into three.[73]

The verbs that Proclus uses to express the relationship between each ruler and race are important. Proclus says that Phanes "establishes" or "founds" his race (*hypostēsai*), which echoes the founding of human dynasties by mythical kings and heroes but leaves vague the exact nature of his contribution. Cronus "rules over" his race (*arksai*), which again fails to connote any specific act of creation.[74] But Zeus, finally, "puts together" the third race (*systēsasthai*). This verb connotes an ordering or arranging of existing materials into a new whole – it is used of a general marshaling his troops, for example, or of joining cities together into a league.

It is possible that Proclus took the first two verbs from the Orphic poem he was summarizing, but the third verb is clearly his own, for *systēsasthai* is never found in poetry – a *bricoleur* composing in that genre wouldn't have used it. What probably first brought *systēsasthai* to Proclus' mind was what he was reading: the passage from the *Republic* on which he was commenting when he told the Orphic story uses a participial form of the verb (*systasan*) in its very first phrase (546a1). This alone probably would not have been enough to prompt Proclus to use it in his summary of the Orphic story, however, for as a rule, *systēsasthai* is not used of cosmogonic or anthropogonic acts; in the phrase from *Republic* 546a1, it refers to the manner in which a state is constituted out of the individuals who inhabit it. But the verb already had significant associations in Proclus' mind. The one place where, contrary to the norm, *systēsasthai* is used to describe cosmogonic or anthropogonic acts is Plato's *Timaeus* – one of Proclus' favorite works, and one on which he wrote yet another extensive commentary. In the *Timaeus*, where creation depends on the demiurge's careful assembling of pre-existing elements into more advanced forms, *systēsasthai* is used numerous times to describe acts of cosmogony and anthropogony.[75] If, while using the Orphic poem to clarify the *Republic*, Proclus was reminded of the *Timaeus*, then he might well have begun reading the Orphic poem through the lens of the *Timaeus* – and thus have developed the idea that the third race of humans had been purposefully built from pre-existing elements (the remains of the Titans) like everything else. If we remember the Orphic tradition that already credited Zeus with creating the physical world and the other gods (a tradition that Proclus himself refers to a few lines after the passage that we are considering here),[76] it becomes even likelier that Proclus adapted Orphic anthropogony so as to make Zeus the deliberate creator of the human race, too. This fourth version of the Orphic anthropogony, in other words, is very unlikely to have appeared earlier than the fifth century CE, and we thus can be confident that the *bricoleur* himself developed an anthropogony in which the emergence of humanity was accidental – lacking both a creator and a deliberate plan.

Putting it all together

Having looked at the parallels for and significance of each part of the Orphic story of Dionysus, we can now step back and review what the *bricoleur* was up to more generally: what were the primary ideas that he wished his *aition* to reflect, and how did he convey them?

Let us begin by considering his sources of inspiration – that is, by reviewing the mythic themes he used and where he is likely to have found them. For heuristic purposes, we can divide them into four types (in reality, some themes could be assigned to more than one type).

1   Mythic themes known from panhellenically famous poetry (especially Hesiod and Homer):

succession of generations, including
    ingestion as a means of both truncating and extending succession or cosmogony
the Titans as enemies of Zeus' order or plan
the birth of defective creatures out of the remains of defective gods
spontaneous birth as negative.

2   Mythic themes that were widely known by at least the fifth century but that are not found in (extant) panhellenically famous poetry:

sparagmos as a Dionysiac means of death
Isis' search for Osiris.

3   Traditions that began locally but that acquired panhellenic fame:

Dionysus' grave at Delphi (at least by the late fourth century BCE)
Persephone's centrality to eschatological happiness (Eleusis)
a mother's loss of her child and its ramifications for humanity (Eleusis).

4   Themes shared by many Greek myths of different kinds:

> the birth of creatures, including humans, out of the earth
> primal error
> corrupted sacrifice and the related theme of subsequent
> regeneration.

The list reiterates an important point: the *bricoleur* drew his themes from well-known myths. The episodes in his story, although new in themselves, reverberated with ideas that would have been familiar to most or all of his listeners; therefore, the story would implicitly make sense to those to whom he was marketing it. This was important because it allowed him to innovate more freely where he needed to. Similarly, by anchoring his story of the first Mormons within the very old tradition of the lost tribe of Israel, Joseph Smith gave it verisimilitude and prepared the ground for his new, bolder claims.

Starting from his stable base, our *bricoleur* was able to make four major innovations. First, he brought Dionysus more firmly into the sphere of deities who were eschatologically important – or in other words, made him a deity around whom a new mystery cult could be developed. The ground work for doing this was already there insofar as Dionysus was associated with the return of ghosts at the Anthesteria, for example, and was said to have retrieved Semele from Hades, but the *bricoleur* developed these promising hints by making the Queen of the Underworld Dionysus' mother and by making his story run parallel to – indeed extend – the story that was already being told to underpin the mysteries performed at Eleusis. At Eleusis, Persephone was the lost child mourned by her mother; in the new story Persephone became the mourning mother. Another innovation was thereby necessitated – Dionysus the lost child had to be revived in some way – and this was accomplished by improvising on one of several other well-known themes. Depending on which particular version of the story we choose to follow, Dionysus' revival parallels that of other children who had been sacrificed and then revived (e.g., Pelops); parallels that of Osiris, whose dismembered pieces were cared for by Isis, a goddess similar to Rhea and Demeter; or draws on the motif of creation through ingestion that is found in many Mediterranean cosmogonies and theogonies. Notably, whichever version we take, Dionysus' revival also serves as an implicit parallel for what the initiates themselves anticipated: they, too, would die but, in somewhat the same fashion as Dionysus, they would win a new existence after death (compare tablets nos. 26 a and b).

Second, the *bricoleur* elevated Dionysus to a position virtually equal to that of Zeus – a move that was essential in the specific context of an eschatologically oriented mystery cult, where Dionysus' role would be more immediately important than Zeus'. The *bricoleur* accomplished this by extending yet another well-known myth – the theogonic succession myth – but he again managed to do so in a way that did not contradict any existing tradition. As a Zeus *manqué* who loses the cosmic throne due to his early death, Dionysus is granted considerable power, but that power is shifted into the realm of death. Like his mother Persephone, Dionysus will wield control over "everything that creeps and moves," but he will do so with reference to a specific aspect of human existence. It might even be said that, for those who are initiated into his cult, Dionysus promises a golden postmortem existence similar to the one he would have brought to the whole cosmos, had his reign not been truncated. Indeed, as we will discuss in more detail in the next chapter, some tablets promise that initiates will enjoy an afterlife like the life enjoyed by Hesiod's Golden Race and Race of Heroes (races that existed before the Titans' dreadful crime gave rise to the current race of humans).

Third, by incorporating the themes of spontaneous generation and generation from defective gods, the *bricoleur's* myth presented humanity as being deeply flawed – or rather, it provided a new and more emphatic explanation for what was already recognized as a basic characteristic of the human condition, a condition from which initiation promised to rescue members of the cult. To do this, the myth also drew on the themes of corrupted sacrifice and primal error. The first two themes are particularly important, because they gave the *bricoleur* an opportunity to move the enactment of the second two into a period *before* the creation of humanity. This was an especially significant innovation insofar as it made the anthropogonic explanation of humanity's wretched condition universally valid, universally applicable. Any *orpheotelestēs*, operating in any part of Greece, could use the myth to persuade potential initiates of the need for ritualized purification to which some of the tablets allude.

Finally, the *bricoleur* linked anthropogony to eschatology, and specifically to the question of postmortem bliss or misery. We tend to overlook how innovative a move this was because it seems familiar from Christian doctrine, according to which actions committed by Adam and Eve before they had conceived the next generation of humans had eschatological ramifications for every individual thereafter, which could be erased only through personal commitment to Christ. But within the context of ancient Mediterranean anthropogony, the link is exceptional.[77] Of course, death itself is strictly for humans, in contrast to gods; one might therefore say that by definition, birth as a human always has eschatological implications. Moreover, given that no Mediterranean religious system makes postmortem existence look appealing, one might say that all anthropogonies implicitly condemn humans to a state of eventual existence that will be unpleasant. But the *bricoleur* developed such eschatological implications into something that could underpin the salvific aspects of a mystery cult by making the very *fact* of human existence an active, ongoing cause of misery for the Queen of the Dead herself. Anthropogony and eschatology were inextricably joined together for the first time; the *orpheotelestai* could argue that every human had to "atone to Persephone" for the "ancient grief" from which humanity arose or risk eternal misery in the afterlife.

4

THE ESCHATOLOGY BEHIND
THE TABLETS

Sarah Iles Johnston

If we are to understand the eschatology behind the Gold Tablets – that is, what the tablets' owners believed would happen to them after they died and why – then we need to keep in mind a point that was developed in the last chapter, where the myths of Dionysus' birth, death, and rebirth are discussed. Namely: those who developed the myths and the rituals that we glimpse behind the tablets were *bricoleurs*, drawing upon and adapting myths and rituals that already existed; the tablets' use of epic diction underscores the extent to which they drew on a large reservoir of shared cultural forms.[1] Any study of the tablets' eschatology, therefore, must plant its roots firmly within what we know of Mediterranean eschatology and related topics more generally. The main portion of this chapter will do that, examining each feature of the tablets within the framework of other narratives and practices wherever possible.

First, however, we need to clarify what kinds of documents these tablets were, and what kinds of information we therefore can hope to derive from them. The tablets comprise two types. Twenty longer tablets are primarily *mnemonic devices*, intended to remind the recently departed soul of what it needs to say and do upon arrival in the Underworld. Tablets nos. 1 and 2 explicitly call themselves "the work of Memory"; a fragmentary line on tablet no. 2 may go on to specify that "this" (meaning the information on the tablet, presumably) must be written when the owner is about to die (line 13:]τόδε γραψ[). Tablet no. 9 tells someone (an Underworld divinity whom the owner encounters?) to "accept this gift of Memory." Many others include instructions about which paths to use in the Underworld, from which bodies of water to drink, and what to say to divinities that the soul will confront. Most of tablet no. 27 is a list of passwords to be spoken, constituting a sort of crib-sheet for the soul's most final of exams.

Eighteen shorter tablets include only the name of the departed (nos. 23,

94

24, 24a, 32, 33, 34, 35, 36), a claim of membership (no. 31 "To Persephone, Poseidippos, pious initiate," cf. nos. 20, 21, 22, 28, and possibly 30) or a single phrase of greeting (no. 37 " Philiste greets Persephone," cf. nos. 15, 17, 38).[2] These are *proxies*, intended to speak on behalf of the soul. At least some of these proxies may also be understood broadly as mnemonic devices insofar as one possible reason that the soul is expected to be unable to speak on its own behalf is postmortem confusion – although we will consider another way of looking at the proxy tablets toward the end of this chapter.

It is important to note that neither mnemonic devices nor proxies are, by their nature, likely to offer continuous narratives about the Underworld and the afterlife in the way that *Odyssey* 11 or the story of Er in Plato's *Republic* does. A grocery list – to use one of the most common sorts of mnemonic devices as a comparison[3] – doesn't tell the casual reader that Beef Wellington is planned for dinner; it only indicates that a fillet of beef, liver pâté, and mushrooms need to be purchased. Nor does a grocery list tell the reader how to roast the beef; or that butter – which the composer of this particular list already has at home – will be needed to complete the recipe. Nor does the list describe what the finished dish will taste like. Like all mnemonic devices, in other words, the grocery list includes only information that its composer considered vital for accomplishing the specific task at hand. Proxies, too, are typically brief and allusive. When a person who will be out of town on the day of an important decision leaves behind a piece of paper that states which way she wishes to vote, she does not include an explanation of why she votes the way she does or what she predicts the ramifications of her choice will be if the vote goes her way. An explanation would be superfluous to the task at hand; a prediction would state what her colleagues probably already know.

In the tablets, too, we should expect to find brief allusions to bigger stories and ritual sequences with which their possessors were familiar, rather than detailed, coherent expositions of those stories and rituals. The costliness of the gold from which the tablets were composed exacerbated this tendency; the fewer words one could get by with, the better. The fact that some lines on the mnemonic tablets were probably excerpted or adapted from a longer poem (or poems) or a longer ritual sequence contributes to their allusive quality as well; a given *orpheotelestēs* or his client might believe that certain portions of a poem or ritual were more important or more difficult to remember than other portions, and yet expect that reminding the soul of those portions would evoke the poem or sequence in its entirety, just as the phrase μῆνιν ἄειδε, θεά evokes the entire *Iliad*. The problem for us is that, unlike the *Iliad*, the poems and ritual sequences that the tablets' phrases once evoked are now lost.

Given all of these circumstances, it is impossible to reconstruct a single, complete, and coherent eschatological system out of the statements on the tablets, even if we supplement them with related information from other sources. But we can attempt to: (1) identify what actions were considered by the creators and owners of specific tablets (or groups of related tablets) to be essential for winning happiness in the afterlife; (2) determine how those actions were similar to or different from eschatologically-oriented actions advocated by other systems of the time – that is, how did the cult(s) behind these tablets define themselves, eschatologically, in contrast to others? and (3) explore how these eschatological actions underpinned, and were underpinned by, the myth that was examined in the last chapter and the rituals that will be examined in the next chapter.

Postmortem geography

Most cultures imagine that the soul of the dead will inhabit a new place, once it has been freed from the body. Failure to be completely freed from the body after death, in fact, is often imagined to trap the soul *between* places, where it wanders forever, unable to rest. This sort of belief fits well into what J. Z. Smith has called the locative worldview – everything has its proper place and the work of religion is to ensure that each thing ends up where it belongs – but even utopian religions, which tend to work toward the release of the soul from the material world and thus, we might imagine, would not consider the disembodied soul to even need a place to dwell, typically picture the soul as moving from here (usually understood as "below") into some other place (usually understood as "above"). And "above" is often filled with objects similar to those "below," such as rocks, rivers, trees, flowery meadows, temples, and palaces. In the Hellenistic apocalypse known as *The Book of the Watchers*, for instance, Enoch is shown all sorts of things similar to earthly features – mountains, rivers, springs, gates, and so on. In the *Apocalypse of Paul*, a product of late fourth-century CE Egypt, the soul travels to a gated community modeled on monasteries of the time.[4] It is usually only the philosophers within a given culture who can envision an absolute cessation of existence after death, an absolute "placelessness" of the soul.

Literature offers elaborate narratives that draw on these ideas. Odysseus sails west to the stream of Ocean, passing through the land of Cimmeria, which is eternally hidden in mist, and coming ashore at the very outskirts of the Underworld, from which vantage point he can observe the souls of the departed going about their business, pleasant or unpleasant (*Od.* 11.13–19). The early Christian *Ascension of Isaiah* describes seven increasingly high and increasingly luminous levels of Heaven, populated by singing angels, thrones of glory, and souls of the righteous. Dante loses his way in a dark forest and ends up touring Hell's Nine Circles, Purgatory, and Heaven, the first of which are filled with imposing landmarks: foreboding gates, chasms, and gulfs, the marshy bog of the Styx. Shorter descriptions of the afterlife can be vividly evocative of physical place as well. Homer emphasizes the remoteness of the Underworld by telling us that Hades is "as far beneath the earth as the earth is beneath the heavens" (*Iliad* 8.16; cf. Hes. *Theog.* 720). Hesiod speaks of the "echoing halls of Hades" and of the brazen fence that encircles Tartarus, the deepest and most dreadful part of the Underworld (*Theog.* 769, 726). Jewish and early Christian images of Hell crop up in numerous texts; Sheol or Gehinnom is referred to frequently as a "fiery pit" with "rivers of fire," inhabited by dangerous beasts.[5]

Rituals connected with death and the afterlife, not surprisingly, also express an interest in Underworld geography, although it is much more practically oriented. The Tibetan Book of the Dead includes descriptions of dangerous or obstructive features of the Underworld, such as a river, and instructions as to how the soul may triumph against them. Rivers that must be crossed are in fact one of the most common features of Underworld geographies; by at least the classical period, popular Greek belief developed the idea that coins buried with the dead would insure that Charon, the infernal ferryman, would transport the soul into the Underworld (Ar. *Ran.* 190–3).[6] Ancient Egyptian "guides to the hereafter" described gates, paths, and waterways, and provided code-words or other information that the soul needed to pass through or over them. Calvert Watkins has drawn our attention to a Hittite text that seems to provide a map for the soul traveling through the Underworld, complete with paths, a river, and a pond.[7]

Thirteen of our twenty "mnemonic" tablets mention geographical features of the Underworld. These come from widely scattered parts of the ancient world – Magna Graecia, Sicily, Thessaly, Crete – and date from the fifth century BCE to the second or first century BCE. If we wished, we could divide these according to the sorts of features they emphasize (paths, trees, bodies of water and meadows), or according to the specific type of advice they convey, but for the moment, what should be noted is the sheer amount of interest in geography itself, which suggests that mapping the Underworld was just as important to the people who created and bought the tablets as it was to anyone else. In other words, at least in this broad sense, the tablets' users were no different from everyone else in their surrounding culture. Given this, our main questions in what follows will be: how and why did the creators of the tablets (or the poem[s] and ritual[s] that underlay them) adapt existing *topoi* concerning Underworld geography, and how was knowledge of that geography expected specifically to aid the soul in transition?[8]

Bodies of water and their markers: tablets nos. 1, 2, 8, and 25

Twelve of the thirteen tablets under consideration are concerned with obtaining water in the Underworld – a very common motif in eschatological narratives and ritual systems all over the world, which tend to presume that the deceased will be thirsty. But our tablets, in contrast to many other texts that use the motif, posit more than one source of water in the Underworld and focus on ensuring that the initiate will drink from the correct, "safe" one (the Lake of Memory) instead of the wrong "dangerous" one (which, as we will see, might be called "the Spring of Forgetfulness"). Thus, tablet no. 1, which is among the more elaborate expositions of this idea, as well as the earliest in date of all our tablets, says:

1   This is the work of Memory, when you are about to die
2   down to the well-built house of Hades. There is a spring at the right side,
3   and standing by it a white cypress.
4   Descending to it, the souls of the dead refresh themselves.
5   Do not even go near this spring!
6   Ahead you will find from the Lake of Memory,
7   cold water pouring forth; there are guards before it.
8   They will ask you, with astute wisdom,
9   what you are seeking in the darkness of murky Hades.
10 Say, "I am a son of Earth and starry Sky,
11 I am parched with thirst and am dying; but quickly grant me
12 cold water from the Lake of Memory to drink."
13 And they will announce you to the Chthonian King,
14 and they will grant you to drink from the Lake of Memory.
15 And you, too, having drunk, will go along the sacred road on which other
16 glorious initiates and *bacchoi* travel.

Tablet no. 2 from Petelia in Magna Graecia and tablet no. 8 from Entella in Sicily are very similar to Tablet no. 1. Tablet no. 25 offers an abbreviated version of the text shared by nos. 1 and 8:

1   You will find in the house of Hades, on the right side, a spring,
2   and standing by it a white cypress.
3   Do not even approach this spring!

4   Ahead you will find, from the Lake of Memory,
5   cold water pouring forth; there are guards before it.
6   They will ask you by what necessity you have come.
7   You, tell them the whole entire truth.
8   Say, "I am a child of Earth and starry Sky.
9   My name is 'Starry.' I am parched with thirst. But grant me
10 to drink from the spring."

Later in this chapter, we will discuss the specific purpose served by the Waters of Memory, as well as the role of the guards, but first we will focus on how the soul is supposed to identify the source of this water.

Three of the four tablets under consideration here (nos. 1, 8, and 25) agree that when the soul of the initiate arrives in the Underworld, it will bear to the right of the house of Hades, as do six tablets from Crete that will be discussed later (nos. 10–14 and no. 16) and a tablet from Thurii (no. 3). The fourth tablet that we are discussing at the moment (no. 2, from Petelia), as well as another tablet from Crete (no. 18), although very similar to the remaining geographic tablets in other ways, diverge in suggesting that the soul will bear to the *left* of the house of Hades when it arrives. Possible reasons for this divergence will be offered below, but for the moment, as we focus on building our larger picture of the eschatological ideas underlying the tablets, we will work from the assumption that the prevailing tradition in the religious circles from which the tablets emerged expected the soul to bear to the right immediately after death.

All four tablets specify that soon after the soul has started down its path in the Underworld, it will encounter a dangerous spring, which is marked by a white cypress tree. Should the soul, then, have veered to the other side of the house of Hades instead, upon first arriving? That is: if the tradition behind the tablets expected that the newly arrived soul would set off down the right-hand path, should it have set off on the left-hand path instead, in order to avoid this spring? No – rather, the soul is instructed to travel further (πρόσθεν) on its original course until it encounters a second body of water (the Lake of Memory). This preference for the right-hand path aligns well not only with the privileging of right versus left in ancient eschatologies and ancient mentalities more generally[9] but also with statements in tablet no. 3:

1   But as soon as the soul has left the light of the sun,
2   Go to the *right*, being very careful of all things.
3   "Greetings, you who have suffered the painful thing; you have
    never endured this before.
4   You have become a god instead of a mortal. A kid you fell into milk.

5 Rejoice, rejoice." Journey on the *right-hand* road
6 to holy meadows and groves of Persephone.

The message, then, is that the soul of the initiate must not only go to the right when it arrives in Hades but must remember to keep going – not to give in to thirst at the first opportunity, however parched it may be.

Three types of souls

If the initiate's soul persists on the right-hand path until reaching the Lake of Memory, then whose soul is imagined to give in at the sight of that first, dangerous body of water? And whose is to be imagined to go to the *left* of the house of Hades (an option implicit in the tablets' specification of the right-hand side)?

Some passages from Pindar and Plato will suggest an answer. In *Olympian* 2, an epinician ode composed in 476 BCE for Theron of Acragas (a Sicilian city not far from where tablet no. 8 would be created about a century later, and in the same general part of the world where tablet no. 1 was created about fifty years later), Pindar suggests that there are three categories of dead: those who committed injustices while alive and who pay the penalty after death in an unspecified place (lines 56–60), those who were good while alive and enjoy a "tear-free existence" in the afterlife in a place where they dwell among the honored gods (lines 61–7), and those who managed to live three lives and three afterlives without committing any injustices, who "travel the road of Zeus to the tower of Cronus, where ocean breezes blow around the island of the blessed and golden flowers blaze forth both from radiant trees and from the waters" (lines 68–80). Well-known heroes such as Peleus, Cadmus, and Achilles end up in this third place as well.

In other words, in *Olympian* 2 Pindar describes a tripartite Underworld with different locales for the bad, the good, and the good who arrive with an extra characteristic that sets them apart from the rest: either they have managed to be good even longer than the other good souls or, like most heroes, they have a special relationship with the gods. Might we not imagine that similarly, in the system behind the tablets, there were three types of souls? The bad, who went to the left of the house of Hades; the good, who went to the right but gave in to their thirst too soon and drank at the first body of water; and the "good-plus" (as I will call them from now on), who continued further along the road to the right? The structure of rewards suggested by our tablets differs from that of *Olympian* 2: in the tablets it seems to be only the good-plus who will dwell alongside the gods; in Pindar, the good dwell among gods as well, although apparently not among the same gods and heroes as the good-plus, and not for so long a period. But the basic idea is the same: in both Pindar and the tablets, the bad, the good, and the good-plus are geographically and experientially separated in the Underworld.

In Pindar, the good-plus win their reward by virtuous behavior. What characteristic qualifies the good-plus for special treatment in the system behind the tablets? To some degree it is allegiance to virtue as well, specifically, to a virtue that the Greeks would have called *sophrosynē*, moderation. It is their ability to resist drinking the first water that they encounter, in spite of their thirstiness, that enables the good-plus to hold out for the Lake of Memory. But it is also the *knowledge* that it is necessary to resist the first body of water that sets the good-plus apart from the good. Insofar as the knowledge was mnemonically preserved on the tablets that the good-plus carried into death, and insofar as both of these things – the knowledge and the tablet – were almost surely acquired during initiation into the mysteries, we can say that it is initiation itself that has set the good-plus apart.

A similar system can be glimpsed behind the fragments of a dirge composed by Pindar, which are embedded in discussions of the afterlife by Plutarch.[10] The fragments suggest that, as in *Olympian* 2, Pindar presented one place in Hades where the pious (*eusebeis*) enjoyed eternal sunshine, red roses, frankincense and fruit trees, gaming, music, and feasts. He also presented a separate place to which those who had lived in an unholy and lawless manner (*anosiōs* and *paranomōs*) journeyed along what he described as "the third road." And by implication, if it was a "third road" that led to the place of punishment, then there must have been yet one more road, leading to one more place – perhaps described by another fragment that survives from the dirge: "happy are all of those who have the good fortune of toil-relieving [initiation] rites (*teletai*)." If so, then here, as in the tablets (and in contrast to *Olympian* 2) Pindar suggests that it was initiation that set the good-plus apart from the merely good.

One more postmortem scheme, presented in Plato's *Republic*, will help to confirm what our readings of Pindar have already suggested about the tablets' eschatology and geography. At the beginning of the story, we meet two types of souls who have recently arrived in an Underworld meadow. One type is those who were virtuous while alive (the good); when these leave the meadow they travel a path rightward and upward to a place of postmortem reward. The other type is those who misbehaved while alive (the bad); when they leave the meadow they travel a path leftward and downward to a place of postmortem punishment. One thousand years later, almost all of the souls re-emerge into the central meadow where they started, now equal in status, for most of the bad have been able to pay for their misdeeds by enduring punishment. Only a few, incurably bad souls are kept back, eternally imprisoned below in Tartarus. In other words, all members of the two original groups, good and bad, are reassessed at this point, but the categories themselves remain in place: it is just that the majority of souls now are good and only a few are bad.

All of the good souls now travel together to a place where each chooses a new incarnation for the next life. At this juncture, both *sophrosyne* and knowledge – specifically the knowledge of what constitutes a good life, as acquired through philosophy – begin to separate the good souls from those who will constitute the category of the good-plus. Whereas some souls choose their new incarnations hastily and badly, distracted by the glittering riches associated with particular lives, those who have learned restraint and who possess knowledge make a more careful choice and enter upon a new life that will be relatively virtuous and free of pain. The challenges are not over yet, however: having chosen their next lives, the souls journey across the scorching Plain of Oblivion and eventually reach the River of Forgetfulness. All of the souls drink from this river, but "those who were not saved by their good sense (*phronesis*) drank more than they needed to and forgot everything [that they had learned]." These souls begin their new life at square zero, no further ahead than they were when they began the previous one. The good-plus, in contrast, drink in moderation and carry some of what they have learned into the next incarnation.

Plato's tale differs from the system we seem to glimpse behind the tablets insofar as not even the good-plus can escape reincarnation; the best one can hope for is a pleasant time while in the afterlife for a thousand years and a better life the next time than one had before. In the tablets' system, the souls of the good-plus probably are imagined to dwell forever among the gods and heroes (more on this below). But Plato's tale clearly does assume that there are three categories of souls – bad, good, and good-plus – and that what distinguishes the good-plus from the good is knowledge and the ability to control one's desires. Thus, we have a third parallel for the tripartite system that I proposed for understanding the roads in the tablets and the souls who travel them. Like Plato's incurably bad souls, the bad souls of the tablets' system probably go to the left of the house of Hades. Good souls go to the right in both cases, but some distinguish themselves further by knowing either where to drink (the tablets) or how much to drink (Plato).

We might wonder why the tablets never explicitly mention the bad souls, their left-hand journey or their loathsome fate. The answer once again lies in the tablets' nature as mnemonic devices and their construction out of an expensive material. There was no need to remind the initiate's soul of what it would have suffered had it not been initiated, so why incur the extra cost to do so? Descriptions of the damned are often found in extended narrations of the afterlife, where they produce lovely

Comparative chart of eschatological systems

System and qualities	Deciding factor(s)	Destination and fate
Olympian 2: the bad	Unethical life	Paying the penalty somewhere in Hades
Olympian 2: the good	Ethical life	Winning rewards somewhere in Hades with gods present
Olympian 2: the good-plus	Ethical life three times over	Winning better rewards at the Tower of Cronus/Island of Blessed; heroes present
Pindar's dirge: the bad	Unethical life	Paying penalty somewhere "along the third road" in Hades
Pindar's dirge: the good	Ethical life	Winning rewards in a pleasant part of Hades
Pindar's dirge: the good-plus	Ethical life plus initiation	Winning rewards in another pleasant part of Hades
Plato: the bad	Irredeemably unethical life	Remain eternally in the lower, left-hand part of Hades and be punished
Plato: the good	Ethical life or redeemably unethical life	Escape eternal punishment but choose next life unwisely and drink deeply of Forgetfulness
Plato: the good-plus	Ethical life or redeemably unethical life, plus philosophic training and self restraint	Escape eternal punishment; choose next life wisely and do not drink deeply of Forgetfulness
Gold Tablets: the bad	Unethical life	Left side of Hades' house
Gold Tablets: the good	Ethical life; drink at first water	Right side of Hades' house; drink of Forgetfulness
Gold Tablets: the good-plus	Ethical life plus initiation; wait for second water	Pleasant place further on to the right with gods and/or heroes; drink of Memory

frissons for readers or listeners, or in extended descriptions of what a particular religious system has to offer, where they serve as frightening points of contrast. Such descriptions may well have been part of the longer Orphic poem(s) from which some of the lines on our tablets were derived – Plato tells us about an Orphic poem according to which the damned wallow in manure and mud for eternity (*Phd.* 69c8–d1) – but inscribed on a Gold Tablet, such descriptions would have been merely a waste of money. The closest we come in the tablets to any mention of souls other than the good-plus is the remark that "the souls of the dead refresh themselves" at the first right-hand body of water, which initiates must avoid. These souls, I have argued, are those of the good. Given that the souls of even the good-plus would be thirsty and confused upon arrival in the Underworld, it was important to make it clear that they must avoid drinking this spring's water – thus, there was a practical reason for including a description of the good souls' location and behavior.

Before we leave our discussion of left paths, right paths and their significance, it should be noted that the general idea of the Underworld having various roads is very common in ancient sources. Outside of the cases that we have just examined, Underworld paths typically are presented as disorienting the newly disembodied soul: in the *Phaedo*, for instance, Socrates says that the journey to Hades is full of treacherous forks and crossroads.[11] Different systems offer different solutions to this quandary: Socrates goes on to say that the wise, disciplined soul will avoid becoming lost by closely following the daemonic guide that comes to meet it upon arrival. Souls that are utterly impure or lawless are shunned by these guides, however, and end up wandering forever in the desolate darkness of the Underworld (an idea that finds an echo in the fact that in tablets nos. 1 and 8, Underworld guards ask the soul what it is seeking in the darkness and murkiness of Hades). Thus, Socrates' solution requires the soul both to prepare for a successful afterlife before death by avoiding bad behavior and becoming pure (whatever "pure" means in this context), and to do the right thing once it arrives in the Underworld by paying attention to the guide. Similarly, the system behind the *Republic* expects the soul to prepare before death by studying philosophy and then to use that preparation to do the right things after death. Pindar seems to offer two different solutions: *Olympian* 2 demands exceptionally virtuous behavior of those who hope to end up among the good-plus whereas the fragments of his dirge indicate that initiation is required instead or as well: the pious (*eusebeis*) who have kept away from lawless and unholy behavior end up in a good place, but *teletai* are required if one wishes to end up in the best place of all.

Our tablets mention nothing that can really be defined as virtuous behavior in the usual sense of that term; some of them, which we have not examined yet, emphasize a need for purity, but it is likely that this is purity of a ritual variety, rather than ethical or moral. It is always possible that the tablets are silent on the topic of virtuous behavior because, as mnemonic devices, they had no reason to waste space recording what had already taken place during the initiates' lifetime – although if adherence to a particular ethical or moral standard were important, we might expect the souls to have been reminded to assert this to the guards who would challenge them, according to some of the tablets. Instead, the initiates must tell the guards that they are of a certain lineage. Outside sources do not add anything more about virtuous behavior. Although some ancient authors associated Bacchic mysteries and Orphic teachings with vegetarianism and the avoidance of wool,[12] these requirements (if they were even followed by those initiates who used the tablets) again characterize ritual purity rather than a wholesale pursuit of virtue.

Moreover, the idea that initiation alone would suffice to guarantee postmortem bliss is not out of step with what we hear about mysteries from other ancient sources: several voices complain that these cults promised salvation to those who had done nothing more than scrape together enough cash to be initiated. These are the critical voices of outsiders, to be sure, but they suggest that mysteries put the emphasis on ritualized actions rather than any on-going moral or ethical improvement in one's way of life.[13] And, whether the mysteries' critics acknowledged it or not, this was in line with the standard attitude in ancient Greek and Roman religions: the proper performance of rites in honor of the gods *was* part of being a virtuous person just as surely as proper treatment of one's parents was.

To sum up: the authors we have examined so far – Pindar, Plato, and the anonymous composers of the tablets – agree in positing a tripartite structure for the afterlife, but disagree as to what, exactly, qualified each kind of soul for each of the three parts. The system underlying the tablets, in which ritualized initiation defined the good-plus, almost surely was the earliest version of a tripartite afterlife; Plato (a philosopher interested in defining and promulgating ethical behavior) and Pindar (a poet who consistently shows an interest in this as well) adapted this older system to their didactic uses, replacing initiation either wholly or partially with virtue and philosophical training.

Eschatological divisions before the tablets

All of this begs the question, however, of what any of these authors were reacting *to*. If Plato, Pindar, and the mysteries posited three categories of dead – bad, good, and good-plus – are we to imagine that mainstream eschatology of their own or earlier periods posited only two categories? If so, what were these categories? Bad and good? Good and good-plus? And, finally, what were the merits of a tripartite system?

Our sources are too spotty to provide definite answers, but we can make some informed guesses. In our earliest Greek narrations about the afterlife, taken from Homer and other epic poems, only the very bad (those who have committed crimes against the gods, such as Tantalus and Tityus) are punished and only the very privileged (those who are related to the gods by birth or marriage, such as Achilles and Menelaus) enjoy bliss. The vast majority of people simply languish away in Hades, neither suffering any particular distress nor enjoying any particular pleasure.[14]

Obviously, these ideas could have laid the groundwork for the expectation that *everyone* would be rewarded or punished after death for what they had done while alive – that is, for a bipartite afterlife based on virtue or its absence. Our earliest expressions of this idea show up in the passages from Pindar that were discussed above: although Pindar actually describes two different versions of a *tripartite* system, the divisions in each version are predicated in part on virtue or its absence. Pindar indicates, therefore, that the concept of postmortem punishment and reward for deeds performed while alive was available by the early fifth century at latest – more or less the same time as the tablets begin to show up. The fact that Pindar's system is a *tripartite* one – that is, we assume, an elaboration of a simpler *bipartite* system – suggests further that a bipartite system had probably been around for quite some time before he composed his poems. Solon (early sixth century) can take us a bit further in this direction, for he provides our earliest certain evidence for the concept of inherited guilt (frg. 13.26–8), which shares with the concept of postmortem rewards and punishments the salient principle that retribution is ineluctable – even if it comes late.[15] Both concepts fit well into the archaic period, which witnessed an increasing awareness of the individual and an increasing concern with questions of personal responsibility. Taken in combination, these observations suggest that the concept of a bipartite afterlife, in which individuals were assigned places according to how they had behaved while alive, developed at some point before the tablets.

But this hypothetical scheme of development implicitly emphasizes the side of the picture that deals with the losers – those who, like Tantalus and Tityus, earned their punishments by willfully committing misdeeds – at the expense of ignoring the side that deals with the winners – those who, like Achilles and Menelaus, received postmortem favors based on divine kinship. The picture could have also been developed to suggest that everyone got either a bad or a good afterlife not on the basis of how they had *behaved* while alive, but on the basis of the *relationship* they had established with the gods, or with particular gods. Those who had forged a special bond that more-or-less replicated the divine familial relationship that Menelaus and Achilles had enjoyed would benefit in the afterlife; those who had not would suffer.

And in fact, the first certain mention we get of a bipartite afterlife points in exactly this direction. In lines 364–9 of the early sixth-century Homeric *Hymn to Demeter*, Hades says to his new wife, Persephone, that by reigning in the Underworld:

> [you] will be mistress of everything that lives and creeps, and will have the greatest honors among the gods; there will be punishment given forever more to those who act wrongly – to those who do not propitiate your might with sacrifices, acting in a pure manner and making the correct offerings.

Most scholars assume that the sacrifices and offerings that Hades mentions refer to those performed during the Eleusinian Mysteries by initiates who hope to reap benefits both here and now and after death. Later, in lines 480–2, the poet of the *Hymn* describes an initiate who has beheld the Eleusinian Mysteries as "blessed (*olbios*) among humans who live on the earth," whereas someone who is not initiated "has no share in these same things after he is dead, down in the musty dark." In other words, there are initiates and non-initiates; the only good behavior that matters for your postmortem prospects is good behavior directed toward the gods, and especially toward Persephone and her mother in the context of the Eleusinian Mysteries. This follows a logic we see elsewhere in early hexameter poetry, whereby the "just" or "correct" life prominently included paying proper cult to the gods and failure to pay it could therefore constitute "injustice" or "incorrect" behavior.[16] By performing the proper rituals, one could create a relationship with these two goddesses that approached the kinship with the gods shared by Achilles and Menelaus.

Thus, there were two eschatological systems available by the late archaic age on which bipartite visions of the afterlife could be built – what might be called the "ethical" system and the "ritualized" system. The first could claim the merit of "fairness" within a world that was increasingly concerned with personal responsibility; the second could claim the merits of expediency and security within a world where everyone knew that few people, if any, lived lives of moral and ethical perfection. The *bricoleurs* behind the tablets brilliantly combined the two, creating a tripartite system that demanded both proper *ethical behavior* (everyone who had been good during life went to the right of the house of Hades after death and everyone who had been bad went to the left) and proper *ritual behavior* (only those who had been initiated into the Bacchic mysteries continued further onward to the right, past the first body of water). The appeal of this combination is attested by Pindar's and Plato's adaptations of it. Plato substituted philosophic training for ritual in his version, but in doing so retained the important point that some sort of special knowledge was required. In his dirge, Pindar retained initiation; in *Olympian 2*, he substituted extraordinary virtue for ritual, but by making the souls of his good-plus join the souls of traditional heroes such as Achilles in their afterlife paradise, he evoked one of the goals that underlay initiation in both the Bacchic and the Eleusinian Mysteries: to establish a close personal relationship with a god, such as the heroes had.[17]

We must pause on one question before we move on: why do tablets nos. 2 and 18, in contrast to all the rest of the geographic tablets, specify that the soul of the initiate will go to the *left* when it arrives in Hades? I will postpone discussion of no. 18 until we have discussed the rest of the Cretan tablets, but in the case of no. 2, I suggest that we can find an answer by looking closely at the differences between its language and the language of nos. 1, 8, and 25. The three latter all include some variation of the phrases: "You will find in the house of Hades, on the right side, a spring, and standing by it a white cypress. Do not even approach this spring! *Ahead* (πρόσθεν) you will find from the Lake of Memory cold water pouring forth . . ." In other words, these tablets make it clear that the dangerous water and the good water are found by the side of the *same* path. Tablet no. 2, in contrast, says "You will find to the left of the house of Hades a spring and standing by it a white cypress. Do not even approach this spring! You will find another (ἑτέραν), from the Lake of Memory, cold water pouring forth . . ." The creator of this tablet does not make it clear whether the second, safe source of water is on the same path as the first, dangerous spring, or on a different path – the right-hand path. We might imagine that he acquired only partial knowledge of what the majority of the tablets suggest was the standard idea – namely, that the good spring was somewhere to the right – and extrapolated from this, quite naturally, that the other, dangerous spring must be on the left. If this hypothesis is correct, it once again underscores how open to modification both the words of the tablets and the ideas that underlay them could be in a system that perpetuated itself through itinerant, independent initiators.

The cypress

The spring from which the dangerous water pours forth is marked not only by the crowd of souls who eagerly drink from it but also by a white cypress (tablets nos. 1, 2, 8, 25). Many descriptions of the Underworld, in ancient Greece and elsewhere, include trees and groves and, given that the cypress has funerary associations in some strands of ancient thought, it is not too surprising that we would encounter this particular tree in the world below.[18] What needs further consideration is why the cypress is white (*leukos*).

Marcello Gigante conjectured that the tree's color might be connected with the white clothing worn by initiates into some mysteries; Bernabé and Jiménez San Cristóbal have pointed to the use of white cloth in burials. Another train of thought has understood the tree's whiteness to signal the inverted nature of the Underworld – trees are not white in the upper world.[19] Most persuasive to my mind, however, is Zuntz's observation that *leukos* can mean not merely white, but brilliantly white or shining. The tree's color, therefore, makes it stand out better in the gloom of the Underworld – a gloom that is explicitly mentioned in several of the tablets (1.9, 3.1, 8.11, and perhaps also 2.14 and 8.3).[20] Similarly, we hear about a white (*leukē*) rock that marks the entrance to the Underworld at *Odyssey* 24.11, and a marvelous island called White (Leuke) where the souls of heroes end up according to the epic *Aethiopis* – it makes sense to understand the heroes' souls as enjoying a place that, in contrast to the rest of Hades, is brightly lit. And, similarly, Pindar and other authors place souls of the blessed and heroes in sunny parts of the Underworld.[21]

Drawing on these associations of whiteness and brightness in the Underworld, we can understand the role of the cypress in two complementary ways. On the one hand, if the Spring of Forgetfulness functions as an attraction for the souls of the ordinary good, who are destined to drink its waters and lose all recollection, then the white cypress serves as an additional lure for them, drawing them toward the water like moths to a candle. On the other hand, if the souls of the good-plus must be sure to avoid this spring, then the white cypress marks the place as dangerous, like a lighthouse beacon. The absence of any such cypress at the Lake of Memory, in contrast, assures the soul of the initiate that this source of water is safe.

A different geography: tablets nos. 10–14, 16, and 29; tablet no. 18

Or *is* the cypress absent from the Lake of Memory? Six tablets from Crete and one from Thessaly state otherwise. Aside from minor differences, six of the Cretan tablets (nos. 10–14, 16) all read:

1   I am parched with thirst and am dying; but grant me to drink
2   from the ever-flowing spring on the right, where the cypress is.
3   "Who are you? Where are you from?" I am a son of Earth and starry Sky.

The Thessalian tablet (no. 29) adds a final line, which we also find in tablets nos. 2 and 8. It reads:

1 I am parched with thirst and am dying; but grant me to drink
2 from the ever-flowing spring. On the right is a white cypress.
3 "Who are you? Where are you from?" I am a son of Earth and starry Sky
4 But my race is heavenly.

Not only does the cypress mark its water source as desirable in these tablets, but that water source is described as a spring, like the dangerous body of water in the tablets we have just examined.

The Greek in these seven tablets is virtually identical to that in the corresponding lines of the tablets we earlier examined. This, plus the fact that the Thessalian tablet adds an extra line that is also found in tablets nos. 2 and 8, suggests that these seven belong in the same group as the four other tablets. Notably, however, the texts of the Cretan and Thessalian tablets, overall, are much shorter than those in tablets nos. 1, 2, and 8 and somewhat shorter than the text in no. 25. Two or perhaps three of the four tablets in the first group date to the fourth century BCE; one dates to the late fifth century BCE. One of the seven tablets in the second group dates to the fourth century BCE, the rest of them date to the second or first century BCE. In other words, the longer examples are on the average at least a century older than the shorter examples. It looks as if scribal abbreviation took place in the process of transmitting (perhaps repeatedly transmitting) these texts – and any time that scribal abbreviation occurs, alterations are likely to occur as well; thus, new meaning is generated, intentionally or unintentionally. The clustering of six of the seven tablets on Crete is especially telling: once an altered exemplum made it on to the island, it set the standard.[22] Thus, the existence of a *second* body of water to the right of the house of Hades fell out of the tradition and the one that remained became the one that initiates were to seek. The generally positive association of the right-hand side would have made this easy to accept; there was no reason that those using the shorter tablets would have suspected that anything was amiss.

But there is one more quandary to consider: tablet no. 18, which is also from Crete, reads:

1 He is parched with thirst and almost dying but grant me to drink
2 from the ever-flowing spring on the left of the cypress.

3 "Who are you? And where are you from?" I am of Earth, mother
   [untranslatable letters] and of starry Sky.
4 Thirst [untranslatable]

Why did the creator of this tablet advocate drinking from a spring on the
left-hand side? We cannot explain this away in the same way as we did
no. 2's apparent divergence; the tablet clearly advocates drinking from
the left-hand spring. It is marginally possible that tablet no. 18's creator
simply made a mistake; the tablet is, as its editor Yannis Tzifopolous
says, very sloppily written, with many other omissions and departures
from the text as we know it from other examples (most noticeably, the
first line is spoken in the third person rather than the first person). And
yet, mistaking left for right in such a crucial context seems unlikely,
however bad one's script or careless one's grammar may be. Perhaps the
orpheotelestēs who sold the tablet innovated purposefully, arguing to
his client that *his* was the correct knowledge, in contradistinction from
what all the other purveyors of tablets were claiming. Apparently, this
innovation didn't catch on, however, given that no. 18 is the only tablet
we have on which (in contrast to no. 2) the left is clearly indicated as the
desirable path.[23]

Guards and their questions

Our four longer geographic tablets (nos. 1, 2, 8, and 25) say that there are
guards standing in front of the Lake of Memory; the guards' presence is
implied in the shorter tablets insofar as these tablets provide variations
of the questions the guards ask and the answers the souls give, as we will
see.

6 Ahead you will find from the Lake of Memory,
7 cold water pouring forth; there are guards before it.
8 They will ask you, with astute wisdom,
9 what you are seeking in the darkness of murky Hades (no. 1)

4 You will find another, from the Lake of Memory,
5 cold water pouring forth; there are guards before it. (no. 2)

8 Ahead you will find from the Lake of Memory
9 cold water pouring forth; there are guards before it.
10 They will ask you, with astute wisdom,
11 what you are seeking in the darkness of murky Hades (no. 8)

4   Ahead you will find from the Lake of Memory,
5   cold water pouring forth; there are guards before it.
6   They will ask you by what necessity you have come. (no. 25)

In three of the four cases, the guards bar the soul of the initiate from drinking until it has answered a question. This also seems to be the case in the remaining instance (no. 2), because the next lines of the tablet repeat the answer that the initiate is to give, just as in tablets nos. 1, 8, and 25.

Guards and guard-like figures are encountered frequently in ancient Mediterranean eschatological texts and in related documents such as ascent and *katabasis* texts (texts in which a living individual temporarily visits the Heavens or the Underworld). Usually, these guards are located at the entrance to a desirable part of the afterlife; sometimes they stand at the entrance to Heaven or the Underworld as a whole, in which case failure to get past them means that the soul will wander forever between the realms of life and death. The guards may be gods, *daemones*, angels, or monstrous creatures such as Cerberus. (We are given no information about what the guards in our tablets are, or even look like; they may be any or none of these things.) Typically, such guards challenge the traveler to do something before allowing him or her to enjoy whatever benefits they are protecting. These challenges may include questions to be answered, evaluations of one's moral worth or one's accomplishments during life, and demands for gifts (for example, giving a "sop to Cerberus"). The soul may respond by establishing its knowledge or other qualifications, by providing the required gift, or simply by frightening the guards – by revealing, for example, that it knows their secret names.[24]

Although the exact formulation of the question asked by the guards in our tablets varies slightly from case to case, it always amounts to asking why the soul is in its current situation – what is it seeking in Hades? By what necessity has it come there? These may evoke for us the questions that Odysseus is asked by three of the souls whom he sees in the Underworld in Book 11 of the *Odyssey* – those souls, however, ask out of wonderment at Odysseus' presence or sheer curiosity, whereas the questions in the tablets take on the flavor of a sentry's challenge.[25] Unlike Odysseus, moreover, the souls in the tablets do not need to address the guards' questions directly; instead, they are reminded to tell the guards who they are and what they require:

10   Say, "I am a son of Earth and starry Sky,
11   I am parched with thirst and am dying; but quickly grant me
12   cold water from the Lake of Memory to drink." (no. 1)

6   Say, "I am a child of Earth and starry Sky,
7   but my race is heavenly. You yourselves know this.
8   I am parched with thirst and am dying; but quickly grant me
9   cold water flowing from the Lake of Memory." (no. 2)

12   Say, "I am a child of Earth and starry Sky,
13   I am parched with thirst and am dying; but grant me
14   cold water from the Lake of Memory to drink.
15   But my race is heavenly. You yourselves know this." (no. 8)

7   You, tell them the whole entire truth.
8   Say, "I am a child of Earth and starry Sky.
9   My name is 'Starry'. I am parched with thirst. But grant me
10   to drink from the spring." (no. 25)

The shorter tablets from Crete and Thessaly include similar statements:

1   I am parched with thirst and am dying; but grant me to drink
2   from the ever-flowing spring on the right, where the cypress is.
3   "Who are you? Where are you from?" I am a son of Earth and starry
    Sky (nos. 10–14 and 16, allowing for minor variations)

1   I am parched with thirst and am dying; but grant me to drink
2   from the ever-flowing spring. On the right is a white cypress.
3   "Who are you? Where are you from?" I am a son of Earth and
    starry Sky.
4   But my race is heavenly. (no. 29)

Part of the answer, "I am a child of Earth and starry Sky," and the variations that accompany it in three tablets, "My name is Starry" and "My race is heavenly," are generally in line with what is said by individuals who confront guards in other texts: the one who desires access often has to prove that he is from a special family or group (cf. also "Earth is my mother" in no. 18). The specifics of the phrase "I am a child of Earth and starry Sky," have occasioned much debate, however. To understand the statement's purpose, we have to start from the oft-made observation that the verse calls to mind line 106 of Hesiod's *Theogony*:[26]

[the gods] who were born from Earth and starry Sky.

Insofar as the lines in the tablets assert that a human (soul) is descended from the gods, they also evoke line 108 of Hesiod's *Works and Days*, in which the first, Golden Race of humans is described:

from the same race [came] the gods and mortal humans.

M. L. West has suggested that this second phrase meant no more than that the gods and mortals started out on equal terms, or that humans lived a life not unlike that of gods, but (as West concedes) the word I have translated here as "same" (the adverb ὁμόθεν) usually implies a blood relationship.[27] Certainly, whatever Hesiod himself intended, the line could have been understood by later audiences to mean that gods and humans were literally related to one another, for the idea is found elsewhere in Greek sources. Pindar's sixth *Nemean*, for instance, begins with the statement "There is one race of men, one of gods, but from a single mother we both draw our breath," and one of Euripides' characters said that humans and animals – and implicitly all gods, given traditional mythological genealogy – have Earth and Sky as common parents (frg. 1004 Kannicht).

The line "I am a child of Earth and starry Sky," then, may have verbally evoked the *Theogony*'s description of the gods, but conceptually it also evoked the *Works and Days*' description of early humans being relatives of the gods. Thus, an ancient reader of our tablets would have understood the soul's declaration that it was a "child of Earth and starry Sky" to mean that it was claiming an affinity – based on both lineage and nature – with the gods. Statements on tablets that we have not yet examined actually claim that the initiate will become a god instead of a mortal (nos. 3.4, 5.9, 9.4) or tell the soul to boast to the gods that it is "of your happy race" (nos. 5.3, 6.3, 7.3). Of the tablets we are examining at the moment, no. 2 says that the initiate will "rule among the other heroes," which, given that a hero frequently was understood to be the child of a god and a mortal, could be understood to mean that the initiate has become at least a junior member of the divine group. The phrase "remembering hero" on a fragmentary part of tablet no. 8 may allude to this expectation as well; if the initiate remembers to do what he or she has been taught to do, then he or she will become a hero. All of this aligns well with an idea developed earlier in this chapter: the aim of initiation, in this and other mystery cults, was to establish a personal relationship between the initiate and one or more gods, replicating as closely as possible the familial relationship between gods and their children, the heroes.

Joining the heroes

We might wonder how those who promulgated the cult and the poems that it used as sacred texts justified this claim, however. As the last chapter discussed, humans of the present age are in trouble precisely because they sprang from the remains of evil Titans who had consumed Dionysus. How could such a creature claim to be related to the gods or heroes? Some scholars have proposed that, since the Titans *were* gods – and were specifically the children of Earth (Gaia) and Sky (Uranus), then their human descendants could be understood as gods, too, but this strains credibility.[28] Why would humans want to remind Persephone or her representatives of their Titanic origins, even if this gave them a distant claim to divinity? Moreover, would anyone describe the Titans who killed Dionysus as a "happy race?"

We can better answer the question by returning to Hesiod. The humans who were described in the *Works and Days* as being of the same descent as the gods were not the humans of our own race (what Hesiod calls the Iron Race), but rather were the very first humans (what Hesiod calls the Golden Race). These blessed people,

> lived like the gods, having carefree hearts,
> apart from all misery and pain. Wretched Old Age
> did not exist, and they enjoyed feasts with
> feet and hands that never failed, apart from all evils.
> Death overcame them like sleep. All excellent things
> belonged to them. The grain-giving earth bore fruit,
> much of it, unstintingly and automatically. They lived in
>   freedom
> and peace, pasturing their lands rich in flocks, dear to the gods.
> But the Earth covered this race.
>
> (lines 112–21)

The race that immediately preceded ours, according to Hesiod – the race that he calls the demigods or heroes, which included such traditional mythic figures as Cadmus, Oedipus, and the warriors who fought at Troy – enjoyed a similar paradise at the ends of the earth, after their deaths:

> They live [at the ends of the earth] with carefree hearts,
> In the Islands of the Blessed, near stormy Ocean.
> Happy heroes, for whom three times yearly
> The grain-giving land bears forth honey-sweet fruit.
>
> (lines 170–3)

In other words, the race of demigods and heroes wins the same sort of existence after their deaths as the Golden Race had enjoyed while still alive. Given that demigods and heroes were considered to be relatives of the gods and therefore, like the Golden Race, to be of the same race, this only makes sense: if the two groups share salient characteristics then they should share rewards as well, even if the timing of the rewards comes somewhat late for the heroes.

The Gold Tablets don't say much about what ultimately awaits the initiate; as mnemonic devices they focus on the task that needs to be done rather than its reward. What little they do say, however, aligns well with Hesiod's paradisiacal vision: the initiates expect to dwell among meadows and groves (3.6, 27.4 and cf. 28, on which the initiate demands to be sent to the *thiasos* of initiates), to enjoy abundant wine (26 a.6 and b.6), to be happy and blessed – gods instead of humans (5.9), to dwell among the blessed (6.7, 7.7, 26a.7) or to live among the heroes, *as* a hero (2.11, perhaps 8.2). In other words, the initiate expects to move, after death, into an existence like that enjoyed by Hesiod's Golden Race while still alive and by Hesiod's race of heroes and demigods after death. Having atoned during initiation for the pre-primal crime from which the current (Iron) race of humans sprang, the initiate has in effect moved him or herself back into the status that humans enjoyed before that crime occurred, at the time the heroic race ruled. Like them, therefore, the initiate will enjoy paradise after death.[29]

Thirst and its quenching

Declaring that it is "a child of Earth and starry Sky," then, is another way for the soul to establish that it has been initiated and thereby has earned a special relationship with the gods. The other phrases that the soul must remember to speak to the guards, "I am parched with thirst. But allow me to drink from the spring," are echoed by eschatologies around the world – as Zuntz noted, even the Inuit dead ask the living to give them ice, "for we are suffering from thirst for cold water."[30] The phrase itself, however, finds no exact parallel in Greek texts. Although the Greeks poured libations to the dead, which may have expressed this idea, and although grave epigrams speak of the dead drinking the Waters of Lethe (to which we will return), outside of Book 11 of the *Odyssey* and Plato's story of Er (which itself probably draws on the cult promulgated through our *bricoleurs*) we hear little about the Greek dead actually being thirsty.[31] Odysseus' actions, moreover, are somewhat problematic *comparanda* for our tablets. Drinking changes the Homeric dead from "witless heads" into creatures who can once again speak as they did while they were alive (that is, it has somewhat the same effect on them as the Waters of Memory will have on the souls of the initiates), but it is blood that the Homeric souls drink rather than water, and its effects are only temporary.

Given, on the one hand, that there are no good *literary* precedents for the Greek dead wanting to drink, and that, on the other hand, the idea of the dead being thirsty is nearly universal, it is likely that the *bricoleurs* simply developed a familiar, popular idea into a form that would have specific implications within their cult. To do so, they focused on the qualities of what the dead would drink. The water that the good-plus will receive is called the Waters of Memory (*Mnemosyne*) and, although none of the tablets specifically states so, the water that the good-plus should avoid logically must be the Waters of Forgetfulness (Lethe).

Forgetting and remembering

And indeed, Waters of Forgetfulness are mentioned not only in epigrams and Plato's story but frequently elsewhere as well.[32] Waters of Memory, in contrast, are almost unheard of outside of the tablets; the *bricoleurs* seem to have invented them, modeling them on the better-known Waters of Forgetfulness.[33] To understand what the Waters of Memory were supposed to do, therefore, it is best to start by asking what the Waters of Forgetfulness were supposed to do. In antiquity, by far the most common assumption was that the dead who drank these waters would forget everything they ever knew. The late sixth-century elegiac poet Theognis already alludes to this when he says, "Persephone provides *lēthē* to mortals, disabling their minds," and many later authors, including Plato, make the point explicitly.[34] A grave epigram from the first century BCE touchingly inverts it: the deceased woman says to her husband "I have not taken my final drink from Lethe in Hades, and therefore I have [my memory of] you to console me even among the perished."[35]

By contrast, logically, those who drink from the Lake of Memory should remember everything about their former lives. What is the value of this, within the eschatology of the tablets? The tablets, which are themselves mnemonic devices, have already reminded the souls of what they must say to the guardians, so it seems unlikely that drinking the water guarantees recollection of special phrases or passwords the initiates will need (further on this below). Nor is it likely that the waters are meant to aid in the recollection of further "road-maps," for if we can judge from line 5 of tablet no. 3, the soul of the initiate will simply continue on the right-hand path until it reaches its final goal. No other tablet implies that further directions are necessary, either.

If we take our cue from Plato, we might imagine that the soul must remember its former life in order to do a better job the next time it is incarnated. As we'll see, some of the tablets that we have not yet examined apparently allude to reincarnation, and a fragment of Pindar connects it with a cult in which atonement is made to Persephone:

> But for those from whom Persephone accepts retribution
> for her ancient grief, in the ninth year she returns their souls
> to the upper sunlight; from them arise
> proud kings and men who are swift in strength
> and greatest in wisdom, and for the rest of time
> they are called sacred heroes by mortals.
> (frg. 133; W. H. Race's Loeb translation, slightly adapted)

The fragment is quoted by Socrates in Plato's *Meno* (81b8–c4), where he uses reincarnation to sustain his argument that learning is really a matter of remembering what one already knows – thus, as in the story of Er, the wise soul will protect its memory after death. Socrates adds that "wise men and women" in charge of "divine affairs" (*theia pragmata*), who are also known as "priests and priestesses" (*hiereis te kai hiereiai*), talk about reincarnation as well, when they attempt to explain the rituals they perform – he probably is referring to the priests and priestesses of mystery cults, among others.[36]

According to this fragment, those who pay retribution to Persephone for her ancient grief – as did the initiates of Bacchic mysteries – do not escape reincarnation, at least not immediately. Rather, they earn better lives the next time around. Perhaps these next lives will be their final lives: if they become what mortals call "heroes," then like other heroes they ought to journey to paradise after their mortal lives are finished. Empedocles, a Sicilian philosopher who was approximately contemporary with Pindar and whose religious outlook shared many characteristics with the system we are discussing, developed such an eschatology. Empedocles claimed to have been through many incarnations himself, including some in which he was a plant or animal. He also claimed that in his current life he was already a god, and that after his next death he would rejoin the rest of the gods.[37] Thus, becoming divine during life could be understood as the last incarnational stop on the way to postmortem paradise. By this analogy, the souls whom Persephone sends up into a new life as heroes are in their final incarnation and will need to die one more time before they escape incarnation altogether. Under this system, paying retribution gets an initiate to the penultimate stage, not the ultimate one.

And yet, using Empedocles' system as a *comparandum* could also suggest that the words of the tablets mean that initiates will be released from the cycle of reincarnation *this* time – not after the next incarnation.[38] Many tablets imply that the disembodied soul has already joined the ranks of the gods or demigods – the initiate's declaration that it is a "child of Earth and starry Sky," for example (nos. 1, 2, 8, 10–14, 16, 18, 25, 29) and the declaration to the initiate that it "has become a god instead of a mortal" (no. 3). Furthermore, one of the "purity" type tablets, which are yet to be discussed, talks about escaping from the "difficult circle," which most scholars understand as the circle of incarnations.[39]

It is possible, particularly in the context of a cult promulgated by itinerant priests, that more than one solution was offered. The general idea was that initiation would bring an enhanced eschatological status – this was borrowed from the better established Eleusinian Mysteries. Metempsychosis, which was very much in the air during the late archaic period in Greece,[40] could have been grafted on to this by our *bricoleurs* – and let us not forget that the myth that underpinned the Dionysiac mysteries centered on a god who himself experienced a sort of reincarnation, suffering death at the hands of the Titans and then being reborn from Semele's womb. Perhaps the earliest *orpheotelestai* guaranteed only that the initiates would move up in incarnational status by paying retribution to Persephone for her ancient grief, without promising any escape from the circle altogether; perhaps subsequent promulgators of the cult increased its appeal by guaranteeing permanent release. Perhaps some of them even developed eschatologies that did not include a need to be reincarnated at all. If we imagine a competitive context in which different *orpheotelestai* passed through the same cities in turn, or even lived in the same cities for extended periods, then we might expect at least some of them to have developed new and more attractive eschatologies as time went on. The striking fluidity of beliefs concerning metempsychosis that we find in sources from the late archaic through early Imperial periods (the periods over which our tablets stretch) confirms that we would be wrong to seek complete homogeneity among any of its theorists; this is typical of rituals and beliefs that lie outside of civic religion, which never develop the same canonical, nearly static nature as those inside.[41]

But if the Waters of Memory are not intended to help the soul of the initiate do better in its next life, then what is their purpose? Plutarch may provide a clue. Discussing the lovely meadows where the souls of the pious end up, he says "those who dwell there pass their time together recalling and speaking of the past and the present" (*De lat. viv.* 7.1130.c). In an eschatological system where the geography of the Underworld echoes that of the upper world and the blessed are rewarded by eternal feasts like those they enjoyed while alive – including the feasts that initiates undoubtedly celebrated at the end of their initiation[42] – we shouldn't be surprised that the ability to remember one's corporeal life (or at least the good parts of it) is considered a boon: nothing is so welcome in death as the imitation and recollection of life, to judge from the frequency with which these activities show up in eschatologies world-wide. The epigrammatic statement made by a dead wife to her husband – that her recollection of him comforts her in Hades – is one specific instance of a broader motif. The *topos* of recollection after death goes back to the earliest sources, in fact; Plutarch invokes it when discussing fragments from the Pindaric dirge that we have already examined; and in the *Odyssey*, the dead long for a taste of blood so that they can cast off the torpor that makes them "witless heads," unable even to recognize those who visit from the land of the living. Once they have drunk, they long for nothing so much as to speak with Odysseus about their pasts. Socrates, in defending death as one of the highest of blessings, looks forward to an afterlife in which he will converse with the great men and women of the past about their experiences – an expectation that assumes they have retained their memories (*Ap.* 40c–41c). As imperfect as corporeal life is, in other words, people find it hard to let go of the idea that it is the standard to which all other existences should aspire. The nearly universal expectation that the dead are obsessed with watching the living – benignly or enviously – speaks to this idea as well.

In sum, the Waters of Memory that the tablets promise to initiates probably guarantee simply that they will arrive in paradise with their recollections intact, unlike those who drink from the Waters of Forgetfulness, and that they therefore will be able to enjoy their rewards fully.

Initiates and bacchoi

Once the soul has safely made it past the guards and has drunk from the Waters of Memory, it proceeds to its final destination (at least in this round of incarnation, and perhaps forever). Continuing in their geographic manner, the tablets tell us that the soul travels down a "sacred road" that other "initiates and *bacchoi*" have traveled before (no. 1.15–16) to the "holy meadows and groves of Persephone" (no. 3.6) where it will "rule among the other heroes" (no. 2.11). We have already discussed the fact that the meadows evoke the paradisiacal existence that is often found in eschatological and other contexts and the significance of the soul's inclusion among the heroes. What remains to be considered is the description of the road as being that on which "other glorious initiates (*mystai*) and *bacchoi* travel," which implies that there is a single place where all properly prepared souls end up. This is logical enough – but what is the difference between *mystai* and *bacchoi*?

It is possible that the words are synonymous; I have used the word *mystai* and its most common English translation ("initiates") to refer to members of Dionysiac cults throughout this book, and *mystai* could be used that way in antiquity as well (several of our other tablets use the word, in fact: 20, 21, 22, 28, and 31). By this reading, the author of the tablet used two words instead of one for emphasis. It is also possible, however, that *mystai* is used here in its original, more restrictive sense, to refer to Eleusinian initiates. As Fritz Graf has shown elsewhere, the eschatological hopes of initiates into Eleusinian and Dionysiac mysteries were virtually identical – no surprise, if the latter were reacting to and adapting the former. Given this, it would not be remarkable if at least some of the *orpheotelestai* preached that Dionysiac initiates would end up in the same part of the Underworld as their Eleusinian brothers and sisters. For that matter, some people were initiated into *both* cults. This created a potentially sticky eschatological problem that could be brilliantly solved by decreeing that they all ended up in the same place. Certainly, we can say now that the technology of the tablets was available for adoption by other cults; the tablets from Roman Palestine (Appendix 3) indicate this, as does, perhaps, tablet 8a, which probably should be understood as attesting to a cult in honor of Demeter and Persephone.

Purity

Until now, we have concentrated on what I called the thirteen "geographic" tablets (nos. 1, 2, 3, 8, 10–14, 16, 18, 25, 29). Now we will turn to what I call the "purity" tablets. The keys to success in the geographic tablets were knowing where to go, what to drink and what to say to the guards about one's pedigree; in the purity tablets, it is still important to know what to say, but the emphasis will lie on establishing the nature of the initiate's soul, which has been changed during the process of initiation, and the soul will speak to the Queen of the Underworld herself, rather than her guards. There will be some overlaps between these and the other tablets; my divisions are heuristic and it is important to keep in mind that the ideas and rituals that underlie the two types are not necessarily mutually exclusive.[43]

The tablets in the "purity" group are nos. 5, 6, 7, and 9. The first three of these come from a single burial mound in Thurii (Lucania) and date to the fourth century BCE. They start with the line:

I come pure from the pure, Queen of the Chthonian Ones

Tablet no. 9, which was created six centuries later than the others and which was found in Rome, begins:

> She comes pure from the pure, Queen of the Chthonian Ones.

Tablet no. 9 has adapted the formula found on the earlier tablets: whereas nos. 5, 6, and 7 seem to remind the souls of what to say, no. 9 instead seems to speak on behalf of the soul. The three older tablets are mnemonic devices, in other words, and the fourth is a proxy.

The soul declares that not only is it pure itself, but it has come from a group of other pure individuals – other initiates, we assume.[44] But of what nature is this purity? *Katharos* and its cognates cover a wide range of ideas, from pure in the sense of "unmixed" (e.g., water or gold) to pure in the sense of what we would call "being of pure [good] morals." Somewhere in between lies what can be called ritual purity – being in a fit state to approach the gods, because one has been ritually freed from such things as blood-guilt and the lingering stain brought on by childbirth or contact with a corpse. What all of these meanings and most other uses of *katharos* and its cognates share is the implication that one is "free of" something that would otherwise pollute one; *katharos* is more about the *absence* or *removal* of something than the presence of something, in other words.[45] It seems reasonable to conjecture that in the case of the tablets' owners, whatever burden they claim to have been freed from is still carried by other, non-initiated humans: Plato says that whereas the non-initiated are believed to lie in mud and mire in the afterlife, those who have been initiated and cleansed (*kekatharmenoi*) will join the gods.[46] Initiation itself, then, has purified and freed the souls who make this declaration to Persephone.

It is likely that the burden from which the initiates have escaped is the ancestral blood-guilt that all humans inherited from the Titans, which has put humanity in Persephone's bad graces. The declaration of purity is made first and foremost to Persephone herself, and in all three tablets, she is given a central role in the soul's salvation ("Now I come as a suppliant to holy Persephone," nos. 6 and 7; "I have sunk beneath the breast of the Lady, the Chthonian Queen," no. 5). Tablets nos. 26a and b, which share some characteristics with the purity tablets, as we'll see, remind the soul to "tell Persephone that the Bacchic One himself released you," which suggests that the mysteries that used the tablets focused on a story involving both Persephone and Dionysus – which can only be the story of Persephone's giving birth to Dionysus and his subsequent murder by the Titans, given that no other story links the two divinities.

Eucles and Eubouleus

All four of the purity tablets continue with variations of a second line, in which the speaker addresses other divinities as well:

Eucles, Euboleus and the other immortal gods (no. 5)

Eucles and Euboleus and other gods – as many *daimones* (as do exist) (no. 6)

Eucles and Eubouleus and the gods and other *daimones* (no. 7)

Eucles and Eubouleus, child of Zeus (no. 9)

Others have discussed the problems of scribal transmission in this line. Whatever the changes from version to version, however, it appeals to Eucles and Eubouleus (whose name is spelled in a variety of ways in these lines), and to the gods as a whole. Most scholars agree in identifying Eucles, whose name literally means "of good fame," with Hades, who in cult is sometimes referred to euphemistically as "Klymenos," or "famous." "Eubouleus," whose name means "of good counsel," is identified in ancient sources with Zeus and with Dionysus (e.g., at Orphic *Hymn* 30.6, Plut. *Quaest. Conv.* 7.9, 714c), and is an independent divinity in Eleusis, who has connections with the Underworld.[47] Given that tablet no. 9 explicitly describes Eubouleus as the "son of Zeus," we can guess that in all four cases this name refers to Dionysus.[48] Thus, in the purity tablets, the soul begins by making its declaration to Persephone, then goes on to include two other deities who will be of vital importance to its postmortem happiness, and finally includes the gods (and heroes) in general.

Joining the gods

The third line of tablets nos. 5, 6, and 7 is:

For I also claim to be of your happy race.

The fourth (and final) line of no. 9 makes a similar statement, but personalizes it with the name of the deceased woman to whom the tablet belonged:

Caecilia Secundina, come, by law grown to be divine.

Both are variations of a theme that we encountered already in the geographic tablets: the initiate claims to be of the same race as the gods, or even to have become a god herself. The same interpretation that I proposed there works here as well: through initiation, the soul has purged itself from the stain shared by the current, "Iron" race of humanity – the race that sprang from the remains of the Titans – and has thereby become equal to members of an earlier, happier race, such as those that Hesiod called the Golden Race and the race of demigods and heroes. These three lines (lines 1–3 in tablets nos. 5, 6, and 7 and lines 1, 2, and 4 in tablet no. 9), then, are roughly equivalent to the soul's claim, in the geographic tablets, that it is a "child of Earth and starry Sky."

At this point, the tablets diverge a bit. Let us start by finishing no. 9, the shortest and latest of the group. In its entirety, it reads:

1   She comes pure from the pure, Queen of the Chthonian Ones.
2   Eucles and Eubouleus, child of Zeus. "But accept
3   this gift of Memory, sung of among mortals."
4   "Caecilia Secundina, come, by law grown to be divine."

The third line has no exact verbal parallel in any other tablet, but its first half thematically resembles the statement found at the beginning of tablet no. 1 and the end of tablet no. 2, "This is the work of Memory." The speaker of the line – which seems to be the tablet itself, acting as proxy for a soul that is unable to speak – declares its own function: the tablet preserves what must be said to those whom the soul meets in the Underworld and then says it on the soul's behalf, as do the shorter proxy tablets that we will examine below. But the request that the divinities "accept" this gift of Memory (the tablet) suggests that the tablet may also have been understood as a *symbolon* in the physical sense – that is, like the clay, bone, or wax tokens that sometimes were used to prove a person's identity in the world of the living, the tablet proves, by its very existence, that the soul who possesses it is an initiate. Tablet no. 9, then, utilizes ideas found in other tablets, but in an abbreviated form and with a somewhat different method.

Lightning

The fourth and subsequent lines of the longer tablets read:

4 But Moira overcame me and the other immortal gods and the star-
flinger with lightning.
5 I have flown out of the heavy, difficult circle,
6 I have approached the longed-for crown with swift feet,
7 I have sunk beneath the breast of the Lady, the Chthonian Queen,
8 I have approached the longed-for crown with swift feet.
9 "Happy and blessed, you will be a god instead of a mortal."
10 A kid I fell into milk. (no. 5)

4 I have paid the penalty for unrighteous deeds
5 Either Moira overcame me or the star-flinger with lightning.
6 Now I come, come as a suppliant to [holy] Persephone
7 so that she may kindly send me to the seats of the pure (nos. 6 and 7)

The line about Moira ("Fate") draws on a Homeric formula that is used to describe the deaths of the heroes Patroclus and Heracles and the bad luck of the hero Odysseus. Thus, for example, at *Iliad* 18.119, Achilles says that Heracles was overcome by Moira and the anger of Hera. The phrase means that the span of a particular person's life (his Moira) ran out but that the direct agent of his or her death was a specific god or human. The use of the formula in our tablets subtly underscores what we already noted earlier: the soul of the initiate is likened to a traditional hero and will eventually join other initiates and heroes in an Underworld paradise.

In the tablets, the direct agent who works with Moira must be Zeus, the flinger of lightning *par excellence*; the term that I have translated as "star-flinger" is used of Zeus (and only Zeus) in Homer, Hesiod, and later texts. But what does the soul hope to accomplish by claiming that its bodily life was terminated by Zeus' lightning? Of the various possibilities discussed by scholars, three have drawn particular attention.

The first argues that the three people who used this verse on their tablets – all of whom were buried in a single tumulus – really were struck by lightning. We can neither prove this nor disprove this, but even if they were killed in this way, the phrase would still have to mean something *within* the context of the ritual, the myth, or both. Otherwise, the three initiates' special mode of death would not have been recorded.[49]

The second suggestion draws on one of the four versions of the Orphic anthropogony, according to which humanity arose from the ashes of the Titans whom Zeus punished by incinerating them with lightning.[50] To be "struck by lightning," then, means to pay for one's misdeeds with one's life.

Asclepius similarly was incinerated by Zeus' lightning after Hades complained that Asclepius was using his medical skills to resurrect too many dead people.[51] In another version of the Orphic anthropogony, however, the Titans are killed in such a way that their blood drips upon the ground, which would seem to exclude incineration. In a third version, the Titans' blood and dismembered limbs are mixed together and *then* struck by lightning; lightning itself does not cause their death. Our sources for all three versions of the myth are late; it is impossible to guess which version(s) were available at the time that these tablets were created. But more importantly, we must ask why the initiate would want to identify himself with the Titans. Although it is for their crime that the initiate ritually pays a penalty during initiation, and although the initiate considers himself, like all humans, to be the Titans' *descendant*, there is no reason that he would want to *be* a Titan. On the contrary, everything suggests that initiates sought to purge themselves of this association.

The third suggestion brings us back to Asclepius. His death by lightning may have been a punishment for thwarting the decrees of Fate (Moira), but it was also the cause of his apotheosis: after his fiery death he rose to Olympus and became a god. Similarly, Semele, according to some late versions of the myth, did not spontaneously ignite at the sight of Zeus but rather when she was struck by his lightning. Eventually, she, too, rose to Olympus. In one version of Heracles' story, his pyre, from which he rose to Olympus, was ignited by his father's lightning bolt.[52] To be struck by lightning is yet another way of joining the gods and the heroes, in other words.[53] Walter Burkert has argued that the word "Elysion," which is one term for a postmortem paradise among the Greeks, is derived from *enēlusios*, which means "struck by lightning." Even natural objects that were struck by lightning, such as trees and rocks, were considered sacred.[54]

Being struck by lightning, then, often combines the idea that the individual has committed a transgression egregious enough to merit death – Semele and Asclepius both strayed outside the bounds of acceptable human ambition – with the promise that this particular way of paying for the transgression will purify and refine the transgressor, thereby qualifying his or her soul for inclusion in the divine or heroic realm. If we apply this idea to the statements in tablets nos. 5, 6, and 7, we see that it expresses essentially the same expectation as we found in other tablets, which promise that the soul of the initiate will join the company of gods and heroes. Moreover, given that fire, especially heavenly fire, is a cleansing agent, death by lightning also aligns with the primary theme of these particular tablets – purity.

The "heroic" interpretation of the initiate's claim to have been struck by lightning that I have just offered need not completely exclude the interpretation that focuses on the fate of the Titans. Rather, the fate of the Titans serves as a contrast to the fate of the initiates and of the heroic figures in whose tracks the initiates follow. Whereas the Titans, who were enemies of Zeus and Dionysus, were completely destroyed by lightning, a hero (that is, a human of a race earlier than the Titanic race of humans) or an initiate (that is, a human who has participated in the proper rituals) might undergo the same ordeal and emerge from it quite differently. The line that immediately precedes the statement about Moira and the lightning in tablets nos. 6 and 7 hints at just such a differentiation: "I have paid the penalty for unrighteous deeds." That is, the initiate has performed whatever ritual was necessary to be cleansed. What were these deeds? The word I have translated as "penalty" (*poinē*) is highly suggestive. As Rose and Bernabé noted, when used negatively it is virtually always connected with blood crimes, such as murder. It is also the word used in the fragment of Pindar that we have discussed several times, which almost surely refers to the Titans' murder of Dionysus and humanity's subsequent obligation to atone for it.[55] In sum, the line in our tablet about paying the penalty for unrighteous deeds probably means that the initiate has atoned to Persephone. Having thus been freed of his or her Titanic burden, the initiate might be struck by lightning and end up not like the Titans but rather like the heroes.

Circles and crowns

In tablet no. 5, the statement about Moira and the lightning is immediately followed by:

5   I have flown out of the heavy, difficult circle,
6   I have approached the longed-for crown with swift feet

Line 5 is usually understood to refer to the circle of reincarnation; a fragment of the Orphic *Rhapsodies* echoes this line, in fact, by explicitly calling reincarnation a "circle." Proclus, commenting on this part of the *Rhapsodies*, specifies that escape from the circle was afforded by initiation into the mysteries of Dionysus and Kore (*OF* 348).

The initiates who carried these tablets, then, expected to enjoy something like what Pindar promised to the good-plus in *Olympian* 2; in contrast to the souls of even the good-plus whom we meet in Plato's story of Er, these initiates will never again be compelled to enter into bodily form but will exist forever in a paradisiacal place. The next line is first and foremost a metaphor: to "approach the longed-for crown on swift feet," alludes to athletes who were given crowns upon winning a race – thus, it means to achieve what one attempts. The image may also evoke another type of crowns, however: those worn by participants at symposia (including, says Plato at *Resp.* 363c4–d2, the symposia that mysteries claim initiates' souls will enjoy after death; cf. Pindar *Ol.* 2.72–5).

Breasts and kids

The next lines on tablet no. 5 are:

7 I have sunk beneath the breast of the Lady, the Chthonian Queen,
8 I have approached the longed-for crown with swift feet.
9 "Happy and blessed, you will be a god instead of a mortal."
10 A kid I fell into milk.

The meaning of line 9 is clear, but lines 7 and 10 have occasioned debate – line 10 more debate than any other line in all the tablets.

In a general sense, the meaning of line 7 is unproblematic: the initiate is claiming a close relationship with Persephone. At issue is the significance of the phrase "sunk beneath the breast." Some have suggested that the line signifies the initiate's rebirth from Persephone, either into a new life or into a new existence after death. This seems unlikely; the word I have translated here as "breast" (*kolpos*) can mean "womb," as well, but the specific phrase "to sink beneath the womb" makes little sense obstetrically.[56] More promising is the interpretation that begins by noting epic parallels for the phrase: Demeter holds and protects the Eleusinian princeling beneath her breast (Hom. *Hymn Dem.* 187), Thetis protectively receives into her bosom both Dionysus and Hephaestus (*Iliad* 6.136, 18.398). Somewhat similarly Teucer runs to his brother Ajax for protection in battle and "plunges under him like a child under his mother" (*Iliad* 8.271). In short, our line would seem to mean that the initiate has won Persephone's protection.[57]

This leaves us with "a kid I fell into milk." Some scholars have looked eastward, suggesting that it alludes to the Jewish dietary law that forbids cooking animals in their mothers' milk – although it is not clear why this would be an appropriate model for our initiate. A Ugaritic ritual in which a goat is cooked in milk has also been adduced, although again it is not clear what the relevance to our initiate would be.[58] Other scholars adduced the fact that according to a few ancient sources, there is some connection between Dionysus and goats – and concluded that the initiate, who was equated with Dionysus by being likened to a young goat, was experiencing rebirth.[59] Whatever other problems it had, this solution is in any case no longer workable, given the variations of the line that are in the newer Pelinna tablets, which mention a bull and a ram falling or leaping in milk as well. Although Dionysus was sometimes equated with a bull in antiquity, there is no evidence that he was imagined as a ram. A third theory saw a reference to the Milky Way in the phrase and posited that the initiates expected, as "children of starry Sky," to find their postmortem bliss in the sky. This is unlikely, given that everything else in the tablets and related literature points to a subterranean location for the initiates' paradise.[60]

The best theory understands the phrase as a proverb expressing happiness. To "fall into milk," or "leap into milk" means to be in the midst of abundance, or to make a new beginning (further on milk and blessedness, see now the Getty Hexameters).[61] Particularly in the context of the preceding lines on tablet no. 5, and even more so in the context of the Pelinna tablets to be examined below, the line makes general sense as part of a *makarismos* – a statement of the initiate's bliss. (It is possible that the phrase had other, subtler connotations as well, which may have varied according to which animal was specified, but we cannot recover them.)[62]

Let us return now to tablets nos. 6 and 7. After the line about Moira and lightning, we read:

6   Now I come, come as a suppliant to holy Persephone,
7   so that she may kindly send me to the seats of the pure.

The meaning here is straightforward and repeats what we have found elsewhere: the initiate supplicates himself or herself before the Queen of the Underworld (here described by her Homeric adjective holy, *hagnē*) and she then sends him to join the other souls of the good-plus.

Purity tablets – summation

The aim of the purity tablets, like that of the geographic tablets, is to help the soul establish that it is one of the "good-plus," who should be allowed to join other members of that group in the paradisiacal part of the Underworld. In each case, set phrases that must be spoken to Underworld figures prove that the soul has been ritually purified during initiation and has thereby been freed of the stain carried by other humans – the stain caused by the Titans' murder of Dionysus. In the geographic tablets, this takes the form of the soul claiming that it is no longer a member of the race of humans that Hesiod would have called the "Iron Age" but instead belongs among the heroes and demigods; in the purity tablets, the soul asserts that its purity qualifies it to live among the gods and heroes.

It is arguably possible that the two programs I have described separately (the geographically-oriented and the purity-oriented) were parts of a single, longer sequence of actions and statements undertaken by each initiate's soul in the Underworld. We might imagine, as did Zuntz, that the soul first confronted the guardians at the Lake of Memory and, having successfully refreshed itself from those waters, went further down the "road that other *mystai* and *bacchoi* travel" to the "meadows of Persephone" where it had to declare its purity to the "Queen of the Chthonian Ones" herself.[63]

But should we try to tidy things up so neatly? There are two possible objections. First, if we work from the assumption that the creators of the tablets inscribed upon them whatever they thought the souls had to remember, including the precise forms of statements that had to be spoken to authority figures, then it would be strange to find only half of those statements preserved in any given instance. That is to say: if the soul had to pronounce specific phrases first to the guards and then to Persephone, why would the creators of the geographic tablets presume that the souls were likely to forget what they had to say to the guards but not what they had to say to Persephone? We have already considered a possible answer to this form of the question: namely, that once the guards had allowed the soul access to the Waters of Memory, it would remember, on its own, what it had to subsequently say to Persephone. But for the converse question – why the creators of the purity tablets presumed that the souls were likely to forget what they had to say to Persephone but not what they had to say to the guards – we cannot do the same. At best, then, we would be left hypothesizing that the geographic tablets represent a further development of what was an originally simpler eschatological narrative, in which the soul confronted only Persephone. We have no reason to think this was the case.

Second, in other tablets that we have not yet examined, we encounter different passwords or key phrases that the soul must pronounce to Persephone (nos. 26 a and b). If we pursue the hypothesis of a single sequence of actions, of which each tablet represents an episode, then these words and phrases present a problem. Must the lines on nos. 26 a and b be spoken to Persephone in addition to those we read on the purity tablets? If so, why aren't all of them included on all the purity tablets? Tablet no. 27 presents a variation of the same problem, as it includes yet other words to be spoken to an unidentified Underworld figure, as does no. 28.

Clearly, the better answer is that all of these words and phrases represent variations within a broader pattern. Different *orpheotelestai*, operating in different parts of the Greek world at different times, shared the idea that the soul would have to pronounce something to Persephone or her representatives, but either deliberately or through the accidents of transmission of a tradition that was primarily oral, they diverged with respect to specifics.[64]

What does all of this imply about the materials for which the tablets serve as mnemonic devices? At the beginning of this chapter, I suggested that the tablets alluded to episodes in longer stories and ritual sequences with which the initiates were familiar and that they had particular reasons to remember. But this needn't mean that we must posit the existence of a single poem (say, a single Orphic *Katabasis*), from which all of the metrical lines on all of the tablets were taken: there were almost surely several such poems in circulation.[65] To take two parallel examples, we know that there were several different poems that narrated Demeter's search for her daughter, each of which had some claim to canonical status in its own time and place, and several different Orphic theogonies in circulation as well.[66] Nor need we posit the existence of a single ritual sequence; indeed, in the case of a religion that was promulgated by independent, itinerant priests, such singularity would be remarkable. What we *should* expect to find is a consistency of broader ideas, and that we do: the tablets we have examined so far share the expectations that there is a special place in the Underworld for Bacchic initiates (shared with the heroes and perhaps the initiates of other mysteries as well) and that reaching it requires the use and display of knowledge obtained during initiation rituals performed before death.

The Pelinna and Pherae tablets

Until 1987, most scholars understood all tablets to fall into one of two groups, more or less like those I have been using so far: the geographic (often called the "B" group, following Zuntz) and the purity (often called the "A" group). The publication of two tablets from Pelinna (nos. 26 a and b), which were found symmetrically placed on the chest of a woman buried in the late fourth century BCE, erased that distinction, for they included a new version of a formula that we saw already in tablets nos. 3 and 5, which Zuntz put in group A, and variations of statements from nos. 1 and 2, which Zuntz put in group B.[67]

For our purposes, some parts of these tablets can be treated briefly. Lines 3 through 5,

3 Bull, you jumped into milk.
4 Quickly, you jumped into milk. [missing from no. 26 b]
5 Ram, you fell into milk.

are an extended version of the *makarismos* formula we saw already in tablets nos. 3 and 5. Line 6, "you have wine as your fortunate honor," is primarily an extension of this *makarismos*, echoing Plato's description of the "symposium of the blessed" that some mystery cults promised (which is particularly appropriate for Dionysus' initiates, given his familiar role as the god of wine), but it also serves as a lead-in to line 7, which is found on only one of the two tablets:

7   And below the earth there are ready for you the same offices (or rites) as for the other blessed ones.

This is a variation of the final lines we saw in tablets nos. 1, 2, 6, and 7, which promise that the soul of the initiate will join other such souls or heroic figures in a special part of the Underworld.

The most interesting lines on the tablets from Pelinna are 1 and 2:

1   Now you have died and now you have come into being, O thrice happy one, on this same day.
2   Tell Persephone that the Bacchic One himself released you.

Line 2 has been interpreted elsewhere by Fritz Graf, with the help of an Orphic fragment found in Damascius (*OF* 350). Damascius says:

Dionysus is responsible for deliverance and for this very reason the god is called Deliverer. And Orpheus says:

People send perfect hecatombs
in all seasons during the whole year,
and they perform rites, seeking deliverance from unlawful ancestors.
But you [Dionysus], having power over them, whomever you wish
You will deliver from difficult suffering and limitless frenzy.

As Graf concludes, "the tablets from Pelinna put [the story of Dionysus, Persephone, and the Titans] firmly into the context of Bacchic mystery cults and define the function of this mythology in living religion (as opposed to pseudepigraphical and Neoplatonist speculation)."[68] The model, then, is this: Dionysus, under whose aegis the Bacchic mysteries operate, releases souls from the burden that the Titans' crime placed on all humans. Once this has been done, (which happens while the initiate is alive), the soul of the initiate will have the right to declare its special status to Persephone after death and thereby win her favor in the afterlife.[69]

The first line is more difficult to interpret. It would be tempting to think of metempsychosis, were it not for the fact that the subject is expected to be pleased by this turn of events ("O thrice-happy one!"): the typical reaction prompted by passage into a new incarnation is one of disappointment and complete escape is the highest *desideratum*. This observation, combined with the tablet's emphatic statement that the death and new existence are happening "on the same day," suggests that "coming into being" does not refer to a regular sort of corporeal life but rather to a new sort of "life" that the initiate will find within the Underworld, which will include the feasting and sharing of memories in Persephone's meadows.[70]

The Pelinna tablets, then, share several features with other tablets, notably the function of reminding the soul to declare something to an Underworld authority (in this case Persephone herself) in order to establish its identity as an initiate and therefore its right to pass into paradise. Our next tablet, found in Pherae and dating to the late fourth century BCE (no. 27), performs the same task, but much more tersely:

1   Passwords: Man-and-
2   child-thyrsus. Man-and-child-
3   thyrsus. Brimo, Brimo. Enter
4   the holy meadow, for the initiate
5   is redeemed.
6   GAPEDON

The tablet starts by reminding the soul of exactly what it must say – and here, we find no elaborate phrases concerning purity, lineage, or relationship to Dionysus but rather two single words, each of which is spoken twice. This variation – which is further away from what we saw in the geographic and purity tablets than the variation found in the Pelinna tablets – underscores the relative freedom with which some *orpheotelestai* adapted the cult they promulgated. The first word seems to be built from four others: *andr-*, the root of the Greek word for "man"; *kai*, meaning "and"; *paido-* meaning "child"; and *thyrsos*, the term for a staff used in Dionysiac ritual. The second is "Brimo," the name of a local goddess who is here and elsewhere equated with Persephone.[71] Once these words are spoken, an unidentified respondent declares that the initiate has paid retribution,[72] and therefore may enter the paradisiacal meadow. This aligns well with what we have seen elsewhere. The final line of the tablet is untranslatable and inscribed upside down. The other tablet from Pherae (no. 28), works by a similar logic. The tablet reminds the soul to declare that it must be sent to join the band (*thiasos*) of initiates (*mystōn*), because it has participated in rituals dedicated to Demeter Chthonia and the Mountain Mother (further on these two tablets, see Appendix 2).

Mnemonic tablets: summation

All of the mnemonic tablets assume that the soul will be confronted by authority figures in the Underworld and converse with them. Knowing what to say will establish the right of the soul to pass into paradise. There is a considerable amount of variation as to what words or phrases will do the trick, but in one way or another, all of them prove that the soul was initiated into Dionysus' mysteries while alive, in the course of which it erased from itself the stain of the Titans' crime. In the geographic tablets, which seem to have been developed by someone with a taste for Hesiodic mythology, this involves the soul claiming that it has made itself equal to the heroes who dwelt on the earth before the current age of humans. In the purity tablets, the soul more straightforwardly states that it is pure, although it may claim affiliation with the divine race as well. In both types of tablets, we are given glimpses of the promised paradise, in which other initiates – perhaps including those from Eleusis – and heroes dwell.

There are two main differences between the types of tablets: (1) The geographic tablets, as a group, give us a more detailed picture of the Underworld than do the purity tablets, drawing on the common *topoi* of confusing roads and potentially dangerous bodies of water. In contrast, the purity tablets focus more closely on Persephone's right to determine the fate of the soul, which is particularly central to Dionysiac and Eleusinian mystery cults. (2) The purity formula, as we see it in tablets nos. 5, 6, and 7, focuses almost exclusively on what must be said rather than on what must be done; the geographic tablets include elements of both. Seen in this context, the tablets from Pherae fall more easily into the purity group than the geographic group – even though they lack any clear statement about purity.

Against the backdrop of the other tablets, one feature of the tablets from Pelinna stands out as strikingly odd; these tablets include far more statements addressed *to* the soul than *by* the soul. With the exception of line 2 ("Tell Persephone that the Bacchic One himself released you"), the Pelinna tablets can scarcely be called mnemonic devices, in fact, at least in the same sense that we have used the term mnemonic in this chapter. We might hypothesize that the creator of these particular tablets innovated upon a technology that he had borrowed: he continued to draw on Orphic poetry and Bacchic cult to inscribe lines that seemed important to him, his client, or both, but did not make the tablet mnemonic. We might call it a "remembrance" – a token that reminded the initiate of what she had learned without a clearly practical purpose.

Proxy tablets

The remaining eighteen tablets (nos. 15, 17, 20–4, 24a, 28, 30–8) were probably meant to serve as proxies, speaking on behalf of the initiate rather than reminding the initiate of what to say. This certainly seems to be the case for those that carry only the name of the deceased, like a toe-tag in the morgue (nos. 23, 24, 24a, 32, 33, 34, 35, 36). We can imagine that Persephone or her deputy was to read these labels and consult a list of initiates to see whether the name appeared there. Those on the list made it into paradise; others were excluded.

Other proxies go further. Some try to make their point more clearly by spelling out the cultic identity of the deceased: "To Persephone, Poseidippos, pious initiate" (no. 31), "Dexilaos (is an) initiate" (no. 21), "Philon (is an) initiate" (no. 22); similar is no. 30, which declares that the deceased woman is pure and sacred to Dionysus Bacchius (and compare no. 28). Tablet no. 20 is particularly interesting because it has only the single word "initiate" inscribed upon it; it must have functioned like a theater ticket, admitting whoever possessed it. Perhaps some *orpheotelestai* had ready-made bundles of these to hand out to those who had paid to be initiated; perhaps some *orpheotelestai* were, themselves, functionally illiterate and unable to produce more personalized tablets. Three tablets offer greetings to Persephone or to Persephone and Pluton (another name for Hades in this context), or to the Lord (Hades). Tablets nos. 15 and 17 go no further than that ("Greetings to Pluton and Persephone," "To Pluton and Persephone") and again, as with tablet no. 20, we might imagine that some *orpheotelestai* kept supplies of these ready at hand. Tablets nos. 37 and 38 are personalized with the initiate's name ("Philiste greets Persephone," "Philotera greets the Lord").[73]

These proxy tablets, as a group, raise the question of what sort of eschatology lay behind them. Although it is always dangerous to make arguments from silence, it seems unlikely that the souls who owned them were expected to make special declarations to Persephone or anyone else, or to make decisions about which road to take or which body of water to drink from – if the soul was expected to be unable to remember (or speak) his or her own name after death, then it is hard to imagine how the soul could be expected to remember anything else, unaided. The proxy tablets come from locations scattered all over Greece, covering at least two centuries, and so we cannot ascribe the change to some local, isolated variation in the cult. It's hard not to infer that some *orpheotelestai* either didn't know or didn't care about the more complex eschatological doctrines that we reconstructed based on the longer, mnemonic tablets. For these *orpheotelestai* and their clients, perhaps, initiation was the first and only task to be performed to guarantee paradise. Once this had been accomplished and a certificate of completion – a tablet – had been issued, the soul had nothing further to worry about and nothing further to do. If this is correct, then it highlights the ease with which not only desirable ideas but also desirable technologies (in this case, inscribing important words on small gold tablets) adapt themselves in new cultic settings.

Having reviewed the eschatological concepts that underlie both types of tablets (mnemonic and proxy) and taken at least an initial look at the motive that underlay their production, we still are left with the question of how the tablets ended up in the graves where they have been found. Under what circumstances were they distributed? And how do those circumstances of distribution fit into other information that we have about what happened during Dionysiac mystery rites? Our next chapter will address these topics.

5

DIONYSIAC MYSTERY CULTS
AND THE GOLD TABLETS

Fritz Graf

The tablets as ritual texts

The texts of the Gold Tablets contain details that imply a ritualized, performative background. The most important indication is their metrical structure. Basically, all texts are in hexameters: ancient scholars, beginning with Plato's uncle Critias, regarded Orpheus as the inventor of this metre.[1] Some texts are entirely hexametrical, such as the Hipponion tablet (our no. 1); others also contain short passages that are non-metrical. These passages are best explained as ritual acclamations inserted into a hexametrical frame.[2] The smaller tablet from the Timpone Grande in Thurii (our no. 3) contains a sequence of acclamations that move from hexameters to prose and back to hexameters (I underline the non-metrical parts and normalize the Greek spelling):

χαῖρε παθὼν τὸ πάθημα τὸ δ'οὔπω πρόσθε ἐπεπόνθεις.	3
θεὸς ἐγένου ἐξ ἀνθρώπου· ἔριφος ἐς γάλα | ἔπετες.	4
χαῖρε, χαῖρε· δεξιὸν ὁδοιπόρει	5
λειμῶνας θ'ἱεροὺς καὶ ἄλσεα | Φερσεφονείας.	6

Greetings, you who suffered the painful thing; you have never
  endured this before.
You have become a god instead of a mortal. A kid you fell into milk.
Rejoice, rejoice. Journey on the right-hand road,
to holy meadows and groves of Persephone.

Line 3 continues the hexameters of the beginning of the tablet; line 4 combines two unmetrical statements; the unmetrical double χαῖρε then leads back to something that has no certain meter but a peculiar rhythmic structure. In the dramatic progression of the text, this is an acclamation addressed to the successful soul after her arrival in Hades.

But this combination of hexameter and prose is not confined to what Olivieri and Zuntz had labelled the A texts. The same is visible in the Pelinna texts (our nos. 26a, b). Here again, two hexameters are followed by three unmetrical lines that, furthermore, are a variation on line 4 of the Thurii tablet:

> Bull you jumped into milk.
> Quickly, you jumped into milk.
> Ram, you fell into milk.

The following rhythmical address could be seen as a sequence of two choriambics followed by a spondee, or as the end of a hexameter.[3] It leads again back to a hexameter that ends the text: here too, the ritual acclamations are framed by the hexametrical narration.

On the surface of these texts, the speaking voice praises the soul for having attained her goal, the new life after death in eternal bliss. It is surprising that these acclamations are not couched in hexameters. After all, the hexameter is the dominant metrical form in these tablets. The direct speech of the speaking voice expresses itself in hexameters, and the words that the soul has to speak in front of infernal guards or judges are also hexametrical – not only when they use an indirect narration, as in the Pelinna text, but also when they purport to be the direct speech of the deceased, as in all the other texts. There is only one explanation for this complex structure: the unmetrical acclamations reproduce ritual formulae that have been integrated into an earlier hexametrical text.

This must mean that these texts were meant for oral performance; they were liturgical scripts. Another observation points in the same direction. The first verse of both Pelinna tablets is (I again underline the non-metrical part):

> Νῦν ἔθανες καὶ νῦν ἐγένου, <u>τρισόλβιε</u>, ἄματι τωῖδε.
> Now you have died and now you have come into being, <u>O
>   thrice happy one</u>, on this same day.

This should be hexametrical, but it jars: τρισόλβιε with its three short syllables is one syllable too long. But we achieve a regular hexameter when we replace τρισόλβιε with the two short syllables of the word μάκαρ; both words occur in the acclamations of initiates and are more or less synonymous.[4] Metrical mistakes are common in the tablets. Some are unintentional, for example when a negligent or hasty scribe left out one or several letters; this is easily corrected, and it does not mean that the text was pronounced without the missing sounds. Other "mistakes" result from intentional changes, although they are less easy to spot, because they do not render the Greek faulty or unintelligible; and sometimes they even preserve the original hexameter. I will give one example only. Did the scribe of the Hipponion tablet think of Hades or of Persephone when he wrote ΒΑΣΙΛΕΙ in line 14, with a clear empty space afterwards? That is: did he mean βασιλῆϊ, or do we have to change the last word to βασιλεί<αι>, with the same metrical value? To phrase it differently: did the scribe forget the syllable AI after he had written the closely similar syllable EI, or did he really associate the guardians with the king, not the queen? Evidence from outside the text cannot provide us with a clear answer. Hades appears as a main actor on the Toledo vase (see Figure 4, p. 64),[5] and two Cretan tablets address Hades and Persephone as equals, with the king preceding the queen.[6] But at least in Orphic mythology, Persephone is much more important than her husband; she runs the Underworld.[7] The text itself might help us to decide: there is enough empty space after the word to suggest that the scribe meant what he wrote; it does not follow, however, that other scribes did not introduce the queen instead of the king. To come back to the case in hand: τρισόλβιε certainly is an intentional change, since it is a good Greek term found in similar contexts (see note 4), but it is much more emphatic than the simple μάκαρ or ὄλβιε. This emphasis can be seen as yet another sign of orality: if the verse is addressed to the initiate in a ritual context, a higher emphasis on the blessing makes some sense. The oral performance could easily gloss over the metrical problem, as we all are aware when we add improvised stanzas to a song.

On the other hand, the identity of the speaking voice is no immediate help in this question.[8] In some texts – the ones from Thurii and from Crete – the voices belong to the deceased: they claim purity for themselves and ask for water.[9] But in most tablets we hear a different voice. It is the voice of an omniscient and somewhat didactic guide who addresses the soul on its way through the Underworld; he describes the critical points and tells it what to do, what to avoid and what to say. But he also acts as a master of ceremonies who utters acclamations, praising the soul at crucial stages, and he promises future bliss. One can understand this, and has regularly done so in the past, as the voice of Orpheus, the poet who has seen it all and is addressing the initiate to let her participate in his knowledge: this turns the texts into snippets from a *katabasis* poem.[10]

At the same time, given the acclamations, the voice can be understood as belonging to someone who speaks during a ritual; and I very much would argue for such an understanding. But what ritual? Because we deal with deceased initiates, it could be either a funeral or an initiation ritual, or it could be both at the same time, in the sense that the funeral re-enacted parts of the initiation rite. All three possibilities have been proposed by scholars at one time or another. Initiation has been proposed from early on, well before the Hipponion and Pelinna texts were found.[11] Reacting to this view (which he called "phantasies"), Günther Zuntz argued for a "Pythagorean *missa pro defunctis* celebrated at the burial of those who took the tablets with them to the other world."[12] Christoph Riedweg proposed a combination of the two: "in the sepulcral rite, the deceased initiate is addressed by a mystery priest."[13] This diversity of opinions calls for a new analysis of the evidence.

Bacchic initiation rites

Generalities

The deceased persons who were carrying the Gold Tablets had been initiated into a mystery cult. The use of the term *mystai* in the Hipponion and the Pherae texts (our nos. 1 and 27) as well as in some of the very short texts leaves no doubt about their status,[14] and it can be generalized for all the Gold Tablets. The first tablet from Pherae even bears the title *symbola* "passwords," and has these words – the enigmatic composite word *andrikepaidothyrson*[15] and the divine name Brimo – repeated as if in a dialogue between guardian and initiate.[16] Similar passwords are known from several other mystery cults; Albrecht Dieterich collected them a century ago, and not much new material has accrued since.[17] The mystery cult in which the bearers of the Gold Tablets were initiated was Dionysiac. The Hipponion text juxtaposes *mystai kai bacchoi* "initiates, and especially those of Dionysus."[18] The Pelinna texts are even more outspoken: they refer to Dionysus as the god whose help was decisive in gaining access to a better postmortem existence; the tablets themselves have the shapes of ivy leaves, and the deceased woman had the statuette of a maenad in her grave.

In fifth-century Greek, the term *mystēs* is attested for persons who were initiated into the Eleusinian Mysteries, those of Dionysus and, perhaps, of Cybele.[19] The noun *mystēria* designates both the Eleusinian and the Samothracian cults; perhaps it started as the name of the Eleusinian festival and then was transferred on to the comparable Samothracian cult.[20] The underlying ritual – *myēsis* "initiation," or simply *teletē* "ritual" – changed the status of the person who underwent it, but it did not always introduce a person into a formal group. Nor did it always lead to the same expectations: Eleusinian and Bacchic initiates expected a blessed afterlife, initiates of the Samothracian Great Gods expected safety at sea, those of the Corybantes, relief from depression.

In order to understand the tablets as ritual texts, we need to look at details of Bacchic mystery cults; intentionally, the net will be cast rather wide, so as to catch as much information as possible, and other mystery cults will occasionally be adduced as well. Much of the evidence for Bacchic initiation rites is iconographical, and it comes from the late Hellenistic and the Imperial epochs; the range of monuments comprises the (late Hellenistic) frescoes of the Villa dei Misteri in Pompeii, the Augustan stuccoes in the Villa Farnesina in Rome, sarcophagi, reliefs, and paintings from Imperial times. As always with this type of information, its interpretation is heavily debated.[21] Literary texts are earlier, but they are allusive at best; inscriptions rarely talk about rituals.[22] Egyptian papyri preserve the edict of Ptolemy IV Philopator and the liturgical fragment from Gurôb; the former is general, the latter tantalizingly fragmentary – and could have been read by Ptolemy.[23] The corpus of the Orphic *Hymns* belonged to a mystery association in Western Asia Minor; it is more important than many scholars think, although its date is uncertain, but it surely belongs to the Imperial epoch, and to the second rather than the third century.[24] We would know more if we could treat Euripides' *Bacchae* as firm evidence for the Dionysiac initiation of Pentheus, as Richard Seaford has argued.[25] But his thesis is fraught with problems, even if we accept that initiation into a city *thiasos* could be relevant for initiation into private mysteries – which might well be the case: it is plausible (but not more than plausible) that the private cults worked with elements of the city cult. More problematical is the fact that Seaford's argument uses two main strategies, parallelism with other mystery cults, especially Eleusis, and a general pattern of initiation rites, neither of which moves his thesis further than to assert that Pentheus' death resonates with the ritual pattern of initiation. This is interesting as far as it goes (and not altogether unexpected), but it does not help our problem. We would be better off if we could find confirmation for his assertion that: "For Dionysiac initiation ... there is evidence of a mock sacrifice of the initiand."[26] If this were true, we would better understand why death rites and initiation rites seem to collapse into one in the case of the Gold Tablets. But the evidence for such an assertion disintegrates under closer scrutiny.[27]

Even when we cast the net widely, the methodological problems are formidable. As with all mystery cults, details about the rites are not easy to come by: the rites were kept secret, and the central, emotional experience could not be communicated at all, as Aristotle already knew (frg. 15 Rose). In the case of the Bacchic mysteries, there are two further problems. On the one hand, to use fragmentary information spread out over time and space lands us with an artificial construction that presumably was never historical reality: there must have been changes between late archaic southern Russia or southern Italy and Imperial Rome, if only due to the disappearance of the charismatic specialists at some time during the later Hellenistic period.[28] On the other hand, it is far from certain that everything we can piece together about Bacchic mystery rites applies as well to Orphic rites and to those of the users of the Gold Tablets (which might or might not be the same thing), especially if we allow for the inventiveness of the individual itinerant specialists who had to rely on their own ritual ingenuity in their battles with rival specialists and *polis* cults.

Orphic versus *Bacchic*

The ancient evidence for the relationship between the two areas of ritual is somewhat contradictory and rather hazy. In a famous passage, the historian Herodotus uses them as more or less synonymous terms: Orphic and Bacchic rites, he asserts, were in reality Egyptian and Pythagorean.[29] If taken seriously, this statement involves two parallel diachronic developments, and a theory about the true authorship of at least some of Orpheus' writings. Whereas the worshippers of Dionysus assert that their rites were founded by Orpheus, the historian implies that Pythagoras learned them from the Egyptians and that the worshippers of Dionysus learned them from writings of Orpheus that "in reality" were Pythagorean texts. Implicitly, he agrees with his contemporary Ion of Chios who "attributed some of Orpheus' writings to Pythagoras."[30]

Later authors agree with such a connection between Orpheus and Bacchic rites, including the historical derivation. Diodorus of Sicily confirms Orpheus' role and expands on it in a passage that in its substance goes back to early Hellenistic times.[31] At the end of his long narration about Dionysus, Diodorus focuses on his own version of Dionysus' adventures in Thrace that we know already from the sixth book of the *Iliad*. After being helped by a certain Charops against the impious Lycurgus, Dionysus installed Charops as king of Thrace and taught him his mystery rites; Charops handed them down to his son Oeagrus, and Oeagrus in turn to his son Orpheus. Orpheus "made many changes in the practices: for that reason, the rites that had been established by Dionysus were also called Orphic." The story explains the unity of *Orphica* and *Bacchica*: in the same way as Demeter, arriving from abroad, taught her mysteries to the aristocrats of Eleusis who became the local priestly families, the foreign god Dionysus taught his mysteries to a human king who then handed them down to his grandson; here as elsewhere, cultural innovation and its innovator come from abroad.[32] But unlike the Eleusinian Mysteries, which were never called anything other than Eleusinian or Demetrian, the mysteries of Dionysus could also be called Orphic, not just Dionysiac or Bacchic, because Orpheus had reformed what he had inherited. Diodorus does not tell us whether there were also unreformed, un-Orphic mystery rites of Dionysus. The way he tells the story, it does not seem likely.

Similarly, when introducing Alexander's mother Olympias, Plutarch in his *Life of Alexander* identifies Bacchic and Orphic maenadic cults, at least in Macedonia. "All women up there [i.e., in Macedonia] are devoted to the Orphica and the ecstatic rites of Dionysus from old, and they are called Clodones and Mimallones."[33] In this cult, Olympias handled large snakes that crept out from under ivy leaves or from the *likna*, the winnowing fans used in the cult, or they wound around the *thyrsoi*, the ritual wands of the maenads. *Thyrsoi* and *likna* are the regular implements of Bacchic mysteries, the *liknon* usually containing the image of a phallus (see below). Plutarch connects this somewhat loosely with the snake that was found in Olympias' bed more than once; in the back of his mind, he might remember Zeus' incest with Rhea-Demeter and with Persephone in the shape of a snake that might well have been known already at the time of the Derveni Papyrus.[34]

Thus, according to these later writers, Bacchic and Orphic mystery rites are coextensive. This might go well beyond the reality of maenadism in the archaic and classical periods, however; the custom of designating members of Dionysiac associations as *mystai* and their rites as *mystēria* seems to be known only in the Hellenistic period.[35] The maenads are attested well before we hear of mystery rites, and the rituals of the *thiasoi* were often embedded in the ritual structures of the polis: the relationship between the ecstatic cult of Dionysus and the Bacchic mysteries was more complex than Diodorus or Plutarch intimate, and it might have radically differed in different places and at different times.

A verse of Orpheus known already to Plato, furthermore, makes a fundamental differentiation between two groups of ecstatic worshippers:

Many are the thyrsus-bearers, but few are the *bacchoi*.[36]

Among the ecstatic worshippers of Dionysus, then, there was a small, very special group, and Orpheus addressed only them – this at least was the self-definition of "Orphic" Bacchic cults in the classical age. Again, that might have changed over time, with all Bacchic mystery cults being regarded as Orphic, or Diodorus and Plutarch might have exaggerated their point.

Purification, eschatology, and madness

All mystery initiations had a purificatory component, although again its role and its emphasis differed from cult to cult.[37] In Eleusis, purification was achieved through a preparatory collective bath in the sea and the sacrifice of a piglet; in the rites of Isis, an individual bath performed by the priest but in a public bath house prepared the novice for the ritual;[38] in the Corybantic rites, the initiates were formally bathed by the priest or the priestess, as part of a larger ritual sequence.[39] In all these rites, purification is preliminary and prepares the initiate for contact with the divine, as in other rituals that provided such a contact, from sacrifice to incubation.

Besides this preliminary purification, the overall initiation rite could have a cathartic function as well; this is especially true for ecstatic rituals. Ecstasy was understood as being purificatory by itself, cleansing the soul from the disturbances and constraints of daily life. Originally this cleansing was connected with eschatological concerns; then it was transferred to the soul's cleansing from the guilt accumulated by injust deeds.[40] For the Corybantic rites, Plato explained how ecstatic song and flute music could rid the soul of anxiety and other disturbances that were understood as faulty movements of the soul, by forcing it to participate in the violent but regular movement of the music; implicitly, he assumed the same for Bacchic rites.[41]

Whereas the Corybantic rites in Plato seem perfectly respectable, the practitioners who offered other, more individual initiation rites were not, as his description in the *Republic* shows:

> Begging priests and seers go to rich men's doors and make them believe that they, by means of sacrifices and incantations, have accumulated a treasure of power from the gods that can expiate and cure with pleasurable festivals any misdeed of a man or his ancestors, and that if a man wishes to harm an enemy, at little cost he will be enabled to injure just and unjust alike, since they are masters of spells and enchantments that constrain the gods to serve their ends. ... And they produce a hubbub of books of Musaeus and Orpheus, the offspring of the Moon and the Muses, as they affirm, and these books they use in their rites, and make not only ordinary men but states believe that there really are remissions of sins and purifications for unjust deeds, by means of sacrifice and pleasant entertainment for the living, and that there are also special rites for the defunct (*teteleutēsasi*), which they call functions (*teletai*), that deliver us from evils in that other world, while terrible things await those who have neglected to sacrifice.
>
> (*Republic* 364b–365a, adapted from W. C. Greene)

The text introduces the itinerant specialists who were the vehicles for the diffusion of Bacchic mysteries all over the ancient world. Plato describes their initiation rites as "pleasurable festivals" and "sacrifice and pleasant entertainment": he is sarcastic and thus not interested in describing them in more detail, but his audience must have been aware of what he meant. Several centuries later, Livy's account of the events that led to the Bacchanalia affair in Rome in 186 BCE echoes Plato's language.[42] Besides the binding spells that the specialists offered to Plato's wealthy contemporaries, which do not concern us here, their rites focused on calming the fears their clients felt regarding the world of the dead.[43] These rites helped to bring peace to restless dead ancestors, whose evil deeds led them to interfere with their living descendants,[44] and they procured a better after-life for those who were still alive but who might fear that the old stories about punishment after death were true after all, as old Cephalus did at the beginning of the *Republic* (330d). For their rites, these practitioners relied on books of Orpheus and Musaeus: the specialists were, to use a rare Greek term, *orpheotelestai*, "ritual performers or initiators of Orpheus."[45] A few paragraphs later in the same dialogue, Plato summarizes his argument: "The sons of the gods who became poets and prophets" argue that the "functions" (what we would call "initiation rites," *teletai* in Plato) and the "gods of deliverance," *lysioi theoi*, had great power to protect one against punishment after death.[46] Thus, the rites put emphasis on the afterlife. Among the *lysioi theoi*, Dionysus was the most important: according to the Pelinna texts (no. 26), the deceased had to tell Persephone that "Dionysus himself delivered me (*elysen*)." When the initiators' business went well, they might decide to stay in residence for a while: one of the three *orpheo-telestai* whom we see in action, the professional who plays a supporting role to Theophrastus' *Superstitious Man*, has set up shop in Athens and is regularly consulted by individuals for their daily needs, especially concerning matters of ritual purity. Purity is a major concern of these rites. In Plato's description, they purify "from past evils," and we have already seen the importance of purity in Bacchic mystery cults. The initiates' own claim to purity also lurks behind Theseus' sarcasm when he chastises his son in Euripides' *Hippolytus* (953f.): Hippolytus, Theseus maintains, claims to be a vegetarian and has "Orpheus as his Lord when he worships the ecstatic god (*bakcheuein*) and honors the smoke[47] of many books"; but this pious surface hides a deeply debauched and wicked person, to whom not even his father's wife is sacred. Nothing compels us to understand the term *bakcheuein* here in anything other than its literal sense: Theseus depicts his son not only as a vegetarian who lives according to the books of Orpheus, but also as an initiate into Bacchic mystery rites.

The nexus of Bacchic mysteries and eschatology is attested already in the later part of the sixth century BCE. Heraclitus of Ephesus threatened the "night-roaming *magoi, bacchoi*, maenads and initiates (*mystai*)" with fiery punishment after death; by doing so, he sarcastically turned their beliefs against them.[48] His list combines male and female Dionysiac initiates and their itinerant initiators, whom he likens to the Persian priests, the *magoi*, who were well known and feared, hated, or despised in Persian-occupied Ephesus of Heraclitus' time.[49]

Another description of an *orpheotelestēs*, this time from Hellenistic times and preserved in Philodemus' treatise *On Poems*, represents him playing a hand-drum (*tympanon*), as a proverbial maker of empty noise.[50] The *tympanon* is the instrument of ecstatic rites, of the Mother of the Gods, the Corybantes, and of Dionysus Bacchius and his maenads,[51] "the invention of Mother Rhea and myself," as Dionysus says in Euripides' *Bacchae*.[52] As such, the *tympanon* is a constant attribute of maenads in literature and in Dionysiac iconography.[53] Philodemus shows that it was also the instrument played by the Bacchic initiator. Plutarch does the same: he describes how king Ptolemy IV Philopator, a great enthusiast of Dionysiac rites, took up the role of a Bacchic initiator, "performing initiations and with a *tympanon* in his hand begging for money (*ageirein*) in the royal residence."[54] This well illustrates Plato's image in the *Republic* where he describes the ritual specialists as "begging-priests" (*agyrtai*, from the same root) and their rites as "pleasurable festivals."

This same nexus of initiation rites, purification, Dionysus, and the Great Mother appears also in Dionysiac myths that might well go back to the archaic age; the Phrygian Mountain Mother Cybele was worshipped in Greece already in the later part of the seventh century BCE.[55] Apollodorus' *Library* contains the story of how Hera drove young Dionysus mad (3.5.1 = 3.33). "He wandered through Egypt and Syria . . . and arrived at Cybela in Phrygia: there, after he had been purified by Rhea and learned the rituals (*teletai*), he received from her the ritual paraphernalia"; the *tympanon* was part of this. The story is alluded to in Plato and Euripides and goes back to the *Europia*, an epic poem by one Eumelus, whom the Greeks dated as early as Homer. "Dionysus" (Eumelus is cited as saying) "was purified in Cybela in Phrygia by Rhea and received from her the rites and the entire outfit."[56] Rhea is just another name for the Mother of the Gods, who also is called Cybele. According to the medical treatise *On the Sacred Disease*, Cybele is among the divinities who cause madness:[57] this explains why Dionysus turns to her for healing. The story closely connects ritual purification and the teaching of initiatory rites: it is the etiological myth for Dionysiac initiation. To outside observers, however, this ritual appeared to be not very different from the rituals of Rhea-Cybele. Both rituals aimed at an altered state of consciousness for the participants. In both cults, this state expressed itself in the same way, in orgiastic, ecstatic song, music, and dance, and the two divinities and their cults were connected during the fifth century BCE at the latest.[58] The god is the victim of madness, which his rites would then heal. Plato plays with the same story of Dionysus' madness as the etiological myth for his rites, but turns these rites, and the invention of wine, into the god's vengeance on the human race, for a reason he chooses not to tell us (*Leg.* 672b). In both cases, however, the stories address the ecstatic cult of Dionysus.

It is in a poem attributed to Orpheus that we read that Dionysus heals madness (*oistros* – that is, a frenzied state of mind, not the quiet dejection of depression); this madness has not been wantonly inflicted by a god, but follows from the unjust deeds of "lawless ancestors." Someone (Orpheus?) addresses Dionysus in these verses:[59]

People send perfect hecatombs
in all seasons during the whole year,
and they perform rites, seeking deliverance from unlawful
    ancestors.
But you [Dionysus], having power over them, whomever you
    wish
You will deliver from difficult suffering and limitless frenzy.

Damascius, the Neoplatonic commentator who cites these verses, adds that this is the reason that the god is called *Lyseus* "Deliverer." I do not know whether the "lawless ancestors" are the ancestors of all humanity, the Titans, or closer ancestors whose evil deeds caused madness in their descendants; they might be both. Plato was thinking of concrete ancestors as objects of the rituals in the passage from the *Republic*. In a passage from the *Phaedrus*, he similarly attributes the cause of madness to the anger of one's ancestors and makes its healing dependent upon "prayers and worship of the gods, from which purifications and intitiations (*teletai*) are derived that make it [the soul] healthy for the present and all the future time."[60] The Orphic adaptation of Dionysiac purification turns it into an instrument of personal psychic well-being and eschatological hopes. There must have been other texts ascribed to Orpheus that dealt with the same nexus; according to the list of Orpheus' works in the Byzantine lexicon *Suda*, there was a poem called *Thronismoi Metroioi kai Bakchika*, "Enthronements of the Mother and Bacchic Things." The *thronismos* was an initiation rite in which a neophyte was at the center of a frightening ecstatic dance: did this poem narrate Dionysus' initiation into the cult of the Mother?[61]

Madness is also important in the prayers that are contained in the Orphic *Hymns*: several prayers to a specific divinity ask for madness to be healed. In the hymn to Corybas (the singular of "Corybantes"), the god is asked to put an end to his wrath and to stop sending terrifying visions. The Corybantes could send madness, but their rites were also used to heal madness, at least in fifth- and fourth-century Athens, where they reminded observers of Bacchic rituals.[62] The hymn to the Titans more specifically asks them "to ward off the difficult anger, if one of the chthonic ancestors should approach our houses," that is for protection against restless dead that might cause psychic troubles.[63] Similar prayers are addressed to Pan and to the Eumenides, well-known agents of psychic disturbances:[64] Pan sends panic fear and sudden madness, the Eumenides can punish specific crimes with madness, as Orestes learned.[65] The cult group for which the collection of Orphic *Hymns* was written was Bacchic; again, healing from madness and Bacchic cult coincide.[66]

Images of rituals

More information is contained in Bacchic images. The image that is most often repeated shows an erect phallus in a winnowing basket (Greek *liknon*), either carefully covered by a cloth, as in the painting from the Villa dei Misteri in Pompeii, or dramatically revealed to a shocked female, as in a late mosaic from Cuicul-Djemila (Algeria).[67] Scholars debate whether this phallic exhibition is symbolic or whether it was a part of the ritual scenario, and if so, whether it was the central *mystērion* or a preliminary rite only.[68] Diodorus makes the actual worship of the phallus into the center of the mysteries that the Greeks took over from the Egyptian cult of Osiris: when Typhon dismembered Osiris and scattered his pieces all over Egypt, his phallus got special attention, and Isis instituted the worship of its image: "Therefore the Greeks . . . worship this body part in the mysteries, rituals (*teletai*) and sacrifices of this god (i.e., Osiris-Dionysus)."[69] Dionysus *Liknites*, "Dionysus in the *liknon*" receives a hymn in about the middle of the corpus of Orphic *Hymns*, that is, towards the very center of its ritual scenario: this underscores the importance of the ritual.[70] If rumors about such a rite triggered the accusation of ritual rape in the Roman Bacchanalia, as is possible, we could move its attestation within a private Bacchic group back a century,[71] and if Diodorus faithfully reproduced the late fourth-century historian Hecataeus of Abdera, we would arrive at the time of the first Ptolemy.[72] Phallic presentation, however, is central to Dionysiac processions even in the late archaic age, where it is public and highly visible; the mysteries adopted and privatized a public ritual.

Iconography reveals other details that are missing from the literary record. There are scenes in which a novice is instructed, either by someone reading to him from a book scroll (Villa dei Misteri) or explaining the images of a relief triptychon (Villa Farnesina).[73] A sarcophagus shows the purification of a veiled initiate with a burning torch.[74] Ecstatic Bacchic music is alluded to in the frequent images of hand drums (*tympana*) and sometimes of flutes.[75] There are also images of libations and sacrifices on an altar, bringing home the insight that not everything in the panoply of the mysteries was strange and unusual; sacrifice and libation are, after all, the "staple rituals" of ancient religion.[76] Wine, finally, plays its part as well: in one of the Farnesina reliefs, a satyr fills a crater with wine, while a youthful initiate turns his back toward this scene: this must be the preparation for the final celebration after initiation. A similar scene appears in several later pictures as well;[77] and the building that housed a Bacchic association in Hellenistic Pergamon yielded a dedicatory inscription according to which one Carpophorus dedicated a large crater and an altar-table to Dionysus *Kathegemon*.[78] In the rites of the Corybantes and of Sabazius, a god who was very close to Dionysus, the crater was so important that it named a ritual, the *kraterismos* – which was presumably focused again on the ritual consumption of alcohol.[79]

Much earlier, the initiation scene on an Attic black-figured pelike (a wine jug) in Naples, dated to about 500 BCE, might belong to the same Bacchic ritual. On the right, two youths with laurel wreaths are sitting next to each other on a couch, facing a table heaped with pieces of meat and with a full bread basket under it; a bearded man with a wine-skin and myrtle twigs in his left hand and a drinking cup in his outstretched right hand addresses the youths; on a pole next to him, there is a relief (showing the Dioscuri, according to Beazley); the word MYΣTA ("the two initiates") is written across the entire scene.[80] The scene has usually been understood as Eleusinian; some even saw it as representing the drinking of the *kykeon*, the specific Eleusinian sacred drink that broke the initiates' long fast when they arrived in Eleusis.[81] The wine-skin contradicts this interpretation, and wine makes Eleusis difficult anyway: Demeter rejected wine in favor of the *kykeon* in the etiological narration of the Homeric *Hymn to Demeter*.[82] Bacchic mysteries thus seem preferable for this late archaic image.

Only one other, equally tantalizing, bit of information is pre-Hellenistic. The Derveni commentator, who is pre-Platonic in philosophical outlook if not date,[83] is aware of a preliminary sacrifice that the initiates (*mystai*) offer to the Eumenides "in the same way as the *magoi*."[84] The *magoi* offered cakes and libations of water and milk as part of a sacrifice that they perform "as if they were paying a penalty"; the aim of their rite was to placate dead souls that might otherwise "be in the way." The rite of the *magoi*, then, is purificatory and heals damage done by vengeful ghosts.[85] The *magoi* in this passage are itinerant purification priests of the type that Heraclitus and Plato scoffed at. If the initiates belong to the same religious world, they must be Bacchic, "Orphic." But this is far from certain: the Derveni author presents to us a list of rituals to support his assertion that "prayers and sacrifices placate the souls (of the dead)" – first the incantations, sacrifices, and libations of the *magoi*, then the preliminary sacrifice of the initiates, and finally a preliminary bird sacrifice by whoever sacrifices to the gods. Theoretically, the initiates could belong to the Eleusinian Mysteries: we know from Athens of wineless libations to the Eumenides, although not in an Eleusinian context,[86] and Empousa "She Who Gets in the Way" is a demon who frightens Eleusinian initiates.[87] Given the very strict Eleusinian secrecy, however, an author might have hesitated to use this ritual for his proof (except, that is, if he was Diagoras the atheist, as Richard Janko argued).[88] The name Eumenides, furthermore, is panhellenic and was equated with the local, Athenian name of Semnai Theai only in the course of the fifth century.[89] The goddesses had links to the dead; any initiate who was about to come into contact with that other world was well advised to enlist their benevolence. If we can trust Plato, the Bacchic, "Orphic" mysteries were much more concerned with the ghost world than were the Eleusinian ones: this might argue for such a preliminary sacrifice before the Bacchic initiation.

Later texts 1: The Gurôb Papyrus

None of these rites – phallic presentation, sacrifice to the Eumenides – or their effect – to heal madness – is reflected in the Gold Tablets: their place in the scenario of Bacchic mystery rites still eludes us. We come closer when we look at a liturgical text preserved in a third-century BCE papyrus from Gurôb, a Lower Egyptian town at the entry to the Fayûm. We have only a miserable scrap of a larger text: only parts of two columns are preserved.[90] Besides being heavily damaged, the papyrus lacks any context besides the fact that it refers to rituals of a Greek-speaking cult group in Ptolemaic Egypt; all other inferences have to be drawn from the text itself. This is true only under the assumption that we really deal with a ritual text and not with part of a longer theoretical treatise such as the Derveni Papyrus with its descriptions of rituals and allegorical explanation of an Orphic theogony; the overall structure of the text seems to suggest such an assumption.

The structure of the preserved text combines discursive portions with liturgical speech in direct citations; the discursive portions in turn appear to be mainly ritual directions. The key word "ritual" or "initiation" appears early in the fragment ("because of the initiation," teletē, col. i 3). A first invocation follows immediately; we discern traces of hexameters: "Save me, Brimo, me . . ., Demeter and Rhea . . . and armed Curetes" (col. i 5–7). In this first invocation, Dionysus does not appear: we move in the circle of Rhea-Cybele and her helpers, the Curetes, who performed an armed dance around baby Zeus. Brimo is often understood as the Thessalian form of Hecate, but she also appears in a ritual formula connected with the Eleusinian Mysteries as the mother of a mighty child, that is, as Demeter whose Eleusinian son would be Plutus, "Wealth," rather than as Persephone and her son Dionysus; in rare contexts, however, Brimo is identified with Persephone.[91] The Curetes in turn are invoked in the corpus of the Orphic Hymns as the Samothracian gods who invented the mystery rituals – that is, if we take Ephorus' story into account, the source of the Orphic mysteries.[92] The very beginning of the Gurôb invocation is tantalizingly incomplete; perhaps it reads: "[Recei]ve my [gift] as a retribution for the fath[ers' deeds]" – which lands us again in the nexus of unjust ancestors, madness as punishment for their deeds, and the ecstatic rituals of Cybele and Dionysus that heal madness. After a line that is destroyed beyond restoration, there follows, still as part of the invocation, the exhortation "to perform beautiful sacrifices" (9). Two of the sacrificial animals are the ram and the billy goat (10); then we discern "immense gifts" (12). The ram is often sacrificed to Persephone, the billy goat as often to Dionysus.

In what follows we discern more detailed instructions for the sacrifice of a billy goat (13), perhaps at a riverbank, which could only refer to the Nile (12). An instruction to "eat the rest of the meat" follows (14): sacrifice and meal belong together, as in any Greek cult. After two very difficult lines, we catch the word "prayer" as introduction to a second hexametrical invocation: the speaker addresses another set of divinities; Eubouleus is the only well-preserved name (18). Somewhat later, but still in the same invocation, Demeter and Pallas appear in the genitive (21). The next line asks for divine salvation: "King Erikepaios, save me."[93]

The next line juxtaposes the name of Dionysus and the word *symbola*, (ritual) "tokens," in what is not hexametrical verse and thus presumably not a direct invocation (23). The following line preserves the formula "god through the bosom." "In the Mysteries of Sabazios, 'god through the bosom' is the token for the initiates," says Clement of Alexandria (*Protrepticus* 2.16.2). He gives it a sexual reading, since the Greek word *kolpos* can mean both "bosom" and "female lower body," including the genitals: the rite mimics the incest of Zeus with Persephone, the result of which was the first birth of a bull-faced Dionysus.[94] Sabazius and Dionysus are closely related, as are Sabazius, the Corybantes and the Great Mother: all preside over ecstatic cults, all with the exception of Dionysus originated in Asia Minor, especially Phrygia and Lydia, whence the ecstatic Dionysus came back to Thebes as well, according to Euripides' *Bacchae*. What in reality are well-defined cults collapse here into one complex scenario. This is far from being negatively defined syncretism, rather it is creative cultic innovation. Similar combinations occur not only in the imagination of Christian polemical writers such as Clement, but already in the thinking of theologians and practitioners of mystery cults in the fifth century BCE, as the Derveni papyrus suggests.[95]

Whatever the details, the Gurôb text seems to deal with details of "Orphic" rites whose aim was salvation from afflictions. The next line has "I drank, donkey, cowherd." This sounds like a password (Greek *synthēma*), as attested in several mystery cults either to enter the sanctuary or to access the next-higher intiatiory degree; the first Pherae tablet (our no. 27) contains such a password in what seems to be a ritual context, and most other tablets treat utterances by the initiates as passwords that give access to otherwise forbidden parts of the Underworld. The self-designation of the Gurôb initiate as cowherd, *boukolos*, inserts him firmly into Bacchic mysteries, where *boukolos* designated a mid-range initiate.[96] "I drank the *kykeon*" is part of the Eleusinian password, "I ate from the hand drum (*tympanon*), I drank from the drum (*kymbalon*)" belongs to the password of Meter Mysteries.[97] The term *synthēma* appears in the next line, confirming the ritual character of the passage. Besides knowledge of the password, the initiate had to have certain objects, tokens (*symbola*[98]) of the rites. "I have been initiated into a large number of Greek mystery cults," said Apuleius (*Apology* 55), when asked what he kept secret and wrapped in a handkerchief: "I carefully guard certain signs and mementos (*signa et monumenta*) that the priests gave me." They reminded him of the rites, and he might have had to use them if he wanted to enter a religious group in which he was not yet known. After a line of direct speech that eludes me (27 "and what was given to you for your consumption": are we still talking about a sacrifice, or about another part of the password?), the text mentions a basket (28) and certain objects – a cone, a spinning top, knucklebones, and a mirror. The basket occurs again in an Eleusinian password;[99] all the other objects are toys, and they all are connected with the story of how the Titans killed the first Dionysus. Hera or the Titans "allured him with toys and a mirror";[100] or, according to hexameters attributed to Orpheus and cited by Clement of Alexandria, they used "a cone and a spinning top and toys with flexible limbs [i.e., puppets] and golden apples from the Hesperides";[101] others add a ball.[102] The mirror reappears on a scene of the fifth-century CE ivory pyxis in the Museo Civico Archeologico di Bologna that presents scenes from the life of Dionysus: the child Dionysus is shown sitting on a throne with the armed Curetes dancing around him and a robed female figure, presumably Hera, kneeling close by and holding a mirror up to the boy (see Figure 5).[103] But we need not look only at such a late object. A late sixth-century BCE bronze mirror with a Bacchic inscription comes from a grave in Southern Russia, and its inscription repeats the Bacchic ritual shout "*euai!*"[104] A myth tells us that a surprised *euai!* was the reaction of the Titans when they saw their first mirror.[105] The information comes from a poem on the *Teletai of Dionysus* that was ascribed to Pythagoras' daughter Arignote, thus proving the important ritual role the mirror had in Dionysiac initiations.

With regard to the myth and cults of Dionysus, the Gurôb text accomplishes several things. First, it demonstrates that this Egyptian group of initiates had a complex mythology that combined different ecstatic deities, not unlike the mystery association that used the Orphic *Hymns*, but well before their time.[106] Secondly, it attests to the toys that were used to distract the young god, and does this several centuries before their first explicit literary attestation. The toys imply the myth of Dionysus' murder at the hands of the Titans: this local initiation ritual was modeled on the Orphic myth.[107] Thirdly, the text makes clear that this Egyptian group was neither an exception nor an aberration in a foreign country. Firmicus Maternus, who wrote in the earlier part of the fourth century CE, describes a Cretan ritual of Dionysus; he follows a euhemerist source of early Hellenistic date that in turn transforms an earlier narration.[108] This euhemerist

Figure 5 Ivory pyxis with Dionysiac scenes, sixth century CE. Museo Archeologico Civico di Bologna, inv. no. PCR12 © Bologna, Museo Civico
Archeologico.

perspective turns Zeus into a Cretan king whose son and presumptive
heir and successor was Dionysus – with the problem that the heir was
born from an adulterous relationship. This had consequences: while Zeus
was away, his legitimate wife, Hera, bribed Dionysus' bodyguards, the
Titans, seduced the boy with toys, and had him killed by the Titans who
then cooked and ate the child. His sister Pallas (Athena) was able to save
Dionysus' heart; the name Pallas was derived from its palpitations (we saw
that the Gurôb text mentions her as well). The irate and aggrieved father
killed the Titans, fashioned a gypsum image of his adored son, put the
preserved heart in it, built a temple around it and made the boy's peda-
gogue, Silenus, the priest of the new cult. The Cretans in turn celebrated a
biannual festival "in which they perform in sequence everything that the
dying boy did or suffered." The rest of his description, however, cannot be
taken literally:

> With their teeth they tear a living bull apart, evoking the cruel
> meal in their annual commemorations; in the secret depths of the
> forests, they imitate the madness of a raving soul with dissonant
> howls, as if the crime was not the result of evil premeditation,

but of insanity. In front [of the procession], they carry the box in which the sister hid his heart, and with the sound of flutes and the rattling of the drums, they imitate the toys with which the boy was deceived.

The euhemerist interpreter whom Firmicus follows here discusses a biannual Bacchic rite. It began with a procession through the town that led the celebrants out to the forests, with the *cista mystica* (the box with the secret ritual objects) in front. In the forests and on the mountains far away from the city, the initiates performed ecstatic dances and ate raw meat (*omophagia*). The Gurôb text takes the myth much more literally than Firmicus' source: no toys are symbolically imitated by music, the toys are instead manipulated during the ritual.

This does not mean that the Egyptian mystery cult was a purely local affair, characterized by a "local brand of syncretism," as scholars have assumed. The combination of an ecstatic Dionysus with an equally ecstatic Cybele goes back to the archaic age; in the late fifth century BCE, it was familiar enough that Euripides could devote a choral ode to it (*Helen* 1301–68). More importantly for us, the first tablet from Pherae (our no. 27) contains the *symbola*, or "passwords," of the rites. I realize, by the way, that the semantic distinction between *synthēmata* and *symbola* as between tokens and passwords is somewhat tenuous. Originally, both terms referred to an object, such as a ring, that warranted the recognition of a business obligation between strangers even after generations. The partners broke the ring in half; each kept his part and handed it down to his successors; at the end, the successors established their identities and obligations by "holding together," *syntithēnai* or *symballein*, the two pieces. In the Pherae text, the tokens of recognition were the words *andrikepaidothyrsos* and Brimo. The name Brimo recurs in Gurôb col. i 5; the Pherae password resonates with *Irikepaios* in Gurôb col. i 22. Brimo is a name for Demeter and is attested in several texts ascribed to Orpheus,[109] Erikepaios is another name for Dionysus and is, at the same time, a primeval being in Orphic theogony.[110] The second Pherae text (our no. 28) combines Demeter Chthonia and the Mountain Mother (also called Rhea and Cybele) into a group that again recalls the Gurôb pantheon and where Bacchic mysteries are not far away (see Appendices 2, 4 no. 3).

Some of these elements appear also in other cults. The mystery cult presided over by the mother of the orator Aeschines performed purifications at night and processions by day, according to a disparaging description by his rival Demosthenes (*On the Crown* 259). Aeschines read the sacred books and performed the nightly rituals among which the use of a mixing bowl and a deer skin was important; they ended with the exclamation "I escaped evil, I found the better." During the day, he led the *thiasos* in a procession that looks very Bacchic (wearing of ivy and of the *liknon* are mentioned) but uses not only the Dionysiac shout *euoi* but also invocations that recall the Anatolian gods Sabazios and Attis, the companion of the Mountain Mother. All this looks like a ritual bricolage based on a Bacchic template, not unlike the rituals visible in the Gurôb Papyrus or in our no. 28 from Pherae; the religious entrepreneuse at its head, incidentally, is known as the sister of the seer Cleobulos (died *c.* 370 BCE), a closely related religious specialist: this sort of undertaking stayed in families, as also the evidence from the Roman Bacchanalia shows. To make it more intriguing, a papyrus of the later third century BCE narrates a hitherto unknown aetiological story of the rites of Sabazius, the older form of Dionysus (Obbink 2011a); the story strongly recalls the Orphic *Hymns* 39 and 40 and suggest that mythical and ritual bricolage might be connected with Orpheus. An altar from Hierokaisareia in Lydia, in the hinterland of Smyrna and dated to the second century CE, was dedicated to Dionysus Erikepaios by a hierophant:[111] this local mystery cult had connections not only with Bacchus but with Orphic texts where Erikepaios alone appears. So did a contemporary mystery cult for Dionysus Bromius in nearby Smyrna: its hexametrical sacred law calls the rites *Bakcheia*, Dionysiac festival. The law forbids, among other things, the eating of a heart or beans, and explains this somehow (the text is damaged) by reference to the Titans. The main concern of this Smyrnaean group was ritual purity: to be pure, the text claims, would prevent the anger (*mēnima*) of the dead. The defiling events ranged from abortion and contact with neighbors in whose house someone had recently died to eating forbidden food.[112]

Later texts 2: the Orphic Hymns

This brings me to the so-called Orphic *Hymns*, a corpus of seventy-eight texts from a town somewhere in Western Asia Minor, not too far from either Smyrna or Pergamum. I have talked about the *Hymns* already in the general context of madness. Ritual details are rare in the corpus, aside from the fumigations that accompany the recitation of each hymn, but the liturgical use of these texts in the rites of a Bacchic initiation group that claimed relationship with Orpheus is beyond any doubt. Among the different ways that the corpus of the *Hymns* is organized, the performance of a nightly ritual is important.[113] The first hymns address Hecate Prothyraia, "She at the Doors," (*h.* 1) and Night (*h.* 2), the final hymns invoke Mnemosyne/Memory (*h.* 77) and Dawn (*h.* 78): the ritual begins at the doors of the shrine and spans the entire period between nightfall and dawn. Mnemosyne is specifically asked "to awaken for the initiates the memory of the sacred rite and to send away forgetfulness of it": the initiates can lead a pure life only if they remember what they experienced and learned during the rite, and perhaps they will need this memory again when they die, as some of the tablets (especially nos. 1, 2, and 8) imply.

In addition to the prayers that ask for healing from madness incurred outside the rituals (see above), there is another risk of madness: the initiates are afraid of being driven mad during their ritual performances. Several prayers address a specific divinity and pray for her to manifest herself as *euantetos*, "good to meet." This always refers to a specific ritual context in which the divinity is invoked, and to a phenomenon well attested for several mystery cults. The ritual experience of meeting a divinity during the altered state of consciousness induced during the rite can be violently frightening, either because the gods can send apparitions that frighten the initiate,[114] or because the madness induced during an ecstatic rite is more than just a blessing. As several myths tell us, the god Dionysus could push his victims to terrible deeds: Agave and her sisters killed Pentheus, the Minyads slaughtered their babies. This prayer thus attests both to the importance of ecstatic experience during the rites, and to its ambivalence. The means by which the altered state of consciousness ("ecstasy") was induced, however, remain unclear; the traditional methods – wine and violent dance movements – seem the likeliest choices.[115]

The hymn to Semele (*h.* 44) is the only hymn in the entire corpus that explicitly refers to a ritual act and its etiology. Persephone, the text says, created for Semele

> an honor (*timē*) among mortal humans at the time of the *trietēris*, when they celebrate your labor when you bore Dionysus, the sacred table, and the pure mystery rites (vv. 6–9).

This describes one of the rituals performed during the biannually recurring major festival of Dionysus. Semele's motherhood is honored with what might be public sacrifice: a gloss in a Byzantine lexicon gives the festival's name as "table of Semele."[116] The hymn closely connects the mysteries with her: Persephone, the Lady of the Bacchic Mysteries and first mother of Dionysus, gave a place of honor to the second mother of her only son.[117] To talk about "Semele's labor" is remarkable: in the traditional myth, the pregnant Semele died well before she could give birth and suffer labor, and Zeus snatched the baby out of her smoldering body. Thus, the term is either a benign circumlocution for her cruel death, or this specific mystery group told a happier birth story. Several centuries later, the ivory pyxis in Bologna also depicts what seems to be a very normal birth of Dionysus; the iconography, however, is unclear enough to make a decision as to whether it portrays Semele or Persephone impossible.[118]

The Gold Tablets and mystery rites: summation

It is high time to draw together a long discussion. Not much in the ritual of Bacchic mystery cults can be traced back to the Gold Tablets, although both the cults and the tablets go back to a pre-Hellenistic, presumably late archaic date.[119] Heraclitus is the first author to attest to Bacchic initiations with an eschatological bent; Pindar's allusion to the Orphic myth of Dionysus (frg. 133) is next, followed by Herodotus' remarkable silence concerning the myth of Osiris, which must be understood as reflecting secret Greek beliefs related to the dismemberment of Dionysus. The initiates expected to continue their festivities in the afterlife, as the Pelinna texts (our no. 26 a, b) explicitly promise: "You have wine as your fortunate honor." As the crater that is represented in some images implies, ritual wine-drinking was important at a later stage of initiation, presumably at its end. Plato made fun of this ritual and the eschatological belief that resulted from it, when he described the "banquet of the pure" with its eternal drunkenness, as a promise given by "Musaeus and his son" (that is, by either Orpheus or the Eleusinian Eumolpus)[120] – but these banquets mirrored the banquets of Bacchic, "Orphic" initiates.[121]

Other things are even more generic. In the texts from the Timpone Piccolo in Thurii (our nos. 5–7), the deceased stress their purity ("I come pure from the pure"): this fits the general importance of purification as a goal of the ritual.[122] In the Hipponion text (our no. 1), the deceased will proceed along a sacred road together with the other initiates: this recalls both Bacchic and Eleusinian processions. Bacchic processions led the maenads through the town out to their dancing and celebrating "on the mountain," as a famous Milesian inscription has it,[123] and as Firmicus Maternus describes happening in Crete;[124] the Eleusinian procession led outwards, from the city of Athens to the sanctuary of Eleusis.[125] In his transformation of the Eleusinian procession that Aristophanes stages in *The Frogs*, the ritual again will lead the initiates to their dancing grounds in ever-green and flowery meadows: the tablet from the Timpone Grande (our no. 3) holds out the promise of Persephone's grove and meadow, and the first Pherae text (no. 27) promises these meadows as well. The images of the afterlife are the same in the literary discourse about Bacchic and Eleusinian expectations; our strict separation of them projects Christian longing for orthodoxy or scholarly desire of consistency.[126]

If the way in which the afterlife experience is imagined is modeled after Bacchic rituals, we can go a step further. The overall situation is one in which a deceased person confronts either stern guardians or Persephone and her infernal court; the correct password – a reference to one's divine, pre-Olympian origin (Hipponion, Petelia, Thurii, Crete), or to Dionysus' intercession (Pelinna) – will open up the path to eternal blessings, and acclamations may accompany this success. The suspicion that this reflects actual ritual experience can be substantiated, at least in a generic way. In death, Plutarch says (frg. 178), the soul "undergoes the same experiences as those who are initiated into the great mystery rituals; this is why the word *teletē* 'initiation rite' echoes the word *teleutē* 'end, death' and the reality of initiation echoes the reality of death." In this reading, at least the emotional and presumably also the ritual progression of initiation plays out the factual and emotional experience of death. But its emotional center is not physical death but rather the descent to the Underworld, the confrontation with the powers down there, and, finally, the successful arrival among the other blessed initiates. This ritual process must also include instructions about what to avoid, and especially about what to say. This is why the Pherae text (no. 27) adds the injunction "enter the sacred meadow" after the passwords: the ritual's and the soul's afterlife travels are the same. There is no need to go back to Eliade's idea that initiation rites take rebirth literally, even if some details could be read in this way:[127] the Pelinna texts (no. 26) and an Olbia bone tablet (Appendix 4 no. 1A) insist on the sequence life–death–life, and the enigmatic milk-formula in Thurii and Pelinna recalls the use of milk in the mysteries of Attis, which a late source understands as a reference to a new birth.[128] But it is impossible and unnecessary to turn this into a general theory. You only die once: the ritual death during initiation pre-empts and cancels out the future physical death.

Bacchic funerary rituals

A famous inscription from the middle of the fifth century BCE, found in Cumae in Italy, reserves a portion of the local cemetery for Bacchic initiates only:

> It is not lawful for someone to lie here if he has not become an initiate of Dionysus.[129]

This could attest to not much more than the custom common among many later religious associations of guaranteeing the burial of their members; in Hellenistic and Roman times, this very often was the main function of such associations.[130] Dionysiac groups did the same, as inscriptions demonstrate, although they rarely owned a specific burial plot.[131] The Cumae inscription seems somewhat too early for this, moreover; one generally assumes that such associations resulted from the urbanization and high mobility of Hellenistic Greece, where people moved far away from the family or clan groups that would have provided burial and grave cult for them, had they stayed home. If one then asks for a different reason that the Cumaean initiates of Dionysus Bacchius had their common burial ground, one answer imposes itself: these initiates had their very specific burial rites and thus wanted their graves to be separated from the graves of other people.

But were there specific Bacchic rites for the dead? A few details argue at least for some differences between the burial customs of Orphic initiates of Dionysus and those of other Greeks. In the second book of his *Histories*, Herodotus talks about the Egyptian use of linen garments, and he adds:

> This agrees with the customs known as Orphic and Bacchic, which are in reality Egyptian and Pythagorean, for anyone initiated into these rites (*orgia*) is similarly forbidden to be buried in wool.[132]

It is Herodotus' theory that these customs "in reality" are Egyptian and Pythagorean, that is, brought from Egypt by Pythagoras. But Herodotus himself observed them not in Pythagorean circles (at least not exclusively), but in Orphic and Bacchic mystery groups. "Orphic and Bacchic" in this text is furthermore a *hendiadys*, a double term referring to one and the same religious group: they performed Bacchic rites, but followed the books and instructions of Orpheus, their "prophet," to use Burkert's term. Orpheus is a poet about whose age or even existence Herodotus has his doubts, as he said not much earlier in the same book: the identification of Orphic with Pythagorean must mean that Herodotus, like Ion of Chios, regarded Pythagoras (or a Pythagorean) as the author of the ritual texts ascribed to Orpheus.[133]

Plato, by contrast, as we saw, made a clear distinction between two groups of Bacchic worshippers: the many who bear the *thyrsus* and the few who really are *bacchoi*, ecstatic followers of the god; he based his statement on a hexameter of Orpheus.[134] He attributes this dichotomy to "people who deal with initiations," ritual specialists, and he even adds a sample of their teachings: "These people tell us that, whoever arrives in Hades without being initiated will lie in mud, but those who arrive purified and initiated will be together with the gods." His specialists, whom I confidently would call *orpheotelestai*, claimed a special eschatological status for their clients; this status depended on the ritual purity that the clients had gained through their initiation. This resonates with the Thurii tablets' emphasis on purity and deification, and their promise of an afterlife enjoyed in the groves and meadows of Persephone.

The Thurii tablets can teach us yet more. The grave in the Timpone Grande revealed not only the double tablet, one wrapped around the other, with the wrapper (our no. 4) still defying the ingenuity of modern readers. The excavation also revealed that this same grave was the focus of an ongoing cult: the locals, or some of them, worshipped the deceased as a hero (see Figure 2, p. 53). Furthermore, when the excavator Francesco Cavallari opened the main tomb on March 23, 1879, he found "*un bianchissimo lenzuolo*," "a very white shroud" lying over the cremated remains of the deceased. As soon as the excavators touched the shroud, however, it turned to dust. Thus, it is impossible to determine from what sort of material this shroud was made. In the light of the Herodotean passage, I think linen is very likely.[135]

Aristotle's pupil Hermippus talks about another burial custom, this time Pythagorean. "They did not use cypress wood for caskets, because Zeus' scepter is made of this wood" – which means that one should not bring elements of the world of the living into the realm of the dead. Iamblichus repeats this and seems to think that, together with cedar, laurel, oak, and myrtle, the cypress was a tree that humans used to honor the gods. He adds that there was also "some other, mystical reason" which, because the reason was mystical, he does not divulge.[136] The only mystical reason we know of is found in the Gold Tablets: the cypress is standing next to the fountain whose waters prevent one from enjoying a blessed afterlife: it is a tree to be avoided.[137] This time, Pythagoreans and Orphic initiates of Dionysus share a specific ritual detail,[138] and like the prohibition of wool, it contradicts common Greek use: the Athenians, at least, buried the dead of the first year of the Peloponnesian War in caskets of cypress wood.[139]

White garments or caskets that avoid using cypress do not by themselves make for a special burial rite, of course; neither does the presence of a Gold Tablet in a grave. All of these things are details that express Bacchic initiation, but they do not necessarily mean that one must change the burial rites that are customary in a city or a family: such a change of traditions would have been unwelcome in the societies of the ancient world. As if to confirm this, not one of the graves that contained a Gold Tablet has exhibited features that pointed to a burial rite contradicting ordinary Greek burial practice. Nor can we detect uniformity among the graves that held Gold Tablets even as to basic rites.[140] Some burials, such as the ones in Thurii, were preceded by cremation,[141] others were burials by inhumation; the Thurii graves were covered by a mound (and at least in the case of Timpone Grande showed traces of later grave cult), most others were simple cist graves; only the deceased woman in Pelinna was buried in a stone sarcophagus. Specificity, if at all, was expressed by items added to a grave, such as the white shroud in Timpone Grande or the statuette of a maenad in Pelinna. Such additions have been found also in graves that did not contain Gold Tablets, such as a marble egg with a statuette of Helen inside or, on larger scale, a terracotta statue group of Orpheus and the Sirens, from two Metapontine graves,[142] or the splendid silver and gold crater that contained the remains of the deceased in the Derveni B grave:[143] all of these items have been convincingly connected with Orphic afterlife beliefs. The Etruscan sarcophagus lid that depicts a maenad most likely meant that the deceased was initiated into Bacchic mysteries, too;[144] we would also assume that the Orpheus vase in Basel (Figure 3, p. 63) and the Toledo Underworld vase (Figure 4, p. 64) came from the graves of initiates.[145] The Toledo vase shows the pact between Hades and Dionysus, the Basel vase depicts Orpheus singing in front of a seated man in an *aedicula*; the man holds a rolled text in his hand, the equivalent of a Gold Tablet. Eschatological hope need not be expressed by texts alone; and if these vases had not been deprived of their contexts, other grave items might have helped us to understand the deceased's hopes better. In short, adherence to Dionysiac or "Orphic" mysteries could be marked by a large and varied number of grave goods. The Gold Tablets were only one possibility among many others. The problem is larger than one might think, however: as long as we lack a comprehensive statistical analysis of each cemetery, the relevance of such items is difficult to gauge, given that significant deviations from a norm are almost impossible to spot.[146]

Even when focusing on the Gold Tablets alone, there is no uniformity either of text or of burial custom throughout the Greek world. Most tablets treated in this book have a coherent text of a certain length; even the short Cretan texts, with their three lines only, contain a complete text, as do the greetings to Hades and Persephone. But then there are the very short pieces that contain nothing more than a personal name and, sometimes, the added description of the deceased as an initiate. Some of these tokens from Crete are gold coins that have been flattened and inscribed; others again are altogether devoid of any writing. These different variations are attested in clusters: the most prominent cluster is the group of short Cretan tablets; several tablets with personal names alone come from Achaea, others again from Crete. Thus there were local customs, and one suspects that these customs were shaped by the resident specialist or by the memory he left behind (see above, Chapters 3 and 4). One should also bear in mind that not every initiation had to be performed by a professional. A recently published inscription for the cult of the Corybantes in Erythrae assumes that sometimes an initiate – a *kekorybantismenos* – would in turn perform an initiation; similar delegation of the initiation rite to non-professionals can be observed in Bacchic cults.[147] In the absence of an itinerant *orpheotelestēs*, the same can be imagined for our groups, and the empty or short texts might well attest to this, as well as to the concomitant lack of a book from which to copy a longer text.

The way in which the tablets were buried with the dead similarly varied.[148] What counted was the fact that the initiates had their texts with them; otherwise they might have become lost in the Underworld. In most of the cases where we have an archeological record, the tablets were found next to the right hand of the body; this corresponds to the Basel vase where the seated grave owner holds a rolled text, and to a lost papyrus roll from Callatis that was found next to the hand of a skeleton.[149] The two Pelinna tablets were placed symmetrically on the chest of a deceased woman's body, the Hipponion tablet was placed either in the mouth or again on the chest of the body it accompanied.[150]

This leads me to the very small tablets that are only minimally inscribed. There are at least eighteen such pieces that range from normally one word only, a personal name, to four (nos. 15 and 31).[151] The only obvious information on a ritual contained in them is the designation *mystēs*, "initiate," that appears three times in Achaia (nos. 20, 21, 22) and once in Pella (no. 31): the person thus designated underwent an initiation rite.

It is unclear which mystery cult might have been involved; Matthew Dickie, who first drew our attention to the objects, identified some of them as myrtle leaves rather than the somewhat similar but larger laurel leaves, and connected them with Dionysiac cult.[152] Things are more complex, however.

Out of eighteen pieces, only seven have been described as leaves by their excavators. Five others are unquestionably rectangular; the rest are somewhat ambivalent: is a piece that is described as "almond-shaped" (no. 22), "rhomboid" (no. 23), or "ellipsoid" (no. 17) in reality a badly executed leaf, and does the archaeologist's description of it as *elasma*, "metal piece" (no. 35) imply a rectangular shape? Specific shapes seem to cluster in specific regions: the two naturalistic leaves with a middle ridge and a short stem come from Dion/Pella (no. 31), other but markedly smaller leaves come from Aigion (nos. 20–22), Elis (no. 24), and again Pella (no. 32); another piece from Pella is a small disk (no. 33). All other Macedonian texts are written on small rectangular pieces of gold foil, whereas of the two Cretan texts, no. 15 is rectangular and no. 17 long oval. Not all measurements are available; where we have them, they show a typical range between 20 and 40 millimeters in length and about 12 millimeters in width; only the two naturalistic leaves are larger, over 80 millimeters long and around 25 millimeters wide.

All this taken together can be understood to mean that it was not that relevant whether a piece was somewhat leaf-shaped or rectangular, or even round. More consistent is the placement inside the skull, which in a few cases suggested to the excavator that the gold piece served as Charon's coin.[153] This fits with the theory proposed by Yannis Tzifopoulos for the smaller Cretan tablets, that they were put on the mouth of the deceased as *epistomia*, "mouth covers," a custom that survived into Christianity; it is tempting to conclude that in this position even the short texts were meant to perpetuate the voice of the deceased.[154] Some of these *epistomia* follow roughly the outline of the lips and are long ovals or ellipses, others are narrow rectangles. The leaf shape can be seen as a simple coincidence with the shape of the lips – and it might well be that small rectangular gold tablets served the same purpose, such as nos. 10–15, 23, 38 or the uninscribed 8a with its image of Demeter and her daughter. On the other hand, nothing prevented the use of naturalistic leaves from a gold crown to which an inscription had been added. [155] It might be that the characteristics of the two inscriptions on these leaves are the result of this secondary use: one is rather hastily inscribed with a name, on the other one the letters are composed of dots pushed into the gold: these reused leaves might have been somewhat thicker than the regular gold leaves and thus more difficult to inscribe. We will never know whether the users (or their initiator) depleted a gold crown as a handy source for gold leaves, or whether this was the rest of an honorary or ritual crown; given the uniqueness, the former seems somewhat more likely. At any rate, a Bacchic crown would not be made from laurel or olive, but from myrtle: the shorter of the two naturalistic leaves actually comes from a man's grave that also contained a myrtle crown.

What about the connection with a mystery cult? Given the irrelevance of the shape, it is impossible to argue for a specific mystery cult from a specific sacred plant. The only certainty is given by the pieces that use the term *mystēs*: three such pieces come from Aigion (nos. 20–22), one from Pella/Dion (no. 31). Additionally, one might argue with the Dionysiac finds from Macedonia: one text comes from a grave with a grave-couch (*klinē*) decorated with Dionysiac images (no. 35), and two of the Pella texts (nos. 31 and 32) come from a cemetery where another contemporary grave contained another grave-couch with Bacchic imagery.[156] The Cretan *epistomia* share most of the text with longer gold leaves and thus must belong to the same religious world. By extension, we might assume the same for all very short texts – and at the same time keep in mind that we deal with a rather fluid cultic environment: the Syracuse tablet no. 8a that represents a Janus-headed goddess, most likely Demeter and Persephone rolled into one, joins the Pherae tablet no. 28, another text that talks of *mystai*, in opening the Dionysiac circle towards Demeter and related female goddesses. We have to allow, then, for ritual bricolage on the template of the Bacchic mysteries, or even the possibility that the technology of the tablets – the idea of writing a message on a gold leaf that then was carried by the deceased to the other world – could be adopted by other mystery groups. The gold tablets from Palestine published in Appendix 3 are probably a case in point.

So far, we cannot spot much deviation from ordinary Greek custom. There is, however, some evidence for Dionysiac grave rites that must have seemed unusual to ordinary Greeks, although these rites did not leave direct traces in the archeological record. A few inscriptions and literary epigrams attest to a joyous Bacchic dance around the fresh grave. As the Hellenistic poet Dioscorides (mid-second century BCE) put it in one of his epigrams:

> Scatter white lilies over the grave and beat the usual drums
>   (*tympana*) around the tombstone of Aleximenes;
> Let stream the locks of your long hair, maenads,
> and let them whirl around the city at the Strymon!
> To these tender tunes the city often danced, while he
> played sweet sounds to your shouts.[157]

Many centuries later, the poet Nonnus still shares this feeling, in a long passage where he narrates the burial of Dionysus' friend and companion Staphylus. During the rite, Staphylus' friend Maron (the same man who gave Odysseus special Thracian wine) gets up and offers "reels and jigs at your tomb . . . I will dance for Staphylus after death."[158] One suspects that this has to do with the certainty that the dead Staphylus is on his way to a blessed existence that outdoes all human bliss. "For you I dance a revel upon your grave, Staphylus," sings Nonnus' Maron, "you who are both alive and not breathing." This paradoxical formulation evokes the Pelinna tablets: "Now you have died and now you have come into being, O thrice happy one, on this same day"; rites of ecstatic joy seem more appropriate than rites of abject grief and mourning.

This is unusual. Although initiation into mystery cults brought hope for those left behind, we rarely hear of joy at the grave. Even when they expect bliss for the deceased, the survivors express their own grief, as they do in another Dionysiac grave epigram, a late Hellenistic text from Macedonia written for a young boy:

> While we are tormented by our grief, you live, restored to life in Elysium [. . .]. Whether, according to Fate, in the flowery meadow, among the assembly of the Satyrs, the initiates marked [i.e., tattooed] for Bacchus demand you for themselves, or the basket-bearing nymphs equally demand you to lead their festal ranks with torches preceding, be now anything your age has brought you . . .[159]

Thus, Bacchic initiates may have had very special burial rites, expressing joy about the life to come as well as grief about the life that had been lost. This does not mean that the rituals of which the tablets were a part were performed on the grave; if taken seriously, everything we know about them effectively contradicts such an assumption. It was the initiation rite with its "joy and play" that instilled certainty about a better life after death; the tablets that gave such tangible expression to this expectation must have been handed over then and there. But this expectation had consequences for the burial rite: far from emphasizing the grim end of life, it celebrated the "god-given beginning" of an afterlife that included Bacchic dances.

Orphic communities

Common cemeteries such as the one in Cumae need stable communities: in order to acquire land and to defend it against intruders, there must have been a well-established and continuous association of *bacchoi* in fifth-century Cumae. Such communities would have been more likely to develop their own rituals than single individuals would have been. The evidence for such communities, however, is scanty. Mystery initiation does not necessarily introduce one into a group or community; initiates of the Samothracian gods could form associations in their hometowns, but this was optional. As to Bacchic mysteries, there is more evidence for groups than just the inscription from Cumae; most of it dates to the Hellenistic and Roman Imperial epochs.[160] Ordinarily, we are unable to connect them with Orpheus, however, and Plato's description of the itinerant practitioners seems to make the initiation rite an entirely private affair of isolated individuals. The one exception is the Olbian bone tablet that mentions *Orphikoi* (with some debate about the reading): perhaps these *Orphikoi* were a local community who used these small tokens to recognize each other. Several decades earlier, Herodotus attests to ecstatic Bacchic cult groups in this city (4.79), and a Bacchic mirror dedicated by a woman and a man, a father and his daughter, might even be seen as the earliest attestation (late sixth-century BCE) of the Orphic myth of how the Titans lured young Dionysus to his death with a mirror.[161] The distribution of the Gold Tablets is harder to use as evidence for communities. Many of the tablets' find-spots are isolated, although they lie within larger cemeteries: such is the case with the Hipponion text. This pattern points to isolated individuals. Other tablets cluster together, most notably those from Crete or the tiny tablets from Hellenistic Aigion (Achaia), but also the four texts from Thurii – the only cluster for which we have a clear archeological record. This might point to small local communities, or simply to the prolonged presence of an *orpheotelestēs* in one place (the two things can, but need not, be different); the samples are not large enough to prove either possibility.

Initiation or burial rites? A summary

The bearers of the Gold Tablets were initiates who underwent a special rite that was understood as mainly cathartic, purificatory; the purification was aimed at securing for them a better lot after death (see Chapter 3). The detailed analysis of our evidence for Bacchic initiation rites showed that they, too, were understood as having a cathartic function. But this function had a somewhat different scope, according to Bacchic mythology or ritual texts, such as the Orphic *Hymns*: they were intended to heal madness, *mania*. Orphic anthropogony, however, provides a bridge between these two seemingly different goals, eschatological hopes and healing of madness: as the fragment of Orpheus cited by Damascius shows, Dionysus Lyseus, the Deliverer, is connected with the healing of both.[162]

All of this is very general only. The texts that most clearly allude to specific rituals, the two tablets from Pelinna, find some parallels in Bacchic rites, where the drinking of wine marked the final stage of the ritual. There is no trace of a rite that we could connect with the making and giving of the Gold Tablets, nor is there evidence for special burial rites that could resonate with the Pelinna texts: Bacchic revelry over the grave is far different from the solemn *makarismos* in the Pelinna texts. And at least in the cases where we cannot assume a stable and sizable community (such as one has to assume for Cumae or Olbia), specific burial rites are rather unlikely: adherence to "Orphic" mysteries expressed itself in the composition of grave goods or some other details of the grave, not in special rites. This makes it very likely that the Gold Tablets preserve traces of a ritual scenario that was part of the bearers' initiation and that prepared them for the role they had to play once their souls had left their bodies and entered "the dark realms of Hades."

6

ORPHEUS, HIS POETRY, AND SACRED TEXTS

Fritz Graf and Sarah Iles Johnston

In this final chapter, we will take up two topics. The first is the identity of Orpheus, the legendary poet credited with transmitting the stories that we examined in Chapter 3, some portions of which were probably quoted by the Gold Tablets. The second is the very nature of those stories. Ancient authors mention *hieroi logoi*, "sacred stories," in connection with particular cults or religious rituals, including some that are related to the tablets. Some modern scholars have gone further and called the tablets themselves *hieroi logoi*. We will consider whether this definition is correct and, more generally, how the concept of "sacred story" may enhance our understanding of the tablets.

Who was Orpheus?

In the tightly-knit network of family relations that is the hallmark of Greek heroic myth, Orpheus is an outsider. His mother was a Muse, usually identified as Calliope; his father was either a Thracian king or, in a few accounts, the god Apollo himself; this makes another musician, Linus, the lyre teacher of Heracles, his half-brother.[1] Beyond this, there is no part of the genealogical network into which Orpheus would fit; it is doubtful whether he ever appeared in the *Catalogue of Women*, the pseudonymous late archaic epic poem transmitted as a work of Hesiod, which constructed this network.[2]

Orpheus the Argonaut

From very early on, however, Orpheus may well have played an important role in another and much older epic narrative than the *Catalogue of*

Women, the *Voyage of the Argo*. In his traveler's tale, Odysseus refers to the "*Argo*, sung by all" (*Od.* 12.70) – the story was famous and familiar already to Homer's audience. But it never received the dazzling treatment that Homer gave to Odysseus' travels; the two epic versions of Jason's voyage that we possess, one written by the Greek poet Apollonius of Rhodes (*c.* 250 BCE), the other by the Roman poet Valerius Flaccus (*c.* 70 CE), are both learned and somewhat pedantic, lacking the luster of Homer's narrative power. We do not know, moreover, whether Orpheus was among the Argonauts already in pre-Odyssean versions of the story; over time the list of crew members grew longer because the story attracted all sorts of local heroes.

It seems likely, however, that the Argonauts needed a singer all along, not only to call the beat of their oars, but also to out-sing the dangerous Sirens. A sculpture group from Delphi, dated to between 570 and 560 BCE, shows two singers and two other crew members aboard a ship; next to the prow stands a horseman. An inscription identifies one of the singers as Orpheus (ORPHAS); the ship must be the *Argo*, the horseman one of the Dioscuri; the three other crew members remain anonymous.[3] We might feel tempted to retroject Orpheus' participation into these earlier narratives, if it were not for the second singer. His name was inscribed as well, but is lost now; some scholars identify him as Philammon, the father of another Thracian singer, Thamyris, whom the *Iliad* mentions.[4] Philammon has close ties to Delphi and one can assume that he owed his place on the *Argo* to Delphic story-telling.[5] But the historian Pherecydes of Athens (born around 480 BCE) attests to Philammon's presence among Jason's crew as well;[6] this version thus had wider currency than just in Delphi. Still, the doubling of the singers on the Delphic metope could be read as a sign of how important and therefore old Orpheus' presence in the story was.

Unfortunately, earlier images are even more difficult to evaluate. An early Attic black-figure vase in Heidelberg (about 580 BCE) shows a singer with his harp between two Sirens: Hildegund Gropengiesser understood the picture as the first attestation of Orpheus the Argonaut confronting the Sirens, while other scholars preferred to regard it as an ornamental frieze composed of figures that are common on this sort of pottery.[7] A similar uncertainty surrounds an Etruscan vase painting from the first half of the seventh century BCE, thus almost contemporary with the *Odyssey*: it shows a lyre player among dancing warriors. If this represents a scene from Greek myth, it might well be Orpheus among the Argonauts, as Erika Simon thought; the local nobles could have understood the story as a mythical representation and legitimation of their world and values. It could also, however, be the direct representation of an aristocratic ritual.[8]

Orpheus the foreigner

Orpheus' lack of genealogical connections in early Greek myth goes together with his foreign origin: the Greeks were accustomed to regard Orpheus, like other famous musical heroes such as Musaeus and Thamyris, as being Thracian. From Athenian vases to late antique mosaics, images could depict Orpheus in a foreign, "Thracian" costume, or at least a "Phrygian" cap that denoted barbarian foreigners. But there were also always images that represented him as Greek – not least the many vase paintings that depicted him singing among Thracians, where the contrast is marked.[9] When pressed for details, Greek narrators sometimes named the Thracian heartland in what is now Southern Bulgaria, to the north of the Rhodope Mountains, as the country from where Orpheus came and where he even had an oracle; he was said to belong to the tribe of the Odrysians, a tribe with which the Athenians made a treaty in 431 BCE. Orpheus the Odrysian must reflect this political alliance.[10] The same political event is mirrored in an epigram that purports to come from Orpheus' grave and that sheds a surprisingly positive light on the Thracian singer: he "invented letters and wisdom for humanity," and was killed by Zeus' lightning, not by Thracian women.[11] Other sources made him a member of the Cicones, a mythical Thracian tribe that settled in eastern Macedonia, around the city of Ismaros, and that was allied with the Trojans; Odysseus sacks their city but suffers heavy losses when the barbarians attack his drunken sailors.[12] This could either be an older story, following the conventions of epic story-telling, or a later reaction to the perception that an Odrysian Orpheus was anachronistic.

But Orpheus had even closer ties with a region of southern Macedonia in the foothills of Mt Olympus, called Pieria; the region originally was settled by Thracians.[13] The Pierian town of Leibethra housed a small wooden image of Orpheus, a *xoanon* that was said to have sweated when Alexander the Great set out for the conquest of Asia – the statue did so not out of concern for Alexander, but "because he would perform deeds worthy of song and fame that would cause much sweat and work for the singers."[14] According to the late Hellenistic author Conon, Orpheus, "king of the Macedonians and Thracians," suffered his death in Leibethra, torn to pieces by the local women whose husbands he had alienated from them. In order to atone for this killing, the Leibethrians buried Orpheus' head in a splendid *temenos* and offered him cult "as if to a god," but excluded all women from the sanctuary. At some time between Alexander's death and the Imperial epoch, the neighboring and larger city of Dion took over: Pausanias saw Orpheus' grave there, transferred from Leibethra after a flood had destroyed the lesser town because of the carelessness with which the Leibethrians had treated the grave.[15] In the political reality of Roman Greece, Dion incorporated Leibethra as a suburb; Pausanias thus reports the myth told in Dion to justify their annexation of the grave. Whatever, then, the historical value of these stories may be, they attest to the claims that Leibethra, Dion, and its region made on Orpheus. Pieria shares with Orpheus the ambivalence of being Greek and foreign at the same time, and it shares with him a connection with the Muses: Pieria was also the place from where the Pierids (either the Muses or their rivals) came.

Orpheus the singer

All of this makes Orpheus a poet, or rather a mythical representative of *mousikē*, the combination of instrumental music, song, and dance that was the hallmark of civic life in the cities of archaic Greece; although it flourished in the early democracies no less than in the aristocratic cities, it was modeled on aristocratic ideals. Orpheus' instrument was the lyre, the instrument that any Greek aristocrat was expected to master; Homer's Achilles, a prototype of the aristocratic young warrior, plays the lyre to console himself, whereas Heracles, as the caricature of the traditional aristocrat, killed his lyre teacher, Linus, out of frustration.[16] As with Achilles, whom Homer represents as singing heroic poetry to the accompaniment of his lyre, with Orpheus the emphasis is on the words and not on the music: Pindar calls him "father of songs," and his name opens a canonical list of four early Greek poets that we can trace back to the sophist Hippias of Elis (late fifth century BCE): it comprises Orpheus, Musaeus, Hesiod, and Homer, in that order.[17]

Orpheus is thus the perfect image of the singer in the aristocratic circles of archaic Greece: he plays the lyre and sings among the all-male group of young heroes who sailed out with Jason. But whereas these aristocrats were all tied to their lands, as their heroic ancestors were tied to their graves in the cities or on the estates, the singers had no such connections. Like seers, healers, and carpenters, with whom Homer combines them in a list of itinerant professionals, singers wandered from city to city and from court to court, offering their services to whoever wanted them and paid them well (*Od.* 17.383–5). This "essential foreignness" helps to explain why Orpheus, Thamyris, or Musaeus was a Thracian without genealogical ties in the web of Greek heroic mythology. The mythical paradigm of the singer in Greek archaic society makes them as itinerant and vagrant as the historical singers were. At the same time, these specialists are part of the fabric of Greek society: to make them Thracians, coming from the neighboring barbarians who were thought to have lived as far south as Mt Olympus, expresses such an ambivalent status.[18] Another hallmark of archaic Greek society was homoerotic relationships: they characterized the education that a young aristocrat underwent.[19] Thus, it is no surprise that both Orpheus and Thamyris were credited with the invention of homosexuality.[20]

Unlike Homer, however, Orpheus was never thought to have composed large narrative epics, at least in archaic and classical Greece; the version of the voyage of the *Argo* that he tells in his own voice, from the point of view of a participant, was written during the Imperial age and distances itself explicitly from all other poetry of Orpheus.[21] His specialty was, like Hesiod's, theogonic poetry, such as the text that is interpreted in the Derveni Papyrus.[22] The unidentified allegorist of this "Derveni Theogony" was an intellectual who lived in the later part of the fifth century BCE; we do not have enough information to determine how much older the theogony itself is. Other theogonies were credited to Orpheus, too; they all coalesced into the huge *Theogony in Twenty-four Rhapsodies* from which Neoplatonist philosophers cited many hexametrical fragments.[23] Besides the theogony, the Derveni allegorist cites *Hymns* by Orpheus that mention Demeter, Rhea, and Cybele. Other mythic poets such as Musaeus were credited with a similar range of works: fifth-century Greeks, it seems, perceived their earliest poets as being mainly concerned with the gods. Far from being mere entertainers, they were authorities on the divine world. Herodotus' famous statement – that "Homer and Hesiod gave the Greeks their gods" – has to be read in this light: he follows up his statement with a polemical remark that "the so-called earlier poets [that is Orpheus, Musaeus, etc.] in reality lived later than these men, I think."[24] Obviously Herodotus' audience was used to seeing Orpheus and Musaeus in the roles in which he casts Homer and Hesiod.

Orpheus the magician

But there is more to Orpheus than just poetry, as there is more to *mousikē* than just entertainment or status representation. In early Greek thinking, the poets' words possessed a power that went well beyond that of ordinary speech: they captivated and charmed (*thelgein*) the souls of their listeners.[25] In Orpheus' case, this power went well beyond the fascination of poetic entertainment. The poet Simonides (late sixth/early fifth century BCE) described how Orpheus had power even over nature: "Countless birds were flying over his head and the fish jumped straight out of the blue sea when he sang his beautiful song." Later authors would add that even trees and rocks gathered around the singing Orpheus.[26]

It should not surprise us that the singer of such powerful words was soon understood as a magician whose spells – *epōidai*, a variation of *ōidai* "songs" – could perform all sorts of strange deeds, as soon as magic was conceptualized as something special during the late sixth century BCE.[27] If anything, it should surprise us that the notion of Orpheus as a magician was not more widespread than it was in classical and later Greece. The satyrs in Euripides' *Cyclops* know of spells by Orpheus that could move the red-hot stake into the eye of the Cyclops who kept them prisoners.[28] This is a comic version of something more serious, but in their despair, the satyrs wildly exaggerate Orpheus' much more circumscribed power: it usually is confined to healing spells. In his *Alcestis* of 438 BCE, Euripides has his chorus sing about the unyielding power of Ananke, "Coercion" or "Destiny": "I have found nothing that is stronger than Destiny, neither the medicine contained in the Thracian tablets that the voice of Orpheus has inscribed, nor the remedies that Apollo has given to the sons of Asclepius, to heal the manifold suffering of mortals."[29] This reference to written Thracian spells is isolated, and the ancient expounders of Euripides debated what he meant exactly.

Mousikē, however, is only one aspect of archaic song-culture; *goēteia*, the song that connects the living with the dead, is the other one.[30] Diodorus of Sicily, following the fourth-century historian Ephorus, says that

> the Idaean Dactyls were born in the region of Mt Ida in Phrygia; they migrated with Mygdon to Europe. Being *goētes*, they spent their time with spells (*epōidai*), initiations and mystery cults. When they were living about the island of Samothrace, they quite frightened the indigenous inhabitants with all these things. At this time also, Orpheus became their student, although his different nature had first driven him to poetry and music; and it was he who first brought initiations and mystery cults to the Greeks.[31]

As early as the sixth century, the Dactyls were connected with metallurgy and with magic and the remedies to magical spells. The combination of blacksmith and sorcerer is attested throughout the world and stems both from the marginality of a specialist in a somewhat uncanny craft and the organization of blacksmiths into secret societies; the mystery cults of the Dactyls, as of the Samothracian and Lemnian Cabiri with whom they were early identified, show traces of such archaic groups.[32] Other mystery cults such as those of Eleusis or Dionysus, were more concerned with the afterlife and sought the contacts with the world of the dead – again a type of contact that the *goēs* could establish: he was primarily concerned with the passage between the two worlds. The Greek term *goēs*, after all, derives from *goös*, "the "lament" that helped ritually to ensure that the dead would complete this passage; from this early function, the *goēs* retained his key role in communicating with the dead.[33]

Orpheus the *goēs*, however, is much more an initiator than a sorcerer. In the "fluid triangularity between music, mysteries, and *goēteia* that operates in all directions,"[34] Orpheus was closer to music and mysteries than to magical spells. Healing is almost the only province of Orpheus' magic; in Pliny's comprehensive history of magic, Orpheus is credited with having spread healing magic from Thrace to Greece, and even here Pliny has some reservations.[35] The hero whose divine knowledge became more pronounced over time could not be a practitioner of damaging spells; only the satyrs in the *Cyclops* and Plato make this connection, the latter in a rather vague way, when he rails against the "begging priests and seers" who used "a hubbub of books of Orpheus and Musaeus" to perform initiation rites and binding spells.[36]

Orpheus the initiator

Orpheus, Ephorus said, introduced mystery cults into Greece, having learned initiations from the Dactyls; performing initiation into mystery cults, then, is a craft that can be learned and that relies, among other things, on powerful words and songs; implicitly Plato, in the passage just cited, made the same claim. Orpheus is regularly portrayed as the founder of mystery cults and their initiator; he was, as the geographer Strabo has it, "an itinerant wizard (*goēs*) who first peddled music along with divination and mystery rituals, but later thought more highly of himself and attracted crowds and power."[37] Strabo (or his source) imagined Orpheus as one of the seers and begging priests berated by Plato, but one whose mystery rituals gained a much wider acceptance than those of others. Orpheus' reputation as an inventor of mystery cults is well established in the later fifth century, although it is not always clear which cults a particular author has in mind when speaking of this reputation.[38] Hellenistic and later authors, at least, agree that he introduced the mystery cult of Dionysus, but perhaps as early as the fifth century, he was connected with the Eleusinian Mysteries; Pausanias adds that he founded the mysteries of Hecate on the island of Aegina and those of Demeter Chthonie in Sparta.[39]

One is tempted to understand this role of Orpheus in mystery associations as an innovation modeled on his role as a singer among groups of young aristocrats in archaic Greece, influenced by the rise of *goēteia* during the archaic period.[40] Already Ephorus read the story in this way when he constructed Orpheus as a singer turned *goēs* and initiator through the teachings of the Dactyls – this construction stresses the poetic role of Orpheus and reduces the goetic side to mystery cults, leaving aside entirely the role in magic that at least the Dactyls played. Orpheus' role as a singer and initiator survives in yet another representation in a story told by Conon about Orpheus' activities in Leibethra, which led to his violent death; this time, he performs initiations for an all-male group, which resonates with the connotations of Cabiric and Dactylic rites. According to this story, Orpheus, the king of Macedonia and Thrace, assembled his warriors around himself and performed secret rites (*orgiazei*) in a special building into which they were not allowed to bring their weapons.[41] The wives of the warriors surprised the unarmed assembly and killed its leader, "because he did not let them participate in the rites, or perhaps for other reasons"; some ancient authors understood these other reasons as Orpheus' introduction of homosexuality into this warrior society. This story combines the topics of male warrior groups, mystery initiations, and possible homosexuality. It invites an evolutionary reading: it preserves memories of archaic civic customs, as attested among the backward Dorian cities of Sparta and Crete whose citizens met for common dinners in their men's houses (*andreia*) and who practiced homoerotic initiation rites, but it reads those memories in the key of more recent initiations into private mystery rites.[42] It also reminds us of what we know about the secret society of Pythagoras and its Thracian imitation by his former slave Zalmoxis.[43] The two readings do not contradict each other: Pythagoras adapted both aristocratic customs and the private cult of the Great Mother to his own purposes:[44] together with Epimenides and Empedocles, he belonged to a group of charismatics in archaic Greece who combined all sorts of ritual lore with authoritative insights into the nature of the world and the divine.[45] In many respects, Orpheus is modeled on their examples. Already in the fifth century, Greek intellectuals understood this and claimed Pythagoras or some Pythagorean as the true author of Orpheus' poems.

Orpheus and Eurydice

The power, but also the final futility, of poetic song is one of the themes of what would become Orpheus' main myth: the story of his love for Eurydice, her death on their wedding-day, his descent into the Underworld to win her back, his initial success by means of his music, his subsequent loss of her again because he could not observe the conditions under which Eurydice had been restored to him, and, finally, his retreat into the wilderness of Thrace, where he suffered a violent death at the hands of mad women – in some versions Dionysus' maenads and in others the Thracian women whose warrior husbands he had enchanted.[46] Full and lengthy narrations of this story are surprisingly late in our texts: they are preserved only in Vergil's *Georgics* and Ovid's *Metamorphoses*. The story as such is considerably older than the end of the first century BCE, however. Its first attestation again is iconographical: a relief depicts Orpheus looking back toward Eurydice, who is just about to be led away by Hermes. The relief is preserved in several Roman copies and thus must have been famous among Romans; its original, however, belonged to an Athenian monument of the later fifth century BCE, perhaps the altar of the Twelve Gods in the Athenian Agora.[47] Plato and some Hellenistic authors allude to the same story, in several variations that are not always in agreement with one another, even as to the name of Orpheus' wife. It was Vergil's and Ovid's versions that canonized the myth for posterity, down to the present day.

From its first attestation, the center of the story is Orpheus' descent into Hades to fetch Eurydice. This story belongs together with a series of tales told on both sides of the Pacific rim; all these tell of how a person entered the realm of the dead in order to bring back someone they loved (lover, wife, or sister) and of how an initial success turned into its opposite because of the rescuer's thoughtless behavior.[48] But this does not guarantee that the Greek story antedates the classical epoch. Although "in the fifth and fourth century more than one poem was known about Orpheus' descent into Hades,"[49] no author and no image attests to Orpheus' descent or any other aspect of the Eurydice myth before the fifth century BCE. Vase paintings with Orpheus in the Underworld became very popular in fourth-century southern Italy, but are absent from fifth-century Athenian pottery. Instead, Athenian vases repeatedly represent the death of Orpheus at the hands of Thracian women[50] – presumably for political reasons, given the importance of Thrace for Athenian politics and economy; the same reason explains the "correction" of the story that had Orpheus killed by Zeus' lightning, thus saving the Thracians' allies from embarrassment.[51] We have no guarantee that Orpheus' gruesome death was always part of the myth of Eurydice, and at least Conon can dissociate the two, as we shall see. To make things even more opaque, on a fresco painted in Delphi in about 450 BCE, the Athenian Polygnotus depicted Orpheus in an Underworld grove of Persephone together with the Thracian singer Thamyris and the Phrygian flute-players Olympus and Marsyas – but without any trace of Eurydice:[52] for Polygnotus, Orpheus in the Underworld did not necessarily evoke the myth of Eurydice, but rather ranked him among other famous, deceased musicians.

All of this poses a problem for the assumption that the texts of the Gold Tablets come from one or more late archaic hexametrical poems that narrate Orpheus' descent (katabasis) to the Underworld. The problem is not insurmountable, given that one can always posit the existence of such poems alongside other myths about Orpheus and other poems credited to him. Moreover, Orpheus' connection with the world of goēteia and consequently with the realm of the dead fits the archaic age much better than the fifth century.[53] Whatever the chronology, the story makes Orpheus the one poet who entered Hades, sang in front of its rulers and inhabitants, and came back to tell the tale. It thus invites and legitimizes the creation of hexametrical *katabasis* poems narrated in the first person singular – in other words, autobiographical reports by someone who had seen it all. Such poems, again, are absent from the direct record, but they can be reconstructed with some plausibility.[54] In the catalog of his own works, which he presents at the beginning of the so-called Orphic *Argonautica*, Orpheus claims that "I told you also what I saw and perceived when I went the dark way of Taenarum into Hades, trusting in my lyre and driven by love for my wife."[55] Certainly, such a poem or poems were well known during the first century BCE, for Diodorus Siculus argued that what Orpheus had presented as memories of his *own* trip to the world below had really been transformed from rites he had seen while traveling in Egypt (1.92.3) – the same place from which he had borrowed the orgiastic rites that he introduced to Greece. And the poems were undoubtedly much older than this: among the works ascribed to Orpheus, the title "Descent into Hades" (*eis Hadou Katabasis*) appears in the allegorical work *On the Poems of Orpheus* by a certain Epigenes, whose date is debated: he is cited by Clement of Alexandria (*c.* 200 CE), but he might be earlier than Callimachus[56] and is perhaps identical with a pupil of Socrates; as such, he is among the writers surmised to have written the allegorical explanation of the Derveni theogony.[57] At about the same time, Plato had his Socrates describe how the souls of the non-initiates were punished after death, according to "some clever mythologist, presumably a Sicilian or Italian." This points to an Italian or Sicilian *Descent* poem that was connected with mystery cults; we hear of a certain Orpheus of Camarina (a Sicilian town) as the presumed author of such a poem.[58] Thus, a *Descent* poem (or several such poems) might well be one among the many books attributed to Orpheus that had become accessible to Greek readers during the fifth century BCE and that started a debate about the real authorship of these poems (many Greek intellectuals must have shared Herodotus' feeling that the works ascribed to the mythical poets were in fact later than Homer and Hesiod). In Euripides' *Hippolytus*, Theseus accuses his son of being a hypocrite who ostensibly followed an ascetic doctrine of moral purity as prescribed by the books of Orpheus, but secretly lusted after his stepmother.[59] Half a century later, Plato complained about the "hubbub of books of Orpheus and Musaeus" that were used by itinerant ritual specialists (*Republic* 364c–e). Euripides' contemporary Ion of Chios ascribed many of Orpheus' books to Pythagoras, whereas Epigenes named specific Pythagoreans, such as a certain Cercops whom he credited with having written the *Katabasis*, implicitly correcting Ion because Pythagoras had left no writings; Pythagorean authorship fits perfectly with Plato's "clever Sicilian or Italian."[60]

Orpheus' voice and the words of the tablets

Orpheus, then, was a singer, magician, initiator, and visitor to Hades who was credited, probably by the classical period at the latest, with composing poems that conveyed eschatologically important information. Some of these poems were considered *hieroi logoi* – that is, "sacred stories" – in antiquity, and some were transmitted in books on which cultic activities were centered. It wasn't only Orpheus' eschatological works that might be characterized as *hieroi logoi*, however; Plutarch calls the Orphic story that the cosmos emerged from an egg a *hieros logos* and both this and a plural form of the phrase (*Hieros Logos, Hieroi Logoi*) were titles of cosmogonical and theogonical poems attributed to Orpheus; these included the episodes connected with Dionysus that we examined in Chapter 3 as well as other episodes.[61] Nor have we yet exhausted the possibilities: Lucian portrays Orpheus as having taught astrology to the Greeks through *hieroi logoi*, for instance (*Astr.* 10; cf. *OF* 718–82). That *hieroi logoi* might also include both ritual prescriptions and explanations of ritual prescriptions, is shown by Herodotus' famous comment:

> It is contrary to [Egyptian] religious custom to be buried in a woolen garment or to wear wool in a temple. This agrees with the customs known as Orphic and Bacchic, which are in reality Egyptian and Pythagorean, for anyone initiated into these rites is similarly forbidden to be buried in wool. A *hieros logos* is told about these things. (2.81 = *OF* 650)

Leaving aside the tangled issue of whether Orphic = Pythagorean and Bacchic = Egyptian in this passage or, rather, all of them equal each other,[62] one thing is clear: certain Orphic rituals (and for that matter, Bacchic rituals) were explained by *hieroi logoi*.

A question of definition

A broad variety of topics were covered by *hieroi logoi*, then, including eschatology, cosmology, theogony, astronomy, ritual, and more. What do all of these topics have in common? And more importantly, how does the way in which *hieroi logoi* discuss them differ from the way in which they are discussed in other, "non-hieratic" venues? What, in short, is a *hieros logos*, either according to the ancients or according to those of us who now look at the matter from a distance of more than 2000 years?

For a long time there was a tendency for scholars to answer these questions from the perspective of the culture into which most of them had been born – the predominantly Judeo-Christian culture of the Western world. Accordingly, *hieroi logoi*, "sacred stories" or "sacred texts" (a phrase that the Christian fathers used of their holy scriptures) implicitly comprised authoritative, canonical writings in which the central beliefs and history of a religion were set down.[63] By this reckoning, neither Greek nor Roman "mainstream" religions could be said to have real *hieroi logoi*. Their religions, which focused much more on the correct *performance* of certain acts such as sacrifice ("orthopraxy") than on correct *belief* ("orthodoxy")[64] had neither any need nor any desire to record what a person was supposed to think or feel as he or she practiced its rituals. As for history, most Greek and Roman religions were strongly local in their focus. A given town might have stories about how particular cults or rituals had come into existence, but these were of interest primarily to the inhabitants or to unusually curious travelers such as Pausanias. Such local "histories," moreover, were open to quite a bit of change as the need or the whim arose. The story of Iphigenia, which was associated with the cult of Artemis at Brauron, sometimes ended with Iphigenia's death, sometimes with her miraculous transportation to the land of the Taurians, and sometimes with her transformation into the goddess Hecate. Sometimes, the girl associated with the cult wasn't even called Iphigenia. And even when the basic "plot" of a myth remained stable, poets changed details from version to version; the gods were understood to take particular delight in new compositions sung in their honor. "Canonical" sacred histories therefore were unlikely to exist even at the local level.

Another trait that earlier scholars often ascribed to *hieroi logoi* was that they had been divinely "revealed" to primordial figures such as Moses. In the early nineteenth century, this characteristic encouraged Max Müller to attempt to enlarge the category of "*hieroi logoi*" beyond Jewish and Christian texts. Müller argued that many Eastern texts were just as sacred as the Bible, largely on the basis of their reputation as revealed wisdom.[65]

Müller's endeavor, although admirable in its intention to move *hieroi logoi* out of exclusively Western circles, had the side effect of making virtually any text with any connection to religion "sacred."[66] The fifty volumes of his *The Sacred Books of the East* included law-codes, hymns, ritual statutes, stories about the gods, wisdom literature, etcetera. On a similar tack, classicists could begin to argue that the ancient Greeks had sacred texts, too: the poems of Hesiod and Homer. Not only were these "canonical" insofar as they had reached a stable form by at least the early classical period, but also, as Herodotus famously had said in the passage to which we have already referred:

> Homer and Hesiod are the poets who composed our theogonies
> and described the gods for us, giving them all their appropriate
> titles and offices and powers. (2.53)

Yet, were Homer and Hesiod's poems really "sacred" texts? In actuality,
we learn little from these authors about religious acts or beliefs that were
central to Greek religions: how a sacrifice is to be performed, for example,
or how concepts of *miasma* worked. Nor can the information that they
give us about the gods really be considered canonical: in some passages,
for instance, Hephaestus' wife is said to be one of the Charites, and in
others Aphrodite.[67] And finally, if one reads the Herodotean passage in
its full context, one discovers that the Greeks didn't necessarily assume
that information contained in Homer and Hesiod was actually *Greek*,
anyway:

> In ancient times . . . the Pelasgians offered sacrifices of all kinds,
> and prayed to the gods, but without any distinction of name
> or title – for they had not yet heard of any such thing . . . Long
> afterwards, the names of the gods were brought into Greece
> from Egypt and then the Pelasgians learned them . . . From that
> time on, therefore, the Pelasgians used the names of the gods
> in their sacrifices, and from the Pelasgians the names passed to
> the Greeks. And so it was only the day before yesterday that the
> Greeks came to know the origins and the forms of the various
> gods, and whether or not all of them had always existed; for
> Homer and Hesiod are the poets who composed our theogonies
> and described the gods for us, giving them all their appropriate
> titles and offices and powers.

Herodotus' comments essentially reflect what we have already suggested:
mainstream Greek religion had little interest in creating canonical texts
for itself.

Having determined that earlier scholarly definitions of "sacred text" are
not quite adequate to the task at hand, let us start anew, from what the
ancients themselves said. As we will see, in some respects the ancient definition agrees with that of modern scholars, but in others it does not.

The first thing we might notice is that ancient *hieroi logoi* are often
presented, implicitly or explicitly, as *explanations* for what is done in a
ritual, why a given god is portrayed as he or she is, or why some other
aspect of the world is the way that it is.[68] Thus, for example, Herodotus
(in whose works we find our earliest uses of the phrase) mentions the
following:

1   a *hieros logos* about why puppets used in celebrations of Dionysus have large genitals that can be made to move (2.48.3)

2   a *hieros logos* about why Athenians make their herms ithyphallic – which is recited during the Samothracian mysteries (2.51.4)

3   a *hieros logos* about the festival of lamps at Saïs in Egypt, which explains why it is celebrated and why on a particular night (2.62)

4   a *hieros logos* about why certain groups prohibit the use of wool in burials (2.81.2; the passage was quoted above, p. 177).

Many later uses of the phrase are similar to these (e.g., Paus. 2.13.4 and 8.15.4, Plut. *De Is. et Os.* 353d), but later uses also refer, as we have seen, to extended narratives about such things as the creation of the cosmos and the nature of the Underworld. Even at the risk of slipping back into Müller's too catholic definition, then, it is tempting to begin from the observation that in ancient Greece at least, virtually any narration that explained or described the nature of "divine things" was a candidate for hieratic status.

But the obvious problem is that this definition could embrace many narrations that the Greeks never characterized as *hieros*, as far as we know. Every cult and every ritual had an *aition* – a narration about why certain practices had come into existence – so why weren't all of them called *hieroi*? What further distinguishing factors can we pinpoint?

Supplementarity, secrecy

Albert Henrichs suggested that *marginality* was one of the decisive characteristics, noting that *hieroi logoi* often were associated in antiquity with practices that the Greeks believed had been borrowed from foreign cultures, or with groups such as mystery cults.[69] Drawing particularly on the latter association, Henrichs also noted that most *hieroi logoi* were cloaked in *secrecy*. He suggested that it was partially for reasons of secrecy, for instance, that Ptolemy IV required all Bacchic initiators to seal copies of their *hieroi logoi* when they handed them in to his ministers,[70] and that it was for reasons of secrecy that Herodotus and Pausanias never narrated any of the *hieroi logoi* that they mentioned.

But perhaps this is approaching things the wrong way around. Although Henrichs is certainly correct that *hieroi logoi* are most often associated with what modern scholars categorize as marginal groups and that knowledge of *hieroi logoi* was often restricted, not all marginal or secret groups had *hieroi logoi* – the three qualities are not inextricably linked to one another. It may be more useful, then, to ask what properties *hieroi logoi*, marginality, *and* secrecy had in common that led to their frequent collocation.

And indeed, as a first step in this direction, we need to separate the quality of marginality from that of secrecy. Not all religious groups that kept secrets can be called "marginal": most aspects of the Thesmophoria, for example, were hidden from men, and yet this festival was so firmly entrenched at the center of Greek life that husbands were required to finance their wives' participation in it. The Eleusinian mysteries, too, kept secrets to which only initiates were privy, and yet the mysteries were an enormous point of Athenian pride, central to Athenian identity. Nor did all religious groups that were marginal keep secrets: so far as we know, for instance, the cult of Bendis, which catered largely to Thracians living in Athens, was transparent in its conduct. A reputation for secrecy could marginalize a cult, and, conversely, marginality could give rise to rumors of secret behavior, but the two things do not always go together, in ancient Greece or anywhere else.

As a second step, we can now consider, independently, the connections between marginality and *hieroi logoi* and secrecy and *hieroi logoi*. In many cases, in antiquity, part of what defined a religious group as what we would call "marginal" was the fact that participation in its rituals was optional, in contrast to participation in "mainstream" cults, which were central to civic identity and in which, therefore, virtually all members of a polis took part. Although members of such a group might believe that the rituals they performed were crucial for winning such rewards as a happy afterlife, outsiders viewed what the groups did as *supplemental* – perhaps usefully supplemental, but supplemental nonetheless: outside of the core practices in which everyone was expected to participate.

Marketing the supplemental is a tricky business. On the one hand, the fact that it is supplemental is a boon – it can be presented as offering something "extra" and therefore special. Those who possess supplemental knowledge or skills are privileged. On the other hand, something that is supplemental cannot validate itself by claiming to be part of the tried and true – part of what, in ancient Greek religion, were referred to as *ta patria* and *ta nomima* ("the ancestral practices" and "the customary practices"). One solution to this quandary, which has been used by religious innovators throughout history, is simultaneously to insist that supplemental practices are in reality *old* and yet to concede that they were only recently *rediscovered* – that is, that they had been temporarily lost and forgotten (consider, for example, Joseph's Smith's "rediscovery" of Mormon doctrines, as discussed in Chapter 3). This is where *hieroi logoi* often come in, for *hieroi logoi* typically purport to preserve material of great antiquity. Whereas public cult in Greece looked to an unbroken chain of repeated practice to preserve itself, then, supplemental cult often looked to words – *logoi* – that had originally been uttered by famous poets and then miraculously survived the centuries.

This helps to explain why, from an early period, many Greek *hieroi logoi* circulated in written form. If the information conveyed by a *hieros logos* was to be understood as old, then the gap between that *logos'* original composition and its subsequent rediscovery had to be secured; the possibility of anything having corrupted the *logos'* integrity during the period that it was lost had to be eliminated. Two possible means of accomplishing this were available. Either religious innovators had to be "re-inspired" so as to "re-recite" the poems to which they laid claim, ("reactivating" the original voice behind the *hieros logos*, to borrow a phrase Henrichs uses to describe chresmologues reading from oracle collections)[71] and thus setting in motion a new string of oral performances; or physical documents on which those poems had been recorded at the time of their original performance had to be produced.

Both methods were probably used by the *orpheotelestai*. We know that some people whom we might call *orpheotelestai* also offered their services as *manteis*, a profession that often attracted those with a talent for prophetic inspiration.[72] Why shouldn't one or more of these *manteis* become inspired, as well, with long-forgotten Orphic *hieroi logoi*? But the late archaic and classical periods were also a time when re-discovered documents exerted a certain fascination: chresmologues pored over collections of oracles allegedly compiled by legendary prophets such as Bacis and Musaeus, for example.[73] Orphic writings such as those that Euripides' Theseus describes as promoting doctrines of purity may similarly have been copied from a document ascribed to the hand of Musaeus, Orpheus' amanuensis.

Having written copies of *hieroi logoi* offered another advantage as well. In mainstream civic cult, where *ta patria* and *ta nomima* were the watchwords of authenticity, people grew up witnessing the rituals that they would someday perform themselves. Long observation by relatively stable audiences guaranteed preservation. Similarly, the *aitia* associated with most mainstream cults were freely repeated; every Athenian girl surely knew the story of Erigone and the reason for the rituals held in her honor long before she reached an age where she performed them herself.[74] The ritual practices and stories contained in *hieroi logoi*, in contrast, were known to a relatively small group – the initiates of a mystery cult or even, as in the case of the Andanian mysteries, the members of a single family who served as its priests.[75] Moreover, many members of such groups joined them only in adulthood. Under such circumstances, preservation of cultic lore – much less preservation of the *ipsissima verba* of the poet who had conveyed it and whose mythic status as an inspired poet validated it – could best be guaranteed through writing. The legend of how an Argive man named Epiteles had recovered the sacred writings of the Andanian mysteries of the Great Goddesses is a perfect example:

a dream told him where to dig and in that spot he discovered a bronze urn filled with inscribed sheets of tin, supposedly buried three centuries earlier. The writings on tin were subsequently copied into "books" (*biblia*) by the priestly family that ran the mysteries and were declared "valid for all time to come" (Paus. 4.26.7–27.5).[76]

To sum up thus far: the "marginality" of groups associated with many *hieroi logoi* can better be understood as "supplementarity" – that is, these groups offered additional benefits that mainstream cults did not. To authenticate and validate those benefits, as well as to preserve their traditions, such groups, which were not embedded in *ta patria* of mainstream cult, looked instead to *hieroi logoi*.[77]

Let us turn to the second characteristic that Henrich noted was often associated with *hieroi logoi*: secrecy. One of the most common reasons that religious groups invoke secrecy is the necessity of preventing information from falling into the hands of people who might intentionally or unintentionally use it improperly – people who are uninitiated, who are the wrong gender, or who are members of the wrong family, for example. Whatever was conveyed through secret *hieroi logoi*, then, is likely to have been information that could be *used* in some fashion – these were not simply stories told for the sake of the telling alone. Obviously, ritual instructions fit this definition, but so does a cosmogony, for example, if the cosmogony justifies a ritual or enhances its effect.[78]

These observations suggest another possible characteristic of *hieroi logoi*, then: broadly speaking, *hieroi logoi* had practical applications – and, if the rituals of a particular group needed to be kept secret, then it is only logical that the *hieroi logoi* that accompanied them would have had to be kept secret as well. Of course, secrecy within such groups inevitably took on another function as well, which was usually unacknowledged (perhaps even unrecognized) by its members: shared secrecy bound the group together more firmly. If, as we noted above, supplemental religious groups marketed themselves by promising something "extra," then claims of secrecy and the insider/outsider dynamic that such claims promoted were valuable tools.

One more topic needs further consideration before we move on to the specifics of the Gold Tablets and their possible status as *hieroi logoi*: the relationship between *hieroi logoi*, as we have just defined them, and other *logoi* connected with religion – the latter category including, for instance, etiological myths that were widely known.[79] Often, the two categories overlapped. For example, everyone knew the story of Hades' kidnapping of Persephone and Demeter's search for her daughter; it was the subject of several famous hymns in antiquity, including what we now call the Homeric *Hymn to Demeter*, and was referred to in other publicly performed texts such as Euripides' *Helen*.[80]

And yet, we know that there were also versions of this myth, associated with the Eleusinian Mysteries, whose details were not available to the general public. These versions were considered *hieroi logoi* and in some cases even attributed to Orpheus.[81] Similarly, we know that authors such as Pindar and Callimachus alluded to at least portions of the story of Dionysus that we have been calling "Orphic" in this book – but these versions did not reveal all the details that were available to initiates.[82]

There seems to have been a two-tiered system, in other words. There were versions of certain stories that were *not* kept secret and that were *not* limited to supplemental groups (i.e., they were not what we would include under the term *hieroi logoi*) and then there were versions of those same stories that were kept secret and were kept limited – stories that we would define as *hieroi logoi*. In some cases, such as the story of Demeter and Persephone, the un-hieratic *logos* surely developed first and the *hieros logos* later, when the supplemental cult developed. In other cases, such as the story of Dionysus, it is likely that the *hieros logos* developed first (under the direction of the *bricoleurs*, who also developed the cult itself). Enough of the story's basic plot soon became known, however, to make non-hieratic versions available. Under either scenario, the additional material provided in the hieratic versions of these stories is what enabled those who knew them to reap the benefits of the cults with which they were associated. Again, supplementarity is the key concept here; the *hieroi logoi* offered not something utterly *different* from the stories available to everyone; rather, they offered something *extra*.[83]

What sort of supplemental information are the Orphic *hieroi logoi* likely to have provided? Probably, as some scholars have suggested, those that narrated the story of Dionysus' birth, death, and rebirth included, for example, details about which particular toys the Titans had used to lure Dionysus away from his guardians – details that we now find in the Gûrob Papyrus, embedded in what look like the *legomena* of a ritual.[84] We can make further guesses, as well: eschatologically-oriented *hieroi logoi* (including those called *Katabasis* and *The Lyre*), probably included specific instructions about where to go and what to do in the Underworld – some of which we now find embedded in some of our tablets. Other Orphic *hieroi logoi* probably comprised ritual prescriptions for initiation ceremonies, perhaps including *legomena* that subsequently would be repeated after death ("A kid, I fell into milk"; "I come pure from the pure") and instructions as to how one should be buried ("no wool"). The statement that Aeschines read aloud from a book when his mother performed private initiations, perhaps into a cult of Sabazios/Dionysus ("I escaped from evil, I found the better," Dem. 18.259), is probably an example of one *legomenon* taken from a *hieros logos*.[85]

By these standards, the Gold Tablets are not themselves *hieroi logoi* any more than is the Gûrob Papyrus; rather, both the tablets and the papyrus preserve portions of *hieroi logoi*. But if we move outside of this relatively strict definition of *hieros logos*, there is one more quality of some of the tablets – the proxy type tablets, as we called them in Chapter 4 – that may mark them as *hieroi* in quite a different sense. Namely, they "speak" the *logoi* that are inscribed upon them and in doing so, accomplish acts of religious significance, winning the initiates who possess them admission to desirable parts of the Underworld.

Interestingly, here we have passed from what Sam Gill has called the "informative" function of texts into a "performative" function.[86] The first category, into which most sacred texts fall, focuses on explaining things, describing things, and passing on instructions about how to do things. The second focuses on causing things to happen by virtue of the text's very existence; as has often been noted, many amulets and other forms of "magical" spells fall under this rubric. The Orphic *hieroi logoi* – those poems that we now possess only in fragments – were by and large informative, even if they incorporated performative material (e.g., *makarismoi* and other pronouncements that would been made during initiation or funerary rituals). The mnemonic type of Gold Tablets were also informative, insofar as they reminded the initiates of what the *hieroi logoi* had told them to do and say in the Underworld – although they, too, may have incorporated parts of formulaic *makarismoi* that had been pronounced while the initiate was alive or that would be pronounced (a second time?) after the initiate was dead. The proxy-type tablets, in contrast, do not seem to look back, at least in any direct manner, to an informative text. Instead, by greeting Persephone or pronouncing the initiate's name, they instantly effect the desired change: like a key, they open the Underworld doors through which the initiate wishes to pass.

If the formulation that we have just offered is correct, then two things follow. First, any secure categorization of *hieroi logoi* looks less and less likely. Even if we can define with some satisfaction what the ancients meant by that term, and even if we can, as historians of religion, create a heuristically useful series of characteristics for what *we* mean when we say "sacred texts," we have to concede that the phenomenon, broadly construed, played a greater variety of roles than either definition admits. Secondly, and more importantly, we have to concede that the types of roles that sacred words played were very fluid. The technology of writing something that was eschatologically important on a small sheet of gold was probably used first to produce what we have been calling the mnemonic tablets, but was adapted for a use that, to us at least, looks quite different in its approach and in some of its underlying assumptions – about the

state of the disembodied soul, for example. To take another, more hypothetical example, we also might consider to what degree the identity of the
person doing the writing qualified a tablet (or any other physical text) as
hieros. We say "hypothetical" because our information on this topic is very
sparse. We assume that the wandering *manteis* and *agyrtai*, whom Plato
credits both with the performance of individual mystery initiations and
with the creation of curse tablets, and whom we typically identify with
orpheotelestai, given that they validate their practices through the books
of Orpheus and Musaeus,[87] were responsible for creating most of the
physical tablets – that is, for inscribing upon the sheet of gold the words
the initiate would need after death. But what if some of the simpler, proxy-
type tablets were created by the initiates themselves, either for themselves
or for other members of their family? Is the ritualized environment in
which we presume that the *orpheotelestēs* created the tablet crucial to the
tablet's hieratic status or not?

Such questions must remain open – but in any case, their value probably lies more in their posing than in any answers we might offer; the
openness of their answers underscores again the provisional, fluid nature
of any definition or model into which we might try to fit a given religious
practice or belief. This is all the more the case, as we have emphasized
several times in this book, in a situation where the practices and beliefs
are crafted, and then periodically recrafted as they spread throughout the
Greek world, by individuals who had particular, conscious aims in mind –
and who worked under limits imposed by the circumstances of marketing
the supplemental.

But as we close this discussion, and this book, it would be good to think
one last time about Orpheus as we portrayed him at the start of this
chapter: somewhat foreign to Greek eyes, but by no means abnormal
or aberrant; firmly entrenched in Greek heroic myth and yet set apart
from other heroes by virtue of his musical accomplishments; like other
heroes a survivor of *katabasis* – but unlike them, responsible for having
set down the knowledge he attained in the Underworld for the benefit of
those who came later. Orpheus, in short, is an extraordinarily apt figure to
stand behind not only the new cult and myth that entered Greece at some
time during the late archaic period, but behind the concept of *hieros logos*,
which was itself novel and, as we have seen, somewhat exotic to Greek
eyes. Homer would surely have been too staid a figure onto which to graft
these new ideas; Hesiod, as least as we glimpse him through what little
remains of his poetry, would have been too circumspect. The Orpheus
whom our *bricoleurs* inherited was a remarkably plastic *bricolage* himself,
changing, as the circumstances demanded, from a singer of heroic poetry
to a singer for the dead, from a traveler to Colchis to a traveler to Hades.

Appendix 1

ORPHISM IN THE TWENTY-FIRST CENTURY

Fritz Graf

As we saw in the introductory History of Scholarship, during the twentieth century scholars were oscillating between an understanding of Orphism as an almost church-like religious system, a sect in the modern sense of the word (scholars such as Macchioro or even, less extremely, Guthrie),[1] and the rejection of any importance that Orpheus and Orphism had on Greek religion (most prominently expressed by Wilamowitz). This constellation mirrored the way scholarship on mystery cults had been oscillating between understanding them as the most important feature of Greek religion (Creuzer 1812) and a much more modest reading that saw them as just one small part of it (Lobeck 1828). Like our ancestors in the early twentieth century, most contemporary scholars seem again to lean toward a moderate definition that ascribes some importance to Orphic texts and religious specialists connected with them, against the minimalist approach of Linforth and Zuntz, who rejected any religious phenomenon that could be called Orphic. But by now the textual foundation for any position has become much better: spectacular finds such as the Derveni Papyrus and the growing number of gold tablets have helped, as has the steady increase in texts and interpretations of Hellenistic poetry and mythography that show a presence and perception of Orphic texts already among the scholar-poets of the third century BCE; Plato's interest in Orpheus no longer seems isolated and unusual. We have also learned from the mistakes of earlier scholars. Unlike them, even among contemporary maximalists, no one talks about "Orphic religion" or claims that early Christianity depended for its soteriology on Orphism or "Orphic mysteries." To derive Christianity directly from pagan mystery cults has been revealed as an ideological stance; when religions are understood as systems, the Bacchic mysteries are a sub-system among many others, with Orpheus "the singer, magician, initiator and visitor to Hades" (above, p. 177) belonging to more than one of them.[2]

Thus, given Orpheus' multifaceted persona, there is no question of a uniform Orphism in whatever sense; perhaps it is better – avoiding the ugly modernism and returning to Greek – to say that there is no question of a uniform and free-standing phenomenon covered by the term *Orphika*, "things that belong to Orpheus," a term as old as Herodotus. In what follows, I want to understand exactly what the term covered. Since the Neoplatonic perception of Orpheus and the things connected with him was crucial for Orpheus' reception in later thinking, as both the success of Comparetti and the excesses of Macchioro show, it makes sense to start with the late antique Neoplatonists, to work backwards in time from them. This does not imply that the early twentieth-century scholars were utterly dependent on the late antique Neoplatonists: the Florentine Neoplatonists had an important role in this chain of transmission, but scholars rarely acknowledged their debts to Ficino and his colleagues, and more modern research is still needed.[3]

I

To me, the key figure in the Neoplatonic shaping of *Orphika* is Proclus, the most prolific and, in the centuries to come, the most influential head of the Athenian Academy; he was born in 412 and presided over the Academy from 432 to his death in 485. The last head of the Academy, Damascius, two generations removed from Proclus, is of some importance as well; born in 485, he led the School from about 515 to the closing of the Academy in 529 and died after 538. In a chance remark, Proclus refers to the seminars (*synousiai*) on Orpheus by his teacher Syrianus, in which Syrianus gave an allegorical reading of the Orphic theogony that aligned it with the way he was understanding Plato (*In Platonis Timaeum*, vol. 1 p. 314): the passage explains the myth of Zeus swallowing Phanes as designating him as the sole and unique creator god, and Proclus remarks with some satisfaction that "Plato too has these notions about Greatest Zeus," as his *Kratylos* shows. Proclus' student Marinus recalls that he too read Orpheus with his teacher, but he also recalls that Proclus told him that he never studied Orpheus' poems with Syranius, but read his teacher's commentaries (*hypomnēmata*) on them, because Syrianus died before he could organize such a seminar (Marinus, *Life of Proclus* 26). Whatever happened, Orpheus was an important topic of study, and already Syrianus had established the methodology used by Proclus; we do not know enough about his teacher Plutarch, the founder of the last line of Academic philosophers, to tell whether he had already established the methodology, but it seems likely.

The poems they read were theogonies, *genealogiai* (Proclus, *In Timaeum*, vol. 3 p. 160) or *theogoniai* (ibid., vol. 4 p. 21); Damascius even gives us the description of "Rhapsodic Theogonies" that in other sources is explained as "Theogony in Twenty-four Rhapsodies," namely one complex theogonical poem that combines the length of the *Iliad* and the *Odyssey*; only Nonnus' poem on Dionysus in forty-eight books, written presumably during Proclus' life-time, would exceed this. In these theogonies, Dionysus' birth, death, and rebirth played an important role, as we saw (above pp. 73–8), but as the remark on Zeus swallowing Phanes shows, it is far from being the only theogonical incident.

Two assumptions underlie the interpretative methodology of Syrianus and his successors. One is that Orpheus' poetry has a meaning that is hidden under the sometimes surprising or shocking narrative surface, such as Zeus swallowing another god, Phanes; this is at least as old as the fifth-century BCE commentary on a theogony of Orpheus preserved in the Derveni Papyrus, and it is in a way the prime reason for allegorizing myths. The corollary is that Orpheus was "really" a philosopher of deep and stunning wisdom, a true *theologos* and writer of *theologia*, as Proclus quite often writes, someone whose work talked about the gods and who had true knowledge about them. His philosophy was seminal for the philosophy of these Neoplatonists, on a par with the Chaldaean Oracles, another work of theological poetry. But Orpheus was not alone: Syrianus and his followers refer to *Orphikoi*, men connected with Orpheus. In the texts we have, they never explain who these *Orphikoi* were and when they were thought to be living; all we hear is that they clad their philosophical wisdom in theogonical poetry, and thus must have been near-contemporaries of Orpheus. If one relies on language, it is obvious that the *Orphikoi* were to Orpheus what the *Platonikoi* were to Plato, a group of followers who thought of themselves as being part of a group and who shared the philosophical system and the way of expressing it (in their case not in discursive prose but in theogonical poetry). But the *Platonikoi* were much better known, since they were much more recent: they were philosophers such as Albinus and Numenius (whom we call Middle Platonists), or Plotinus and his students Porphyry and Iamblichus (to us the Neoplatonists). There is however a much longer chain of tradition (*paradosis*): the Middle Platonists hark back to Plato, and between Orpheus and Plato there were Pythagoras and the Pythagoreans who in turn followed Orphic concepts (Syrianus, *On Aristotle's Metaphysics* 11.35, on Empedocles); and Plato relied on them. In Proclus' words:

Whatever the Greeks thought about the gods (*theologia*) derives entirely from Orpheus and his initiation (*mystagōgia*): first Pythagoras learned from Aglaophamus about the mysteries of the gods, then Plato received perfect knowledge of these things through the Pythagorean and Orphic writings. (*In Timaeum*, vol. 1 p. 25)

This is why the interpretation of a verse by Orpheus can be checked against Plato.

In other words: the late Neoplatonists imagined a school that one could call Orphism, and they did so by projecting their own philosophical habits and their own social structures into their foundational past: this is why they needed not just a founder, Orpheus, but a group of followers, *Orphikoi*; an anonymous sixth-century "Introduction to Platonic Philosophy" – a set of lectures for young students – even constructs a first philosophical school, "the poets' school, whose heads were Orpheus, Homer, Musaeus, and Hesiod," followed by the Milesian ("the Ionic") and the Pythagorean schools, then the Platonists, Stoics, Epicureans, Peripatetics, and New Academy. The late Neoplatonists thus went back to the very roots of Greek philosophy, and in doing so they read and interpreted the written works of Orpheus and the Orphics, *ta Orphika grammata* (Proclus, *Theologia Platonica*, vol. 1 p. 26) in the same way they read and commented on Plato's written dialogues, and the *Chaldean Oracles*. After Syrianus' death, Proclus studied his commentaries (*hypomnēmata*) on Orpheus, as he studied Porphyry's and Iamblichus' interpretations of the *Oracles*. He would himself have written a commentary on Orpheus' poems if a dream had not warned him off several times; instead, he simply added copious marginal notes to his teacher's commentaries. Compared to the key role of texts, ritual was irrelevant, despite Orpheus' earlier fame as initiator into mystery cults. When Proclus talks about Orpheus' "introduction to the mysteries," *mystagōgia*, he uses the ritualistic term figuratively, and he also talks about the *mystagōgia* of Pythagoras, Parmenides, or Plato: the Platonic tradition had a long history of using mystery terminology figuratively, and the word family connected with *mystagōgos* was extremely popular among late antique and Byzantine Christian writers. Only his student and biographer Marinus tells us that Proclus also made frequent use of "Orphic and Chaldaean purification rites" – whatever they were.[4]

Some elements of this reconstructed system are older than Syrianus and his followers. *Orphikoi* as cosmological poets appear already in Iamblichus and in a two uncertain authors who might be later:[5] at least the notion of a group of followers of Orpheus goes back to the earlier Neoplatonists. In a very different form, the idea was already around in the late fifth and early fourth centuries, when the Euripidean Theseus accuses his son Hippolytus of leading an ascetic life informed by Orpheus' books, and when Plato talks about "the Orphic life-style" and describes "seers and mendicant priests" who sell their rituals in which they use the books of Orpheus and Musaios. But these men are no Orphics in the sense of an organized body, a philosophical or religious sect, they are what later sometimes are called *orpheotelestai*, ritual entrepreneurs who sold mystery initiations, purification rites, and binding spells and which we discussed in Chapter 5.

The notion that Orpheus' poems were encrypted philosophical texts is as old, but again in a different sense. We find the first extensive decoding of a theogony of Orpheus in the Derveni Papyrus; its author is an unknown philosopher who must have been a contemporary of Socrates or Plato. In the short theogonical poem that he explains, he finds a physical theory that is close to the materialist views of Anaxagoras that foreshadow atomism. For this interpreter, then, Orpheus was not writing about theology and metaphysics but about physics; but like his contemporaries, he must have understood Orpheus as the oldest poet, in a succession that passes through Mousaios (his disciple) to Hesiod and Homer.

It needed Platonism to move Orpheus into another, less wordly direction. Although Plato himself referred to Orpheus, the idea that he was heavily dependent on him is not attested before the Neoplatonists; Plutarch could still claim that Plato made fun of Orpheus' ideas. Almost a century later, the Christian writer Clement of Alexandria, himself a Platonist of sorts, claimed that Plato got his idea of the immortal soul from Pythagoras, who in turn learned about it in Egypt; Orpheus was the main influence on Heraclitus, not on Plato (*Strom.* 6.2.27.1–3). At about the time of Plotinus, in the third century CE, in the introductory chapter of his history of Greek philosophers, Diogenes Laertius rejects the idea of some scholars that Orpheus was a philosopher, because he did not think that Orpheus described the gods in a philosophical way. Obviously, Diogenes did not think he could read divine actions in Orpheus' poems as encrypted philosophy, and he certainly would not have claimed that the singer had influence on Plato's philosophy – unlike the Pythagoreans who, after all, were still very active in Plato's time.

II

Thus, Orphism in the sense of a coherent theological system entertained by a group of thinkers around Orpheus, the *theologos*, is late. But there is another, implicit, sense that expresses itself in several ways that are much earlier than the Neoplatonists. We can see this in the reference to *Orphikoi* as authors of texts (in Apollodorus of Athens in mid-Hellenistic times),[6] in the description of religious specialists as *orpheotelestai*, "ritual specialists following Orpheus" (as early as Theophrastus, Aristotle's student), and in Plato's idea that there were *bioi Orphikoi,* a way of living an especially pure life inspired by Orpheus (*Laws* 6.782c). There is also the caricature of the Euripidean Hippolytus as a dubious Bacchic ascetic, whose lord is Orpheus (*Hipp.* 953), and Herodotus' understanding that certain *Bakchika* and *Orphika*, "things Dionysiac and Orphic," had to do with specific sepulchral rites (that is, with afterlife beliefs) and were "in reality Egyptian and Pythagorean," imported by the traveler Pythagoras from Egypt (2.81). This "Orphism" is more diffuse, it is more based on rituals than on theology, but it nevertheless is also reflected in a common myth, the result of mythical bricolage in the late sixth century.

The importance of texts thought to have been written by Orpheus – an attribution incidentally questioned in the age of the sophists that had a clearer idea of the development of Greek literature, as we saw above (p. 142) – is not the only element common to the phenomena I have just listed. There is the use of such texts for rituals of purification and initiation, some of which promised special bliss in the afterlife; there is also a closeness to the life style of the extreme Pythagorean ascetics, a close connection with the Dionysus of the mystery cults that were said to have been introduced by Orpheus, and a prevalence of theogonical mythology including the myth of two multiple births – and thus at least one violent death – of the mystery god Dionysus. All of this does not add up to a religious system in the sense the Neoplatonists reconstructed, even less to a religious movement or sect, as some modern scholars have suggested. The main agents were mostly itinerant *orpheotelestai* who sold all sorts of rituals. Some of them – such as the author of the Derveni text – also offered an allegorical interpretation of Orpheus' text. Another such allegorist is the anonymous "wise man" who explained to Socrates the story (told by an "ingenious teller of myths, perhaps a Sicilian or South Italian") of the water-carriers in Hades (Plato, *Gorgias* 493a); Sicily and Southern Italy might point to Plato's idea, adopted from Ion of Chios or his fellow student Epigenes, that some Italian Pythagoreans wrote religious poems under the name of Orpheus. The customers of these specialists were affluent members of the elite, some at least sophisticated enough to appreciate a philosophical interpretation of such a text and take it along to the grave. It is impossible to tell whether the *Orphikoi* of Philodemus, the authors of such texts, were identical with some of the itinerant specialists. Given the fluidity of the texts and their connection with local cults – see especially the two texts from Pherae – such an identity is plausible, but not always necessary: the Derveni author is clearly not the person who wrote the short, hymn-like theogony he used in his rites and of which he offers an interpretation. Nor do we know who the early bricoleurs were who shaped the mythical narration of Dionysus. Thus, even in the fifth and fourth centuries, "Things Orphic" had clear contours and were much more than the weird and incoherent phenomena contemporary minimalists claim them to be.

We talked about how this bricolage happened and what its elements were (see above, pp. 90–3); there is no need to return to it, except to stress that the key elements of the story we hear about in the Neoplatonic sources are already attested in Euphorion (early third century) and have been plausibly postulated in an allusion found in a lost writing of Plato's student Xenokrates and, more than a century earlier, in a famous fragment of Pindar. They help us to understand what is going on in the gold tablets, as, for example, the analysis of the Pelinna tablets demonstrated. The radical but isolated skepticism towards the early existence of this mythology, expressed by Radcliffe Edmonds, seems unjustified; Alberto Bernabé and Albert Henrichs have refuted Edmonds's arguments, as have we in this book. Besides a tendency to discredit or disregard early evidence, these objections are problematic for two basic reasons: they are based on an anachronistic assumption that Macchioro's Christianocentric projection of original sin into the myth of anthropogony is still valid, and they do away with a context, reconstructed from sometimes late evidence, in which the avowedly fragmentary evidence makes sense, leaving behind not much more than isolated fragments. Macchioro's projection was the result of the ideological trench wars of the late nineteenth and early twentieth centuries, and no scholar we know would side with this position nowadays; nor does Luc Brisson's demonstration that Olympiodorus uses alchemical terminology unravel the entire myth; it only impacts one detail (Brisson 1992). The reconstruction, as the history of scholarship has shown, was made necessary by new texts, namely the gold leaves from Thurii, situated by Comparetti in a reconstructed context that still is ours. Its correctness is proven by the fact that more recently found texts such as the tablets from Hipponion, Pelinna, and Pherae make coherent sense only against the background of this reconstruction. The deeper methodological question is whether scholars prefer to work with reconstructed contexts to explain the findings, or whether they feel comfortable with "a heap of broken images." Conscientious reconstruction in order to find an explanatory context for data is, in our view, a fundamental task of historical scholarship when confronted with fragments; to refuse this task runs the risk of reducing history to antiquarian data collection.

From a different set of arguments, Renate Schlesier does not accept any connection of the gold tablets with Orpheus: "neither the name of Orpheus nor the adjective *orphikos* appear on the tablets."[7] This position overlooks the relative uniformity of the texts over space and time, which argues for (a) people who spread ideas and practices and (b) texts that preserved the tradition. Itinerant specialists and texts ascribed to Orpheus are the most economical hypothesis for accounting for these characteristics. The fluidity of the texts is exactly what one would expect in an environment where adaptation to local markets was as important as the main selling point, a great traditional poet as legitimator of the textual truth. But there is no reason to expect Orpheus' name on the tablets. The deceased bearers are no *Orphikoi* – they have no need to be *Orphikoi*, after all. Rather, the deceased are *bacchoi* or *bebaccheumenoi*. It was not the identity of the poet but the religious identity of the deceased that was relevant for post-mortem status; and this religious identity is often enough expressed, from the simple *mystēs* to the much more concrete *bacchos*, not to mention the divinities (mainly Dionysus, Persephone, and Plutus, but also Demeter and Meter) whom the deceased expected to be her or his protector.

Appendix 2

THE TABLETS FROM PHERAE

Sarah Iles Johnston

The two tablets from Pherae (nos. 27 and 28) present some remarkable details that depart from our other examples. At the time of this book's first edition in 2007, we were able to include only a text and translation of no. 28; here I further discuss its significance and its relationship to no. 27.[1] Together, the two tablets suggest that a variation of the Bacchic mysteries that was marked by strong ties to Demeter and Persephone and to a goddess who was called, among other things, "the Mountain Mother," developed in the region of Pherae at some time prior to the beginning of the third century BCE. The promulgators of this cult combined Bacchic mysteries as they were known throughout Greece with aspects of Demeter's mysteries, divinities from local cult, and ideas taken from Orphic poems.

These two tablets are similar to the "purity" type of tablets insofar as the soul is expected to declare its qualifications in order to be admitted to the desirable part of the Underworld (called "holy meadows" in no. 27 and identified as a *"thiasos* of initiates" in no. 28).[2] We find similar statements about the soul's membership in groups of the elite on several other tablets as well (1.15–16, 2.11, 3.6, 6.7, 7.7, 26a.7). No. 3's mention of "holy meadows and groves of Persephone" is particularly close to no. 27's "holy meadows"; and no. 1's mention that the soul will join "other glorious initiates (*mystai*) and *bacchoi"* is close to no. 28's mention of a *thiasos* of initiates (*mystōn*); the word *mystēs* is also found on several of the very short tablets (20, 21, 22, 31).[3] Thus, nos. 27 and 28 share not only a technology with other gold tablets found throughout the Greek world, but also vocabulary and a general spirit.

Yet they depart in certain ways as well. Let us start with no. 27, and the two passwords (*symbola*) that the soul is supposed to pronounce to someone in the Underworld. The first password, *"Andrikepaidothyrson,"* which I translated in Chapter 1 as "Man-and-child-thyrsus," refers to some aspect of Dionysus, as the "thyrsus" part makes clear. Beyond this we cannot go with certainty.[4]

But more can be said about the second password, "Brimo." This name – which makes its first appearance in any Greek text on this very tablet – belonged to a goddess who was at home in the area around Lake Boebeis in the region of Pherae: Propertius mentions "Brimo, resting by Lake Boebeis, a virgin goddess by Mercury's side," and one of the epithets that Lycophron gives Brimo is "goddess of Pherae."[5] A fuller version of the story to which Propertius alludes is passed down by the lexicographical tradition and by the scholiast to Lycophron's *Alexandra*:[6] Hermes became enamored of the goddess and attempted to rape her. She reacted to this by screaming at him so terribly that he was frightened away; it was for this reason that she received the name Brimo (supposedly from the verb "ene*brim*aomai," the lexicographers and scholiast add, which means to bellow with anger or indignation).

The story assumes that another goddess acquired "Brimo" as a new, additional name – and the narrators declare that this goddess was Persephone. This identification is also expressed in Cicero's allusion to the story: "[Mercury] is said to be in a state of constant sexual arousal, inspired by the sight of Proserpina." The lexicographers go on to add that Hecate could also be called Brimo.[7] This triple equation is reflected by the few earlier authors who mention Brimo – sometimes they use the name to refer to Persephone, and at other times to refer to Hecate in her Underworld role. Indeed, Apollonius of Rhodes, who uses the name twice, identifies Brimo as the "queen of the dead," i.e., Persephone, in the first case, and as Hecate in the second. Lycophron first calls the goddess "Obrimo"[8] and equates her with "Kore who dwells below the earth," and then calls her Brimo and equates her with "the triple-formed daughter of Perses," i.e., Hecate.[9]

But Brimo enters Greek literature rather late – in fact, Apollonius, who wrote half a century after the creation of tablet no. 27, marks her literary debut.[10] It may be that, coming tardily into broader Greek awareness, the identity of this goddess was malleable enough to be blended as needed with Hecate as well as with Persephone – who, after all, had herself already begun to be identified with Hecate by the fifth century.[11] In magical spells of later antiquity, where the name Brimo appears more often than it did in earlier literary passages, it is either included in groups of words that are meant to be spoken in the same way as "Brimo" is in tablet no. 27 (that is, as part of a password to prove the speaker's possession of secret knowledge and thus to win the cooperation of the gods) or is one of many epithets for a goddess who has connections with the Underworld but who is hard to pin down to a single identity.[12] "Orpheus," however, in his late antique *Argonautica*, clearly uses "Brimo" as a name for the mother of Dionysus:

Then, [I sang of] the offspring of powerful Brimo, and the destructive acts of the Giants, who spilled the baneful seed of their race from the heavens, begetting the men of old, from which point on, the race [of mortals] was always on the earth. (17–20)

I then sang of the genesis and division of the younger ones among the blessed [gods], of Brimo and Bacchus, and of the destructive acts of the Giants, and of the many-tribed race of feeble mortals. (428–31)

In two other, late instances, "Brimo" is understood to refer to Demeter. First, Clement of Alexandria shifts the story of attempted rape and angry response from Persephone and Hermes onto Deo (Demeter) and Zeus; Arnobius and Eusebius repeat that story.[13] This evokes old tales according to which Demeter became angry after Poseidon raped her, and as a result assumed either the epithet "Erinys," ("Angry") or the epithet "Black."[14] These stories (one version of which circulated already in early epic poetry) may have encouraged the migration of a tale originally told about an angry Persephone on to Demeter. Tellingly, in Clement's story of Demeter and Zeus, the attempted rape succeeds, as it does in the old stories of Demeter and Poseidon, but in the story of Persephone and Hermes, the rape is averted.

Second, the church father Hippolytus claims that at the high point of the Eleusinian Mysteries, the hierophant shouted "Lady Brimo has given birth to a son, Brimos." This has been understood by most modern scholars to refer to Demeter and a son whom she had borne – a favorite scholarly conjecture for the identity of this son is Plutus ("Wealth"),[15] whom Hesiod tells us was Demeter's son by Iasion and whom, according to the Homeric *Hymn to Demeter*, Demeter and Persephone send to the doorsteps of those who have been initiated into their mysteries.[16]

But there is a problem here. Hippolytus understands "Brimo" and "Brimos" to be synonyms for "strong" (*ischura* and *ischuros*) and therefore explains the passage as meaning "a strong mother has given birth to a strong child." Some lexicographers similarly offer either *ischuros* or *obrimos* (a poetic variation of "*brimos*," meaning "strong") as synonyms. But when "*brim-*" words mean "strong," the connotation is always one of overwhelming, and sometimes terrifying, strength: *brimazō* means to bellow like a bull or roar like a lion; *brimaomai* and *embrimaomai* mean to snort with anger or speak out in indignation. A passage from the Homeric *Hymns* that uses the noun *brimē* to describe the birth of Athena from Zeus' head captures the sense of this word family well:[17]

197

All the immortals watched in awe, as before aegis-bearing Zeus she sprang quickly down from his immortal head with a brandish of her sharp javelin. A fearsome tremor went through great Olympus from the power (*brimē*) of the grey-eyed goddess, the earth resounded terribly all around, and the sea heaved in a confusion of swirling waves. (Hom. *Hymn* 28, M. L. West's translation, slightly modified)

And Brimo herself can be overwhelming, too: in one of Apollonius' passages the nymphs draw back in fear at her arrival, and Lucian portrays her as bellowing (*ebrimēsato*) alongside Cerberus in the Underworld.[18] A name formed on the *brim-* root, then, is not one that we would naturally associate with so pleasant a god as Wealth, whom a peaceful, placated Demeter offers to initiates as a reward.

We cannot be sure how much of what Hippolytus tells us is accurate: he has taken his information from a Gnostic tract that in turn focuses on an older pagan commentary on a hymn to Attis.[19] The phrase "Lady Brimo has given birth to a son, Brimos" may not come from the Eleusinian Mysteries at all, then, in spite of what Hippolytus said – and if it does come from an Eleusinian context, it may not refer to Demeter and her child, as modern scholars have assumed. If we look for a god for whom "Brimos" is an appropriate epithet, Dionysus in fact presents himself as a highly suitable candidate: he was famous for manifesting himself in overwhelming and sometimes terrifying ways, for which he received epithets such as Bromios (cf. *bromos,* a loud and furious noise).[20] If we assign "Brimos" to Dionysus and "Brimo" to the goddess with whom the name was most often associated, Persephone, we have "Lady Persephone has given birth to a son, Dionysus" – in other words, a reference to the myth on which Chapter 3 of this book focused, which underpinned the Bacchic mysteries.

How might this make its way into Hippolytus' discussion of the Eleusinian Mysteries? It is possible that Hippolytus confused information about the Eleusinian Mysteries with information about the Lesser Mysteries, which were performed in the Athenian suburb of Agrai about seven months before the Eleusinian Mysteries and which were linked with the Eleusinian Mysteries in ancient perception and practice. At some point during the classical period the Lesser Mysteries came to be thought of as a preparatory stage for the Eleusinian Mysteries, during which the future initiate was purified.[21] The late antique grammarian Stephanus of Byzantium tells us that the Lesser Mysteries included "reenactments of things concerning Dionysus," and the historian Duris (fourth to third century BCE) spoke of the "goddess Demeter coming to attend *her daughter's* mysteries" in Agrai. The scholiast to Aristophanes' *Plutus* states that the

Eleusinian Mysteries belonged to Demeter and the Lesser Mysteries to Persephone.[22] A declaration about Persephone giving birth to Dionysus would be perfectly at home under such circumstances.[23]

Such a pronouncement need not necessarily go back to the earliest stages of the Lesser Mysteries; if I am right that Brimo entered broader Greek awareness relatively late, the pronouncement (at least in the language that Hippolytus transmits it) would have been added after the name became associated with Persephone. And indeed, any attention paid at the Lesser Mysteries to Persephone and Dionysus as a mother–child pair would by definition post-date the development of the rituals and myths that we have examined in this book, which we suggest arose during the late archaic or early classical period. The sanctuary near the Ilissos River where the Lesser Mysteries were held was originally dedicated not to Demeter but rather to Meter,[24] who, as I will discuss shortly below, had an old attachment to Dionysus that included the idea that she had purified the young god, taught him how to perform initiations, and given him the paraphernalia with which to do so. Possibly, it was because of this old association with Meter that Dionysus first became involved with whatever happened at the Lesser Mysteries.

In any case, given that a majority of our attestations make "Brimo" an alternative name for Persephone, I shall assume that it is Persephone who is meant in tablet no. 27. (I eliminate Hecate as a candidate because she played no role in Bacchic mysteries as far as we know, and played only a minimal role in the Orphic poetry that narrates Dionysus' birth, death, and revival.[25]) On other tablets we examined in this book, Persephone appears more or less in the same role and on the same level as Hades: she is a ruler of the Underworld to whom a soul must present itself and its credentials for safe passage. In contrast, as a "name to conjure with" in the *symbola* of tablet no. 27, Persephone/Brimo is intimately tied to the guarantee of a happy afterlife that the Bacchic mysteries promised. The practitioner who created this tablet, at some time around the end of the fourth or beginning of the third century BCE in Pherae, offered a form of mysteries that brought Persephone more to the fore than she usually was.

Perhaps one or more ritual practitioners developed this strand of Bacchic mysteries in response to an already established importance of Brimo and her identification with Persephone in the area around Pherae, but we should remember that in the liturgical text preserved by the Gurôb Papyrus – which is about half a century later than the Pherae tablets and was found in Egypt[26] – Brimo also appears alongside Dionysus, as well as alongside two other goddesses who appear on our other tablet from Pherae, as we will see. If this strand of Bacchic mysteries originated in Pherae, then either it spread abroad relatively quickly or we have lost earlier traces of its existence. The utter absence of "Brimo" in our sources earlier than the Pherae tablet suggests that the first alternative is probably correct.[27] And this, in turn, suggests that the practitioner(s) working in Pherae innovated in a manner that ensured their particular product would find plenty of support in myths and rituals that were already familiar not only locally but throughout the Greek world. We would do well, in other words – not only when thinking about tablet no. 27 but also when considering no. 28 and the combined picture the two might offer – to look to well-known, established practices and stories as possible sources of influence.

The goddesses mentioned in the hexameters of tablet no. 28 are Demeter, under the title "Chthonia," and the "Mountain Mother," a goddess often called more simply the "Mother," or "Cybele," and often identified with Rhea[28] in literary sources, as well as, occasionally (but again only in literary sources), with Demeter.[29]

What do we know of mysteries in honor of Demeter Chthonia and the Mountain Mother? The epithet "Chthonia" most immediately evokes Demeter's role as the central figure in a long-lived and widely known cult in the city of Hermione in the southeast Argolid, which existed from at least the late archaic period and was still around at the time of Pausanias.[30] Most aspects of the festival that we hear about in our sources were open to all, but Demeter Chthonia's close association in Hermione with Clymenus (the local euphemism for Hades) and Kore, which goes back at least as far as the late archaic period, makes it probable that mysteries with an eschatological slant were celebrated there as well; in a hymn, the Hellenistic poet Philicus mentions giving *dora mystica* (gifts connected with mysteries) to Demeter Chthonia, Persephone, and Clymenus. A famous entrance to the Underworld was located near Demeter's precinct in Hermione, and local legend said it had been the Hermionians who told Demeter what had happened to Persephone.[31] All of this suggests that any mysteries connected with Demeter Chthonia in Hermione would have been explained by the same story as those at Eleusis: Demeter's loss of her daughter to Hades and her eventual reunion with that daughter. Pausanias tells us that there was also a cult to Demeter Chthonia in Sparta; he claims it was derived from the more famous one in Hermione, but the Spartans themselves said it had been founded by Orpheus – which again points towards eschatological mysteries, and particularly to mysteries similar to those at Eleusis, which were anchored by hexameter poems attributed to Orpheus. Such poems travel, carrying their gods along with them.[32] We also know that the late archaic poet Lasus (who was from Hermione) composed a hymn in honor of Demeter Chthonia and Kore, "the wedded wife of Clymenus," that became known far and wide,[33] and that by the Hellenistic period the epithet "Chthonia" was the stuff of learned poetry.[34] Even if there was no pre-existing cult to Demeter Chthonia in Pherae in the late fourth century, then, a ritual practitioner could have introduced the goddess with the expectation that his audience would be familiar with her.

Our earliest evidence for initiatory rituals of the Mother connects them exclusively with those of Dionysus – indeed, she is said to have started Dionysus on his initiatory career.[35] According to a scholiast on the *Iliad*, the epic poet Eumelus, who is usually dated to the late eighth or early seventh century BCE, said that Dionysus was purified by Rhea on Mount Cybela in Phrygia (i.e., in the territory traditionally associated with the Mother), after which Rhea taught him how to perform initiations (*teletai*), gave him the paraphernalia (*diaskeuē*) he needed to do so and appointed him to disperse those initiations throughout the world.[36] The *Bacchae*'s chorus of celebrants, following an itinerant priest who is bringing Diony-sus' rituals from Phrygia to Thebes, essentially repeats Eumelus' story as they sing out:

> Blessed is he who, being fortunate and knowing the *teletai* of the gods, leads a pure life and joins his soul to the *thiasos*. Perform-ing Bacchic rituals with holy purifications in the mountains, and correctly celebrating the *orgia* of the Great Mother, Cybele, shaking the thyrsus up and down and being crowned with ivy, that one serves Dionysus. (73–82; cf. 120–34)

Apollodorus gives us an additional detail: Dionysus was in need of purifi-cation by Rhea because Hera had driven him mad.

None of this necessarily has anything to do with *eschatological* mysteri-es. The word *teletē*, which I am translating as "initiation," could refer to any number of rites that introduced an individual into a new group or a new status; we have no reason to think that what Eumelus describes Rhea as doing, and teaching Dionysus to do, was intended to enhance one's postmortem possibilities. Indeed, given Eumelus' date, ascribing escha-tological significance to Rhea's *teletai* here would make them the earliest eschatological mysteries of all, predating our evidence not only for explic-itly eschatological Bacchic mysteries but also for the Eleusinian Mysteries. We should instead stick to what Eumelus and Apollodorus tell us: Rhea's *teletai* (which Dionysus adopted as his own) purified and thereby freed the initiate from madness. These functions do develop associations with eschatology; as Plato and other authors tell us, purification (and especially purification through Bacchic *teletai*) cures madness in part by assuaging the anger of the dead who are responsible for sending it. This is understood to benefit the individual both in the here-and-now and in the hereafter, when he himself enters the ranks of the dead.[37] All of these associations also circle around the Lesser Mysteries in Agrai, as it happens; not only were the Lesser Mysteries celebrated in a locale originally dedicated to the Mother (and set during a month in which other purificatory rituals took place), they also, at least in later times, gave Dionysus a prominent role. Furthermore, according to myth, they were founded to purify Heracles from blood guilt so that he could be initiated at Eleusis – and he wanted to be initiated so that he could safely confront the dangers of the Underworld, including its unhappy dead, when he descended to fetch Cerberus. (Analogously, purification and subsequent initiation at Eleusis promised initiates safety against ghosts and demons, both during the initiation ceremony itself and later, as they journeyed through the Underworld after death.[38]) We might conjecture that at some point, as eschatological concerns grew more important in Greece during the later archaic age, what was originally a purificatory cult of Meter and Dionysus in Agrai became increasingly oriented towards postmortem preparations and was eventually swallowed up by the highly successful Eleusinian complex. Similarly, we might also conjecture that, during the later archaic period, Bacchic *teletai* that originally focused on purification and release from madness developed an additional eschatological focus such as we see in the gold tablets. This would have been an additional reason for Dionysus to become more closely associated with Persephone (or vice versa, depending on the causal scheme one adopts).

At any rate, when the hexameters of tablet no. 28 mention the *orgia* and *telē* of the Mountain Mother, the most natural way to understand this is as a reference to what she had taught Dionysus when she purified and instructed him; in other words, it is another way of saying that the tablet's owner had undergone some variety of Bacchic initiation, which, by the time of the tablet's creation, certainly focused on eschatological concerns.[39] Not that this merely amounts to a difference of wording, however: the ritual practitioner was free to choose the verses he put on the tablet, and I presume that his choice implies a corresponding emphasis on the Mother within the ritual he promulgated and the myths that underpinned it. Ritually, this might mean that he included an enthronement of the initiate in the middle of a circle of frightening, ecstatic dancers. The Byzantine lexicon known as the *Suda* mentions an Orphic poem called *Thronismoi Metrooi kai Bacchika – Enthronement [Rituals] of the Mother, and Bacchic [Rites?]*; a passage from Plato mentions initiations in which people acting the part of Corybantes danced around an enthroned initiate; another passage from Plato indicates that this frightening dance was thought to produce mental calm.[40] The Corybantes, who were often equated with the Curetes, were connected in cult with both the Mother and Dionysus, and in myth were said (like the Curetes) to have guarded the infant Dionysus.

The Gurôb Papyrus mentions the Curetes in the same breath as Brimo, Demeter, and Rhea.[41]

Let us return to the broader issue of how to read tablet no. 28 and its claim of initiation into rites of both Demeter Chthonia and the Mountain Mother. It is possible that the owner of tablet no. 28 had been initiated into two separate mysteries and wished to claim credit for both: one honored Dionysus and the Mother, the other honored Demeter Chthonia. Alternatively, it is possible that a ritual practitioner operating in the region of Pherae[42] innovated not only by shifting the emphasis within his Dionysiac rites towards the Mother, but also by adding elements from other mysteries and from poems that circulated panhellenically. The second scenario seems likelier than the first: surely a ritual practitioner fashioning a tablet would mention only those mysteries that he himself marketed.[43] The co-existence of Demeter Chthonia and the Mountain Mother on tablet no. 28, then, implies the existence of a single cult involving both deities (as well as Dionysus, without whom the Mother had no mysteries at this time), and the existence of an accompanying aitiological myth that gave each of them a significant role.[44] The propinquity (both temporal and spatial) of tablet no. 27 suggests we should bring Brimo into the mix, too. Here we probably deal in part with the influence of an important local cult upon Bacchic mysteries. But the influence, as the ritual practitioner shaped it, had more than local resonance: once again, we would do well to remember the Gurôb Papyrus, which gathers these divine figures – Brimo, Demeter, Rhea/Mother, and Dionysus (as well as the Curetes) together into a single liturgical context.

What sort of myth might bring all of these divinities together? There are two ways to explain the presence of the Mother. First, as we have just seen, there was a very old tradition according to which Dionysus had been purified of madness and then received his initiatory knowledge and accoutrements from Rhea. But as we saw in Chapter 3, there was also a tradition concerning Dionysus' rebirth, according to which Rhea reassembled the pieces of the dismembered god and restored him to life.[45] Our earliest evidence for this tradition comes from Euphorion (mid-third century BCE) – that is, about half a century later than the Pherae tablets and contemporary with the Gurôb Papyrus – which is itself another instance of a myth-and-ritual cocktail mixed by an independent ritual practitioner. Philodemus and Diodorus tell us that this story was a favorite of the Orphics, which suggests that it was narrated in poetry attributed to Orpheus that could have circulated widely. If the postmortem fate of the Bacchic initiate was analogized to that of the god who died and was reborn, then the goddess who facilitated the god's rebirth could be understood to have eschatological importance for the initiates as well.

The two traditions share a theme and a salient detail. Thematically, in each case Dionysus is rescued from destruction by Rhea – madness, left unchecked, destroys the individual and those around him, as many myths of Dionysus make clear. Indeed, in myths involving Dionysus, madness may more particularly lead to destruction through dismemberment – the very state from which Rhea rescued the young god. The salient detail is Hera, who in each case is the motive power behind the god's destruction: she urges on the Titans who dismember him and she drives him into the madness from which Rhea must purify him.[46] The two traditions, then, seem to be different mythic expressions of a broader idea according to which Rhea/the Mother is charged with protecting Dionysus from Hera and her assassins, and with regenerating him – and thereby with protecting and regenerating his initiates, specifically, I assume, through rituals of purification.

But what of Demeter Chthonia? If Persephone/Brimo is Dionysus' mother, and Rhea/the Mother is something of a foster-mother, then what role is left for Demeter to play in any foundational myth that underpinned rituals in Pherae? If I am right that any mysteries honoring Demeter at Hermione or Sparta drew on the familiar story of her loss and recovery of Persephone, then it is a fair guess that Demeter Chthonia played the role of Persephone's mother anywhere else that her name was carried as well, including Pherae and Gurôb. We deal, then, with a myth that joins together the tale of Demeter and Persephone, which was closely associated with Demeter's mysteries; the tale of Persephone and Dionysus, which was closely associated with the Bacchic mysteries; and one or more tales that narrated the important roles that Rhea/Mother had played in Dionysus' youth. In Chapter 3 I suggested that the *bricoleur(s)* who created the myth of Persephone and Dionysus were in effect offering a sequel to the well-known story that underlay Demeter's long-established mysteries in Eleusis. The mythic complex that I am now suggesting was antecedent to tablets nos. 27 and 28 (as well as the Gurôb Papyrus)[47] went even further than that. Rather than narrating only the sequel to Demeter and Persephone's myth, it presented a multi-generational saga, beginning with Persephone's rape and Demeter's grief, continuing with Persephone's delivery (and loss) of Dionysus, and finishing with Dionysus' revival, purification, and education by Rhea. It is likely that the practitioner who brought all of this together supported it with one or more Orphic poems; the hexameters on tablet no. 28 may be drawn from one of those poems. The fact that references to all of these mythic events are found within liturgical texts (the Pherae tablets and the Gurôb Papyrus) indicates that the cults in question were correspondingly multi-generational in their divine focuses. As such, they could market themselves as offering the best of the Eleusinian Mysteries and the Bacchic mysteries in a single package.

Lucian's portrait of Alexander of Abonuteichos as a *bricoleur* of mysteries who drew together this-and-that, parodic though it is, may not be far off the mark.[48]

A note on reconstructing the text of no. 28 [F.G.]

Line 1: The missing text at its end consists of two syllables, the first long, the second long or short. Bouraselis in Parker and Stamatopoulou 2004: 11 suggested ἰδοῦσα as part of the periphrastic construction ἔχω . . . ἰδοῦσα for the resultative perfect, "I have seen." Although it would introduce what I call the "initiatory perfect," this is problematical, for several reasons: the periphrastic perfect is a prosaic construction; "to see" for the mystery experience is confined to Eleusis; and the text scans only under the assumption of an elision with hiatus immediately after the elision between ἔχω and ὄργια. Ferrrari 2007 rejected this and supplied an adjective such as σεμνά, an alternative solution mentioned but rejected by Parker and Stamatopoulou for reasons of syntax. [Βάκχου], our supplement in the first edition, was also suggested but again rejected for syntactical reasons by Parker and Stamatopoulou 2004: 110; Bernabé, however, adopted it in his edition and defended it in a 2008 paper.

Line 2: Several scholars (including Walter Burkert orally) solved the metrical problems around τέλη with the assumption of a haplographic mistake; Parker and Stamatopoulou 2004, Bernabé's and our edition adopted this and printed τε <τέ>λη. Palaeographical reasons recommend it, but τε connects the two divine names, not the two nouns, with the particle in an unusual but not impossible position in third place: the usual second place would have resulted in an unmetrical construction, Δήμητρός τε Χθονίας. τέλη is either an apposition to ὄργια, or the two words are juxtaposed without a connector; in any case, they have to be synonymous or nearly synonymous. Ferrari 2007 objected to this because of the position of τε and because he could not see how τέλη could be synonymous with ὄργια; he suggested τελέσαι and connected it with ἔχω in the meaning "I am able to perform." This is impossible because it creates a very awkward meaning: it is not the initiate who is able to initiate but the priest. D'Alesssio and Battezzato, as cited by Ferrari, suggested τελέσας instead and connect it with ἔχω. This is only marginally more satisfactory: it cleans up the connectors without recourse to the assumption of an apposition ("I have the sacred tokens, having performed . . ."), but leaves the transitive verb τελέω without the necessary object or constructs ὄργια as object of both ἔχω and τελέσας; if we again assume a periphrastic perfect instead, we run into the same problem of this construction in our text as in the syntax of Parker and Stamatopoulou, this time aggravated by the wide separation between auxiliary verb and participle. Either way then the syntax is very difficult; and palaeography strongly argues against changing τέλη in this way: the text is otherwise carefully written and easy to read, and even if because of a crease there are minor problems with the initial κ of καί, the η of τέλη is clear.

Thus, no solution is really convincing. Coming immediately after ἔχω, ὄργια should be connected with it as its object; then it almost necessarily must have the well-attested meaning of a physical ritual object, here a token that admits the initiate to the blessed life (most likely that token is our tablet itself). τέλη on the other hand cannot be a synonym of ὄργια in the sense of tokens: τέλη are physical objects only when brought as taxes or, in a metaphorical use in Sophocles and Euripides, objects offered as a sacrifice, a sort of tax for the gods (Soph. *Trach.* 237; Eur. frg. 327 N²). In the final line of the Pelinna tablet (no. 26a) τέλη is what awaits the initiate who has just been admitted, and what all the other happy deceased have; it is either "(honorary) office" (i.e., the positive result when one has reached one's τέλος, "goal") or "rituals" that the initiates perform eternally, as a (poetical) variation of τελετή . To say "I have my token, the rituals of the gods" in the sense that the token signifies the ritual of the two goddesses (both those already performed and, by extension, those to be celebrated in the Underworld) is not impossible but daring at best. At any rate, we then need to fill the lacuna, perhaps with an adjective qualifying ὄργια, although Sarah's reflections above would allow one to think of "the tokens of Bacchos, the rituals" – or even, with hiatus and synizesis, ὄργια᾽ Ὀρφέως.

But one could arrive at an easier syntax if one assumes a syntactic break in the lacuna. This removes the need to think of the key nouns, ὄργια and τέλη, as synonyms that are constructed in an asyndetic or appositional relationship, but it comes at the price of an obligatory enjambment at the end of the line. This is not impossible; see Hipponion (no. 1) lines 8–9, Entella (no. 8) lines 11–13, or Rome (no. 9) lines 2–3, where, however, the syntactic break is always accentuated by ἀλλά. I can see two solutions. The first is to take up Bouraselis' ἰδοῦσα, not as a periphrastic perfect but as explaining where the token came from: "having seen the rituals." This makes several assumptions: the initiate was feminine, the double hiatus before and after ὄργια is unusual; τέλη in the sense of mystery rite is only attested in tragedy; and "to see" a mystery ritual is confined to Eleusis (although Demeter Chthonia brings us close to that).

If these exceptions appear to be a problem, a relative construction would be another solution, although there are metrical problems. The easy solution ἔχω ὄργια παρ᾽ ὧν . . . τέλη – with τέλη as in the final Pelinna promise: "the tokens from which (I will have) the (future) rewards/

rituals" – does not scan, ἔχω ὄργια ἐξ ὧν . . . does, but with hiatus; so does the more artificial [ὧν ἔξ], if one feels bothered by the hiatus. [ἀνθ' ὧν] works even better, although again with hiatus. In inscriptions, it often means "in exchange for" – typically in honorary decrees that list someone's benefactions "for which" the honors are conveyed, i.e., where there is a non-oppositional causal nexus between benefaction and honor, as there is a similar nexus between the token that demonstrates the initiation and the otherworldly achievement.

To sum up: A haplographic mistake in line 2 imposes itself as the most likely solution, but there is no fully convincing supplement for line 1. A syntax that provides for a pause solves the syntactic and semantic problems; among the possible supplements, [ἰδοῦσα] or [ἀνθ' ὧν] appear most likely. Given that all the ends of the tablets look towards the future, the latter would be my favorite.

Appendix 3

THE TABLETS FROM ROMAN PALESTINE

Fritz Graf

A very small and locally circumscribed group of eleven gold *lamellae* from graves invite comparison with the Bacchic Gold Tablets, although they come from a different epoch and geographical area, namely mid-Imperial Palestine. Four of them are small rectangular gold leaves, seven are strips of thin gold foil; they all date from the second or third century CE according to the letter forms; most come from the art market and lack a reliable archaeological context. The seven longer pieces are narrow rectangular bands with an inscription that is usually framed in a so-called "tablet with handles" (*tabula ansata*), a common frame for many private Roman inscriptions from the Imperial epoch; it imitates the shape of earlier bronze tablets whose handles served to mount them between two wooden posts, or simply to hold them while reading. They contain a common formula, written in the Greek of the period, that addresses the deceased. In its full form it reads "Take heart, so-and-so: nobody is immortal" – in Attic spelling (which is rarely the spelling of these late texts): θάρσει, NN, οὐδεὶς ἀθάνατος. Not all texts used the full formula, although θάρσει, the key term, is never omitted. We give a list of the known texts:

Group 1: Full formula

Tablet no. 1: Cologne, Niessen collection, from Beth Djibrin/Eleutheropolis: gold strip, inscription in a central square. M. Siebourg, *Archiv für Religionswissenschaft* 8 (1905), 391 no. 1.

> θάρσι, Εὐγε–
> νή, οὐδὶς ἀ–
> θάνατος.

> Take heart, Eu-
> genos, no one is im-
> mortal[1]

Tablet no. 2: Geneva, Musée d'art et d'histoire, from Beth Djibrin/Eleu-theropolis: gold strip, with a central rectangle that carries the inscription. W. Déonna, *Syria* 4 (1923), 224.

ᵛᵛᵛθάρσι, Πέ—
τρε, οὐδὶς ἀ—
θάνατος.

Take heart, Pe-
tros, no one is im-
mortal

Tablet no. 3: Bonn, Akademisches Kunstmuseum, from Jerusalem: *tabula ansata*. M. Siebourg, *ARW* 10 (1907), 393 no. 1 = Peter Thomsen, *Die lateinischen und griechischen Inschriften der Stadt Jerusalem und ihrer nächsten Umgebung* (Leipzig: Hinrich, 1922), 113 no. 208a.

θάρσι, Ε—
ὐγενή, ο—
ᵛὐδεὶςᵛ
ἀθάνατ—
ος.

Take heart, Eu-
gene, no
one is
immort-
al

Tablet no. 4: Salt Lake City, Harold B. Library of the Brigham Young Uni-versity, without provenance: rectangular gold tablet with irregular edges, 30 mm high and 55 mm wide. L. H. Blumell, "A Gold Lamella with a Greek Inscription from the Brigham Young University Collection," *Zeitschrift für Papyrologie und Epigraphik* 177 (2011), 166–8.

θάρσι, Ἡρα-
κλίανε, ᵛοὐ-
δὶς ἀθάνα-
ᵛᵛᵛτος.

Take heart, Hera-
klianos, no
one is immort-
al

Group 2: Half-formula

Tablet no. 5: Cologne, Niessen collection, from Beth Djibrin/Eleutheropolis: gold strip, inscription in a central square. M. Siebourg, *Archiv für Religionswissenschaft* 8 (1905), 391 no. 2.

θάρσει,
Εὐγενή,
ΟΥΓΕΝΗ

Take heart,
Eugene,
OUGENĒ

Tablet no. 6: Bonn, Akademisches Kunstmuseum, from Jerusalem: fragmentary *tabula ansata*. M. Siebourg, *ARW* 10 (1907), 394 no. 2 = Peter Thomsen, *Die lateinischen und griechischen Inschriften der Stadt Jerusalem und ihrer nächsten Umgebung* (Leipzig: Hinrich, 1922), 113 no. 208b.

θάρσι,
Εὐγε-ᵛ
νή.ᵛᵛᵛ

Take heart,
Euge-
ne

Tablet no. 7: In private possession; found in a sarcophagus in el-Nathroun-Anwas/Nicopolis: a rectangular gold strip, 28 mm high and 23 mm wide, perhaps a *tabula ansata* with the handles broken off. Pierre Benoit, *Revue Biblique* 59 (1952), 253.

θάρσι,
Νικό-
μαχε.

Take heart,
Niko-
machos

Group 3: Only the imperative

Tablets nos. 8–11: Fik in Palestine, from a grave: four rectangular gold labels. P. Benoit, *Revue Biblique* 59 (1952), 256.

θάρσι.

Take heart

This formula, both in its longer and its shorter forms, and with some variation in the imperative that sometimes replaces θάρσει ("Take heart") with the synonymous εὐψύχει ("Be of good spirit"), is widely attested in stone inscriptions from the entire Imperial epoch and beyond.[2] They are especially widespread in the area between Syria and Arabia, but we know many examples from Anatolia (in decreasing numbers from east to west) and Egypt, and markedly fewer further west, on the one hand from the eastern shore of the Adriatic Sea with a thin inland spread that reach Pannonia (modern-day Hungary), and on the other hand from North Africa, Sicily, and mainland Italy, with an accumulation around Rome (and with a rather thin spread to Gaul and Germany). This diffusion seems to reflect a pattern of emigration and diaspora of Levantine people (Syrians and Palestinians) to the west, with central Anatolia, Sicily, and Rome as main areas of attraction, and the north coast of Africa plus Sicily and the eastern shore of the Adriatic Sea as the two main travelling routes. On the stones, the formula is independent of any religious affiliation and appears on what seem pagan gravestones and sarcophagi as well as what are clearly Jewish and Christian grave monuments, including Coptic ones. Sometimes there is an addition that points to their monotheistic background: "It is God alone who is immortal," ὁ θεὸς ὁ μόνος ἀθάνατος.[3]

On these grave stones, the formula expresses the fact that death is part of the lot of every human being and thus should not be terrible and frightful; the imperative θάρσει "take heart" is used as an admonition in a difficult situation that will end well.[4] A few texts clarify this by short additions to the main formula. One text has: "Many (died) before you, many after you: nobody is immortal" (πολλοὶ πρὸ σοῦ, πολλοὶ μετά σε · οὐδεὶς ἀθανατος);[5] another one: "Nobody is immortal; even Herakles died" (οὐδεὶς ἀθάνατος· καὶ ὁ Ἡρακλῆς ἀπέθανε). One instance points to its ritual use in an acclamation to the deceased: a long grave epigram for an actress from Aquilea ends with the statement: "Your stage colleagues tell you: be courageous, Bassilla, nobody is immortal" (οἱ σύσκηνοὶ σου λέγουσιν · "εὐψύχει, Βάσσιλλα, οὐδεὶς ἀθάνατος").[6] This makes one wonder whether the formula was not really used in an acclamation as part of the burial liturgy: with it, the survivors thus comforted each other as much as they did the deceased person; John Chrysostom attests to such a ritual among his Christians.[7] This is confirmed by the few cases where a sometimes rather elaborate grave inscription in Latin closes with the formula in Greek.[8] On the other hand, there is no attempt preserved to turn the Greek formula into Latin as well: the grave liturgy with which these immigrants from the east were accustomed was in Greek and remained Greek even if the formula was inserted into a Latin grave text.[9]

The formula on the stones has been the subject of scholarly debate; surprisingly enough, the gold tablets were never included in these discussions. In a foundational study of 1936, Marcel Simon argued for an eschatological meaning of this liturgical acclamation and an origin in a mystery cult. He argued for an origin in the cult of Osiris and Isis, based on the famous acclamation during what is a ritual of resurrection: θαρρεῖτε μύσται τοῦ θεοῦ σεσωσμένου ("take heart, O initiates, for the god has found salvation"); although Firmicus Maternus, who preserves this text, does not name the god, Simon with others connected the description with the mystery cult of Osiris; others conjectured Adonis.[10] However this may be, scholars by now hesitate to connect the grave acclamations with any specific mystery cult; given the semantics of θάρσει, however, the positive tone of the proclamation holds good nonetheless. As Pieter van der Horst phrased it: "The exhortation ... probably meant 'to encourage the deceased to meet the dangers involved in the passage to the next world courageously'."[11]

This must be true to an even higher degree for the gold tablets: unlike the stone inscriptions above ground that addressed the passers-by and let them participate in the good hope of the deceased, the gold tablets in the grave addressed the deceased only, in a form that must have been thought of as much more durable than the grave stones. Since none of the texts was found in an undisturbed context, we cannot know where in the grave or on the body these texts were. Two of them had holes on the small sides and have evoked the image of a diadem that was tied to the head of the deceased. If such a diadem is comparable to a crown, one can imagine that these dead expected to participate in a banquet of the dead; this again is attested in several mystery cults.

Nor do we know what religious group they belonged to. Some of the stone inscriptions from Palestine have been connected with Jewish communities that kept a certain distance from the purely Rabbinic communities in Galilee; but they are not unthinkable in a pagan context as well.[12] This fits the gold texts as well: they come from three cities outside Galilee – Aelia Capitolina, Eleutheropolis, Nicopolis – that mainly were inhabited by Greeks, Romans and Romanized Jews with very mixed but mainly polytheist religious adherence.[13] Among the personal names on the tablets, only Petros is most likely Jewish or Christian; Nikomachos and Heraklianos are possible in any religious context – nothing prevents us assuming that the people buried with these texts were Jews or Christians, but they do not have to be either.

Four of the seven tablets address a person called Eugenē; we understand this as the vocative of the late Greek feminine form, "noble."[14] This word is found only twice elsewhere in inscriptions, both times again in the *tharsei*-formula: more precisely both occurrences are on the same undated, but late grave stone from the hinterland of Syrian Apameia.[15] This cannot be a coincidence, and we wonder whether we deal with an honorific title for women rather than with a personal name: in this specific eastern group, a woman would simply be addressed as "noble one" whereas men retained their individual names. Parallels to this, however, are absent. But if it was the custom of a small religious or social group, our lack of knowledge is not surprising: even if an ancient writer happened to record such a group, he would not have mentioned a minor social custom.

However this may be, again we deal with what might be a more or less specific group of worshippers that used gold tablets to preserve eschatological hopes. Given the survival of this technology in Bacchic groups until perhaps the early third century CE, as demonstrated by the tablet of Caecilia Secundina from Rome (no. 9), it is conceivable that a Palestinian group adopted it consciously from these groups; one religious specialist would have sufficed to make this transfer in the same way as, according to Livy, one itinerant religious specialist was enough to spread Bacchic mysteries to Rome. The alternative – spontaneous parallel development – sounds less likely, given the availability of a Bacchic model.

Appendix 4

ADDITIONAL
BACCHIC TEXTS

Translations by Fritz Graf

1 The Olbia bone tablets

Several rectangular bone plaques, polished, with rounded corners, *c.* 5 cm by 4 cm, 0.5 cm thick; three of them are inscribed, none shows traces of wear:[1]
Ed. princ. Rusyayeva 1978; new edition after the photographs in West 1982; new readings and interpretation in Vinogradov 1991. See Dubois 1996: 154 no. 94a–c; *OF* 463–5 (see Figure 6, p. 215).

Tablet A

Top, starting at the upper part of the left side

    βίος θάνατος βίος
        ἀλήθεια

bottom

    Διό(νυσος) Ὀρφικοί or Ὀρφικόν (the edge is damaged)

    Life death life
        truth
    Dio(nysus) Orphics [or Orphic]

Verso is blank

A recto

B recto   B verso

C recto   C verso

Figure 6 Drawings of the Olbia tablets, after *Vestnik Drevnei Istorii* 143 (1978), p. 89, fig. 6.

Tablet B

Top line:

εἰρήνη πόλεμος
ἀλήθεια ψεῦδος
Διόν(υσος)

Bottom left corner: A

Peace war
truth lie
Dion(ysus)

Verso:

Drawings: a rectangular shape with seven compartments, each containing a small oval; next to it a zig-zag (inverse Σ with a downward stroke
through its top); at the bottom a snake-like line.

Tablet C

Διο(νυσο)
ἀλήθεια (both words end at the right margin)
σῶμα ψυχή

Dio(nysus)
truth
body soul

σῶμα Vinogradov 1991: 79 who also adds [ψεῦδος . . . before ἀλήθεια

Verso:

Drawing of two triangles, attached at their points and lying horizontally.
The right triangle is open on its right side; a horizontal stroke extends
from the top corner of the left triangle; resembling a "folding chair with a
fleece" (West).

2 Bacchic inscriptions from Olbia

2.1

Bronze mirror, presumably made in Olbia, from a grave in Olbia, *c.* 500
BCE; with a careful inscription in Ionian letters along its edge:

Δημώνασσα Ληναίō εὐαὶ καὶ Λήναιος Δημόκλō εὐαί.

Demonassa daughter of Lenaeus, euai! and Lenaeus son of
Damoclus, euai!

Dubois 1996: 143 no. 92 (with earlier bibliography).

2.2

Attic black-figure vase stand, 5th cent. BCE; on its lower outside a graffito
in letters of about 300 BCE, written in two concentric circles.[2]

Outer circle:

Καλλίνικος Φιλ[ονί]κου, [Ποσει]δώνιος Σωκρατί(ο)υ, Ἡροσῶν
Φιλοξένου, Δημήτριο[ς] Σωκράτου, Φίλων Σωκράτου, Βορεϊκοὶ
θιασῖται.

Kallinikos son of Philonicus, Poseidonios son of Sokratios,
Heroson son of Philoxenos, Demetrios son of Sokrates, Philo
son of Sokrates, members of the northern thiasus.

Inner circle:

βίος βίος ᾿Απόλλων ᾿Απόλλων ἥλιος ἥλιος κόσμος κόσμος
φῶς φῶς

Life life Apollo Apollo sun sun order order light light

Dubois 1996: 155 no. 95.

3 The Gurôb Papyrus

Papyrus in Trinity College, Dublin; P. Gurôb 1; mid-3rd cent. BCE.
Col.i, right side with line ends preserved

. . .] having everything that he finds	
. . . let him] collect the raw (meat)	
. . .] on account of the ritual.	
"[Receive my gift] as the payment for law[less ancestors . . .	4
]Save me, Brimo, gr[eat	
]and Demeter [and] Rhea [	
]and the armed Curetes [. . .]	
]that we . . .	8
] so that we will perform beautiful rites	
] . . . ram and he-goat	
] immense gifts."	
] and along the river	12
ta]king of the he-goat	
] . . . let him eat the rest of the meat	
] . . . let him not watch	
] . . . , dedicating the chosen	16
] . . . **Prayer:**	

"I call [Protogo]nos (?) and Eubouleus,
] I call the wide [Earth
] . . . the dear ones. You, having parched . . .   20
of De]meter and Pallas to us
Eubou]leus, Irikepaios, save me
hurler of lightn]ing . . . one(?) Dionysus. **Passwords:**
] . . . god through the bosom   24
] . . . I drank [wine?], donkey, herdsman
] . . . token: above below for the . . .
] and what has been given to you for your consumption
in]to the basket, and again   28
c]one (or spinning-top), bull-roarer, knuckle-bones
] mirror

Col. ii, of which only the extreme left part (beginnings of the lines) is preserved, is too damaged to lend itself to any attempt at a translation; one
can perhaps see "pray" ii 11, "drink[ing wi]ne"(?) ii 12, "I see" ii 17, "to
consume" ii 23, "journey" ii 25.

J. G. Smyly, *Greek Papyri from Gurōb* (Dublin, 1921), no. 1; *OF* 31 Kern;
R. A. Pack, *The Greek and Latin Literary Texts from Greco-Roman Egypt*
(Ann Arbor, 2nd edn. 1965), no. 2464 (translation West 1983: 170f.); new
edition and commentary Hordern 2000; *OF* 578.

4 The Edict of Ptolemy IV Philopator

P. Berlin 11774 verso; 250–200 BCE.

On the order of the king,
the persons who initiate to Dionysus all over
the countryside shall sail to Alexan-
dria (those who live between Alexandria and Naucratis   4
by the tenth day after this decree has been
set up, and those beyond Naucratis
by the twentieth day), and they shall sign in
with Aristoboulos in the Archive by the   8
third day after their arrival, and they
shall right away indicate from whom
they inherited the cult outfit, up to three
generations, and deposit their sacred text, sealed,   12
and each shall sign (it) with his proper
name.

Wilhelm Schubart, *Amtliche Berichte aus den Königlichen Kunstsammlungen* 38 (1916/17), 190 (photo); idem, in: *Aegyptische Urkunden aus den Königlichen Museen zu Berlin, Griechische Urkunden*. Vol. VI: *Papyri und Ostraka der Ptolemäerzeit*, ed. W. Schubart and E. Kühn (Berlin, 1926), no. 1211 (*BGU*); *Sammelbuch griechischer Urkunden aus Ägypten*, vol. 3, 1926/27, no. 7266 (*SB*).

The edict has often been discussed; the best (although somewhat technical) discussion still is Zuntz 1963/1972.

The attribution to Ptolemy IV Philopator (reigned 222–205 BCE) is based on this king's interest in Dionysiac rites (see Chapter 6 n. 54). According to some papyrologists, paleographic considerations would rather argue for a date in the mid-230s, under his father, Ptolemy III Euergetes (reigned 246–222 BCE).

NOTES

1 THE TABLETS: AN EDITION AND TRANSLATION

1 An exception is the complex and still somewhat enigmatic text from Thurii, our no. 4, where we thought it necessary to give somewhat more technical details than elsewhere.

2 See Schwyzer 1950: 237f.

3 "L'unica classificazione certa sembrerebbe geografica," Scalera McClintock 1991: 396f.

4 This book is an up-to-date version of his earlier edition, *Le lamine d'oro 'orfiche'* (Milan, 1993) which is a private edition that is difficult to find but contains the most splendid photographs of the texts anywhere. The more recent text contains fewer photographs; it has been translated into French for the collection Budé (Paris: Les Belles Lettres, 2004).

2 A HISTORY OF SCHOLARSHIP ON THE TABLETS

1 The metrical appendix contains a still valuable account of the development of the hexameter in Greece, see Pfeiffer 1976: 179. For more on Orpheus, see our Chapter 6.

2 See the essays in Warden 1982; for the Florentine Neoplatonists see also Klutstein 1987.

3 The Romantic philosophers, however, could agree; see F. W. Schelling, *Über die Gottheiten von Samothrake* (1815), Engl. Brown 1977.

4 Lobeck 1829: 229–783.

5 While Sir William Hamilton has been the topic of many books, including Susan Sontag's *The Volcano Lover*, James Millingen's life remains unexplored; typically enough, Wilton and Gignamini 1996, the catalogue of an exhibition on the Grand Tour at the Tate Gallery, contains several references to Sir William and two to his second wife, the alluring Emma Hart, but none to

his engraver; Jenkins and Sloan 1996 is equally reticent. Millingen published engravings of Greek vases, collected and published medals of Napoleon and was a member of the French Académie des Inscriptions et Belles-Lettres and of the Prussian Academy. I am not sure whether he was also the Dr James Millingen who, after Lord Byron's death (either in Missolonghi or, more plausibly, when the embalmed body of Byron had been returned to England awaiting the then refused burial in Westminster Abbey), examined his feet, see the note of Byron's editor in Prothero 1904, no. 4, note 1.

6 Letter of Carlo Bonucci to Eduard Gerhard, May 30, 1834; reprinted in Pugliese Carratelli 2001: 69f.; Bonucci writes "Io l'ebbi in mano, prima di lui, e per la differenza di alcuni piastri non l'acquistai."

7 *Corpus Inscriptionum Graecarum*, vol. 4, no. 5772; Kaibel 1879, no. 1037.

8 See Bottini 1992: 56–8.

9 Marshall 1911: 380 no. 3155.

10 *Notizie degli Scavi di Antichità* (*Not. Scav.*) 1879: 156–9 (with pls. 5 and 6); 1880: 152–62; a long analysis in Bottini 1992: 27–51.

11 On Comparetti, see *Dizionario Biografico degli Italiani*, vol. 27 (1982), 672–8; Marzi 1999.

12 *Dizionario Biografico degli Italiani*, loc. cit.

13 A new Italian edition, with an introduction by Giovanni Pugliese Carratelli, Florence 1989.

14 *Virgilio nel Medio Evo*, 1872, English 1885; a recent English edition was published in 1997 by Princeton University Press, prefaced by Jan Ziolkowski.

15 Comparetti 1882.

16 Plat. *Resp.* 364c–e; for more on this passage, see below Chapter 6.

17 *Not. Scav.* 1880: 158.

18 Dieterich relies on Gebhardt 1893; the text was first published a year earlier by Urbain Bouriant, a member of the French School in Cairo, cf. Bremmer and Czachesz 2003.

19 On Albrecht Dieterich, see Betz 2003: 14–26, following the biography with which Richard Wünsch introduced Albrecht Dieterich's *Kleine Schriften* (1891).

20 On Erwin Rohde, see Crusius 1902, Cancik 1985, Kaller 1994.

21 The complex publication history of these four Cretan tablets (three of them more or less identical variations of the short form, the fourth an address to Hades and Persephone) is explained by Comparetti 1910: 37. The four texts were acquired by the Austro-Hungarian consul in Rethymno, Trifilli, and were said to come from Eleutherna "ove dovettero esser trovate da qualche villico certamente in antichi sepolchri; sul luogo però e modo del trovamento egli non aveva alcuna precisa notizia." Trifilli showed them to the Italian archeologist Federico Halbherr who made drawings and sent them to Comparetti in 1894. He had also sent another drawing of one tablet to André Joubin who was a fellow of the French School in Athens in 1889; Joubin published it in the 1893 issue of the *Bulletin de Correspondance Hellénique* (see Joubin 1893). Trifilli also showed the tablets to J. L. (later Sir John) Myres – a Craven fellow of the British School in Athens in 1892–5 who was travelling in Crete with Arthur Evans, keeper of antiquities at the Ashmolean

Museum, on his quest for the elusive Minoan texts. Myres also made copies, and when Joubin published one text, Myres immediately sent his reading of the other three texts to the *Bulletin*, where they were printed in the same year 1893, although misspelling his name as "M. J. L. Myre, de Magdalen College" (see Myres 1893). Then, Trifilli donated all four texts to the Greek National Museum from where Gilbert Murray obtained yet another set of drawings for his *Critical Appendix* in Harrison 1922: 660f., where he published three of them. Comparetti finally published Halbherr's very accurate drawings in his 1910 collection; Margherita Guarducci then reproduced Halbherr's drawings in *Inscr. Cret.* 2.

22 Harrison 1922: 473.

23 Whereas Orpheus was absent in Diels' earlier collection, *Poetarum Philosophorum Fragmenta* (1901).

24 Three-quarters of a century later, Giorgio Colli still did the same, in Colli 1977.

25 Wilamowitz 1931/1932: vol. 2, 192–207; the quotation on p. 199.

26 "Der Qualm des Orphismus ... liegt schwer über dem Licht der alten Götter wie zu Zeiten des Iamblichos," Wilamowitz 1931/1932: vol. 2, 202. To which Father Lagrange retorted: "Mais alors il faut renoncer à expliquer les textes anciens, ne tenir aucun compte d'une tradition formelle," Lagrange 1937: 7. The same polarity still characterizes the debate between Edmonds 1999 and Bernabé 2002.

27 Ernst Maass had his problems with Wilamowitz, or perhaps the other way round. Maass published his dissertation in Wilamowitz' series *Philologische Untersuchungen*. Years later, Maass incensed Wilamowitz because of a private scandal, and the relationship cooled radically, see Calder and Kirstein 2003: vol. 2, app. IV pp. 720–1.

28 See Smith 1990.

29 To give just one example for how unreflectedly a minor scholar projected Christian assumptions on Orphism: in his edition of the first Cretan tablet, the editor, A. Joubin, describes the *orpheotelestai* as "ces apôtres de l'orphisme qui parcouraient le monde en enseignant les mystères," Joubin 1893: 123. On the topic, see esp. Edmonds 1999.

30 For a more recent critical review see Wiens 1980.

31 See the author's remark on p. 366 of the first edition ("les événements ont retardé cet achèvement jusqu'à la présente année 1919"); its title-page bears the date 1914.

32 They are, in his order: "Dionysiaka," *Atti Acc. Arch. Napoli* (1917); "Orphica," *Riv. Indo-Greco-Italica* 2–3 (1918); "Dionysos Mystes," *Atti Acc. Scienze Torino* (1918); "Il rito funerario Orfico," *Archivio Storico della Sicilia Orientale* (1919); *Zagreus. Studi sull'Orfismo* (Bari, 1920); *Eraclito. Nuovi studi sull' Orfismo* (Bari, 1922); *Orfismo e Paolismo* (Montevarchi, 1923), Chapters 1 "L'Origine Orfica della cristologia Paolina," 2 "L'essenza del mistero," 3 "Il dio degli Orfici," 4 "Verso i prati di Persefone"; "Orphism and Paulism," *Journal of Religion* (1918); "La catabasi Orfica," *Classical Philology* (1928).

33 Harnack 1920/1924; 1923.

34 See Schneider 1928, 1936, and Schneider and Clough, 1929.

35 Albeit as the result of a somewhat bizarre affair. The young Mircea Eliade, then still in Bucharest, had read Macchioro's books on Orphism in the mid-1920s and even published on Heraclitus and Orphism (see Macchioro's *Eraclito. Nuovi Studi sull'Orfismo*, Bari, 1922); the two entertained a regular correspondence, and Eliade visited him in the spring of 1927 during his first trip to Italy; in a subsequent article on this trip in a Romanian newspaper, he included Macchioro's personal remarks about the Fascist regime. As a consequence of what Eliade later called his "naiveté," Macchioro was interrogated by the police and removed from his post; see Eliade 1981: 94 (Heraclitus and Orphism), 125-7 (the visit).

36 http://www.biblebelievers.net/False Teaching/kjcathei.htm.

37 See the review of such websites in http://craigcunningham.com/dewey/part3.htm.

38 "La religion chrétienne a été revelée par Dieu par la voie de l'histoire," Lagrange 1937: 1; "peut-être a-t-on exagéré l'importance dans l'antiquité des religions à mystères," p. 2.

39 Lagrange 1937: 136: "Nous groupons ce que nous avons à dire de ce sujet, le centre de l'orphisme, autour des lamelles d'or trouvées dans des tombeaux."

40 Martin P. Nilsson, closer to Wilamowitz than to the French tradition, was more cautious, without, however, denying to Orphism the name of a religious movement, see Nilsson 1935.

41 Dodds 1951: 148. The small book of Moulinier 1955 tries a less negative attitude, reacting more to Loisy and Boulanger than to Linforth (whom he cites once) and Dodds.

42 Nilsson 1967/1955: 680 note 1; 1961: 235-8. The one exception is Guarducci 1977: 258-70.

43 Zuntz 1971. Skepticism made its impact on the educated general public as well, as an anonymous review in the *Times Literary Supplement* on May 25, 1984, 597 shows: "An insubstantial religion constructed by scholars out of myths, cults, verses, and ritual connected with his [sc. Orpheus'] name, ... Orphism is now obsolete."

44 Zuntz 1971: 383.

45 At least among the textual evidence preserved to us; but we have to rely on these texts, otherwise our methodology becomes arbitrary.

46 Our no. 27. On Brimo, see Chapter 5 n. 91.

47 Our no. 28.

48 Text no. 3 in our Appendix 4.

49 Text no. 1 in our Appendix 4.

50 *Ed. princ.* Rusyayeva 1978; new edition after the photographs, West 1982; see also West 1983: 18-20.

51 Announced with text samples in Kapsomenos 1964 and Kapsomenos 1964/65; a first Greek text appeared without an editor's name as "Der orphische Papyrus von Derveni," *Zeitschrift für Papyrologie und Epigraphik* 47 (1982), after p. 300 (basically the text the Greek editors had sent to selected scholars); an English translation of additional text by André Laks and Glenn W. Most in Laks and

Most 1997: 9–22; a new translation in Janko 2001; tentative Greek texts in Janko 2002 and Betegh 2004; the excavation report in Themelis and Tsouratsoglou 1997; two book-length studies: Jourdan 2003 and Betegh 2004; the official edition: Kouremenos et al. 2006.

52 Bottini 1992 was able to collect an impressive archeological dossier on "archeology of salvation" ("*archeologia della salvezza*"); Ricardo Olmos, in Bernabé and Jiménez San Cristóbal 2001: 283–341 gives a somewhat idiosyncratic collection of archeological documents. Graepler 1997 cautions us not to overtax the archeological evidence.

53 Basel, Antikenmuseum und Sammlung Ludwig; Schmidt et al. 1976: 7 no. 6; see Schmidt 1975 and 1991.

54 Toledo Art Museum, Toledo OH; *LIMC* 7 (1994), 315 no. 70; Johnston and McNiven 1996.

55 J. Paul Getty Museum, Malibu, California; Bottini and Guzzo 1993.

56 Outside the still small circle of scholars on Greek religion, vague denominations survive much longer: the otherwise highly perceptive and innovative Graepler 1997: 180 still calls the tablets "orphisch-pythagoreisch," thus proving his own insight that "auf die archäologische Forschung haben diese neuen Impulse jedoch noch kaum eingewirkt."

57 See Burkert 1987 and Smith 1990.

3 THE MYTH OF DIONYSUS

1 Olympiodorus *In Phd.* 1.3 (41 Westerink)= *OF* 304 I, 318 III, 320 I. Olympiodorus is commenting here on Plat. *Phd.* 62b.

2 Pindar: frg. 133 and see Lloyd-Jones 1985; Plato: see citation of the most important passages and discussion in Bernabé 2002. Bernabé is also excellent on the reconstruction of the myth as a whole; I have followed him closely when creating the summary of the myth that I offer below. Also still helpful is Linforth 1941: 307–64, although I do not agree with all of his conclusions. Edmonds 1999 and Brisson 1992 have argued against the existence of the myth as a whole in antiquity; in my opinion, Bernabé 2002 persuasively counters them. See also Henrichs 2011.

3 *OF* 280–3 and 296–300.

4 *OF* 301–11. In some versions, Hera held the mirror herself. See Chapter 5 n. 103.

5 *OF* 312–13.

6 *OF* 318, 320.

7 The last part of this statement – that each human contains a bit of Dionysus – is found only in the passage from Olympiodorus we have just examined and again at Olympiodorus *In Phd.* 8.7 (123 Westerink = *OF 320* III and 576 V); Damascius *In Phd.* 1.4–9 (31 Westerink = *OF* 299 II) and 1.166 (99 Westerink); and Proclus *In Cra.* 77.24. It may well be a Neoplatonic invention, as most modern scholars agree: Linforth 1941: 329–31, West 1983: 166, Brisson 1992: 493–4, Edmonds 1999: 40–2; cf. however Bernabé 2002: 405–7 who more positively suggests that the Neoplatonists would not have developed this idea if Orphic

sources had not at least hinted at it. The first part of the statement – that humans carry the stain of the Titan's crime – is found elsewhere, including Plut. *De esu carnium* 1.7, 996b and other authors cited in *OF* 318 and 320. Bernabé 2002 discusses in depth the age of this part of the myth, reaffirming that it can already be seen behind references made by Pindar, Plato, and Xenocrates (Pind. frg. 133 = Plat. *Meno* 81b; Plat. *Leg.* 701b and 854b, *Phd.* 62b, *Cra.* 400c; Xenocrates frg. 20 = Damascius *In Phd.* 1.2 [29 Westerink].) Cf. Henrichs 2011.

8 This topic is discussed in West 1983: 94–100, Lloyd-Jones 1985, Johnston and McNiven 1996, and Bernabé 2002: 413–18 and see also Bernabé 1999. Some of the most important passages supporting the idea are Pind. frg. 133; Diod. Sic. 5.75.4; schol. Lucian 52.8 (212.22 Rabe); the Gurôb Papyrus (text no. 3 in our Appendix 4); *OF* 350 (= Damascius *In Phd.* 1.11 (35 Westerink); Proclus *In Ti.* III 297.3 as quoted in *OF* 34 III.

9 *OF* 59, 322, 326, 327, 328. Bernabé, in his edition of the fragments, does not accept what he includes as *OF* 59 as being "Orphic," but rather includes it under a rubric called *fabulae de Baccho et Titanibus traditio altera*, because he thinks that the sequence of events it represents differs from that described in genuinely Orphic fragments. As I will discuss below, I do not think we should aim at the reconstruction of one particular "Orphic" story but rather should assume that several versions may have been in circulation at any given time.

10 *Prot. Jas.* 17–20 (in circulation by the second century).

11 Smith 1990. Edmonds 1999 overplays the point. See also Graf's discussion in our Chapter 2.

12 Most recently, Bernabé, 2002: 416–18; cf. Henrichs 2011. See also Rose 1936 and 1943, Lloyd-Jones 1985. West 1983: 137 includes the story in his reconstruction of the Eudemian Theogony, dating to the fourth century. No other incident in Persephone's biography has any connection with the human race; no other incident could require humans to pay Persephone requital. Moreover, as Bernabé notes (following Rose 1943), the Greek word that I have translated as retribution (*poinē*) almost always refers to requital for a blood-crime; the only other known incident in Persephone's mythic biography that caused her grief, her rape by Hades, was not a blood-crime. We find what look like allusions to Orphic beliefs elsewhere in Pindar as well; see Lloyd-Jones 1985 and Bernabé 1999. Arguing against the common interpretation of the fragment was Edmonds 1999: 47–9. Linforth 1941: 345–50, considers other interpretations, but concludes that "there is a high degree of probability of Rose's interpretation." Most of Linforth's reasons for hesitating to accept the interpretation completely have been well addressed by subsequent scholars.

13 *DK* 22 B 14 = Clem. Al. *Protr.* 2.22.2–3. The fragment joins together in a list "*nuktipoloi* (night-wanderers): *magoi, bacchoi, lenai* and *mystai* (initiates)." Clement introduces it in the midst of his condemnation of all who perform mystery initiations.

14 West 1983: passim with a summary on pp. 259–63.

15 See West 1983: 7–29, Parker 1995, Riedweg 1995, Bremmer 1999a and 2002: Chapter 2.

16 Plat. *Resp.* 363c–366b; Eur. *Hipp.* 952–4; Theophr. *Char.* 16.12; Hdt. 4.79. Cf.

Plut. *Apophth. Lacon.* 224e and Philodemus *On Poetry* 1.181; also, col. xx of the Derveni Papyrus, which seems to refer to *orpheotelestai* or something very similar. The fragment of Heraclitus cited in n. 13 is harder to be sure of: it mocks those it lists, but we cannot be certain that *bacchoi* are initiates into a Dionysiac mystery cult, as opposed to other sorts of Dionysiac worshippers or that *mystai* does not mean Eleusinian initiates.

17 I borrow the term *bricoleur* from Lévi-Strauss 1962: 16–36. For other recent applications of the term to ancient experts in myth and religion, see Frankfurter 2002 and 2003.

18 Exceptions are *aitia* for some cults that were instituted during the historical period at the command of the Delphic Oracle, for example, or cults attributed to historical, even if legendarily embroidered, figures such as Solon of Athens.

19 In the pages that follow, I will speak of the creator(s) of the myth of Dionysus in the singular ("author," "*bricoleur*," etc.). Although we cannot know whether there were one or several at the beginning, certainly, as time went on, a number of *bricoleurs* adapted the myth in different directions to suit their aims.

20 Hdt. 7.6.3. See also Dillery 2005.

21 Alexander of Abonuteichos: The ancient source is Lucian's *Alexander or the False Prophet*. Among modern discussions, see Lane Fox 1986: 241–50 and Jones 1986.

22 Joseph Smith: Bloom 1992: 77–128, Krakauer 2003: 52–82, 95–114, 123–33, 191–225.

23 Johnston 1999a: 63–71.

24 On the artistic representations, see Carpenter 1997: 62–4.

25 Diod. Sic. 4.25.4. The myth of Dionysus' descent to claim Semele from the Underworld is also told by Apollod. *Bibl.* 3.5.3, Paus. 2.31.2 and 2.37.5, and Plut. *De sera* 27 566a. The myth serves as an *aition* of a cult at the Alcyonian Lake in Amymone near Lerna (Paus. 2.37.5 and further sources and discussion in Sir James Frazer's notes in the Loeb edition of Apollodorus, vol. 1, pp. 332–3). Other mentions of Semele's ascent to Olympus with Dionysus' help (but without mention of Hades) are Charax *FGrH* 103 F 14, Aristides 41.3, Philostr. *Imag.* 1.14, and *Anth. Pal.* 3.1. Pind. *Ol.* 2.25–7 mentions that she died and then ascended to the company of the gods, but does not explicitly say that Dionysus was responsible for her rescue. Later authors make Zeus or his lightning the means of her ascent: Diod. Sic. 5.52, Achilles Tatius 2.37.4, Nonnus *Dion.* 8.409 and 9.206. In the passage from Plutarch, the road by which Dionysus leads her up travels through bands of reveling souls taking part in much the same rewards as mystery initiates typically do in the afterlife.

26 Bremmer 1997.

27 In describing these births as "first," "second," and "third," Philodemus is not implying that they occurred in this order in a composite myth; he is interested in delineating the various ways that myth narrated the birth of Dionysus without any particular concern for chronology. Cf. Rudhardt 2002: 493–5.

28 Rhea reviving Dionysus: Euphorion frg. 53 De Cuenca = Philodemus *On Piety* (P. Hercul. 247 III 1 ff., p. 16 Gomperz = *OF* 59 I); Philodemus *On Piety* (P. Hercul. 1088 XI 14 ff., p. 47 Gomperz = *OF* 59 II); Cornutus *Nat. Deor.* 30

(58.6 Lang = *OF* 59 IV). Cf. Appendix 2 and Henrichs 2011. On Euphorion, see the edition, translation, and commentary of B. Acosta-Hughes and C. Cusset (Paris, 2012) frg. 53, who note that Dionysus was a divinity who particularly interested the poet, and that he surely treated this event as well in his *Dionysus*.

29 Demeter reviving him: Diod. Sic. 3.62.8 = *OF* 59 III. Note also that Bacchylides made it Rhea who restored Pelops to health after he had been cut up into a cauldron by his father (frg. 42 = schol. Pind. *Ol.* 1.26). Perhaps Bacchylides also influenced the Orphic *bricoleur* or perhaps Bacchylides was influenced by him, depending on how early this version circulated. Further on Rhea's connection with Dionysus and his mysteries, see Appendix 2 and cf. Henrichs 2011.

30 See West 1983: 72, 107, 131–2, 217.

31 Hecataeus of Miletus *FGrH* 1 F 300 = Hdt. 2.144. Hecataeus of Abdera later maintained that Orpheus had introduced the mysteries of Osiris and Isis into Greece under the names of Dionysus and Demeter (Diod. Sic. 1.96.4, *FGrH* 264 F 25); cf. Diod. Sic. 3.62.1 and West 1983: 26.

32 Hdt. 2.59. Rhea and Demeter were equated with one another, moreover, by the fifth century: Melanippides *PMG* 764; Eur. *Hel.* 1301, *Phoen.* 685, *Bacch.* 275; Telestes *PMG* 809 and see West 1983: 81–2, 93, and 217 for their equation specifically in Orphic contexts.

33 Cf. the remarks of West 1983: 140–1.

34 Pentheus: Aeschylus' treatment of the story is mentioned in Aristophanes of Byzantium's *hypothesis* to Euripides' *Bacchae* (= Aesch. frg. 183 Radt); it is shown on late sixth- and early fifth-century vases such as Boston 10.221 (Euphronius) and Berlin: Ch. inv. 1966: 18. Orpheus: Aeschylus' *Bassarae* (Eratosth. *Cat.* 24) and on early fifth-century vases such as Cincinnati 1979.1 and Louvre G416 (Hermonax). The Minyads: discussed at Dowden 1989: 82–4 and Johnston 1999a: 68–70 (the main sources, Plut. *Quaest. Graec.* 299e–300a, cf. *Quaest. Conv.* 717a, are late but the story is older). Actaeon: for his role as an offender of Dionysus, Johnston and McNiven 1996. The main ancient sources are Stesichorus *PMG* 236; Hes. *Cat.* frg. 346 M-W, now confirmed by P. Mich. inv. 1447 verso; Acusilaus *ap.* Apollod. *Bibl.* 3.4.4.

35 Even here we must be careful not to oversimplify things, for the Greek and Egyptian goddesses do rather different things. Rhea or Demeter creates an orderly assemblage of Dionysus' scattered limbs (the verb is *syntithenai* in Philodemus, citing Euphorion, and *synarmozein* in Diodorus) and then revives the dead god. Once reborn, Dionysus mediates between mortals and the rulers of the Underworld. In contrast, although Osiris is dismembered, the pieces of his body remain together in the sarcophagus where Seth first trapped him; it is Isis herself who scatters the pieces after she discovers the sarcophagus, distributing them among the nomes of Egypt to ensure that Osiris is worshipped everywhere. Osiris is not resurrected; he becomes a god of the Underworld and remains there. Both the Greek and Egyptian goddesses introduce slaughtered gods into new roles, but those roles have different implications for humanity. Isis' presence in Osiris' story surely made the option of including Rhea or Demeter in Dionysus' story more appealing, but it was probably not the main reason that a poet or *bricoleur* first did so.

36 Damascius *In Phd.* 1.129 (81 Westerink) = *OF* 322 II. Olympiodorus *In Phd.* 7.10 (113 Westerink) = *OF* 322 III may be referring to the same story when he says that when the myth tells of Apollo assembling the pieces of the dead Dionysus, he was making him "whole again." Olympiodorus then compares the story to the *anodos* of Kore/Persephone. Cf. also Proclus *In Ti.* II 198.10 = *OF* 322 IV. This story may be associated with a cult of Apollo Dionysido-tus in Phlya that Pausanias mentions at 1.31.4; these may be connected with mysteries held there, on which see Graf 2003: 241–62, esp. 246. The Phlyan mysteries seem to have had connections to Eleusis. Yet other late antique sources speak of Dionysus emerging whole again from the assembled pieces without mentioning any other god's involvement: Macrob. *In Somn.* 1.12.11 = *OF* 326; *Myth. Vat.* 3.12.5; Nonnus *Dion.* 24.28–49; Origen *C. Cels.* 4.17.

37 Clem. Al. *Protr.* 2.18.1–2 = *OF* 322 I; Callim. frg. 643 Pf. and Euphorion frg. 13 De Cuenca = Tzetzes ad Lycoph. *Alex.* 208 = *OF* 36; Damascius *In Phd.* 1.129 (81 Westerink) = *OF* 322 II; cf. Proclus *In Ti.* II 197.24 and II 198.5 = *OF* 311 II and 322 IV. For inclusion in the Eudemian or an earlier theogony, see West 1983: 74, 96, 140–1 and more generally all of his Chapter 5.

38 Philochorus = *FGrH* 328 7; Dinarchus = *FGrH* 399 F 1 = *SH* 379 B. See also Plut. *De Is. et Os.* 35, 365a and Clement of Rome, *Recognit.* 10. For discussion see West 1983: 150–2; Burkert 1983: 123–5. At first glance, it may seem as if a grave of Dionysus precludes the idea of his rebirth. But we cannot expect myth – especially myth that has been developed by one or more *bricoleurs* – to play by the rules of strict logic. Moreover, a god's death is never permanent: Zeus had a grave on Crete but clearly was not "dead" in any lasting sense.

39 *OF* 314–16, 326–7.

40 Nonnus *Dion.* 24.48 ff. = *OF* 326 III; Proclus *Hymn* 7.11–15 = *OF* 327 II; Hyg. *Fab.* 167 = *OF* 327 III. Cf. Lucian *Salt.* 39 = *OF* 327 VI, which ties together the two Dionysuses (the son of Persephone and the son of Semele) without speci-fying how they are linked. Some scholars have rejected the possibility that this tradition is Orphic (apparently on the strength of the fact that Semele does not appear in Kern's collection of "Orphic" fragments) but her presence in the Orphic *Hymns* compels us to reconsider this point, as Rudhardt 2002 has convincingly argued. Also notable is the fact that Aristid. *Or.* 41.2 = *OF* 328 I describes the story of Semele's conception of Dionysus and the fetus' gestation in Zeus' thigh as a tale told by Orpheus and Musaeus; Proclus *In Ti.* III 99, 17 = *OF* 328 III says the story was told by *hoi theologoi* using *mystika onomata*. A version of the story that is even more familiar to modern readers is that Zeus himself swallowed the heart before he made love to Semele; many scholars of the past one hundred years have mentioned it. However, as Martin West already saw (1983: 162 n. 80), there is no evidence for this in ancient sources at all; it seems to have been the accidental invention of H. J. Rose, in his edition of Hyginus and cf. Rose 1928: 51.

41 Clem. Al. *Protr.* 2.18.1, and quoted by Euseb. *Praep. evang.* 2.3.25.

42 Kumarbi: *The Song of Kumarbi* §§5–18; Cronus: Hes. *Theog.* 453–500; Zeus: Hes. *Theog.* 886–900.

43 Sokolowski 1955: no. 84 (= *I. Smyrna* 728 = *SGOst* 05/01/04), l. 13.

44 Cf. Rudhardt 2002. Aristid. *Or.* 41. 2, Proclus *In Ti.* III 99.17 and I 407.22–408 = *OF* 328 I, III and 329 I.

45 This topic is extensively discussed by Detienne 1979: 68–94; some of my observations will draw upon his analysis. He returned to the topic in 1989a.

46 Arn. *Adv. Nat.* 5.19 (273.9 Marchesi) = *OF* 312 III and Clem. Al. *Protr.* 2.18.1–2.

47 Most of the ancient descriptions of how Dionysus was divided into pieces can conveniently be found together in *OF* 209–12 Kern (they are scattered among many different fragment entries in Bernabé). Among those using *sparagmos* or a cognate are: Diod. Sic. 5.75.4, Lucian *Salt.* 39, Olympiodorus *In Phd.* 1.3 (41 Westerink), Damascius *In Phd.* 1.4 (31 Westerink) and Proclus *In Prm.* 808.25, *In Cr.* 109.19, *In Alc.* 344.31. Some ancient authors use the verb *merizō* or *diamerizō*, which simply means "divide into portions" with no implication of how the division is accomplished. Nonnus is more specific, mentioning a type of knife (*makhaira*) that is used in sacrifice.

48 *OF* 312. It is important to note that in all versions of the myth, the Titans do, in fact, cook Dionysus' flesh. *Omophagia*, the act of eating raw flesh that often follows *sparagmos* in Dionysiac myths and that stands in utter opposition to sacrifice, does not occur here (Detienne 1979: *passim* and 1989a). On the method of cooking (boiling then roasting) see Detienne 1979: 74–9 and Burkert 1983: 89n.29.

49 Tantalus: Pind. *Ol.* 1.24–53, Bacch. frg. 42 Snell-Maehler, Eur. *IT* 386–8 and *Hel.* 388–9, etc.; Lycaon: Eratosth. *Cat.* 8 = Hes. frg. 163 M-W, Lycoph. 480–1, Ov. *Met.* 1.199–243, Hyg. *Astr.* 2.4.1, Apollod. *Bibl.* 3.8.1, etc.; Thyestes: Aesch. *Ag.* 1191–3, 1219–22, and 1583–1611, Accius 220–2, Sen. *Thy.* 749–88, etc.; Astyages and Harpagus: Hdt. 1.119; Christian stories: see full discussion in Frankfurter 2006. Discussion of the stories of Tantalus and Lycaon with further *comparanda* at Burkert 1983: 83–134.

50 Initiatory elements in the stories of Pelops and Lycaon: Harrison 1927: 243–8. Jeanmaire 1939: 562–3, Burkert 1983: 84–103, Wathelet 1986, Moreau 1987. See also now Pache 2004: 92–4 for a re-evaluation of initiatory elements in both stories.

51 Initiatory interpretation of Dionysus story: Harrison 1908/09: 322–8, 1921: xxxiii–xxxiv, 1922: 491–4, 1927: 13–27, Jeanmaire 1951: 390; West 1983: 143–50 etc. Criticisms: Nilsson's review of Jeanmaire in *Gnomon* 25 (1953) 276, Detienne 1979: 80–2.

52 Some of them, notably Jeanmaire 1953: 390, also point to the Titans' smearing of white gypsum on their faces as part of their deception of Dionysus, arguing that this parallels the ways in which elders disguise themselves during initiation ceremonies in some tribal cultures. Detienne rightly dismisses this: 1979: 80–2 (although I do not necessarily agree with the alternative explanation of the gypsum that he offers).

53 Zeus born on Crete: Hes. *Theog.* 477–84 and often thereafter. Curetes: the *Hymn to Zeus* from Palaikastro (see now Furley and Bremmer 2001: 2, 1–20), Callim. *Hymn* 1.52, Apollod. *Bibl.* 1.5, Strabo 10.468.

54 Demeter: Hom. *Hymn Dem.* 239–41 and often thereafter; Isis: Plut. *De Is. et*

Os. 16, 357c; Thetis: Ap. Rhod. *Argon.* 4.869–79, Apollod. *Bibl.* 3.13.6, schol. Lycoph. 178; Medea: Eumelus frg. 23 West = frg. 5 Bernabé (see discussion at Johnston 1997). Other parallels are offered by stories where Medea dismembers and cooks adults in a kettle, pulling them out in a rejuvenated state: the earliest mention comes from the *Nostoi* frg. 6 West; see the *hypothesis* of Euripides' *Medea* for a list.

55 Lycaon and flood: Ov. *Met.* 1.163–252 (although note that the actions of the Giants contribute to Zeus' decision as well, 151–62); Thyestes and sun: Sen. *Thy.* 776–8.

56 Hes. *Theog.* 521–616.

57 Story no. 1: Orph. *Argo.* 17–20, Dio Chrys. *Or.* 30.10, Oppian *Hal.* 5, Julian *Ep.* 89b292 (159.19 Bidez). Story no. 2: Olympiodorus *In Phd.* 1.3 (41 Westerink), Damascius *In Phd.* 1.8 (31 Westerink). Story no. 3: Kaibel *Suppl.* 1036a (Perinthos, second century CE). All of these, plus some further supporting citations, are collected as *OF* 320; see further discussion in Bernabé 2002.

58 The sources are collected and discussed by Gantz 1993: 445–54. Among the most important are Hes. frg. 43a.65 M-W, Xenophanes 1.21 W, Pind. *Nem.* 1.67–9, Apollod. *Bibl.* 2.7.1 and schol. *Od.* 7.59.

59 Most 1997; cf. West 1978 ad loc.; cf. Clay 2003: 81–99, esp. pp. 90 n.30 and 97. Other scholars have suggested that the Ash tree nymphs are to be associated with other negatively charged things, such as the spears that were made from ash wood; these viewpoints are summarized and critiqued by West and Most.

60 Interestingly, as Bömer notes in his commentary on *Met.* 1.151–62, the blood of dreadful gods also can send up creatures who are not so much dreadful as simply marginal. Uranus' blood sends up the Phaeacians (Acusilaus *FGrH* 2 F 4), the blood of the Titans sends up the Hyperboreans (Pherenicus ap. schol. Pind. *Ol.* 3.28c), and the blood of the giants sends up the Ligurians (schol. Lycoph. 1356).

61 These are not the *first* humans – Ovid tells of their creation at the hands of a god in lines 76–88 – but these humans do have their own importance in Ovid's story: it is their bad behavior, in combination with Lycaon's cannibalistic sacrifice, that finally precipitates the gods' decision to wipe out the human race.

62 *Enuma elish* VI, *Atrahasis* I.4. Cf. Heidel 1942: 66–81.

63 Cf. Clay 2003: 97, Loraux 1996: 20–6.

64 I follow all recent editors of Hesiod in rejecting as spurious four lines that are interjected to the text by some manuscripts and usually listed as 173b–e. For discussion, West 1978: 194–5 and Most 1997.

65 More recently, Clay 2003: 95–9 has argued that Hesiod alludes to a world-wide anthropogony in the *Theogony*, drawing on line 50, which states that the Giants and humans are of a single race, which might allude to the story of humans being born from Giants' blood (below n. 69), and on lines 185–7, which describe the birth of Ash tree nymphs from the drops of Uranus' blood; a scholiast to line 187 claims that these nymphs were the mothers of humans. Clay concludes that Hesiod means us to understand the nymphs and the Giants – both products of Uranus' blood – as the parents of humanity. Although I think that Clay reads somewhat too much into these passages – the passages clearly

left room for debate about the origins of humanity already among ancient scholars – I agree with her that line 50 may be an important allusion to the same pattern that I have been tracing in this section – that dreadful creatures, including humans, are born from the blood of dreadful gods.

66 *Enuma elish* tablet VI; *Atrahasis* I; cf. *Enki and Ninmah* 24–43.

67 Plat. *Prt.* 321c–e, cf. Aesop's fables nos. 111, 112 and 120 Chambry. The first four Hesiodic races of humans are created by gods, as well.

68 To take just the earliest attestations of the best-known examples: Deucalion and Pyrrha produce a whole new race of humans by throwing stones upon the earth: Acusilaus *FGrH* 2 F 35, Pind. *Ol.* 9.42–53. The first Thebans spring from local soil after Cadmus planted dragon's teeth in it; Jason later uses teeth from the same dragon to produce earth-born men in Colchis: Pherecydes *FGrH* 3 F 22.

69 Clay 2003: 96–8, in fact, posits that behind this tale of how the giants and Ash tree nymphs were born there lay an anthropogony that Hesiod does not articulate but which his listeners would have known, according to which these two groups (sexually) produced the first humans. If she is correct, this comes close to assigning to humanity the same sort of violent and haphazard origin that the Orphic story assigned to it; Clay's hypothesized anthropogony may well have been a direct inspiration to our *bricoleur*.

70 Powell 2003: 305, also West 1983.

71 Proclus *In Resp.* II 74.26 = *OF* 159.

72 There seems to have been an alternative Orphic tradition in which there were five cosmic rulers: Phanes, Night, Uranus, Cronus, and Zeus – but even here, human races seem to have been associated only with Phanes, Cronus, and Zeus. There are traces of an "Orphic" version with four rulers (Cronus, Zeus, Poseidon, and Hades), although West sees Neopythagorean influence behind it: see West 1983: 70–2, 98, 107 and n. 73 and further at *OF* 174.

73 Particularly telling is the fact that the Orphic story fails to connect a specific metal with the third and final race, which was pressed to cover the third, fourth, and fifth of Hesiod's races, two of which had been connected with metals.

74 Cf., both for Phanes and Cronus, the verb *poieō*, which was used by Hesiod to describe how the gods created the four first races of humanity, and *tithēmi*, which Hesiod used to describe Zeus' creation of the fifth race, which connote much more "hands-on" activities, more direct involvement and volition than either of the two first verbs used in Proclus.

75 For example, it describes the way that the demiurge combined fire and earth to create the cosmos (31b7, 69c1–2), the way he created larger bodies by combining smaller ones (54c7 and d6, 56b2), and the way that each of the two human genders was created by combining the physical body with an animating substance (91a).

76 The fragments from which we can reassemble this story are collected and discussed by West 1983: 88–106.

77 A partial analogy is provided by Hesiod's myth of the Five Ages (*Op.* 110–201). The humans of the Golden Age become holy *daemones* and protectors of mortals after death, the humans of the Silver Age are called blessed after

their death, even if they must spend the afterlife below ground, and some humans of the Heroic Age are sent after death to the Isles of the Blessed where they enjoy a carefree existence. Thus, the quality of each race implicitly determines its postmortem fate, but in contrast to the Dionysiac myth, eschatology is not determined by a single, decisive action. (Further on Hesiod's complex motivations in this passage, see the excellent analysis in Most 1997.)

4 THE ESCHATOLOGY BEHIND THE TABLETS

1 On this see Janko 1984; Zuntz 1971 frequently mentions epic parallels during his discussion of individual tablets as well. On the issue of whether the tablets are "Orphic" – and thus have anything to do with the myth of Dionysus attributed to Orpheus that I discussed in Chapter 3 – see Appendix 1, and (for the counter argument) Schlesier 2001, who also has a very concise reconstruction of the Underworld scenario in the tablets.

2 Dickie 1998 argues that three of these shorter tablets, which mention Posidippus, Philicus, and Euphorion, belonged to known poets of the Hellenistic age.

3 Bernabé and Jiménez San Cristóbal 2001: 247 (= 2008: 230) employ virtually the same analogy, as I discovered only after writing these pages.

4 *The Book of the Watchers* = 1 *Enoch* §1–36, see especially §27–36. For discussion of these and related Jewish and Christian images of heaven, see Copeland 2004. Cf. Himmelfarb 1993.

5 See Himmelfarb 1983 esp. Chapter 4.

6 See further Graf 2004, and for many Mediterranean examples, the chapter on "Death, the Afterlife and Other Last Things," in Johnston 2004: 470–95.

7 Watkins 1995: 277–91.

8 Cf. also the discussion of Edmonds 2004, esp. Chapter 2.

9 See discussion in Bernabé and Jiménez San Cristóbal 2008: 22–4.

10 Frgs. 129, 131a, 130 = Plut. *Cons. ad Apoll.* 35 120c–d and *De lat. vit.* 7.1130c.

11 *Phd.* 107d–108c. Wandering paths through the Underworld are also referred to by Plato at *Grg.* 524a and *Resp.* 614c. Cf. Hegesippus frg. 5 G-P = *Anth. Pal.* 7.545 and more generally on the question, Edmonds 2004.

12 E.g., Hdt. 2.81, Eur. *Hipp.* 952–4, Plat. *Leg.* 782c, Apul. *Apol.* 56. Discussion at Detienne 1979: 59–67 and Burkert 1985: 301–4.

13 E.g., Plut. *De aud. poet.* 4.21, Diog. Laert. 6.39, Julian, *Or.* 7.238; generally on the topic, Graf 1974: 103–7.

14 Punishment of the bad: *Od.* 11.576–600; Menelaus: *Od.* 4.561–9; Achilles: *Aethiopis* Proclus' summary lines 26–8. See discussion in Johnston 1999a: 11–14.

15 There are traces of what may be this idea in Homer (*Od.* 11.436–8) and Hesiod (*Op.* 282–4) as well; see Parker 1983: 201–6.

16 See Richardson 1974: *ad* 371 for discussion.

17 Generally, in suggesting that Plato and Pindar adapted the system that we see in the Gold Tablets, I am countering an earlier suggestion, espoused most ardently by Zuntz 1971: 277–393, that both the tablets and Plato were adapting Pythagorean doctrine. See also discussion at Kingsley 1995: 257–72.

18 Citations for the funereal connections of the cypress are provided by Gruppe 1906: 789-9. See also the discussions by Bernabé and Jiménez San Cristóbal 2008: 26-8 and Zuntz 1971: 373, the latter of whom doubted whether the funereal associations were significant among the Greeks, as opposed to the Romans.

19 Gigante 1975: 223; Bernabé and Jiménez San Cristóbal 2001: 45-6. On the idea of white = abnormal see Pugliese Carratelli and Foti 1974: 120 and cf. Janko 1984: 99, who translates *leukos* here as "ghostly," and Scalera McClintock 1991: 398, who offers "spettrale." Further discussion of all these theories at Bernabé and Jiménez San Cristóbal 2008: 25-8.

20 Zuntz 1971: 385; I do not agree with all his conclusions here, however. Cf. Bernabé and Jiménez San Cristóbal 2008: 27 with n. 81, who develop the idea in the same direction as I do here.

21 On the white rock, compare *Od.* 10.515, which similarly mentions a rock at the entrance to the Underworld without specifying its color. *Aethiopis*: Proclus' summary, 26-8. Sunny parts of the Underworld: Pind. *Ol.* 2.61-2 and frg. 129, Ar. *Ran.* 454-5, etc.

22 I agree here with the conclusions of Janko 1984, against those of Zuntz 1971: 376-83 and 1976. See also Riedweg 1998: 365.

23 Tzifopoulos 2010: 226-31 argues that the substitution of "left" for "right" reflects local Cretan geography.

24 A few of many possible examples: the Egyptian *Book of the Dead* Chapter 145 (discussed by Zuntz 1971: 374-6); *PGM* 4.625-710 (from the so-called "Mithras Liturgy"). Further examples can be found in some of the essays included in Johnston 2004: 470-95.

25 *Od.* 11.92-4 (Teiresias), 11.155 (Anticleia), 11.473-6 (Achilles).

26 Among recent authors discussing the Hesiodic background are Edmonds 2004: 77 and Bernabé and Jiménez San Cristóbal 2008: 39-44 (the latter of whom cite previous treatments and summarize the most important strands of interpretation). Burkert 1975: 89 comes somewhat close to the interpretation I will offer here.

27 West 1978 *ad loc.*

28 Olivieri 1915: 13, Harrison 1922: 587 and cf. 494-5; Comparetti 1882: 116.

29 Cf. the similar analysis of Detienne 1963: esp. 115, who suggests that the Pythagoreans attempted to return themselves to the status of the Golden Race by living lives of ethical virtue; the initiates were taking a ritualized route to the same goal. Cf. also Edmonds 2004: 75-80 who makes an argument somewhat similar to mine, but starts from different presumptions about humanity's origins and inherent nature, with which I do not agree.

30 Zuntz 1971: 377-81; cf. Bernabé and Jiménez San Cristóbal 2008: 29, Edmonds 2004: 47-8. On the motif, see also Déonna 1939. As several scholars have discussed, the thirst of the dead is particularly a motif in the ancient Egyptian guides for the dead (e.g., Zuntz 1971: 370-4); this has tempted some to suggest that the Gold Tablets borrowed the idea from the Egyptians, most recently, Merkelbach 1999. However, as Zuntz already noted, and as Bernabé and Jiménez San Cristóbal have more recently argued (2008: 34-5), it is both unnecessary (given the widespread existence of the motif) and wrong to look

to Egypt for direct precedents. The Egyptians sought water in the afterlife so that they could proceed on their journey; there is no reference in Egyptian sources to the use of water to conserve – or erase – memory in the afterlife.

31 A few grave epigrams from the Roman period offer examples. Kaibel 658, from Rome, asks that Hades give cold water to the soul of a boy who died in the flower of his youth; Kaibel 719, also from Rome, speaks of giving cold water to the soul, and epigrams from Roman Egypt (in Greek) ask Osiris to give cold water to the dead.

32 E.g., Lucian *De Luct.* 5, Catull. 65.5, Verg. *Aen.* 6.703, and see Rohde 1925: 249 n. 21 and 443 n. 37 and Nilsson 1943. We also hear about such things as "gates of *lēthē*" through which the dead pass, and the "House of Lethe," which the dead enter, and the "plain of *lēthē*" over which they travel, which have the same effect as the Waters of Lethe. Discussion and citations at Bernabé and Jiménez San Cristóbal 2008: 30-2.

33 Our only mention of Waters of Memory outside the tablets connects them with the Oracle of Trophonius in Lebedeia (Paus. 9.39.8), where the inquirer drank first from the Fountain of Forgetfulness and then from the Fountain of Memory before making his descent into the shrine – and apparently into Hades – to meet the hero face to face. As Edmonds 2004: 106-8 rightly notes, the functions of the Waters of Memory differ significantly in the two contexts.

34 Thgn. 704-5. Another interpretation, which is offered only by Plut. *De lat. viv.* 1130d-e suggests that the Waters of Lethe cause the souls of the bad to be forgotten by the living. As they are engulfed by its swirling waters, they sink into inglorious obscurity and oblivion. In contrast, the souls of the pious pass the time remembering their own lives while reposing in a meadow that is a place of "glory (*doxa*) and life (*to einai*)" – in other words, they both remember and are remembered. It is only Plutarch who interprets the Waters of Forgetfulness in this way – and he does so, notably, in an essay whose very subject is the question of whether the wise man should seek fame – but his innovation does reflect the common Greek fear of being forgotten after death.

35 *SGOst* 01 01 07 (= Kaibel 204).

36 Plat. *Meno* 81a5-b2. Contra Kingsley 1995: 160-2.

37 Frgs. 102 and 132 Wright; cf. 105, 107, 108 and 133. His more specific claim in frg. 132 that humans in the last incarnational stage manifest themselves on earth as "prophets, minstrels, physicians, and leaders," is very similar to what Pindar says in frg. 133. On the relationships between Empedocles' doctrines and those of our tablets, see also Kingsley 1995: 256-72 and especially Riedweg 1995.

38 Other *comparanda* don't help much. Plato's system suggests that reincarnation will continue indefinitely; *Olympian* 2 makes no clear statement about the good-plus but, notably, claims that the good will remain in their lesser paradise forever; our fragments of Pindar's dirge tell us nothing at all.

39 See discussion with summary of previous views at Edmonds 2004: 94-9.

40 Bremmer 2002: Chapter 2.

41 The poetic license that we must allow Pindar and many of our other sources is

also a problem confronting scholars who would use frg. 133 as ironclad information from which to reconstruct metempsychosis as we see it in the tablets. Who is to say how the ideas that Pindar encountered might have been altered to accommodate the themes of his poem or the views of his patron? Because we have only a fragment of that poem (quoted by Socrates to advance his own arguments), we cannot even begin to guess the answer to this question.

42 Cf. Graf 1974: 98–103, Edmonds 2004: 84–8.

43 Indeed, as Graf shows in the next chapter, purity was probably an overriding concern of all initiates into these mysteries, including those possessing what I have called the "geographic" tablets.

44 As Zuntz 1971: 306–7 notes, we find parallel examples of this construction in Plato, where the psychic horses and charioteers of the gods (and by extension, of humans fit to gaze upon the Ideas) are described as being "good from good [stock]" (*Phdr.* 246a, cf. e.g., Soph. *Phil.* 874).

45 Cf. Zuntz 1971: 307, and generally on Greek concepts of pollution and purity, Parker 1983.

46 Plat. *Phd.* 69c, cf. *Resp.* 533d and see discussions at Zuntz 1971: 307–8, Graf 1974: 103–26, Kingsley 1995: 118–23.

47 Graf 1974: 171–2.

48 Cf. Bernabé and Jiménez San Cristóbal 2008: 102–5.

49 Rohde 1925: 448 n. 54 with 581–2, Zuntz 1971: 316.

50 Ancient citations for this and the other versions of the anthropogony at p. 67; cf. Bernabé 2002. The argument that initiates identified themselves with the Titans is developed in an interesting (but to me, unconvincing) direction by Seaford 1986.

51 Asclepius: Hes. frg. 51 M-W, Stesichorus 194 *PMG*, Acusilaus 2 F 18, Pherecydes 3 F 35, Pind. *Pyth.* 3.55–8, etc.

52 Semele: Achilles Tatius 2.37.4, Nonnus 8.409 and 9.206; Heracles: Diod. Sic. 4.38.4–5, Apollod. *Bibl.* 2.7.7. Cf. Amphiaraus, who did not rise to heaven, but when Zeus' lightning opened a chasm in the earth, which swallowed up his chariot, his horses, and himself, Amphiaraus became a god under the ground (Apollod. *Bibl.* 3.6.8, Paus. 8.2.4). See further examples at Rohde 1925: 192 n. 68 and 581–2.

53 Cf. Edmonds 2004: 74–5.

54 Burkert 1961: 208–13; he precedes me in developing the idea in connection with heroes such as Asclepius. Cf. also Sourvinou-Inwood 1995: 49–52, Kingsley 1995: 257–9. More generally, the idea of apotheosis or sanctification through lightning may be linked to the widespread use of fire as a purifier; to be completely permeated by heavenly fire could mean to be purified of all defects. As Sourvinou-Inwood notes, a related concept underlies the tales in which Demeter, Thetis, and Isis try to immortalize their nurslings by burning away their mortality in a hearth fire.

55 Rose 1943, Bernabé 2002: 417; Pind. frg. 133; see discussion on pp. 80–5.

56 This theory is thoroughly discussed (and dismissed) by Bernabé and Jiménez San Cristóbal 2008: 129–30. Advocates have included Dieterich 1891: 37; Harrison 1922: 593; Burkert 1975: 97, Kingsley 1995: 264–72, Edmonds 2004:

88–91. Festugière 1932: 137 preferred to understand it as a reference to *hieros gamos*. Further discussion also at Zuntz 1971: 319.

57 Jan Bremmer will be publishing another promising interpretation, which understands *kolpos* to refer to a fold in Persephone's dress.

58 See Haran 1979; del Olmo Lete 1981: 440; Burkert 1975: 99. Carolina López-Ruiz will be publishing a new interpretation of these lines' possible relationship to the ancient Near East.

59 Particularly Kingsley 1995: 264–72.

60 See the summary of theories and discussion at Bernabé and Jiménez San Cristóbal 2008: 76–83. See also Faraone 2011 for a different approach.

61 Zuntz 1971: 326–7, Graf 1993: 245–6, Bernabé and Jiménez San Cristóbal 2008: 80–3. For this interpretation, Ael. *VH* 8.8 offers a partial parallel. For milk in the Getty Hexameters, which offers an important parallel, see Jordan and Kotansky, forthcoming, and Johnston, forthcoming.

62 Kingsley 1995: 264–72 more specifically understands it as a reference to rebirth; I cannot agree with him here.

63 Zuntz 1971: 383–5 and cf. the elaborate ritual pattern worked out by Harrison 1922: 588–99; see also the sensible remarks of Riedweg 1998 esp. 365 and 387–9 and the caution employed by Edmonds 2004: 104–8.

64 Cf. the persuasive conclusions of Pugliese Carratelli 1975, who usefully adduces magical texts as *comparanda*, and Bernabé and Jiménez San Cristóbal 2008: 231–3.

65 Cf. Riedweg 1998: 377 and 389, Bernabé and Jiménez San Cristóbal 2008: 231–3, Riedweg 2002. See also our own discussion of Orpheus' works in Chapter 6.

66 On versions of Demeter's search, see Clinton 1986. On Orphic theogonies, West 1983.

67 Graf 1991 and 1993.

68 It is necessary to make one correction of Graf's 1993 analysis here. On p. 244, he understood τοῖσι ("them") in line 3 to refer back to the προγόνων ἀθεμίστων ("lawless ancestors") of line 2 and therefore wondered what power Dionysus had over the Titans themselves. As he now agrees, τοῖσι must refer forward to οἷς ("whomever") of the phrase "whomever you wish," that is, mortals.

69 The same complex of ideas is illustrated on the Toledo vase: Johnston and McNiven 1996.

70 Compare the similar conclusion of Graf 1993: esp. 249–50 and in the next chapter.

71 See Appendix 2.

72 The word that I have translated above as "redeemed," *apoinos*, is cognate with the one that I have translated elsewhere as "retribution," *poinē*.

73 See further the next chapter.

5 DIONYSIAC MYSTERY CULTS AND THE GOLD TABLETS

1 See the sources in *OF* 1029.

2 See already Dieterich 1923: 214 no. V, on the kid-in-the-milk formula.

3 οἶνον ἔχεις εὐδαίμονα τιμήν: either ⁻˘˘⁻ | ⁻ ⁻ ˘˘ | ⁻ ⁻ || or ⁻˘˘ | ⁻ ⁻ | ⁻˘˘ | ⁻ ⁻ ||.

4   ὄλβιος Hom. *Hymn Dem.* 480; Pind. frg. 137a (Eleusis); τρισόλβιος Soph. frg. 837 Radt (Eleusis); μάκαρ Eur. *Bacch.* 72 (Dionysus). See Richardson 1974: 310–14.

5   Johnston and McNiven 1996.

6   Our nos. 14 and 15.

7   See also our no. 37, "Philiste greets Persephone."

8   On the voice Graf 1993: 257f. and especially Riedweg 1998.

9   On these "purity tablets" see above Chapter 4.

10 Without, however, going as far as thinking that we can reconstruct this poem. For more discussion of this point, see below Chapter 6.

11 Harrison 1922: 588–99; Wieten 1915: 95–119, with reference to the Thurii tablets; more in Riedweg 1998: 371; see also Bernabé and Jiménez San Cristóbal 2008: 90–4.

12 Zuntz 1971: 343.

13 Riedweg 1998: 371 ("dass die verstorbene Mystin anlässlich des Totenrituals von einem Mysterienpriester ... feierlich angesprochen wird"); Bernabé and Jiménez San Cristóbal 2008: 89. With regard to the Pelinna tablets, I moved from initiation rite (Graf 1991: 99) to words in a burial that recalled the initiation formulae (Graf 1993: 249f.).

14 Short texts: our nos. 20–2, 31.

15 On its composition, see Sarah Iles Johnston's analysis above p. 133; it also resonates with Erikepaios, a divine name connected with the Orphic Dionysus, see above p. 154.

16 Our. no. 27. Σύμβολα appears also in the Entella text (our no. 7), but its context is lost.

17 Dieterich 1923: 213–18; add the formula from *PGM* LXX.13–15, Betz 1980.

18 The Greek is ambivalent; for another interpretation, see the preceding chapter.

19 Eleusis: *IG* I^3 6 B 5, C 4 39 (*c.* 460 BCE), Eur. *HF* 613, *Anth. Pal.* 9. 147 (the Rheitoi bridge). Bacchic mysteries: Heraclitus, *DK* 12 B 14; extended to initiates of "Idaean Zeus," i.e., presumably of (Rhea-)Cybele, Eur. frg. 472.10 Kannicht. P. Derv. col. vi 8 concerns either Eleusis or Bacchic mysteries, see below.

20 Samothrace: Hdt. 2.51.4. For Eleusis, the term is amply attested in Athenian literature and epigraphy of the fifth century (e.g., Ar. *Ran.* 887; Sophocles, frg. 804 Radt; Eur. *Supp.*173; *IG* I^3 6 B 33. C 9); in its linguistic form and in its use, it is the name of an Athenian festival, which makes it likely that this was its primary use that then was extended to related rituals such as those in Samothrace or of Dionysus Bacchius. For the theory of a transfer from Athens to Eleusis see Graf 1997b.

21 The information is collected in Rizzo 1918; half a century later, Matz 1963 had not considerably more. A new important document is a Hellenistic frieze from Cos, Burkert 1993. Boyancé 1966 radically contradicted Matz, which highlights the methodological problems; "ainsi peut-on faire dire ce que l'on pense aux documents que l'on choisit" – in other words, almost limitless arbitrariness – is the somewhat desperate conclusion of Jaccottet 2003: 1, 126.

22 See the collection of texts in Jaccottet 2003, vol. 2.

23 Edict of Ptolemy: text no. 4 in our Appendix 4 (its date is somewhat debated, Ptolemy III might also be possible); Gurôb Papyrus: text no. 3 in Appendix 4.

24 On the Orphic *Hymns*, see the edition by Ricciardelli 2000, and the rich monograph of Morand 2001.

25 Seaford 1981.

26 Seaford 1994: 282.

27 His points (Seaford 1994: 282 n. 8): (a) Theophr. *De pietate* 3.20 Pötscher talks about the human sacrifices performed by the Bassarids: this is myth, not ritual; no Greek story about human sacrifices presupposes a "mock sacrifice," see Henrichs 1981. (b) Livy 39.10.7 and 13.11 cannot be taken at face value as to ritual details. (c) Theocr. *Id.* 26.29 must not mean more than that even a boy deserves death if he opposes Dionysus, and not only the adult Pentheus; an age of nine or ten is not the typical age for adolescent rites anyway.

28 See Burkert 1993: 260.

29 Hdt. 2.81 = *OF* 651; see below Chapter 6.

30 Ion, *DK* 36 B 2 = Clem. Al. *Strom.* 1.21.131.3.

31 Diod. Sic. 3.65.6. He does not indicate his source. But since this source is, in its main outlook, euhemeristic, it cannot antedate the Hellenistic period: one might think of Dionysius Scytobrachion, often a source of Diodorus, see Rusten 1982.

32 Flückiger-Guggenheim 1984.

33 Plut. *Alex.* 2.7–9, p. 665d–e.

34 The double snake transformation in Athenag. *Pro Christ.* 20, see West 1983: 73–4; on its possible connection with the Derveni Papyrus, see Burkert 2006: 108–9.

35 Jaccottet 2003.

36 πολλοὶ μὲν ναρθηκοφόροι, παῦροι δέ τε βάκχοι, *OF* 576 (embedded in the prose of Plat. *Phd.* 69c; more in Lobeck 1829: 813).

37 See above Chapter 4.

38 Eleusis: Deubner 1932: 72. Isis: Apul. *Met.* 11.23.

39 Engelmann and Merkelbach 1973: no. 206.

40 See Parker 1983: 281–307: the development from Bacchic experience to eschatological concerns was introduced by the Pythagoreans and Empedocles.

41 Plat. *Leg.* 790d–791a ; compare Arist. *Pol.* 1342a7ff. See Linforth 1946.

42 *sacrificulus et vates* Livy 39.8.3.

43 For binding spells in general, see Graf 1997a: 118–74; for the connection of binding spells with the dead, see Johnston 1999a: 36–81, esp. 71–80.

44 Johnston 1999a: 53f., 82–123.

45 The term in Theophr. *Char.* 16; Philodemus, *On Poems* 1.181 Janko (see below n. 48); Plut. *Apophth. Lacon.* 224e; see also above Chapter 3.

46 Plat. *Resp.* 366a–b (= *OF* 574).

47 Betegh 2004: 67f. thinks of "Orphic books burnt on pyres – such as the one at Derveni."

48 *VS* 22 B 14; see Johnston 1999a: 110.

49 See Graf 1997a: 21f., with the developments in Bremmer 1999b.

50 Philodemus, *On Poems* 1.181 Janko (Janko 2000: 400f.) – Ὀρφεοτελεστοῦ τυμπάνωι.

51 Janko 2000: 401 reduces the *tympanon* to an instrument in the cult of the Mother and the Corybantes.

52 Eur. *Bacch*. 59; see the longer narration of how in Crete the Curetes and Corybantes invented the *tympanon* "for me" [the chorus of maenads] and gave it to Rhea, from whom "the mad satyrs" received it, *Bacch*. 120–34; the designation of the satyrs as mad might hint at the myth of Dionysus' madness, see below.

53 See Carpenter 1989.

54 Plut. *Agis and Cleomenes* 54.2. 820d τελετὰς τελεῖν καὶ τύμπανον ἔχων ἐν τοῖς βασιλείοις ἀγείρειν; see also Plut. *Quom. adulat*. 17, 60a.

55 On the history of Cybele see Borgeaud 1996/2004. Burkert 1993: 270–3 prefers a later date for the myth.

56 Eumelos F 11 Bernabé (schol. A Iliad. 6.131), from a scholion in Lycoph. *Alex*. 273. For Plato see below n. 60; Eur. *Cyc*. 3 (Hera sent madness to Dionysus), see also *Bacch*. 130, above n. 52, and above Chapter 3.

57 Hippocr. *Morb. sacr*. 4; see also Eur. *Hipp*. 141–4 (Pan, Hecate, Corybantes, the Mother). On her followers, the Corybantes, who likewise send and heal madness, see below n. 62.

58 See Pind. *Dith*. 2.6–14; Eur. *Bacch*. 120–34 (etiological myth of the *tympanon*: invented by the Curetes/ Corybantes who presented it to Rhea from whom the satyrs obtained it).

59 *OF* 350 Bernabé who suggests either Zeus or the oracle of Night as speaker; see also above p. 164.

60 Plat. *Phdr*. 244d and cf. Johnston 1999a, esp. 107–8 and 130–9.

61 The title: *OF* 605 (see Bernabé's introduction to 602–5); for the frightening ritual: Plat. *Euthyd*. 277d = *OF* 602.

62 Orpheus, *Hymn* 39, 9f. For the healing of madness: Ar. *Vesp*. 119; Plat. *Leg*. 790d–791a; for sending madness: Eur. *Hipp*. 141–4. An overview: Linforth 1946; Dodds 1951: 77–80. Among Orpheus' writings, there was also a *Korybantikon*, *OF* 610–1.

63 Orph. *Hymn* 37. See Johnston 1999a, esp. 107–8 and 130–9.

64 Pan *Hymn* 11.23; Eumenides *Hymn* 70.9; for Pan see also Eur. *Hipp*. 141–4.

65 Pan: Borgeaud 1979: 137–75; Eumenides: Johnston 1999a: 250–87 and often.

66 On the group see Morand 2001: 231–89.

67 Matz 1963: pl. 24.

68 To Nilsson 1957: 95, Matz 1963: 18–21 and Burkert 1987: 95f. it is part of the central rites (Burkert 1987: 96 has the evidence for earlier, non-mystical iconography); Boyancé 1966: 35–45 contradicts and thinks it preliminary only.

69 Diod. Sic. 1.22.7, following an unknown earlier account.

70 Orph. *Hymn* 46, with the remarkable and otherwise unattested myth that Dionysus, borne by Semele and fostered by the nymphs in Nysa, was brought to queen Persephone as "terror for the gods," φόβος ἀθανάτοισι θεοῖσι. Whatever the exact story, the association of this Dionysus and the Underworld is much closer than even in the regular Orphic mythology.

71 Livy 39.8.7 talks about *stupra promiscua ingenuorum feminarumque*, "indiscriminate rape of free males and of females."

72 Jacoby, *FGrH* 264 F 25 includes the passage 1.22.7 in his text of Hecataeus;

after Spoerri 1959. Scholars have become less confident, however, with these attributions.

73 Matz 1963: fig. 6; such triptycha were called "reliefs with doors," πίνακες τεθυρωμένοι; for a much earlier initiation scene with such a "relief with doors" see below n. 80.

74 Villa Medici: Nilsson 1957: fig. 19 = Matz 1963: fig. 22.

75 A flute player e.g. in Matz 1963: fig. 7 (Farnesina).

76 Libations: Matz 1963: fig. 2 (Farnesina), 16: 2 (bowl); pig sacrifice: ibid. fig. 15: 1 and Nilsson 1957: 94 fig. 21 (Arretine bowls), 92 fig. 20b (sarcophagus); cakes or fruit: Nilsson 1957: 83 fig. 15 (relief, Louvre).

77 Matz 1963: fig. 9 (Farnesina), fig. 22 (sarcophagus, Villa Medici: part of the ritual preparation), fig. 31 (sarcophagus, Vatican, Museo Chiaramonti), fig. 38 (sarcophagus, Capitoline Museum). There is a *Krater* among Orpheus' works, *OF* 409-412; it had Dionysiac connections according to Proclus *In Ti.* 41d (III 250, 17 Diehl) = *OF* 335 I.

78 Ohlemutz 1940: 113; other inscriptions issuing from the same group in Jaccottet 2003: vol. 2 nos. 92. 94-99.

79 For the rite: Dem. 18.260 (Sabazius); Engelmann and Merkelbach 1973: no. 206 and Himmelmann 1997 (Erythrai).

80 *ABV* 338.3; Metzger 1965: 28 no. 64 and pl. 9.

81 Harrison 1922: 157 (and Farnell 1907, 240f.); Metzger 1965: 30.

82 Richardson 1974: 224.

83 The philosophy underlying the allegorical interpretation of Orpheus' *Theogony* is pre-Platonic, Burkert 1968: 93-114. Several known authors from the later fifth century BCE have been named as its author, from Epigenes (who wrote *Orphica*) to Stesimbrotos of Thasos and Diagoras of Melos, see Betegh 2004: 64f. None are convincing.

84 Col. vi 8; see Johnston 1999a: 273-9 and Betegh 2004: 85-9.

85 Col. vi 4, in Janko's restoration. On the *daimones empodoi*, see Johnston 1999a: 134-8.

86 The material is in Graf 1980: 218 n. 50; Henrichs 1984: 255-68.

87 See the Empousa in Eleusis, Johnston 1999a: 131-8.

88 Janko 1997.

89 Johnston 1999a: 268f.

90 Now in Trinity College, Dublin. Originally published in 1921 by J. G. Smyly as P. Gurôb 1, Hordern 2000 has presented a new edition. For a translation see text no. 4 in our Appendix 4.

91 The ritual formula in Hippol. *Haer.* 5.8: "As when the hierophant in Eleusis performs his great and unspeakable mystery rites – not castrated like Attis but impotent through hemlock and in general having forsaken any procreation in the flesh – he shouts and roars under a huge fire: 'The Lady gave birth to a sacred son, Brimo to Brimos: which means the Strong One to the Strong One.'" Clinton 1992: 91-4 prefers to connect this with the Thesmophoria; Hippolytus, however, is unambiguous in connecting it with the Eleusinian Mysteries. Demeter as Brimo in Clem. Al. *Protr.* 2.15.1 in a context that talks, like the Derveni Papyrus, about her incest with Zeus but then goes on to the mysteries of Cybele and Attis.

Brimo as a form of Hecate in Ap. Rhod. *Argon.* 3.861f. and Lycoph. *Alex.* 1176; as the secret name of a powerful goddess in the *Greek Magical Papyri* (*PGM* IV.2270, 2291, 2611 of Selene, cp. VII.692; LXX.20 of Hecate Ereshkigal). The ancient commentators on Lycoph. *Alex.* 1176 identified her with Hecate or Persephone. In the theogony sketched in Orpheus' *Argonautica*, she is an early power immediately after Phanes, and perhaps the mother of the Giants, v. 17, again going better together with Rhea or Demeter than with Hecate or Persephone.

92 Orph. *Hymn* 38.6, see Diod. Sic. 5.64.4 = Ephorus, *FGrH* 70 F 104 (see below, Chapter 6 n. 31).

93 Or, depending on the restoration, Eubouleus and Erikepaios:]λευ 'Ιρικεπαῖγε.

94 παῖδα ταυρομόρφον Clem. Al. *Protr.* 2.16.3, citing two iambic dimeters of an anonymous "pagan poet" – an unknown tragedian? The story is already presupposed, but not narrated in the Derveni Papyrus.

95 On the uselessness of a category such as syncretism, see Graf 2004, with the earlier bibliography.

96 The term appears often in Orphic literature; see also Jaccottet 2003: vol. 2, 182–90 and often. Pergamon even had "dancing cowboys."

97 The first: Clem. Alex. *Protr.* 2.21.2; the second: ibid. 2.15.3.

98 For *symbola* see Riedweg 1987: 82–4.

99 Clem. Alex. *Protr.* 2.21.2.

100 Firm. Mat. *Err. prof. rel.* 6.2, discussed in detail above Chapter 3.

101 Clem. Alex. *Protr.* 2.17.2 (= *OF* 306).

102 Lydus, *Mens.* 4.51; he also mentions the use of phalli and clarifies that "the mysteries of Orpheus were celebrated" for the son of Zeus and Semele.

103 Museo Civico Archeologico di Bologna, collezione Palagi. Photo: Kerényi 1976 (a better print in the second German edition, 1994): fig. 66b.

104 Text no. 2.1 in our Appendix 4.

105 West 1983: 157.

106 Morand 2001: 276–82.

107 See the extensive discussion of this myth in Chapter 3.

108 Firm. Mat. *Err. prof. rel.* 6; see West 1983: 172f.

109 On Brimo, see above n. 91.

110 Erikepaios as a name of Dionysus: Orph. *Hymn* 52.6 (together with Eubouleus, 52.4) and the dedication of a hierophant from Hierokaisareia in Lydia, see the following note; as a name of one of the primeval gods (who might be a form of Dionysus): in Orph. *Hymn* 6.4; *OF* 139 and often in Neoplatonic interpretations of Orpheus' theogony, see the name index in Kern *OF*, p. 378 (Bernabé's index has not yet appeared). On the word-formation of *andrikepaidothyrsos* see Johnston, above Chapter 4, p. 133.

111 Keil and von Premerstein 1908: 54 no. 112 = Jaccottet 2003: no. 110.

112 Sokolowski 1955: no. 84 = *I. Smyrna* no. 728 = *SGOst* 05/01/04.

113 In what follows, I summarize a paper given at the conference on Orpheus and Orphism in Palma di Mallorca in January 2005; it will be published in the acts of this conference.

114 Several rites are mentioned in our sources: (1) The Eleusinian Mysteries: Ar. *Ran.* 293 (with scholia); Iambl. *Myst.* 3.31, 178.8–16 des Places; see also Clem.

Al. *Strom.* 4.1.3. (2) The Mysteries of Sabazios as performed by Aeschines' mother, another itinerant specialist: Demosth. 18.130; Idomeneus of Lampsacus, *FGrH* 338 F 2. See the discussion in Johnston 1999a: 131–9.

115 On the physiological connection between maenadic dance and ecstasy see Bremmer 1984.

116 *Lexicon Hesychii* s. v. Σεμέλης τράπεζα.

117 See Rudhardt 2002. Morand 2001: 142–4 is rather helpless, and so is Ricciardelli 2000: 408f. who, however, noted the passage in Hesychius.

118 See above n. 103.

119 We thus confidently re-install Comparetti's early chronology of the Orphic anthropogony that has been attacked, in every generation, by more skeptical scholars, Wilamowitz, Linforth, Zuntz, Brisson, Edmonds: see Sarah Iles Johnston's discussion of the myth in Chapter 3.

120 Plat. *Resp.* 363c–d. When (as I think) Musaeus' son is Eumolpus, we deal with promises that were connected with Eleusis; but in this sort of poetry, eschatological details were wandering between the cults of Dionysus (Orpheus) and Eleusis (Musaeus/Eumolpus), as Aristophanes' *Frogs* clearly shows, see Graf 1974.

121 Or, for that matter, of any Bacchic association; but see the qualifications in Jaccottet 2003: 87.

122 See above Chapter 4.

123 Herrmann 1998: no. 733, hence *SGOst* 01/20/21 and Jaccottet 2003: vol. 2, 250 no. 149; see Henrichs 1969.

124 *De err. prof. rel.* 6.5, see above p. 153.

125 On such centrifugal processions, see Graf 1995.

126 Graf 1974: passim; above Chapter 3.

127 Eliade 1958.

128 Sallustius, *On the Gods* 4.

129 οὐ θέμις ἐντοῦθα κεῖσθαι ἱ μὲ τὸν βεβαχχευμένον Sokolowski 1962: no. 120, dated rather before than after 450 BCE. See also Turcan 1986.

130 See Egelhaaf and Schäfer 2002, Kloppenborg and Wilson 1996.

131 E. g. *IG* II^2 11674, VII 686; *SEG* 31. 633; 32. 488, etc.

132 Hdt. 2.81 = *OF* 651; see below Chapter 6.

133 See above p. 176 with n. 60.

134 Plat. *Phd.* 69c (*OF* 434 III Bernabé).

135 Zuntz 1972: 290, after *Memorie dei Lincei* 3 (1879), 328.

136 Hermippus, frg. 23 Wehrli^2 (= Diog. Laert. 8.10); Iambl. *VP* 155; the list of sacred trees: Iambl. *VP* 154.

137 Thus in the tablets from Hipponion, Petelia, Entella, Pharsalos; see above Chapter 4.

138 Hermippus frg. 23 Wehrli (= Diog. Laert. 8.10); Iambl. *VP* 155.

139 Thuc. 2.34.

140 See the list in Graf 1993: 257f.

141 The partial cremation that looms so large in Macchioro should not be pressed; it is simply a matter of how well the pyre was built. Cremation was also practiced with the Derveni graves A and B, see Themelis and Tsouratsoglou 1997.

142 See Bottini 1992: 70–84.

143 Not the grave with the papyrus, grave A; see Themelis and Tsouratsoglou 1997. For the crater see Yiouri 1978 and Barr-Sharrar 1979.

144 From the Tomba del Triclinio in Tarquinia, now in the British Museum; third century BCE. A drawing and bibliography in Bernabé and Jiménez San Cristóbal 2008: 301–4 (Ricardo Olmos).

145 Basel: Schmidt et al. 1967: 7 no. 6 (amphora S 40) and often, with fig. 11. Toledo: *LIMC* 7 (1994): 315 no. 70; Johnston and McNiven 1996; Bernabé and Jiménez San Cristóbal 2008: 291–3 (Ricardo Olmos).

146 For Tarentum, see the important study by Graepler 1997 that has moved methodology a great step forward.

147 *IG* 12: 6: 2 no. 1197.11; similarly the Bacchic inscription from Miletus, Sokolowski 1955: no. 48.18–20, whereas a Coan inscription permits initiation only by sub-priestesses appointed by the city priestess, Sokolowski 1969: no. 166.23–6.

148 See the list in Graf 1993: 257–8.

149 Schmidt et al. 1976: 33, with the earlier bibliography.

150 It was found on the upper chest, but Guarducci 1974/1983: 80–1 thought it had fallen from the mouth during the decomposition of the body.

151 Without counting the only cursorily published finds from Pella, our no. 36a.

152 Dickie 1998: 84–6.

153 See *Arch. Delt.* 32B (1977): 84, 42B (1987): 153 (Aigion). The two gold coins of Philip II with an inscribed name, found in the skull (i.e., mouth) of a man (Andrōn) and a woman (Xenariste) in two graves near Pieria can be regarded as both gold tablets ("toe tags") and Charon's coins; we did not include them, but see Tzifopoulos 2010: F8 and F9.

154 Tzifopoulos 2010, developing an idea from Gavrilaki and Tzifopoulos 1998.

155 The excavator, N. Lilimpaki-Akamati 1989: 93, assumed it came "from a gold wreath."

156 Grave no. 10 in the East Cemetery of Pella, where our contemporary nos. 31 (grave no. 1) and 32 (grave no. 3) were found, see M. Lilimbaki-Akamati, *Arch. Delt.* 44/46A (1989/91), 94–5.

157 *Anth. Pal.* 7.485 (translation after W. R. Paton's Loeb text).

158 Nonnus, *Dion.* 19.167–98. His knowledge is all the more surprising as Nonnus was a Christian, Willers 1992.

159 *CLE* 1233 = Courtney 1995: 174 no. 184 (whose translation I print, with minor changes).

160 See Jaccottet 2003.

161 Text no. 2 in Appendix 4.

162 *OF* 350.

6 ORPHEUS, HIS POETRY, AND SACRED TEXTS

1 Apollod. *Bibl.* 1.14.

2 West 1985.

3 Maria-Xeni Garezou, *LIMC* 7: 1 (1994), 84 s.v. Orpheus no. 6. See also Vojatzi 1982: 44.

4 Hom. *Il.* 2.594–7.

5 See Anneliese Kossatz-Deissmann, *LIMC* 8: 1 (1997) 982 s.v. Philammon no. 1.

6 Pherecydes, *FGrH* 3 F 26.

7 Black-figured lekythos, Heidelberg inv. 68/1; *CVA* Heidelberg (4) fig. 176; Gropengiesser 1977.

8 Simon 1996; for the underlying methodological problems Menichetti 1994.

9 Maria-Xeni Garezou, *LIMC* 7: 1 (1994), 81–105; singing among Thracians: 84–5, nos. 7–26; as a non-Thracian on late antique mosaics: 93–4 nos. 128–34.

10 The treaty in Bengtson 1975: no. 165; see Thuc. 2.29.2, 97.1–3.

11 Alcidamas, *Ulixes* 24; see Linforth 1931.

12 Orpheus Ciconaeus: *OF* 1121 T.

13 Eur. *Bacch.* 560; Strabo 7.330 frg. 18.

14 The story is part of the novelistic tradition about Alexander, see Plut. *Alex.* 14.8.671f (whence my citation). Arr. *Anab.* 1.11.2 and Ps.Callisthenes, *Life of Alexander* 1.42.6f. give only Pieria. Small wooden statues, however, often worked miracles, see Graf 1985: 298–311.

15 Conon, *FGrH* 26 F 1.45; Paus. 9.30.9–11; for the details see Graf 1987.

16 Achilles: Hom. *Il.* 9.186; Heracles and Linus: *LIMC* 4: 1 (1988), 833 nos. 1666–73.

17 Pind. *Pyth.* 4.176 (among the Argonauts); Hippias *DK* 88 B 6.

18 Whether the story of Orpheus' foreign origin retains a memory of the foreign origin of *goēteia* (Johnston 1999a: 116f.), depends in part on how old the Thracian connection is. Given the lack of information on Orpheus in the early versions of the *Argonautica*, this must remain unknown; Orpheus the Ciconian might be old. And at any rate the puzzling choice of Thrace over, e.g., Phoenicia or Egypt must have a reason that cannot be explained this way.

19 A general account: Dover 1989.

20 Orpheus: Phanocles, *Erotes* 9f. (Powell, *Coll. Alex.* p. 107); Ovid, *Met.* 10.83 etc. (*OF* 1004 T); Thamyris: Apollod. *Bibl.* 1.17.

21 Luiselli 1993.

22 Betegh 2004.

23 West 1983: 227–58.

24 Hdt. 2.53.

25 Parry 1992, Riedweg 2004.

26 Simonides, frg. 567 *PMG*; the same myth is told in a recently published poem of uncertain age, but that its ancient edition connected with Sappho, almost a century older than Simonides, see Groenewald and Daniel 2005: 7–12. Rocks and trees: Ap. Rhod. *Argon.* 1.26–30; Ovid, *Met.* 10.86–105 and 11.1–2. The topic of Orpheus among the animals was very popular on late antique mosaics, Maria-Xeni Garezou, *LIMC* 7: 1 (1994) 90–6, nos. 94–164.

27 See Graf 1997a, Chapter 1.

28 Eur. *Cyclops* 646–8.

29 Eur. *Alcestis* 962–6.

30 On this aspect, see Johnston 1999a: 82–123, esp. 111–18; Johnston 1999b.

31 Diod. Sic. 5.64.4 = Ephorus, *FGrH* 70 F 104; see Strabo 7.330 frg. 18 (below n. 72). – The translation follows C. H. Oldfather's Loeb translation.

32 On blacksmiths and sorcery see Eliade 1978; on blacksmiths, the Cabiri, and secret societies see Burkert 1985: 280f.

33 On the *goēs*, see Burkert 1962 (still valid, despite the adherence to a concept of shamanism that is due to Meuli, Dodds, and Eliade and is outdated by now); Johnston 1999a: 102–11.

34 The image is Johnston's, 1999a: 115.

35 Plin. *HN* 30.7: "I would believe that Orpheus introduced the art to his neighbours because he had made such progress in superstitious healing, if not Thrace, his country of origin, was without any trace of magic" *Orphea putarem e propinquo artem primum intulisse ad vicina usque superstitionis ac medicinae provectum si non expers sedes eius tota Thrace magices fuisset.*

36 Plat. *Resp.* 2. 364 b–c.

37 Strabo 7.330 frg. 18.

38 Ar. *Ran.* 1032; Eur. *Rhes.* 943; Plat. *Prt.* 316d; all are somewhat vague.

39 Dionysus: Diod. Sic. 1.23.2 and often (Lactant. *Div. inst.* 1.22.16 claims that "these rites [the mysteries of Dionysus] are even nowadays called Orphic," *ea sacra etiamnunc Orphica nominantur*). Eleusis: explicitly Theodoret, *Graec. aff. cur.* 1.21, implicitly Ar. *Ran.* 1032 and Dem. *Or.* 25.11, see Graf 1974: 22–39. Ov., *Met.* 11.91 combines Eleusinian and Bacchic mysteries: Orpheus taught them to Eumolpus of Athens and Midas of Phrygia, a co-initiate of Silenus. See also below n. 81 on Eleusinian mythology connected with Orpheus. Hecate and Demeter Chthonie: Paus. 2.30.2.

40 On this rise as, among other things, a result of Eastern contacts, see Johnston 1999a: 111–16.

41 Conon, *Fabula* 45 (*FGrH* 26 F 1.45). See Graf 1987.

42 Bremmer 1991.

43 Hdt. 4.94–6.

44 Burkert 1972: 120–65.

45 See Kingsley 1995.

46 The literature on Orpheus is vast; a first orientation in Warden 1982, Segal 1989, Maurer Zenck 2004.

47 See *LIMC* 4: 1 (1988), 99 no. 5 (five Roman copies), no. 6 (a coin); as to its origin, see Thompson 1952: 60f.

48 Hultkrantz 1957, see also Monnier 1991.

49 Bowra 1952/1970, a careful study of the literary remains of the myth; the citation is on p. 227.

50 See *LIMC* 7: 1, 99 and the lists 85–8, nos. 32–67 (Orpheus' death) and 88–9. nos. 72–84 (Underworld).

51 Alcidamas, *Ulixes* 24; above n. 11.

52 Pausanias 10.30.6–9.

53 Descent and *goēteia*: Johnston 1999a: 114. From a very different angle (Weberian sociology), Bremmer 1999a argued for a date in the late archaic age.

54 See most recently *OF* 707–17, with Bernabé's notes.

55 Orpheus, *Argonautica* 40–3.

56 Clem. Al. *Strom.* 1.21 (*OF* 1128); contradicted by Callimachus according to Harpocration, s. v. *Ion* (*OF* 1128).

57 The identification with the student of Socrates in Linforth 1941: 116–18; author of the Derveni allegory: Kapsomenos 1964/5.

58 Plat. *Grg.* 493a; see, among many others, Burkert 1972: 248 n. 48 ("the myth may have formed part of an Orphic *katabasis*"); Kingsley 1995: 113–15. Orpheus of Camarina: *OF* 1103 T; the Byzantine lexicon *Suda*, which cites this author, has more Italians/Sicilians: Orpheus of Croton, author of "Argonautica and other poems," *OF* 1104; Nicias of Elea, author of *Thronismoi Mētrōioi* (a poem on the mysteries of Cybele and perhaps the Corybantes) and *Bacchica*, *OF* 1102; and Timocles of Syracuse, author of a poem with the title "Salvation" (*Sotēria*), *OF* 1105 (Kingsley 1995: 115 connects it with the Underworld). See also below n. 60.

59 Eur. *Hipp.* 952f. (presumably written in the 430s BCE).

60 Ion *DK* 36 B 2; Epigenes: Clem. Al. *Strom.* 1.21 (*OF* 1128; see *OF* 1101). An Epigenes (the same?) was also the author of a commentary on Ion's tragedies, Athenaeus 11468c. Other Pythagoreans as writers of *Orphica*: *OF* 1100 (Brontinus of Metapontum or Croton), 1106 (Zopyrus of Heraclea), and of course Empedocles, see Riedweg 1995; *OF* 1108 T (Empedocles' grandfather *OF* 1107).

61 The ancient evidence for this is extensive; Bernabé collects it as *OF* 1–378. Discussion at West 1983: 9, 13, 68, etc.

62 See above Chapter 5 n. 132.

63 Leipoldt and Morenz 1953 still deserves reading because of its nunaced phenomenological approach (often disregarded, e.g. in Udo Tworuschka's remark in *Handbuch der Religionswissenschaftlichen Grundbegriffe* 3 (1993), 253; Max Müller's *The Sacred Books of the East* (Müller 1879–1910) is, in its very Romanticism, an emblematic instance of this perspective; to a contemporary writer, sacred texts cannot be but Judeo-Christian, William H. Gass, "Sacred Texts," in Gass and Cuoco 2000: 1–12. Church fathers: citations for use of the phrases *hieroi logoi*, *hierai bibloi*, *hierai graphai*, *hiera grammata* in these authors are collected by Henrichs 2002: 35–6 with nn.122–4.

64 Cf. Parker 1996: 54–5.

65 Müller 1879–1910.

66 A model that even recently was followed by Baumgarten 1998; cf. the remarks of Henrichs 2002: 3 with n. 10 and Graf 2001. We should note that we are using the word "text," as Henrichs 2002 does, to refer to any composition, either oral or written (see Henrichs' discussion of the rationale behind this choice on pp. 4–5 especially).

67 *Il.* 18.382–3 and *Theog.* 945–6; *Od.* 8.268–70.

68 Cf. Henrichs 2002: 31.

69 Henrichs 2002; see also Henrichs 2003 and Henrichs 2004.

70 Ptolemy IV: P. Berlin 11774 verso, text no. 4 in our Appendix 4.

71 Henrichs 2002: 14.

72 The crucial passage for this association is Plat. *Resp.* 364b–365a, which we examined earlier in this chapter; it connects *agyrtai* (itinerant priests) and

manteis with a "hubbub of books" credited to Musaeus and Orpheus that include instructions on *teletai* that release those who participate from penalties in the afterlife. Livy (39.8.4) seems to echo Plato in making his Bacchic initiator a *vates*. Orpheus himself was also portrayed as a *mantis* as well as an initiator: Philochorus *FGrH* 328 FF 76, 77; Strabo 7.330 frg. 18 (who explicitly joins the two professions); Philostr. *VA* 4.14; schol. Ap. Rhod. *Argon.* 2.684. Plat. *Prt.* 316d calls Orpheus and Musaeus experts in *teletai* and *chresmōidia* and Ovid calls Orpheus a *vates* (*Met.* 11.8). Further at *OF* 804-11 with discussion by Bernabé.

73 Henrichs 2002: 10-16; on chresmologues and *manteis* more generally, including the use of written collections, cf. also Dillery 2005. Dillery also makes interesting suggestions regarding the preserved, tattooed skin of Epimenides, who was among other things a *mantis*, suggesting that it was guarded as a repository of (written) prophetic texts; for Epimenides' skin as a book see Bremmer 1993.

74 Or so implies Call. frg. 178.

75 Andanian mysteries: Paus. 4.27.5. Cf. the mysteries of the Lycomidae, which were in the hands of a single family as well, and which claimed to be Orphic in origin and to use hymns composed by Musaeus – *hieroi logoi*? Plut. frg. 24 and *Them.* 1; Paus. 1.22.7 and 1.31.4; cf. Graf 2003: 246.

76 Cf. also Paus. 8.15.1, on *grammata* concerning the mysteries of Demeter in Pheneos, which were periodically taken out, read to the initiates, and then redeposited, and Paus. 2.37.3, on texts connected with the mysteries of Demeter and Dionysus in Lerna, inscribed on a heart-shaped piece of copper. On all of these examples, see Henrichs 2002: 36-41 and Graf 2003.

77 It should be noted that there is some indication that written texts could be connected with "mainstream" religion as well under special circumstances (Henrichs 2003: 54-7).

78 Aristotle's statement (frg. 15 = Synesius *Dio* 10 p. 48a) that one "experiences" the mysteries (*pathein*) rather than "learns" (*mathein*) them has led to the widespread assumption that initiates didn't have to know anything – including such things as the way in which a sacred story might explain a mystery's rituals, even the sacred story itself. But as Burkert 1987: 69-70 has clarified, this is not what the statement means in its context; when Synesius quotes it, he is distinguishing between lower, preparatory spiritual states, in which one must learn, and the highest state in which the soul, properly prepared by its studies, is granted a pure vision (*epopteia*). As Burkert goes on to emphasize, we have substantial evidence suggesting that "transmission" (*paradosis*) of information and learning were vital to the mysteries and that *logoi*, both recited and heard, were central to this process. Chrysippus the Stoic considered the transmission of *logoi* about the gods to be essential to *teletai* (frg. 42 *SVF* II 17).

79 Pausanias implicitly makes this distinction when he uses "*logoi*" repeatedly of tales that he *does* repeat for his readers but "*hieroi logoi*" only twice, of tales that he will *not* repeat (2.13.4 and 8.15.4).

80 Eur. *Hel.* 1301-52 with comments at Borgeaud 1996: 40-1; further on variations of the Demeter story, see Richardson 1974: 74-86 and Clinton 1986.

81 Version of the myth that was special to the Eleusinian Mysteries: Clem. Al. *Protr.* 2.16–19; cf. Plat. *Resp.* 377e–378a, which Burkert 1987: 156 n. 44 rightly, we think, interprets to refer to a secret story told at Eleusis; and Isoc. *Paneg.* 28, which says that only initiates in the Mysteries may learn the story of how the people of Attica received Demeter during her visit. Orpheus as the story's composer: ibid. and probably also *Marm. Par.* 16–17 with emendations (see Bernabé 2004: F 379 with comments, and Linforth 1941: 193–4). Orpheus was also often simply called the founder of the Eleusinian Mysteries: e.g., Eur. *Rhes.* 943–5, Diod. Sic. 1.96 (who includes in his description of Orpheus as founder the comment that Orpheus carried back from Egypt not only the mysteries of Demeter and of Dionysus themselves but also a poem about his journey to the Underworld – a *hieros logos* for use in both of these mysteries?), and Diod. Sic. 5.77.3. Further, see discussion also at Linforth 189–202, Graf 1974: 8–39 and *OF* 510–18. Certainly, poems about the kidnapping of Kore and Demeter's search for her were often attributed to Orpheus in antiquity: Bernabé 2004: 312–35 (with *OF* 379–402). We will never be sure which of these were considered restricted for use in the mysteries alone, however.

82 See Chapter 3.

83 Cf. also the remarks of Burkert 1987: 73.

84 On the Gûrob Papyrus' identity as a *hieros logos*, see Henrichs 2002: 27–9 (where he cites earlier scholars) and Henrichs 2005 (where he comes out somewhat more strongly in favor of this).

85 On Aeschines' book preserving a *hieros logos*, see Yunis 2001: 254. Most scholars presume the cult was in honor of Sabazios, a god identified with Dionysus; for another view, see Parker 1996: 159. More generally on the passage and its importance for understanding *hieroi logoi*, Henrichs 2002: 16–18. More generally on poetry, *hieroi logoi*, and the gold tablets, see Obbink 2011.

86 Gill 1985. Gill's model was usefully taken up and applied to ancient material by Frankfurter 2004.

87 On the identity of *orpheotelestai* and sellers of curse tablets: Plat. *Resp.* 364b–365a and discussion at Johnston 1999a: 105–8; on the likelihood that the sellers of curse tablets were also the ones who inscribed them, see not only the suggestive passage from Plato just cited but also *Leg.* 933a and the many publications of David Jordan, e.g., Jordan 1985 and 1994, which show that large numbers of tablets were inscribed by single, and often well-trained, hands.

APPENDIX 1

1 See Freyburger and Freyburger 2006.

2 Smith 1990.

3 On Eliade and the Neoplatonists, see Johnston 2011a, esp. 63–7. For the crucial importance of the Neoplatonists (next paragraph), see esp. Radcliffe Edmonds III, *Redefining Ancient Orphism* (Cambridge: Cambridge University Press, forthcoming).

4 Dreams advising against a commentary on Orpheus: Marinos, *Vita Procli* 26. *mystagōgia*: Proklos, *Theologia Platonica* vol. 1 p. 25f. and vol. 6 p. 40; on

Platonic use of mystery terms see Riedweg 1987. Purifications: Marinus, *Vita Procli* 18.

5 Iamblichus, in Stobaios, *Anthology* 1.49.38; Achilles Tatios, *Isagoge* 4.42 (an astrological treatise, presumably written before 300 CE); Pseudo-Galen, *Ad Gaurum quomodo animetur fetus* 2.2 (date unclear).

6 Henrichs 2011.

7 Schlesier 2001; see also Schlesier 2003.

APPENDIX 2

1 We again thank Robert Parker and Maria Stamatopoulou for giving us access to their publication of this tablet in time for it to be included in the first edition. I also thank Philippe Borgeaud for his many conversations about the Mother in her various manifestations.

2 Parker and Stamatopoulou 2004: 7 make a strong case for the addressee in no. 28 being Persephone; I would assume the same for no. 27, which, as we will see, uses one of Persephone's names as a password.

3 On the question of what the tablets' use of "*mystēs*" implies, see my comments above, pp. 120–1 and in more depth Parker and Stamatopoulou 2004: 7–9; I hold to the opinion that we cannot determine exactly what the word implied on the Hipponium tablet (no. 1). By the time of Herodotus, at latest, it could also be used for initiations other than those at Eleusis, notably those at Samothrace (Hdt. 2.51). Our first certain uses of the term in connection with Dionysiac mysteries are first century BCE (see Parker and Stamatopoulou 2004: 9), but here again we begin to enter the territory of circular arguments: those who (like the present authors) consider the gold tablets, as a group, to be the product of Dionysiac mysteries would use tablets nos. 20, 21, 22, 28, and 31 to move the Dionysiac association of the word back to the end of the fourth century BCE.

4 There is an intriguing echo here of Irikepaios/Erikepaios, the bisexual primordial king according to the Rhapsodic Theogony, whose name appears in a prayer of the Gurôb Papyrus (see Appendix 4 no. 3 line 22). Chrysostomou 1994: comm. ad lines 1–3 goes further in trying to conjecture a meaning for this word.

5 Prop. 2.2.11–12; Lyc. *Alex.* 1180. In this passage, Lycophron also identifies Brimo with Hecate and the "Zerynthian Queen of Strymon" (i.e., Hecate in her Samothracian guise), on whom I will say more in the next paragraph. The scholiast goes on to explain that the "goddess of Pherae" (i.e., Brimo) is also called Hecate because when Pheraia, the daughter of Aeolos, bore Brimo to Zeus, she threw the infant out onto the crossroads, where she was found by shepherds, who subsequently raised her. Thereafter, sacrifices were made to her at crossroads. The story points to an association with crossroads being one of the salient traits that led to the identification of Brimo with Hecate (cf. schol. Theocr. 2.35/36a, who tells the same story). Artemis was also identified with the goddess of Pherae in Sicyon, Athens, and Argos (Paus. 2.10.7, 2.23.5), although Hesychius tells us that she was a "stranger goddess" (*xenikē theos*) in Athens (s.v. *Pheraia*).

6 *Etym. Gen.* 261 (s.v. Brimo); *Etym. Magn.* 213 (s.v. Brimo), *Etym. Sym.* 1.502

(s.v. Brimo), schol. Lyc. ad. *Alex.* 698 and 1176. Given the general indebtedness of the etymological tradition to Hellenistic works, the source of the story may well go back to that period (during which, as we will see, Brimo makes her first appearances in Greek literature). The scholiast to Oppian *Hal.* Book 1 schol. 360 line 4 and the scholiast to Hesiod *WD* 144ter. equate Brimo with Persephone but do not tell the story.

7   The scholion to Lyc. *Alex.* ad 698 does not equate Brimo with Hecate, but the scholion ad 1176 does.

8   "Obrimo" should be understood as a poetic form of "Brimo" just as the adjective *obrimos* ("strong, mighty") is a poetic form of *brimos*.

9   Ap. Rhod. 3.861; A.R. 3.1211. Lyc. *Alex.* 698, 1176. Luc. *Men.* 20.17 does not identify her with anyone.

10 That Apollonius' two uses of her name may well be her first literary appearances, extant or not, is suggested by the fact that the lexicographers who discuss Brimo cite A.R. 3.862.

11 E.g., Soph. *Ant.* 1199, Eur. *Ion* 1048.

12 In *PGM* 4.2960, the name seems to be a password in a spell that invokes both Hecate and Persephone. In *PGM* 70.21 and *Mag. Suppl.* 96a, 96b, and 96e, her name is a password as well. In *PGM* 7.692, the name heads up a list of names and adjectives such as "earth-breaker," "chief huntress," "Baubo," "night-runner" and "man-breaker." In *Mag. Suppl.* 57 Brimo is identified with Baubo and described as a dog-leader and night-roamer. Only in *PGM* 4.2270 and 2607 does "Brimo" seem to mean "Hecate" – but the goddess described in these passages has acquired so many epithets and names that it is difficult to know how significant any one of them is. (The spell that includes 4.2270 also describes the goddess as "Kore," 2302 and 2344.)

13 Clem. Alex. *Pro.* 2.15.1; Arn. *Adv. Nat.* 20.2–3; Eus. *PE* 2.3.16. Eusebius repeats Clement verbatim. All three authors identify Deo/Demeter/Ceres in this story with Zeus' mother. Arnobius adds the information that Jupiter turned himself into a bull to accomplish his desires.

14 Paus. 8.25.2–10, 8.42; Call. frg. 652; schol. *Il.* 23.346 = Theb. frg. 6C; Apollod. 3.6.8. Cf. also schol. Lyc. *Alex.* 153 and Hsch. s.v. "Arion." Discussion in Johnston 1999a: 258–61.

15 Hipp. ref. 5, 8 – endorsed, after earlier scholars, by Deubner 1932: 85, it has become *opinio recepta*; see for example, Clinton 1992: 91–4.

16 *Th.* 969–74; *HHDem.* 488–9.

17 The poetic word *obrimos* and its compounds (*obrimothumos*, etc.) similarly evoke power that is mighty to a physically overwhelming degree: as warriors, Ares, Achilles, and Hector are described as *obrimos,* and so is Zeus' thunder.

18 Ap. Rhod. 3.862; Luc. *Men.* 20.17.

19 The best discussion of this is Frickel 1984.

20 Cf. the schol. ad Ap. Rhod. 3.861 who suggests that the name "Brimo" may be derived from the *bromos* (crackling roar) that a fire makes – he goes on to support this by citing *Il.* 14.396, which describes the "bellow" (*bromos*) of a fire, and by arguing that Hecate/Brimo is a torch-bearing goddess.

21 Lesser Mysteries as preparation for Eleusis: Plat. *Gorg.* 497C seems to allude to

it, see the scholiast on the passage and further sources cited in Deubner 1932: 70. See also Parker 2005: 341, 343–6; Clinton 2003; Johnston 1999a: 132–6; Burkert 1983: 265–6.

22 Steph. Byz. s.v. *Agra chōrion*; Duris frg. 30 Mueller = Athen. *Deipn.* VI, 253d; schol. Ar. *Pl.* 845. Parker 2005: 344 n. 76 concludes that the claim made by the schol. Ar. *Pl.* is "pure schematism"; I agree that the claim certainly looks too neat and tidy to reflect real practice, but I assume there was some basis for the idea, however artificially it may have been later schematized.

23 This is not to imply that there was dramatization of the birth of Dionysus at the Lesser Mysteries; Graf 1974: 66–78. For the contrary opinion, Clinton 1992: 91–5, who would attach the scene to the Eleusinian Mysteries, perhaps with "Plutus" represented by a sheaf of grain instead of/in addition to an actor playing the role.

24 For the Metroon in Agrai see the fourth-century Athenian historiographer Clidemus, *FGrH* 232 F 9; the temple site is still uncertain. Cf. Parker 2005: 344–5 with notes.

25 *OF* 317 Bernabé and see Johnston 2011: 123–6.

26 For a translation of the Gurôb Papyrus, see Appendix 4 no. 3.

27 I would also note that the earliest two literary authors in which she appears – Apollonius of Rhodes and Lycophron – were fond of incorporating recondite mythological information into their poems. Their eager use of Brimo's name (twice, in each case) suggests she was a relatively new and intriguing figure, still mysterious enough to provide a *frisson* of the exotic.

28 Equation of Rhea and the Mother, e.g., Soph. *Philoct.* 391–8 (here called "Mother of Zeus" = Rhea), [Theocr.] 20.40, Nic. *Alex.* 6–8 and cf. 217–21 and schol. ad loc. Generally, on such equations, Parker and Stamatopoulou 2004: 14–15; Borgeaud 2004: esp. 8–9; Burkert 2004: 104.

29 The earliest clear equation of Demeter with the Mountain Mother is at Eur. *Hel.* 1301–68, where the chorus tells the story that is usually linked to Demeter and Persephone (that is, a daughter's rape and a mother's anger about it) but calls the character who is usually identified as Demeter "The Mountain Mother," "Deo," and "The Mother of the Gods". Notably, the latter part of this passage suggests that this goddess can be appeased through wild nocturnal rituals dedicated to Bromios – i.e., Dionysus. See also Pi. *I.* 7.3–5, which speaks of "Demeter of the Bronze-Cymbals" as the *parhedros* of Dionysus. For the equation of Demeter and the Mother – as well as Rhea, Deo, and Hestia – see also Derveni Papyrus col. XXII and R. Kannicht's commentary on Eur. *Hel.* ad loc.

30 For the Hermionian cult, with further ancient references than I give here, see Johnston 2012; Pirenne-Delforge 2008: 206–7; Ferrari 2007; Parker and Stamatopoulou 2004.

31 Eur. *HF* 615; Str. 8.6.12; Apollod. 1.5.1; Paus. 2.35.9–11.

32 Demeter Chthonia in Hermione: the main texts are Paus. 2.35.5–8 and Ael. *HA* 11.4 = Aristocles *SH* 206 = *FGrH* 436 F 2. Demeter Chthonia in Sparta: Paus. 3.14.5. Philicus = *SH* 676. Orpheus and the Eleusinian Mysteries: Graf 1974.

33 *PMG* 702 = Athen. *Deip.* 14, 624e.

34 Demeter is called "Chthonia" at Ap. Rhod. 4.986–7 (intriguingly, she is said to have taught the Titans how to reap grain); and Deo is called Chthonia by the fourth- or third-century BCE epigrammatist Nicarchus, in a request that she, Pan, and Dionysus protect the flocks, the vines, and the fruit (*AP* 6.31).

35 We have no evidence for independent mysteries of Meter (under any of her names) before the Roman period. Cf. Parker-Stamatopoulou 2004: 14 – but see now also Burkert 2004: 105 on the possibility of a Hellenistic mystery dedicated to the Mother in Phaestos, Crete (*IC* I xxiii 3).

36 Eumelus = frg. 27 West = 11 Bernabé = schol. (D) *Il.* 6.131.

37 Apollod. *Bibl.* 3.35–9; cf. Eur. *Cretans* fr. 79 (Austin) where we hear of mysteries dedicated to Idaean Zeus, to Zagreus (a god identified with Dionysus in literary texts), and to the Mountain Mother – implying that, at least in the literary imagination, the link between Dionysus and the Mother, forged through mysteries, could be found wherever the goddess was worshipped. Cf. also Eur. *Cycl.* 3, Nic. *Alex.* 217 with schol. ad loc.; schol. A ad *Il.* 6.131; schol. ad Lyc. *Alex.* 273, and Borgeaud 2004: 113. In the fragments of his second dithyramb, Pindar describes a *teletē* in Olympus to Bromios that starts "next to the Great Mother" (frg. 70b): Pindar must know of the close mythical and ritual connection. Generally on the connection between the foundation of Bacchic rites and a goddess such as Rhea or the Mother, see above pp. 146–8 and see S. I. Johnston, "Hecate, Leto's Daughter, in *OF* 317," in Herrero de Jáuregui et al. 2011: 123–6. Graf 2010: 167–80. On madness, the dead, and the usefulness of *teletai*, Johnston 1999a: 55–6, 107–8, 129–39.

38 Heracles' initiation and its motivation: Diod. 4.14.3 and 4.25.1, cf. Eur. *HF* 610–13, Apollod. *Bibl.* 2.15.12 and schol. Ar. *Pl.* 1013; see further Johnston 1999a 129–39.

39 Although *thiasos* is not only a Bacchic group and a Bacchic group is not always called a *thiasos* (Jaccottet 2003: 24–8), a *thiasos* is not just any association, but should be defined as a "boisterous and somewhat ecstatic group that enjoys pleasures." For Athens, the orators attest, besides the Dionysiac groups, the *thiasos* of a Dionysos-like divinity organized by the mother of Aeschines that contains sacred books, purificatory and initiatory rites, and better hopes for the future (Demosthenes), or a *thiasos* of Heracles as an association of ephebes (Lysias or Isaeus); since we know that these young men dedicated a drinking cup to their god, this is not far from Dionysus and pleasure seeking. Athenian inscriptions also attest to *thiasos* as a sub-group of phratries; this might be the same as the *thiasos* of Heracles with its boisterous young men, and is at any rate specifically Athenian; on the other hand, the word is never used for Eleusis or Samothrace. Thus, a *thiasos mystōn* that is located in the Underworld evokes Bacchic mysteries. A close parallel (in place more than in time) is a grave epigram from Macedonian Lagina (188/189 CE; close to Thessalonica) that evokes eschatological hopes for the initiate member (*mystēs*) of a Bacchic *thiasos*, SEG 35.751. [F.G.]

40 *OF* 605; Pl. *Euth.* 277d = *OF* 602 and Pl. *Lg.* 790c–e; see also pp. 147–8 above. Cf. Hesych. s.v. *thronōsis*, who, commenting on the passage from Plato, tells us that *thronōsis* was an introductory ceremony for those intending to be

initiated. Burkert 1983: 266–8 would also see a *thronōsis* at the Lesser Mysteries or Eleusinian Mysteries (prefigured in myth by Demeter's sitting upon a
stool in the house of Celeus), but the evidence here is uncertain.

41 The ritual might also have included wine drinking; a fourth-century cult law
from Erythrai for the Corybantes mentions *kraterizein*. See Graf 1984: 320–1.
[F.G.]

42 Parker and Stamatopoulou 2004: 12 and 25–6 assume a *wandering* ritual practitioner. I agree with their underlying presumption – that the practitioner was
probably not a priest serving a long-standing, established local cult – but I see
no reason to assume that he necessarily came from outside the area.

43 Cf. Ferrari 2007: 196–7 (arguing for a single cult) and Parker and Stamatopoulou 2004: 10 n. 27 and 12 n. 37 – citing conversations with Peter Stork
and Henk Versnel, each of whom suggested two different cults – from which
Parker and Stamatopoulou conclude (page 12) that we are dealing with a wandering priest who could perform several separate types of initiations.

44 Contra Parker and Stamatopoulou 2004, who see no Bacchic background to
the tablet, Ferrari 2007 supports a Bacchic association, but from a different
angle than that which I have taken here.

45 Pp. 75–6. On Euphorion, see the edition, translation, and commentary of
B. Acosta-Hughes and C. Cusset (Paris, 2012) frg. 53. I have come to conclude
that, of the different traditions for Dionysus' rebirth that I discuss in Chapter 3,
this was the dominant one, especially in myths and rituals that traced their
lineage to Orpheus; cf. Henrichs 2011: 61.

46 The late antique grammarian Stephanus of Byzantium gives us a third story:
the goddess Ma, whom Stephanus equates with Rhea, received the infant
Dionysus from Zeus, who asked her to care for him. Hera asked Ma who
the infant was and Ma saved Dionysus by lying, telling Hera that it was Ares
(*Ethnica epit.* p. 436 s.v. *Mastaura*). Stephanus' source may have been Philo of
Byblus' *On Cities*, a source he often used, given that the passage I cite comes
from an explanation of how the city of Mastaura ("Ma"-staura) got its name.

47 We may wish to include the two Pelinna tablets here, too (nos. 26a and b)
which are dated to the same period as the Pherae tablets. They come from an
area only about forty miles to the west of Pherae, and give a greater emphasis
than other tablets do to the relationship between Dionysus and Persephone.

48 See also Obbink 2011a, who presents a papyrus text of the second half of the
third century BCE, perhaps of Neanthes of Cyzicus. It contains a version
of Dionysus' birth myths in which Demeter Hipte (a Lydian goddess) protects Sabazius (the first Dionysus?) by inventing the *rhombos*, a tool used in
mysteries and also one of the toys that the Titans use to distract the young
Dionysus. This *bricolage* looks Orphic once again; it corresponds closely to
the Sabazius and Hipte myth contained in Orphic *Hymns* 39 and 40. See also
tablet 8a, which is uninscribed but is engraved with the bust of a Janus-headed
goddess who may represent Demeter and Persephone. The tablet was probably placed in the mouth of a female deceased between the late fifth and early
third century in Syracuse. It probably attests to the adoption into another
mystery cult of a technology pioneered by Bacchic initiators, but it is margin-

ally possible that it comes from a cult where Demeter and Persephone were honored alongside Dionysus.

APPENDIX 3

1 All the translations are by Sarah Iles Johnston.
2 Fundamental Marcel Simon, "Θάρσει οὐδεὶς ἀθάνατος. Étude de vocabulaire religieux," *Revue de l'Histoire des Religions* 113 (1936): 188–206 = Marcel Simon, *Le christianisme antique et son contexte religieux. Scripta Varia* (Tübingen: Mohr, 1981), vol. 1, 63–82; see also P. W. van der Horst, *Ancient Jewish Epitaphs. An Introductory Survey of a Millennium of Jewish funerary Epigraphy (300 BCE–700 CE)* (Kampen: Kok Pharos, 1991), 121–2, and Joseph S. Park, *Conceptions of Afterlife in Jewish Inscriptions. With Special Reference to Pauline Literature* (Tübingen: Mohr, 2000), 47–63.
3 E.g., Yiannis E. Meimaris and Kalliope I. Kritikakou-Nikolaropoulou, *Inscriptions from Palaestina Tertia. Ia: The Greek Inscriptions from Ghor-es-Safi (Byzantine Zoora)* (Athens: National Hellenic Research Foundation, Research Centre for Greek and Roman Antiquity, 2005), 27.
4 Simon, op. cit. 192=68 writes of an "épreuve réelle, pénible, terrible peut-être, mais passagère et déjà virtuellement surmontée."
5 *Corpus Inscriptionum Latinarum (CIL)* III 8899 (Dalmatia, second/third century).
6 *Inscriptiones Graecae (IG)* XIV 2342 = J. B. Brusin, *Inscriptiones Aquileiae* (Udine: Deputazione di Storia Patria per il Friuli, 1991–3), no. 710 (Aquileia, 222–235 CE).
7 John Chrysostom, *Oration on Saint Bernice (PG* 50:2, 634): "we sing psalm over the dead admonishing them to take heart (θαρρεῖν) as to the end".
8 E.g., *Inscriptiones Graecae Urbis Romae (IGUR)* II 743 and 1115 (Rome, undated); *IG* XIV 1474 = *IGUR* III 1171 (Rome, third century CE); *IG* XIV 2277 = *CIL* V 7380 (Tortona, second century CE); *Denkschriften Wien* 189 (1987), 48 no. 8 and *Epigraphica Anatolica* 10 (1987), 99–100 (= *Supplementum Epigraphicum Graecum* 37: 1103) (Phrygia, Apameia; late third–early fourth century CE).
9 See M. Simon, op. cit. 199–200/74–5; Sylvia Cappelletti, *The Jewish Community of Rome. From the Second Century BC to the Third Century CE* (Leiden: Brill, 2006), 182–3.
10 Firmicus Maternus, *De errore profanarum religionum* 22.
11 Van der Horst, op. cit. 122.
12 See esp. Joseph S. Park, *Conceptions of Afterlife in Jewish Inscriptions. With Special Reference to Pauline Literature* (Tübingen: Mohr, 2000), 50–2.
13 See Nicole Belayche, *Iudaea-Palaestina. The Pagan Cults in Roman Palestine (Second to Fourth Century)* (Tübingen: Mohr, 2001).
14 The feminine form εὐγενή "noble" appears in literature for the first time in the fifth-century *Passio Gregorii Illuminatoris* by Agathangelus, chap. 39; it designates a woman in an undated stone inscription from the region of Apameia, see the next footnote.

15 *Inscriptions grecques et latines de la Syrie* 4.1995; once, the person is called "loving her husband" and "loving her children," which clarifies the gender.

APPENDIX 4

1 See also the bone plaques from Berezan, approximately contemporary, but with close connections to Apollo: Dubois 1996: 146 no. 93.

2 For Apollo, see also the previous note.

BIBLIOGRAPHY

Barr-Sharrar, Beryl. "Towards an Interpretation of the Dionysiac Frieze on the Derveni Krater," *Cahiers d'Archéologie Romande* 17 (1979), 55–9.

Baumgarten, Roland. *Heiliges Wort und Heilige Schrift bei den Griechen.* Hieroi Logoi *und verwandte Erscheinungen.* Script-Oralia 110. Altertumswissenschaftliche Reihe 26 (Tübingen: Narr, 1998).

Bengtson, Hermann, ed. *Die Staatsverträge des Altertums.* 2: *Die Verträge der griechisch-römischen Welt von 700 bis 338 v. Chr.* 2nd edn. (Munich: Beck, 1975 [1962]).

Bernabé, Alberto. "Una cita de Pindaro en Platón *Men.* 81b (Fr. 133 Sn.-M.)" in Juan Antonio López Férez, ed., *Desde las poemas homericas hasta la prosa griega del siglo IV d.C. Veintiséis estudios filológicos* (Madrid: Ediciones Clásicas, 1999), 239–59.

Bernabé, Alberto. "La toile de Pénélope: a-t-il existé un mythe orphique sur Dionysos et les Titans?" *Revue de l'histoire des religions* 219 (2002), 401–33.

Bernabé, Alberto. *Poetae Epici Graeci.* II *Orphicorum et Orphicis similium testimonia et fragmenta,* fasc. 1 and 2 (Munich: Saur, 2003 and 2004).

Bernabé, Alberto and Ana Isabel Jiménez San Cristóbal. *Instructions for the Netherworld. The Orphic Gold Tablets* (Leiden: Brill, 2008); originally published as *Instrucciones para el más allá. Las laminillas órficas de oro* (Madrid: Ediciones Clásicas, 2001).

Betegh, Gábor. *The Derveni Papyrus. Cosmology, Theology and Interpretation* (Cambridge: Cambridge University Press, 2004).

Betz, Hans Dieter. "Fragments from a Catabasis Ritual in a Greek Magical Papyrus," *History of Religions* 19 (1980), 287–95, reprinted in *Hellenismus und Urchristentum. Gesammelte Aufsätze* 1 (Tübingen: Mohr Siebeck, 1990), 147–55.

Betz, Hans Dieter. *The "Mithras Liturgy." Text, Translation, and Commentary.* Studien und Texte zu Antike und Christentum (Tübingen: Mohr Siebeck, 2003).

Bloom, Harold. *The American Religion. The Emergence of the Post-Christian Nation* (New York: Simon and Schuster, 1992).

Borgeaud, Philippe. *The Cult of Pan in Ancient Greece,* Chicago: Chicago University Press, 1988); originally published as *Recherches sur le dieu Pan.* Bibliotheca Helvetica Romana 17 (Rome: Institut Suisse de Rome, 1979).

Borgeaud, Philippe, ed. *Orphée et Orphisme en l'honneur de Jean Rudhardt* (Geneva: Droz, 1991).

Borgeaud, Philippe, *Mother of the Gods. From Cybele to the Virgin Mary*, Baltimore, MD: Johns Hopkins University Press, 2004); originally published as *La mère des dieux. De Cybèle à la vierge Marie* (Paris: Seuil, 1996).

Bottini, Angelo. *Archeologia della Salvezza. L'escatologia greca nelle testimonianze archeologiche* (Milan: Longanesi, 1992).

Bottini, Angelo, and Pier Giovanni Guzzo. "Orfeo e le Sirene al Getty Museum," *Ostraka. Rivista di Antichità* 2 (1993), 43–52.

Bowra, Maurice. "Orpheus and Eurydice," *Classical Quarterly* 2 (1952), 113–26, reprinted in *On Greek Margins* (Oxford: Clarendon Press, 1970).

Boyancé, Pierre. "Dionysiaca. A propos d'une étude récente sur l'initiation dionysiaque," *Revue des études anciennes* 68 (1966), 33–60.

Bremmer, Jan N. "Greek Maenadism Reconsidered," *Zeitschrift für Papyrologie und Epigraphik* 55 (1984), 267–86.

Bremmer, Jan N. "Orpheus. From Guru to Gay," in Philippe Borgeaud, ed. *Orphée et Orphisme en l'honneur de Jean Rudhardt* (Geneva: Droz, 1991), 7–30.

Bremmer, Jan N. "The Skins of Pherecydes and Epimenides," *Mnemosyne* 46 (1993), 234–6.

Bremmer, Jan N. "Why Did Medea Kill her Brother Apsyrtus?" in James J. Clauss and Sarah Iles Johnston, eds., *Medea. Essays on Medea in Myth, Literature, Philosophy and Art* (Princeton, NJ: Princeton University Press, 1997), 83–100.

Bremmer, Jan N. "Rationalization and Disenchantment in Ancient Greece: Max Weber among the Pythagoreans and Orphics?" in Richard Buxton, ed. *From Myth to Reason? Studies in the Development of Greek Thought* (Oxford: Clarendon Press, 1999), 71–83 (1999a).

Bremmer, Jan N. "The Birth of the Term Magic," *Zeitschrift für Papyrologie und Epigraphik* 126 (1999), 1–12 (1999b).

Bremmer, Jan N. *The Rise and Fall of the Afterlife* (London: Routledge, 2002).

Bremmer, Jan N., and István Czachesz, eds. *The Apocalypse of Peter* (Leuven: Peeters, 2003).

Brisson, Luc. "Le corps 'dionysiaque.' L'anthropogonie décrite dans le Commentaire sur le Phédon de Plato (1 §3–6) attribué à Olympiodore est-elle orphique?" in *ΣΟΦΙΗΣ ΜΑΙΗΤΟΡΕΣ, "Chercheurs de sagesse." Hommage à Jean Pépin* (Paris: Institut d'Études Augustiniennes, 1992), 481–99.

Brown, Robert F., ed. *Schelling's Treatise on The Deities of Samothrace. A Translation and an Interpretation* (Missoula, MT: Scholars Press, 1977).

Burkert, Walter. "Elysion," *Glotta* 39 (1961), 208–13.

Burkert, Walter, "ΓΟΗΣ. Zum griechischen Schamanismus," *Rheinisches Museum* 105 (1962), 36–55, reprinted in Walter Burkert: *Kleine Schriften* 3. *Orphica et Pythagorica*, ed. Fritz Graf (Göttingen: Vandenhoeck and Ruprecht, 2006), 173–90.

Burkert, Walter. "Orpheus und die Vorsokratiker. Bemerkungen zum Derveni-Papyrus und zur pythagoreischen Zahlenlehre," *Antike und Abendland* 14 (1968), 93–114, reprinted in Walter Burkert: *Kleine Schriften* 3. *Orphica et Pythagorica*, ed. Fritz Graf (Göttingen: Vandenhoeck and Ruprecht, 2006), 62–88.

Burkert, Walter. *Lore and Science in Ancient Pythagoreanism* (Cambridge, MA: Harvard University Press, 1972; originally published as *Weisheit und Wissenschaft. Studien zu Pythagoras, Philolaos und Platon*, Würzburg: Carl, 1962).

Burkert, Walter, "Le laminette auree. Da Orfeo a Lampone," in *Orfismo in Magna Grecia. Atti del 14° Convegno di Studi sulla Magna Grecia (Taranto, 6–10 ottobre 1974)* (Naples: Arte Tipografica, 1975, 81–104, reprinted in Walter Burkert: *Kleine Schriften* 3. *Orphica et Pythagorica*, ed. Fritz Graf, Göttingen: Vandenhoeck and Ruprecht, 2006, 21–36).

Burkert, Walter. *Homo Necans. The Anthropology of Ancient Greek Sacrificial Ritual and Myth* (Berkeley: University of California Press, 1983); originally published as *Homo Necans. Interpretationen altgriechischer Opferriten und Mythen*. Religionsgeschichtliche Versuche und Vorarbeiten 32 (Berlin and New York: De Gruyter, 1971).

Burkert, Walter. *Greek Religion, Archaic and Classical* (Oxford: Blackwell, 1985); originally published as *Griechische Religion der archaischen und klassischen Epoche*. Die Religionen der Menschheit 15 (Stuttgart: Kohlhammer, 1977).

Burkert, Walter. *Ancient Mystery Cults* (Cambridge, MA: Harvard University Press, 1987).

Burkert, Walter. "Initiation/Initiation/Initiation/Iniziazione," in *Thesaurus Cultus et Rituum Antiquorum* vol. II (Los Angeles: The J. Paul Getty Museum, 2004), 91–124.

Burkert, Walter. "Bacchic Teletai in the Hellenistic Age," in Thomas H. Carpenter and Christopher A. Faraone, eds., *Masks of Dionysus* (Ithaca, NY and London: Cornell University Press, 1993: 259–75, reprinted in Walter Burkert: *Kleine Schriften* 3. *Orphica et Pythagorica*, ed. Fritz Graf, Göttingen: Vandenhoeck and Ruprecht, 2006, 120–36).

Burkert, Walter. *Kleine Schriften*, vol. 3. *Orphica et Pythagorica*, ed. Fritz Graf (Göttingen: Vandenhoeck and Ruprecht, 2006).

Calder, William, III, and Robert Kirstein, eds. *Aus dem Freund ein Sohn. Theodor Mommsen und Ulrich von Wilamowitz-Moellendorff: Briefwechsel 1872–1903* (Hildesheim: Weidmann, 2003).

Cancik, Hubert. "Erwin Rohde – ein Philologe der Bismarckzeit," in *Semper Apertus. 600 Jahre Ruprecht-Karls-Universität Heidelberg 1386–1986*, vol. 2 (Berlin: Springer, 1985), 436–505.

Carpenter, Thomas. *Dionysiac Imagery in Fifth-Century Athens* (Oxford: Clarendon Press, 1997).

Carpenter, Thomas H., and Christopher A. Faraone, eds. *Masks of Dionysus* (Ithaca, NY and London: Cornell University Press, 1993).

Clay, Jenny Strauss. *Hesiod's Cosmos* (Cambridge: Cambridge University Press, 2003).

Clinton, Kevin. "The Author of the Homeric *Hymn to Demeter*," *Opuscula Atheniensia* 16 (1986), 47–8.

Clinton, Kevin. *Myth and Cult. The Iconography of the Eleusinian Mysteries*. Acta Instituti Atheniensis Regni Sueciae, series in 8°, 11 (Stockholm: Paul Åström, 1992).

Clinton, Kevin. "Stages of Initiation in the Eleusinian and Samothracian Mysteries," in Michael B. Cosmopoulos, ed., *Greek Mysteries. The Archaeology and Ritual of Ancient Greek Secret Cults* (London: Routledge, 2003), 50–78.

Colli, Giorgio. *La Sapienza Greca*, vol. 1: *Dioniso, Apollo, Eleusi, Orfeo, Museo, Iperborei, Enigma* (Milan: Adelphi, 1977).

Comparetti, Domenico. "The Petelia Gold Tablet," *Journal of Hellenic Studies* 3 (1882), 111–18.

Comparetti, Domenico. "Laminetta Orfica di Cecilia Secundina," *Atene e Roma* 6 (1903), 161–70.

Comparetti, Domenico. *Laminette Orfiche* (Florence: Galletti & Cocci, 1910).

Copeland, Kirsti. "The Earthly Monastery and the Transformation of the Heavenly City in Late Antique Egypt," in Ra'anan S. Boustan and Annette Yoshiko Reed, eds., *Heavenly Realms and Earthly Realities in Late Antique Religions* (Cambridge: Cambridge University Press, 2004), 142–58.

Courtney, Edward, ed. *Musa Lapidaria. A Selection of Latin Verse Inscriptions.* American Philological Association. American Classical Studies 36 (Atlanta, GA: Scholars Press, 1995).

Crusius, Otto. *Erwin Rohde. Ein biographischer Versuch* (Tübingen: Mohr, 1902).

Déonna, Woldemar. "La soif des morts," *Revue de l'Histoire des Religions* 119 (1939), 53–81.

Detienne, Marcel. *De la pensée religieuse à la pensée philosophique. La notion de daïmon dans le pythagorisme ancien* (Paris: Belles Lettres, 1963).

Detienne, Marcel. *The Gardens of Adonis. Spices in Greek Mythology* (Atlantic Highlands, NJ: Humanities Press, 1977); originally published as *Les jardins d'Adonis* (Paris: Gallimard, 1972).

Detienne, Marcel. *Dionysos Slain* (Baltimore, MD: Johns Hopkins University Press, 1979); originally published as *Dionysos mis à mort* (Paris: Gallimard, 1977).

Detienne, Marcel. "Culinary Practices and the Spirit of Sacrifice," in Marcel Detienne and Jean-Pierre Vernant. *The Cuisine of Sacrifice Among the Greeks* (Chicago: University of Chicago Press, 1989), 1–20 (1989a).

Detienne, Marcel. "The Violence of Wellborn Ladies: Women in the Thesmophoria," in Marcel Detienne and Jean-Pierre Vernant. *The Cuisine of Sacrifice Among the Greek* (Chicago: University of Chicago Press, 1989), 129–47 (1989b).

Detienne, Marcel, and Jean-Pierre Vernant. *The Cuisine of Sacrifice Among the Greeks* (Chicago: University of Chicago Press, 1989); originally published as *La cuisine du sacrifice en pays grec* (Paris: Gallimard, 1979).

Deubner, Ludwig. *Attische Feste* (Berlin: Keller, 1932).

Dickie, Matthew. "Poets as Initiates in the Mysteries: Euphorion, Philicus and Posidippus," *Antike und Abendland* 44 (1998), 49–77.

Dieterich, Albrecht. *De Hymnis Orphicis capitula quinque* (Marburg: Elwert, 1891, reprinted in Albrecht Dieterich, *Kleine Schriften*, Leipzig and Berlin: Teubner, 1911, 69–110).

Dieterich, Albrecht, ed. *Eine Mithrasliturgie* (Berlin: Teubner, 3rd edn. 1923 [1903]).

Dillery, John. "Chresmologues and *Manteis*. Diviners and the Problem of Authority," in Sarah Iles Johnston and Peter T. Struck, eds., *Mantikē. Studies in Ancient*

Divination. Religions in the Graeco-Roman World 155 (Leiden: Brill, 2005), 167–231.

Dodds, Eric Robertson. *The Greeks and the Irrational*. Sather Classical Lectures 25 (Berkeley: University of California Press, 1951).

Dover, Kenneth. *Greek Homosexuality*. 2nd edn. (Cambridge, MA: Harvard University Press, 1989 [London: Duckworth, 1978]).

Dowden, Ken. *Death and the Maiden. Girls' Initiation Rites in Greek Mythology* (London: Routledge, 1989).

Dubois, Laurent. *Inscriptions grecques dialectales d'Olbia du Pont* (Geneva: Droz, 1996).

Edmonds, Radcliffe G., III. "Tearing apart the Zagreus myth: A few disparaging remarks on Orphism and original sin," *Classical Antiquity* 18 (1999), 35–73.

Edmonds, Radcliffe G., III. *Myths of the Underworld Journey. Plato, Aristophanes and the "Orphic" Gold Tablets* (Cambridge: Cambridge University Press, 2004).

Edmonds, Radcliffe G. III, ed. *The "Orphic" Gold Tablets and Greek Religion. Further Along the Path* (Cambridge: Cambridge University Press, 2011).

Egelhaaf, Ulrike, and Alfred Schäfer, eds. *Religiöse Vereine in der römischen Antike. Untersuchungen zu Organisation, Ritual und Raumordnung*. Studien und Texte zu Antike und Christentum 13 (Tübingen: Mohr Siebeck, 2002).

Eliade, Mircea. *Birth and Rebirth. The Religious Meaning of Initiations in Human Culture* (New York: Harper and Brothers, 1958), reprinted as *Rites and Symbols of Initiation. The Mysteries of Birth and Rebirth* (New York: Harper and Row, 1965).

Eliade, Mircea. *The Forge and the Crucible* (Chicago: University of Chicago Press, 1978); originally published as *Forgerons et alchimistes* (Paris: Flammarion, 1977).

Eliade, Mircea. *Autobiography*, vol. 1: *1907–1937. Journey East, Journey West* (San Francisco: Harper, 1981).

Engelmann, Helmut, and Reinhold Merkelbach. *Die Inschriften von Erythrai und Klazomenai*, Teil II. Inschriften kleinasiatischer Städte 2: 2 (Bonn: Habelt, 1973).

Faraone, Christopher A. "Rushing into Milk. New Perspectives on the Gold Tablets," in R.G. Edmonds, III, ed., *The "Orphic" Gold Tablets and Greek Religion. Further Along the Path* (Cambridge: Cambridge University Press, 2011), 310–30.

Farnell, Lewis Richard. *The Cults of the Greek States*, vol. 3 (Oxford: Clarendon Press, 1907).

Ferrari, Franco. "Demeter Chthonia and the Mountain Mother in a New Gold Tablet from Magoula Mati," *Zeitschrift für Papyrologie und Epigraphik* 162 (2007), 193–202.

Festugière, André Jean. *L'idéal religieux des Grecs et l'Évangile* (Paris: Lecoffre, 1932).

Flückiger-Guggenheim, Daniela. *Göttliche Gäste. Die Einkehr von Göttern und Heroen in der griechischen Mythologie* (Bern and Frankfurt am Main: Peter Lang, 1984).

Frankfurter, David. "Dynamics of Ritual Expertise in Antiquity and Beyond: Towards a Taxonomy of 'Magicians'," in P. Mirecki and M. Meyer, eds., *Magic and Ritual in the Ancient World*. Religions in the Graeco-Roman World 141 (Leiden: Brill, 2002), 159–78.

Frankfurter, David. "Syncretism and the Holy Man in Late Antique Egypt," *Journal of Early Christian Studies* 11 (2003), 339–85.

Frankfurter, David. "Sacred Texts and Canonicity: Introduction," in Sarah Iles Johnston, ed., *Religions of the Ancient World. A Guide* (Cambridge, MA: Harvard University Press, 2004), 622–3.

Frankfurter, David. *Evil Incarnate. Rumors of Demonic Conspiracy and Satanic Abuse in History* (Princeton NJ: Princeton University Press, 2006).

Freyburger, Gérard, and Marie-Laure Freyburger. *Sectes religieuses en Grèce et à Rome dans l'Antiquité païenne* (Paris: Belles Letters, 2006 [orig. 1986]).

Frickel, J. *Hellenistische Erlösung in christlicher Deutung: Die gnostische Naassenerschrift*. Nag Hammadi Studies 19 (Leiden: Brill, 1984).

Furley, William D., and Jan M. Bremer, eds., trans., and comms. *Greek Hymns*. Studien und Texte zu Antike und Christentum 10. 2 vols. (Tübingen: Mohr Siebeck, 2001).

Gantz, Timothy. *Early Greek Myth. A Guide to Literary and Artistic Sources* (Baltimore, MD: Johns Hopkins University Press, 1993).

Gass, William H., and Lorin Cuoco, eds. *The Writer and Religion* (Carbondale and Edwardsville: Southern Illinois University Press, 2000).

Gavrilaki, Irene, and Yannis Z. Tzifopoulos. "An 'Orphic-Dionysiac' gold epistomion from Sfikaki near Rethymno," *Bulletin de Correspondance Hellénique* 112 (1998), 341–55.

Gebhardt, Oscar von. *Das Evangelium und die Apokalypse des Petrus. Die neuentdeckten Bruchstücke nach einer Photographie der Handschrift zu Gizeh* (Leipzig: Hinrichs, 1893).

Gigante, Marcello. "Per l'esegesi del testo orfico vibonese," *La Parola del Passato* 30 (1975), 223–5.

Gill, Sam D. "Nonliterate Traditions and Holy Books," in Frederick M. Denny and Rodney L. Taylor, eds., *The Holy Book in Comparative Perspective* (Columbia, SC: University of South Carolina Press, 1985), 224–40.

Graepler, Daniel. *Tonfiguren im Grab. Fundkontexte hellenistischer Terrakotten aus der Nekropole von Tarent* (Munich: Biering und Brinkmann, 1997).

Graf, Fritz. *Eleusis und die orphische Dichtung Athens in vorhellenistischer Zeit*. Religionsgeschichtliche Versuche und Vorarbeiten 33 (Berlin: De Gruyter, 1974).

Graf, Fritz. "Milch, Honig und Wein. Zum Verständnis der Libation im griechischen Ritual," in *Perennitas. Studi Angelo Brelich* (Rome: Ateneo, 1980), 209–21.

Graf, Fritz. *Nordionische Kulte. Religionsgeschichtliche und epigraphische Untersuchungen zu den Kulten von Chios, Erythrai, Klazomenai und Phokaia*. Bibliotheca Helvetica Romana 21 (Rome: Schweizerisches Institut in Rom, 1985).

Graf, Fritz. "Orpheus. A Poet Among Men," in Jan N. Bremmer, ed., *Interpretations of Greek Mythology* (London: Croom Helm, 1987), 80–106.

Graf, Fritz. "Textes orphiques et rituel bacchique. A propos des lamelles de

Pelinna," in Philippe Borgeaud, ed., *Orphée et Orphisme en l'honneur de Jean Rudhardt* (Geneva: Droz, 1991), 87–102.

Graf, Fritz. "Dionysian and Orphic Eschatology. New Texts and Old Questions," in Thomas H. Carpenter and Christopher A. Faraone, eds., *Masks of Dionysus* (Ithaca, NY and London: Cornell University Press, 1993), 239–58.

Graf, Fritz. "Pompai und Prozessionen in der alten Welt," in Fritz Graf and Erik Hornung, eds., *Wanderungen*. Eranos-Jahrbuch, Neue Reihe 3 (Munich: Fink, 1995), 85–112.

Graf, Fritz, *Magic in the Ancient World*, (Cambridge, MA: Harvard University Press, 1997; originally published as *La magie dans l'antiquité gréco-romaine*, Paris: Belles Lettres, 1994) (1997a).

Graf, Fritz. "I culti misterici," in Salvatore Settis, ed., *I Greci. Storia, Cultura, Arte, Società*, vol. 2: *Una storia greca. Part 2. Definizione* (Turin: Einaudi, 1997), 309–43 (1997b).

Graf, Fritz. Review of Baumgarten 1998, in *Classical Review* 51 (2001), 281–3.

Graf, Fritz. "Lesser Mysteries: Not Less Mysterious," in Michael B. Cosmopoulos, ed., *Greek Mysteries. The Archaeology and Ritual of Ancient Greek Secret Cults* (London: Routledge, 2003), 241–62.

Graf, Fritz. "The Bridge and the Ladder: Narrow Passages in Late Antique Visions," in Ra'anan Boustan and Anette Yoshiko Reed, eds., *Heavenly Realms and Earthly Realities in Late Antique Religions* (Cambridge: Cambridge University Press, 2004), 19–33.

Graf, Fritz. "Serious Singing: The Orphic Hymns as Religious Texts," *Kernos* 22 (2009), 169–82.

Graf, Fritz. "The Blessings of Madness," *Archiv für Religionsgeschichte* 12 (2010), 167–80.

Groenewald, Michael and Robert W. Daniel. "Lyrischer Text (Sappho-Papyrus)," *Zeitschrift für Papyrologie und Epigraphik* 154 (2005), 7–12.

Gropengiesser, Hildegund. "Sänger und Sirenen. Versuch einer Deutung," *Archäologischer Anzeiger* (1977), 582–610.

Gruppe, Otto. *Griechische Mythologie und Religionsgeschichte*. Handbuch der Klassischen Altertumswissenschaft 5: 2. 2 vols. (Munich: Beck, 1906).

Guarducci, Margherita. "Laminette auree orfiche. Alcuni problemi," *Epigraphica* 36 (1974), 7–31 = *Studi scelti sulla religione Greca e Romana e sul Cristianesimo*. Études préliminaires aux religions dans l'Empire Romain 98 (Leiden: Brill, 1983), 71–96.

Guarducci, Margherita. *Epigrafia Greca*, vol. 4: *Epigrafi Sacre Pagane e Cristiane* (Rome: Istituto Poligrafico dello Stato, 1977).

Haran, M. "Seething a Kid in its Mother's Milk," *Journal of Jewish Studies* 30 (1979), 23–35.

Harnack, Adolf von. *Marcion. Das Evangelium vom fremden Gott. Eine Monographie zur Geschichte der Grundlegung der katholischen Kirche* (Leipzig: Hinrichs, 1920, 2nd edn. 1924).

Harnack, Adolf von. *Neue Studien zu Marcion* (Leipzig: Hinrichs, 1923).

Harrison, Jane Ellen. "The Kouretes and Zeus Kouros. A Study in Prehistoric Sociology," *Annual of the British School at Athens* 15 (1908/9), 308–38.

Harrison, Jane Ellen. *Prolegomena to the Study of Greek Religion*. 3rd edn. (Cambridge: Cambridge University Press, 1922 [1903]).

Harrison, Jane Ellen. *Themis. A Study on the Social Origins of Greek Religion*. 2nd edn. (Cambridge: Cambridge University Press, 1927 [1911]).

Hatzopoulos, Miltiades B. "Λατρεῖες τῆς Μακεδονίας: Τελετὲς μεταβά σεως καὶ μυήσεις," in Aphrodite Avagianou, ed., Λατρεῖες στὴν Περιφέ ρεια τοῦ ἀρχαίου ἑλληνικοῦ κόσμου (Athens: Epistemes Koinonia, 2002), 11–29.

Heidel, Alexander. *The Babylonian Genesis, the Story of Creation* (Chicago: Unversity of Chicago Press, 1942).

Henrichs, Albert. "Die Mänaden von Milet," *Zeitschrift für Papyrologie und Epigraphik* 4 (1969), 223–341.

Henrichs, Albert. "Human Sacrifice in Greek Religion. Three Case Studies," in Olivier Reverdin and Bernard Grange, eds., *Le sacrifice dans l'antiquité*. Entretiens sur l'Antiquité Classique (Geneva: Fondation Hardt, 1981), 195–235.

Henrichs, Albert. "The Eumenides and Wineless Libation in the Derveni Papyrus," in *Atti del XVII congresso internazionale di papirologia (Naples, 19–26 maggio 1983)* (Naples: Centro Internazionale per lo Studio dei Papiri Ercolanesi, 1984), 255–68.

Henrichs, Albert. "*Hieroi Logoi* and *Hierai Bibloi*: The (Un)Written Margins of the Sacred in Ancient Greece," *Harvard Studies in Classical Philology* 101 (2002), 1–59.

Henrichs, Albert. "Writing Religion: Inscribed Texts, Ritual Authority and the Religious Discourse of the Polis," in H. Yunis, ed., *Written Texts and the Rise of Literate Culture in Ancient Greece* (Cambridge: Cambridge University Press, 2003), 38–58.

Henrichs, Albert. "Sacred Texts and Canonicity: Greek," in Sarah Iles Johnston, ed., *Religions of the Ancient World. A Guide* (Cambridge, MA: Harvard University Press, 2004), 633–5.

Henrichs, Albert. "Dionysus Dismembered and Restored to Life: The Earliest Evidence (*OF* 59 I–II)," in Herrero de Jáuregui et al. 2011, 61–8.

Herrero de Jáuregui, Miguel, et al., eds. *Tracing Orpheus. Studies of Orphic Fragments* (Berlin: De Gruyter, 2011).

Herrmann, Peter. *Inschriften von Milet*, vol. 2 (Berlin: Mann, 1998).

Himmelfarb, Martha. *Tours of Hell. An Apocalyptic Form in Jewish and Christian Literature* (Philadelphia: University of Pennsylvania Press, 1983).

Himmelfarb, Martha. *Ascent to Heaven in Jewish and Christian Apocalypses* (New York and Oxford: Oxford University Press, 1993).

Himmelmann, Nikolaus. "Die Priesterschaft der Kyrbantes in Erythrai (Neues Fragment von I.K. 2, 206)," *Epigraphica Anatolica* 29 (1997), 117–21.

Hordern, James. "Notes on the Orphic Papyrus from Gurôb (P. Gurôb 1; Pack 2 2464)," *Zeitschrift für Papyrologie und Epigraphik* 129 (2000), 131–40.

Hultkrantz, Åke. *The North-American Indian Orpheus Tradition. A Contribution to Comparative Religion* (Stockholm: Ethnographic Museum, 1957).

Jaccottet, Anne-Françoise. *Choisir Dionysos. Les associations dionysiaques ou la face cachée du dionysisme*. 2 vols. (Kilchberg: Akanthus, 2003).

Janko, Richard. "Forgetfulness in the Golden Tablets of Memory," *Classical Quarterly* 34 (1984), 89–100.

Janko, Richard. "The Physicist as Hierophant. Aristophanes, Socrates and the Authorship of the Derveni Papyrus," *Zeitschrift für Papyrologie und Epigraphik* 118 (1997), 61–94.

Janko, Richard, ed. *Philodemus On Poems. English and Greek*, vol. I (Oxford: Clarendon Press, 2000).

Janko, Richard. "The Derveni Papyrus (Diagoras of Melos, *Apyrgizontes Logoi?*). A New Translation," *Classical Philology* 96 (2001), 1–32.

Janko, Richard. "The Derveni Papyrus. An Interim Text," *Zeitschrift für Papyrologie und Epigraphik* 141 (2002), 1–53.

Jeanmaire, Henri. *Couroi et Courètes* (Lille: Bibliothèque Universitaire, 1939).

Jeanmaire, Henri. *Dionysos. Histoire du culte de Bacchus* (Paris: Payot, 1951).

Jenkins, Ian and Kim Sloan, *Vases and Volcanoes. Sir William Hamilton and his Collection* (London: British Museum Press, 1996).

Johnston, Sarah Iles. "Corinthian Medea and the Cult of Hera Akraia," in James J. Clauss and Sarah Iles Johnston, eds., *Medea* (Princeton, NJ: Princeton University Press, 1997), 44–70.

Johnston, Sarah Iles. *Restless Dead. Encounters Between the Living and the Dead in Ancient Greece* (Berkeley: University Press of California, 1999) (1999a).

Johnston, Sarah Iles. "Songs for the Ghosts. Magical Solutions to Deadly Problems," in David Jordan, Hugo Montgomery, and Einar Thomassen, eds., *The World of Ancient Magic. Papers from the First International Samson Eitrem Seminar at the Norwegian Institute at Athens 4–8 May 1997*. Papers from the Norwegian Institute at Athens 4 (Bergen: The Norwegian Institute at Athens, 1999), 83–102. (1999b).

Johnston, Sarah Iles, ed. *Religions of the Ancient World. A Guide* (Cambridge, MA: Harvard University Press, 2004).

Johnston, Sarah Iles. "Hecate, Leto's Daughter, in OF 317," in M. Herrero de Jáuregui, Ana Isabel San Cristóbal, Eugenio R. Luján Martínez, Raquel Martín Hernández, Marco Antonio Sanatamaría Álverez, and Sofía Torallas Tovar, eds., *Tracing Orpheus. Studies of Orphic Fragments* (Berlin: De Gruyter, 2011), 123–6.

Johnston, Sarah Iles. "In Praise of the Disordered: Plato, Eliade and the Ritual Implications of a Greek Cosmogony," *Archiv für Religionsgeschichte* 13 (2011), 51–68 (2011a).

Johnston, Sarah Iles. "Demeter in Hermione: Sacrifice and Ritual Polyvalence," *Arethusa* 45.2 (2012), 211–41.

Johnston, Sarah Iles. "Myth in the Getty Hexameters," in C. A. Faraone and D. Obbink, eds., *The Getty Hexameters. Poetry, Magic, and Mystery in Ancient Selinous* (Oxford: Oxford University Press, forthcoming).

Johnston, Sarah Iles, and Timothy McNiven. "Dionysus and the Underworld in Toledo," *Museum Helveticum* 53 (1996), 25–36.

Jones, Christopher P. *Culture and Society in Lucian* (Cambridge, MA: Harvard University Press, 1986).

Jordan, David. "Defixiones from a Well near the Southwest Corner of the Athenian Agora," *Hesperia* 54 (1985), 205–55.

Jordan, David. "Magica Graeca Parvula," *Zeitschrift für Papyrologie und Epigraphik* 100 (1994), 325–33.

Jordan, David and Roy Kotansky, "Ritual Hexameters in the Getty Museum: Preliminary Edition," *Zeitschrift für Papyrologie und Epigraphik* 178 (2011), 54–62.

Joubin, André. "Inscription crétoise relative à l'orphisme," *Bulletin de Correspondance Hellénique* 17 (1893), 121–4.

Jourdan, Fabienne. *Le papyrus de Derveni* (Paris: Belles Lettres, 2003).

Kaibel, Georg. *Epigrammata Graeca e Lapidibus Conlecta* (Frankfurt: Reimer, 1879).

Kaller, Gerhard, "Erwin Rohde," in *Biographisch-Bibliographisches Kirchenlexikon* 8 (1994), 571–3.

Kapsomenos, Spyridon G. "Ὁ Ὀρφικὸς πάπυρος τῆς Θεσσαλονίκης," *Archaiologikon Deltion* 19 (1964), 17–25.

Kapsomenos, Spyridon G. "The Orphic Papyrus Roll of Thessalonika," *Bulletin of the American Society of Papyrologists* 2 (1964/5), 3–12.

Kearn, Emily. *The Heroes of Attica. Bulletin of the Institute of Classical Studies*, Supplement 57 (London: Institute for Classical Studies, 1989).

Keil, Joseph, and Anton von Premerstein. *Bericht über eine Reise in Lydien und der südlichen Aiolis*. Denkschriften der kaiserlichen Akademie der Wissenschaften in Wien. Philosophisch-historische Klasse, vol. 53: 2 (Vienna: Hölder, 1908).

Kerényi, Karl. *Dionysos. Urbild des unzerstörbaren Lebens* (Munich and Vienna: Langen Müller, 1976; 2nd edn. Stuttgart: Klett-Cotta, 1994; Engl. *Dionysos. Archetypal Image of Indestructible Life*, Princeton, NJ: Princeton University Press, 1976).

Kern, Otto. *Orphicorum fragmenta* (Berlin: Weidmann, 1922).

Kingsley, Peter. *Ancient Philosophy, Mystery, and Magic. Empedocles and Pythagorean Tradition* (Oxford: Clarendon Press, 1995).

Kloppenborg, John, and Stephen Wilson, eds. *Voluntary Associations in the Graeco-Roman World* (London: Routledge, 1996).

Klutstein, Ileana. *Marsilio Ficino et la théologie ancienne. Oracles chaldaïques, hymnes orphiques, hymnes de Proclus*. Quaderni del "Rinascimento" 5 (Florence: Olschki, 1987).

Kotansky, Roy. *Greek Magical Amulets. The Inscribed Gold, Silver, Copper, and Bronze Lamellae. Part 1: Published Texts of Known Provenances* (Opladen: Westdeutscher Verlag, 1994).

Kouremenos, Theokritos, George M. Parássoglou, and Kyriakos Tsantsanoglou. *The Derveni Papyrus. Edited with Introduction and Commentary*. Studi e testi per il "Corpus dei papiri filosofici greci e latini," vol. 13 (Florence: Olschki, 2006).

Krakauer, Jon. *Under the Banner of Heaven. A Story of Violent Faith* (New York: Doubleday, 2003).

Lagrange, Marie-Jean. *Les mystères. L'Orphisme*. Introduction à l'étude du Nouveau Testament IV: 1 (Paris: Lecoffre, 1937).

Laks, André, and Glenn Most, eds. *Studies on the Derveni Papyrus* (New York and Oxford: Oxford University Press, 1997).

Lane Fox, Robin. *Pagans and Christians* (Harmondsworth: Viking, 1986).

Leipoldt, Johannes and Siegfried Morenz. *Heilige Schriften. Betrachtungen zur Religionsgeschichte der antiken Mittelmeerwelt* (Leipzig: Harrassowitz, 1953).

Lévi-Strauss, Claude. *The Savage Mind* (Chicago: University of Chicago Press, 1968): originally published as *La pensée sauvage* (Paris: Plon, 1962).

Linforth, Ivan M. "Two Notes on the Legend of Orpheus," *Transactions of the American Philological Association* 62 (1931), 5–12.

Linforth, Ivan M. *The Arts of Orpheus* (Berkeley: University of California Press, 1941).

Linforth, Ivan. "The Corybantic Rites in Plato," *University of California Publications in Classical Philology* 13 (1946), 121–62.

Lloyd-Jones, Hugh. "Pindar and the Afterlife," in *Entretiens sur L'Antiquité Classique* 17 (1985), 245–83, reprinted with addendum in *The Academic Papers of Sir Hugh Lloyd-Jones* (Oxford: Clarendon Press, 1990), vol. 1, 80–104.

Lobeck, Christian August. *Aglaophamus sive de theologiae mysticae Graecorum causis libri tres* (Königsberg: Bornträger, 1829).

Loraux, Nicole. *Born of the Earth. Myth and Politics in Athens* (Ithaca, NY: Cornell University Press, 2000); originally published as *Né de la terre. Mythe et politique à Athènes* (Paris: Seuil, 1996).

Luiselli, Raffaele. "Contributo all'interpretazione delle *Argonautiche Orfiche*. Studio sul proemio," in Agostino Masaracchia, ed., *Orfeo e l'Orfismo. Atti del seminario nazionale (Rome-Perugia 1985–1991)* (Rome: Gruppo Editoriale Internazionale, 1993), 265–307.

Macchioro, Vittorio. *From Orpheus to Paul. A History of Orphism* (New York: Holt, 1930).

Marshall, F. H. *Catalogue of the Jewellery, Greek, Etruscan and Roman of the Department of Antiquities, British Museum* (London: British Museum, 1911).

Marzi, Maria Grazia, ed. *Domenico Comparetti tra antichità e archeologia. Individualità di una biblioteca.* Catalogo di una mostra. Facoltà di Lettere e Filosofia dell'Università di Firenze, dal 28 gennaio al 28 febbraio 1998 (Florence: Facoltà di Lettere e Filosofia, 1999).

Matz, Friedrich. *ΔΙΟΝΥΣΙΑΚΗ ΤΕΛΕΤΗ. Archäologische Untersuchungen zum Dionysoskult in hellenistischer und römischer Zeit*, Abhandlungen Mainz 1963: 15 (Wiesbaden: Steiner, 1963).

Maurer Zenck, Claudia, ed. *Der Orpheus-Mythos von der Antike bis zur Gegenwart. Die Vorträge der Interdisziplinären Ringvorlesung an der Universität Hamburg, Sommersemester 2003.* Hamburger Jahrbuch für Musikwissenschaft 21 (Frankfurt am Main, Berlin, Bern: Peter Lang, 2004).

Menichetti, Mauro. *Archeologia del potere. Re, immagini e miti a Roma e in Etruria in età arcaica* (Milan: Longanesi, 1994).

Merkelbach, Reinhold. "'Die goldenen Totenpässe.' Ägyptisch, orphisch, bakchisch," *Zeitschrift für Papyrologie und Epigraphik* 128 (1999), 1–13.

Metzger, Henri. *Recherches sur l'imagerie éleusinienne.* Publications de la Bibliothèque Salomon Reinach 2 (Paris: Boccard, 1965).

Monnier, Alain. "L'Orphée des ethnologues," in Philippe Borgeaud, ed., *Orphée et Orphisme en l'honneur de Jean Rudhardt* (Geneva: Droz, 1991), 61–4.

Morand, Anne-France. *Études sur les Hymnes Orphiques*. Religions in the Graeco-Roman World 143 (Leiden: Brill, 2001).

Moreau, Alain, "Épouser la princesse. Pelops et Hippodamie," in Georges Ravis-Giordani, ed., *Femmes et patrimoine dans les sociétés rurales de l'Europe méditerranéenne* (Paris: Centre National de la Recherche Scientifique, 1987), 227–37.

Most, Glenn. "Hesiod's Myth of the Five (or Three or Four) Races," *Proceedings of the Cambridge Philological Society* 43 (1997), 104–27.

Moulinier, Louis. *Orphée et l'Orphisme à l'époque classique* (Paris: Les Belles Lettres, 1955).

Müller, Max, ed. *The Sacred Books of the East*, 50 vols. (Oxford: Clarendon Press, 1879–1910).

Myres, John L. Letter to the French School in Athens, published in "Nouvelles et correspondance," *Bulletin de Correspondance Hellénique* 17 (1893), 629f.

Nilsson, Martin P. *Studia de Dionysiis Atticis* (Lund: Möller, 1900).

Nilsson, Martin P. *Griechische Feste von religiöser Bedeutung mit Ausschluss der attischen* (Leipzig: Teubner, 1906).

Nilsson, Martin P. "Early Orphism and Kindred Religious Movements," *Harvard Theological Review* 28 (1935), 181–230, reprinted in *Opuscula selecta linguis Anglica, Francogallica, Germanica conscripta*, vol. 2 (Lund: Gleerup, 1952), 623–83.

Nilsson, Martin P. "Die Quelle der Lethe und der Mnemosyne," *Eranos* 41 (1943), 1–7, reprinted in *Opuscula selecta linguis Anglica, Francogallica, Germanica conscripta*, vol. 3 (Lund: Gleerup, 1960), 85–92.

Nilsson, Martin P. *The Dionysiac Mysteries of the Hellenistic and Roman Age*. Acta Instituti Atheniensis Regni Sueciae, series in 8° no. 5 (Lund: Gleerup, 1957).

Nilsson, Martin P. *Geschichte der griechischen Religion*. Handbuch der Altertums-wissenschaft 5: 2. 2 vols. (Munich: Beck; vol. 1: 2nd edn. 1955, corr. 3rd edn. 1967 [1940]; vol. 2: 2nd edn. 1961 [1950]).

Obbink, Dirk. "Poetry and Performance in the Orphic Gold Leaves," in R. G. Edmonds, III, ed., *"Orphic" Gold Tablets and Greek Religion. Further Along the Path* (Cambridge: Cambridge University Press, 2011), 291–309.

Obbink, Dirk. "Dionysos in and out of the Papyri," in Renate Schlesier, ed., *A Different God? Dionysos and Ancient Polytheism* (Berlin and New York: De Gruyter, 2011), 281–95 (2011a).

Ohlemutz, Erwin. *Die Kulte und Heiligtümer der Götter in Pergamon* (Würz-burg: Triltsch, 1940; reprint Darmstadt: Wissenschaftliche Buchgesellschaft, 1968).

Olivieri, Alessandro. *Lamellae aureae Orphicae* (Bonn: Marcus and Weber, 1915).

del Olmo Lete, Gregorio. *Mitos y legendas de Canaan según la tradición de Ugarit* (Madrid: Ediciones Cristianidad, 1981; Engl. *Canaanite Religion According to the Liturgical Texts of Ugarit*, Bethesda, MD: CDL Press, 1999).

Pache, Corinne Ondine. *Baby and Child Heroes in Ancient Greece* (Urbana and Chicago: University of Illinois Press, 2004).

Parker, Robert. *Miasma. Pollution and Purification in Early Greek Religion* (Oxford: Clarendon Press, 1983).

Parker, Robert. "Early Orphism," in Anton Powell, ed., *The Greek World* (London: Routledge, 1995), 483–510.

Parker, Robert. *Athenian Religion. A History* (Oxford: Clarendon Press, 1996).

Parker, Robert. *Polytheism and Society in Athens* (Oxford: Oxford University Press, 2005).

Parker, Robert, and Maria Stamatopoulou, "A new funerary gold leaf from Pherai," *Arkhaiologike Ephemeris* 143 (2004 [2007]), 1–32.

Parry, Hugh. *Thelxis. Magic and Imagination in Greek Myth and Poetry* (New York and London: Lanham, 1992).

Pfeiffer, Rudolph. *A History of Classical Scholarship from 1300–1850* (Oxford: Clarendon Press, 1976).

Pirenne-Delforge, Vinciane. *Retour à la source. Pausanias et la religion grecque. Kernos* suppl. 20 (Liège: Centre Internationale d'Études de la Religion Grecque Antique, 2008).

Powell, Barry. *Classical Myth*, 4th edn. (Upper Saddle River, NJ: Prentice Hall, 2003).

Prothero, Rowland E., ed. *The Works of Lord Byron. Letters and Journals*, vol. 1 (London: John Murray, 1904).

Pugliese Carratelli, Giovanni, and Giuseppe Foti. "Un sepolcro di Hipponio e un nuovo testo orfico." *La Parola del Passato* 29 (1974), 91–126.

Pugliese Carratelli, Giovanni. "Sulla lamina orfica di Hipponion," *La Parola del Passato* 30 (1975), 226–31.

Pugliese Carratelli, Giovanni. *Le lamine d'oro orfiche. Istruzioni per il viaggio oltremondano degli iniziati Greci* (Milan: Adelphi. 2001).

Ricciardelli, Gabriella. *Inni Orfici* (Milan: Mondadori, 2000).

Richardson, Nicholas, ed. and comm. *The Homeric Hymn to Demeter* (Oxford: Clarendon Press, 1974).

Riedweg, Christoph. *Mysterienterminologie bei Platon, Philon und Klemens von Alexandrien*. Untersuchungen zur antiken Literatur und Geschichte 26 (Berlin and New York: De Gruyter, 1987).

Riedweg, Christoph. "Orphisches bei Empedokles," *Antike und Abendland* 41 (1995), 34–59.

Riedweg, Christoph. "Initiation – Tod – Unterwelt. Beobachtungen zur Kommunikationssituation und narrativen Technik der orphisch-bakchischen Goldblättchen," in Fritz Graf, ed., *Ansichten griechischer Rituale. Geburtstagssymposium für Walter Burkert* (Stuttgart and Leipzig: Teubner, 1998), 359–98.

Riedweg, Christoph. "Poésie orphique et rituel initiatique. Éléments d'un 'Discours sacré' dans les lamelles d'or," *Revue de l'histoire des religions* 219 (2002), 459–81.

Riedweg, Christoph. "Orpheus oder die Magie der *Mousiké*. Antike Variationen eines einflussreichen Mythos," in Therese Fuhrer, Paul Michel, and Peter Stotz, eds., *Geschichten und ihre Geschichte* (Basel: Schwabe, 2004), 37–66.

Rizzo, Giovanni E. *Dionysos Mystes. Contributi Esegetici alle Rappresentazioni di Misteri Orfici*. Memorie della Reale Accademia di Archeologia, Lettere e Belle Arti 3 (Naples: Cimmaruta, 1918).

Rohde, Erwin. *Psyche. Seelencult und Unsterblichkeitsglaube der Griechen*. 2nd edn.

(Freiburg, Mohr, 1898; Engl. *Psyche. The Cult of Souls and Belief in Immortality Among the Greeks*, London: Kegan Paul, 1925).

Rose, Herbert Jennings. *Handbook of Greek Mythology, Including its Extension to Rome* (London: Methuen, 1928).

Rose, Herbert Jennings. "A Study of Pindar, Fragment 133 Bergk, 127 Bowra," in Cyril Bailey et al., eds., *Greek Poetry and Life. Essays Presented to Gilbert Murray* (Oxford: Clarendon Press 1936), 79–96.

Rose, Herbert Jennings. "The Grief of Persephone," *Harvard Theological Review* 36 (1943), 247–50.

Rudhardt, Jean. "Les deux mères de Dionysos, Perséphone et Sémélé," *Revue de l'histoire des religions* 219 (2002), 483–501.

Russo, Cristina. "Dalla morte alla 'vera vita.' Revisione autoptica della lamina di Hipponion," *Epigraphica* 58 (1996), 35–59.

Rusten, Jeffrey S. *Dionysius Scytobrachion* (Opladen: Westdeutscher Verlag, 1982).

Rusyayeva, Anna S. "Orfizm i kult Dionisa v Olvii," *Vestnik Drevneij Istorii* 143 (1978), 87–104 (German summary: F. Tinnefeld, *Zeitschrift für Papyrologie und Epigraphik* 38 (1980), 68–71).

Scalera McClintock, Giuliana. "Non fermarsi alla prima fonte. Simboli della salvezza nelle lamine auree," *Filosofia e Teologia* 5 (1991), 396–408.

Schlesier, Renate. "Dionysos in der Unterwelt. Zu den Jenseitskonstruktionen der bakchischen Mysterien," in Ralf von den Hoff and Stefan Schmidt, eds., *Konstruktionen von Wirklichkeit. Bilder in Griechenland des 5. und 4. Jahrhunderts* (Stuttgart: Steiner, 2001), 157–72.

Schlesier, Renate. "Die Leiden des Dionysos," in Alfred Kneppe and Dieter Metzler, eds., *Die emotionale Dimension antiker Religiosität* (Münster: Aschendorff, 2003), 1–20.

Schlesier, Renate, ed. *A Different God? Dionysos and Ancient Polytheism* (Berlin: De Gruyter, 2011).

Schmidt, Margot. "Orfeo e Orfismo nella pittura vascolare italiota," in *Orfismo in Magna Grecia. Atti del Quattordicesimo Convegno di Studi sulla Magna Grecia, Taranto 6–10 ottobre 1974* (Naples: Arte Tipografica, 1975), 105–37.

Schmidt, Margot, Arthur Dale Trendall, and Alexander Cambitoglou. *Eine Gruppe Apulischer Grabvasen in Basel. Studien zu Gehalt und Form der Unteritalischen Sepulkralkunst* (Basel: Archäologischer Verlag, 1976).

Schmidt, Margot. "Bemerkungen zu Orpheus in Unterwelts- und Thrakerdarstellungen," in Philippe Borgeaud, ed., *Orphée et Orphisme en l'honneur de Jean Rudhardt* (Geneva: Droz, 1991), 31–50.

Schneider, Herbert W. *Making the Fascist State* (New York and Oxford: Oxford University Press, 1928; reprint New York: Fertig, 1968).

Schneider, Herbert W. *The Fascist Government of Italy* (New York: Van Nostrand, 1936).

Schneider, Herbert W., and Shepard B. Clough. *Making Fascists* (Chicago: The University of Chicago Press, 1929).

Schwyzer, Eduard. *Griechische Grammatik*. Teil 1. *Allgemeiner Teil, Lautlehre, Flexion*. Handbuch der Altertumswissenschaft 2, 1. 3rd edn. (Munich: Beck, 1950).

Seaford, Richard. "Dionysiac Drama and Dionysiac Mysteries," *Classical Quarterly* 31 (1981), 252–75.

Seaford, Richard. "Immortality, Salvation, and the Elements," *Harvard Studies in Classical Philology* 90 (1986), 1–26.

Seaford, Richard. *Reciprocity and Ritual. Homer and Tragedy in the Developing City State* (Oxford: Clarendon Press, 1994).

Segal, Charles. *Orpheus. The Myth of the Poet* (Baltimore, MD: Johns Hopkins University Press, 1989).

Simon, Erika, "Argonauten beim Waffentanz," in *Schriften zur etruskischen und italischen Kunst* (Stuttgart: Steiner, 1996), 99–104 (originally published in Dieter Gutknecht, Hartmut Krones, and Frieder Zschoch, eds., *Telemanniana et alia musicologica. Festschrift für Günter Fleischhauer zum 65. Geburtstag.* Michaelsteiner Forschungsbeiträge 17. Michaelstein: Ziethen, 1995, 28–33).

Smith, Jonathan Z. *Drudgery Divine. On the Comparison of Early Christianities and the Religions of Late Antiquity* (Chicago: University of Chicago Press, 1990).

Sokolowski, Franciszek. *Lois sacrées de l'Asie Mineure.* École Française d'Athènes. Travaux et mémoires des anciens membres étrangers 9 (Paris: Boccard, 1955).

Sokolowski, Franciszek. *Lois sacrées des cités grecques. Supplément.* École Française d'Athènes. Travaux et mémoires des anciens membres étrangers 11 (Paris: Boccard, 1962).

Sokolowski, Franciszek. *Lois sacrées des cités grecques.* École Française d'Athènes. Travaux et mémoires des anciens membres étrangers (Paris: Boccard, 1969).

Sourvinou-Inwood, C., *Reading Greek Death* (Oxford: Clarendon Press, 1995).

Spoerri, Walter. *Späthellenistische Berichte über Welt, Kultur und Götter* (Basel: Schwabe, 1959).

Themelis, Petros G. and Ioannes P. Tsouratsoglou. *Οι τάφοι του Δερβενίου* (Athens: Ekdosis tou Tameiou Archaiologikou Poron kai Apallotrioseon, 1997).

Thompson, Homer A. "The Altar of Pity on the Athenian Agora," *Hesperia* 21 (1952), 47–82.

Tortorelli-Ghidini, Marisa, *Figli della terra e del cielo stellato. Testi Orfici con traduzione e commento* (Naples: D'Auria Editore, 2006) .

Turcan, Robert. "Bacchoi ou bacchants? De la dissidence des vivants à la ségrégation des morts," in Olivier de Cazanove, ed., *L'association dionysiaque dans les sociétés anciennes. Actes de la table ronde organisée par l'École Française de Rome (24–25 mai 1984).* Collection de l'École Française de Rome 89 (Rome: Institut Français, 1986), 227–46.

Tzifopoulos, Yannis Z. "Ο Ορφισμός στην Κρήτη," *Teuchos* 10 (1998), 81–96.

Tzifopoulos, Yannis Z. *"Paradise Earned": The "Bacchic-Orphic" Gold Lamellae from Crete,* Hellenic Studies 23 (Washington, DC: Center for Hellenic Studies, 2010).

Vinogradov, Jurij G. "Zur sachlichen und geschichtlichen Deutung der Orphiker-Plättchen von Olbia," in Philippe Borgeaud, ed., *Orphée et Orphisme en l'honneur de Jean Rudhardt* (Geneva: Droz, 1991), 65–76.

Vojatzi, Mata. *Frühe Argonautenbilder* (Würzburg: Triltsch, 1982).

Warden, John, ed. *Orpheus. The Metamorphoses of a Myth* (Toronto: University of Toronto Press, 1982).

Wathelet, Paul. "Homère, Lykaon et le rituel du Mont Lycée," in Julien Ries, ed., *Les rites d'initiation. Actes du colloque de Liège et de Louvain-la-Neuve. 20/21 novembre 1984*, Homo religiosus 13 (Louvain-la-Neuve: Centre d'Histoire des Religions, 1986), 258–97.

Watkins, Calvert. *How to Kill a Dragon. Aspects of Indo-European Poetics* (Oxford: Clarendon Press, 1995).

West, Martin L., ed. and comm. *Hesiod. Theogony* (Oxford: Clarendon Press, 1966).

West, Martin L., ed. and comm. *Hesiod. Works and Days* (Oxford: Clarendon Press, 1978).

West, Martin L. "The Orphics of Olbia," *Zeitschrift für Papyrologie und Epigraphik* 45 (1982), 17–29.

West, Martin L. *The Orphic Poems* (Oxford: Clarendon Press, 1983).

West, Martin L. *The Hesiodic Catalogue of Women. Its Nature, Structure, and Origins* (Oxford: Clarendon Press, 1985).

Wiens, Davon H. "Mystery Concepts in Primitive Christianity and Its Environment," in *Aufstieg und Niedergang der Römischen Welt* 2: 23: 2 (Berlin and New York: De Gruyter, 1980), 1248–84.

Wieten, J. H. *De tribus laminis aureis quae in sepulcris Thurinis sunt inventae* (Leiden, Amsterdam: Clausen, 1915).

Wilamowitz Moellendorff, Ulrich von. *Der Glaube der Hellenen*, 2 vols. (Berlin: Weidmann, 1931/32; reprint Basel: Schwabe, 1956).

Willers, Dietrich. "Dionysos und Christus – ein archäologisches Zeugnis zur 'Konfessionsangehörigkeit' des Nonnos," *Museum Helveticum* 49 (1992), 141–51.

Wilton, Andrew, and Ilaria Bignamini. *Grand Tour. The Lure of Italy in the Eighteenth Century* (London: Tate Gallery, 1996).

Yiouri, Eugenia. *Ο κρατήρας του Δερβενίου* (Athens: Archaeological Society, 1978).

Yunis, Harvey. *Demosthenes. On the Crown* (Cambridge: Cambridge University Press, 2001).

Zuntz, Günther. "Once more the so-called 'Edict of Philopator on the Dionysiac Mysteries'," *Hermes* 91 (1963), 229–39, reprinted in G. Zuntz, *Opuscula Selecta* (Manchester: Manchester University Press, 1972), 88–101.

Zuntz, Günther. *Persephone. Three Essays on Religion and Thought in Magna Graecia* (Oxford: Clarendon Press, 1971).

SUBJECT INDEX

Note: we have not indexed everything in the book – citing every occurrence of "Dionysus," "memory," "Orpheus," and "Persephone," for example, would have been of little help to the reader. We have instead tried to provide pointers to topics that might otherwise be difficult to find. For the single tablets see the *Index of Ancient Texts* s.v. Tablets.

INDEX OF ANCIENT TEXTS

CPSIA information can be obtained
at www.ICGtesting.com
Printed in the USA
LVHW101348251119
638446LV00006B/120/P